ALTERNATIVE CONVENTIONAL DEFENSE POSTURES IN THE EUROPEAN THEATER

ALTERNATIVE CONVENTIONAL DEFENSE POSTURES IN THE EUROPEAN THEATER

Volume 3:
Force Posture Alternatives
for Europe After the Cold War

Edited by
Hans Günter Brauch
Robert Kennedy

With forewords by
Carl Friedrich von Weizsäcker,
physicist and philosopher, and
Paul C. Warnke, former director,
U.S. Arms Control and Disarmament Agency

CRANE RUSSAK
A member of the Taylor & Francis Group
Washington   Philadelphia   London

USA	Publishing Office:	Taylor & Francis 1101 Vermont Avenue, NW Suite 200 Washington, DC 20005-3521 Tel: (202) 289-2174 Fax: (202) 289-3665
	Distribution Center:	Taylor & Francis 1900 Frost Road Suite 101 Bristol, PA 19007-1598 Tel: (215) 785-5800 Fax: (215) 785-5515
UK		Taylor & Francis Ltd. 4 John St. London WC1N 2ET Tel: 071 405 2237 Fax: 071 831 2035

ALTERNATIVE CONVENTIONAL DEFENSE POSTURES IN THE EUROPEAN THEATER:
Volume 3, Force Posture Alternatives for Europe After the Cold War

1 2 3 4 5 6 7 8 9 0   B R B R   9 8 7 6 5 4 3 2

This book was set in Times Roman by Hemisphere Publishing Corporation. The editor was Corinne Naden; the production supervisor was Peggy M. Rote; and the typesetter was Laurie Strickland. Printing and binding by Braun-Brumfield, Inc.

A CIP catalog record for this book is available from the British Library.

∞ *The paper in this publication meets the requirements of the ANSI Standard Z39.48-1984(Permanence of Paper)*

Library of Congress Cataloging-in-Publication Data

Alternative conventional defense postures in the European theater /
  edited by Hans Günter Brauch and Robert Kennedy : forewords by
  Carl Friedrich von Weizsächer and Paul Warnke
    p. cm.
  Includes bibliographic references.
    Contents: v. 3 Force Posture Alternatives for Europe After the Cold War
    1. Europe—Defenses. 2. North Atlantic Treaty Organization—Armed Forces.
3. United States—Armed Forces. 4. Germany (West)—Armed Forces. I. Brauch,
Hans Günter, 1947. II. Kennedy, Robert, 1939.
UA646.A633 1989   *89-22204*
355'03304—dc20   CP
ISBN 0-8448-1728-7

Contents

Part One
SURVEYS OF FORCE POSTURE ALTERNATIVES

Part Two
FORCE POSTURE ALTERNATIVES

Part Three
INTERNATIONAL AND DOMESTIC CHANGES:
Future Roles of Germany and the United States
in the New International Order

Foreword

This volume, edited jointly by the American strategic expert Robert Kennedy and the German peace researcher Hans Günter Brauch, takes up conceptual ideas developed by Horst Afheldt and myself, as well as others on both sides of the Atlantic, since the 1960s. Our aim has been to contribute to the development of concepts that would reduce the danger of a third world war by the creation of more stable structures in the context of a defensively oriented conventional defense posture. In this volume a variety of alternative approaches to European conventional defense, driven for the most part by similar strategic considerations, are presented by German and American experts to a larger international audience.

Changes in the declaratory military policies of former Soviet leadership under Mikhail Gorbachev, which were being reflected in a Soviet move toward "defensive defense," German unification, and the immense political changes now under way in Central and Eastern Europe, require a rethinking of the force structures for European defense in terms of a changing structure of peace and security in Europe. In moving toward a new political structure of peace in Europe, technical force structure designs, such as those developed by Horst Afheldt, Lutz Unterseher, Steven Canby, and others, can contribute to the avoidance of a third world war by overcoming the dilemmas of deterrence, by avoiding a new arms race, and by enhancing a process that will in the long run eliminate the institution of war as a means for the resolution of conflicts.

Over the years, my own ideas on the problems of war and peace have focused on two hypotheses:

1. A third world war was possible under Cold War conditions.
2. It is necessary and possible to eliminate the institution of war.

Logically, both hypotheses are not closely connected. So far, both major powers have succeeded in avoiding the third world war. Some deduce from this the sanguine hope that a nuclear war will never occur. However, deterrence has not and probably never will be able to eliminate totally the possibility of war as an institution. Since 1945 the avoidance of nuclear confrontation offered the yardstick for war prevention. Those wars that did occur were regional conflicts considered highly unlikely to result in a nuclear escalation. It is questionable whether such a global situation can be maintained permanently. Conflict resolution through limited war is a pattern of stability for a specific historical period. Moreover, it may be added that the old approach to nuclear deterrence in Europe, e.g., NATO's former concept of flexible response, was based fundamentally on the threat of limited nuclear use. This is so, in my view, because strategic weapons only deter an opponent's use of his own strategic weapons. Thus an attack that includes the employment of limited nuclear forces cannot credibly be deterred by a major strategic threat. Hence, NATO's former concept of flexible response made it inevitable that limited threats were deterred by the threat of limited use of nuclear weapons.

War prevention by nuclear deterrence can never be absolutely certain. Technical errors are possible, and a single breakdown of control in a century is sufficient to cause a catastrophe. More likely are miscalculations with respect to escalation. Thus in the long run, a deterrence system that relies on nuclear weapons is unacceptable. Nuclear weapons have offered a pause in "great power" conflict that may come to an end tomorrow. They have not provided a framework for a political system that can offer long-term peace and security. Rather they threaten the existence of human kind. We must therefore now focus our efforts on developing a nonnuclear security system.

In Europe, as a minimum one must develop a conventional defense posture that does not rely on the threat of a "nuclear-first" use. However, here a sharp distinction has to be made. Only a purely *defensively* oriented conventional force posture would be better than one that relies on the threat of nuclear use. It would be wrong to believe that the elimination of nuclear deterrence alone would make war less likely. Nuclear weapons have not been sufficient to prevent war. However, they have not been the cause. The return to purely or predominantly conventional defense postures in their more traditional forms, which have included offensive capabilities, could drastically increase the likelihood of war. The traditional approaches to conventional defense enhance the risk of entering into a race between tank and antitank weapons. Thus official NATO plans pertaining to conventional armament modernization will not provide an effective deterrent force. The lesson we have learned from nuclear weapons should not be forgotten, and that lesson must be extended to conventional weapons as well: war prevention, not victory is the task. Even if peace can be maintained, nuclear weapons will remain with us both physically and, even if all of them were destroyed, intellectually. We cannot afford any war, not even a conventional one, in our region. Therefore, conventional force structures must fulfill three conditions:

1. They must not offer any incentive to engage in conventional arms races.
2. They must provide stability during crises, i.e., they must not be structured so as to invite rapid preemptive conventional attacks.
3. They must not offer any targets that invite nuclear attacks.

The force structure design by Horst Afheldt and his colleagues claims to fulfill these three conditions. In his major work *Defense and Peace* (1976), Afheldt offered the framework for fundamental reconsiderations on the conditions under which deterrence can be kept stable. His solution was not the repulsion of numerically superior tank armies by numerically inferior tank armies, not even an arms race in tanks or nuclear antitank weapons, but a defensive defense that would not lead to an arms race. In the late 1970s, this model initiated a lively debate, first in Germany and later in other parts of Europe. In a simplified manner, I have argued that what is clearly needed is a system that does not require the threat of a mutual suicide, as well as one that avoids any inherent pressures for acquisitions, i.e., an arms race. The first requirement is violated by the present countervalue nuclear strategy, and the second by the counterforce strategy.

The first 20 years of NATO strategy were influenced by the relative security of a countervalue strategy, which, at a potential price of unacceptable damage in case of war, provided a low probability that such a war might occur. The last 20 years appear to have been influenced increasingly by counterforce strategies brought about by the increasing weapons accuracy. Counterforce strategies have given impetus to increased arms production and sophisticated, highly mobile, and clearly more capable conventional forces. This has increased the likelihood of war and made an arms race inevitable.

However, Afheldt was not satisfied with the critical attitude of his older study. He wanted to demonstrate in a model that his conditions for a more stable deterrence could be fulfilled. Only such an offer for a problem solution could expect to have any impact on armament decisions. Afheldt's positive proposal was limited to the conventional realm: area defense by "technocommandos" with tank-crushing, precision-guided munitions.

Today, modern high precision weapons permit the development of a truly defensive defense, i.e., forces that have a "structural inability to attack." The typical argument that weapons may be used both offensively and defensively can be made only if one ignores the structure of one's forces. It is true that a single weapon can be used both offensively and defensively depending on the weapons system in which it is integrated. A weapons systems, however, that is deployed on the terrain without any means to transport it forward for an attack is a different thing. A force structure that includes only such "defensive" systems would structurally preclude the possibility of offensive war and also would be unlikely to stimulate a new arms race. Moreover, by a reduction of mutual threat perceptions, it would clearly be a step toward stability.

Defensive defense would be a contribution to the creation of more stable military structures. Perhaps more importantly, it would render the deterrent threat of limited nuclear use unnecessary as a means of deterring war. For reasons of mutual interest, the dialogue among the superpowers should now focus on eliminating the potentially dangerous technical approach to war prevention by examining a new political structure of peace. But toward that goal, intermediary technical structures will be inevitable.

The fundamental goal of this change in awareness (*Bewußtseinswandel*) must be to eliminate the institution of war as a means of resolving conflicts. Is there any chance that this can be accomplished? First, we must stress the word *institution*. An institution is a societal structure that has deliberately been created and recognized by human beings. It is man-made and, in principle, it can therefore be overcome by humans. War has been an internationally legally recognized institution. In a formal sense, it should be possible to delegitimize it by international agreement. This was as major goal behind the League of Nations in 1920 and the United Nations in 1945. Nevertheless the institution of war has yet to be eliminated.

However, in the nuclear age, we must recognize that its abolition is a necessary precondition for the continued existence of humankind. Political common sense requires a major change in attitude. This attitude change must be reflected in the objective contents of culture, in its institutions. This insight must be made a part of public conscience. War can be eliminated as an institution once humankind decides to do so. Humankind in this respect does not mean any human being but those that represent and influence the public conscience.

In a postcold war environment as a consequence of political changes taking place in Europe, war between NATO and Russia appears rather remote. Nevertheless, the task will be with us to eliminate war as an institution through the gradual creation of a new security system in Europe. This book contributes significantly to ċhe important debate that must now take place and is highly commended to those who are interested in a new and more cooperative, highly stable system of security in Europe.

Carl Friedrich von Weizsäcker
March 1992

Foreword

The rapid change in the international political environment has exceeded the ability of Western governments to adjust. Just three years ago, a major debate within NATO had to do with the proposed deployment in the Federal Republic of Germany of a new generation of nuclear missiles with range enough to strike targets in the German Democratic Republic, Poland, Czechoslovakia and Hungary. That target area is today all friendly territory. But the contention is still made that Western Europe needs a nuclear defense and plans proceed for an advanced air-to-surface tactical missile.

At the same time, the inescapable (if somewhat grudging) recognition that the Cold War is over has led Western military leaders to consider new force structures, designed to react rapidly to crises within Europe and to engage in low intensity conflict in other regional areas. The speculation about the nature of these crises has been, somewhat paradoxically, high in hypothesis and low in imagination. It is still grounded on the concept of the inviolability of state borders, engrained in historical consciousness and enshrined in the United Nations Charter.

Developments in the Gulf War and its aftermath illustrate this preoccupation with national sovereignty at the expense of human rights. The international community, acting through the United Nations Security Council, was able to react rapidly and drastically to the Iraqi invasion and occupation of Kuwait, a fellow U.N. member. But organized world response to the subsequent barbarities inflicted upon the Iraqi Shiites in the south and the Iraqi Kurds in the north has been slow and stumbling. Today, the only likely sources of conflict have nothing to do with the classic confrontation between NATO and the former Warsaw Pact. The remaining significance of the ceilings imposed in the treaty limiting conventional forces of Europe (CFE) is the major reduction in the offensive equipment of the Commonwealth of Independent States, and not any need for equality between NATO and the now-defunct Warsaw Pact.

Civil war bubbles near the surface, notably in Yugoslavia, but also in other nations carved out of the Austro-Hungarian and Ottoman empires. The compelling question today is not what weapons are needed to fight and win the Third World War, it is instead how military forces can be structured and organized, most desirably within a United Nations framework, to help bring about peaceful solutions to nationalistic movements within existing borders and to traditional ethnic and religious confrontations.

For this task, the Gulf War provides few if any political or military lessons. As commendable as opposition to international aggression is, the human and material costs of this massive application of military force deprive it of any precedential value. It can be said to have demonstrated again that nuclear weapons have no practical military utility and serve only to deter their use by others. But better ways must be devised to manage conflict, particularly in the much more ambiguous situations that may develop.

The governments of Europe and their North American colleagues need expert help in moving from outdated force postures to a new security structure. The essays in this compendium provide both food for thought and a resounding call for reasoned response to realistic security needs.

Paul C. Warnke
Washington, D.C.
March 1992

Acknowledgments

Hans Günter Brauch appreciates the financial support provided by the Berghof Foundation for Conflict Research for the project "Armaments Dynamics and East-West Conflict in the Atomic Age" that provided the basic institutional support. The German Research Society (DFG) that supported the active participation at the annual conventions of the International Studies Association and made it thus possible that both editors and the publishers could meet to coordinate the preparation of this transatlantic publication project. The Ministry for Science and the Arts Baden-Wüttemberg contributed to the communication costs in the final stages of the editorial process of this volume. Finally Peace Research and European Security Studies, AFES PRESS, supported the project on the German and with its infrastructure. He would also like to thank Robert Kennedy for his insightful comments on his two chapters. Hans Günter Brauch appreciates the permission of the editor in chief of *Soldat und Technik,* Col. Gerhard Hubatacheck (Ret.), to reproduce Figure 9.11, that was first published in German in an Article by Captain Ulrich Weisser in the March 1991 issue of the journal.

Furthermore, Mr. Brauch would like to thank Ms. Diederichs, Head of the Translation Service at the German Foreign Office, for permission to publish the English versions of the German-Soviet and German-Polish Treaties, as reproduced in the appendix. It must be noted that these translations have not been authorized by the partners to the treaties, and should therefore be used for information purposes only.

Robert Kennedy would like to thank John E. Endicott, Director of the Center for International Strategy, Technology, and Policy, Micheal Salomone, Daniel S. Papp, Director of the School of International Affairs at the Georgia Institute of Technology, and John Weinstein for their insightfull comments on chapters in this volume. He also would like to thank Suzanne Revou, the Center Secretary, for her administrative assistance in the process of preparing this last volume.

Both editors would like to thank Mr. Thomas Bast, the documentation specialist of AFES-PRESS, who compiled the index. Last but not least they owe special gratitude to their editor at Taylor and Francis, Mr. Todd W. Baldwin for his patience and support.

Hans Günter Brauch
Robert Kennedy
Mosbach, Germany and Atlanta, Georgia
August 1991

Introduction

This book addresses the security implications of the momentous political and geostrategic changes that have taken place in Europe and the former Soviet Union since 1989. It examines the relevance of the more traditional forms of defense as well as the future appropriateness of nonoffensive or confidence-building defense philosophies and principles, and specific alternative concepts for defense in Central Europe in the post-Cold War era.

Fifty years ago, on June 21 and again on December 7, 1941, first the Soviet Union and then the United States were victims of surprise attacks. The attacks, one by Hitler's Germany, and other by militarist Japan, propelled both into the largest war in history. The "war to end all wars" had, instead, led to yet another. However, even before the attack on Pearl Harbor, President Franklin D. Roosevelt and Prime Minister Winston Churchill met on the battleship H.M.S. *Prince of Wales* in Placentia Bay off of Argentina, Newfoundland. On August 12, 1941, the fourth day of their five-day meeting, they signed the Atlantic Charter, setting forth "common principles . . . for a better future for the world." Among the principles set forth that day were the "right of all peoples to choose the form of government under which they live"; the "desire to bring about the fullest collaboration between nations in the economic field"; and the encouragement of measures "which will lighten for peace-loving peoples the crushing burden of armaments."

The war, however, changed the geostrategic landscape. Europe emerged in shambles. The Soviet Union and the United States emerged as the world's only superpowers. Their historical experience had a long-lasting impact on their postwar strategic concepts and on the force structures and planning of the two competing alliances that would come to dominate the future landscape of Europe. Joseph Stalin, determined never again to see the Soviet Union invaded from Eastern Europe, embarked on a course that ultimately lead to the complete domination of that part of the world by the Soviet Union. Western European, the United States, and Canada, concerned over Soviet expansion, forged a political/military alliance to deter any further Soviet advance. Within a few years, Europe was transformed into the largest peacetime armed camp in history. The dreams of Roosevelt and Churchill had been dashed.

The end of the Cold War, however, has brought new hope for a "better future." Germany has been reunited. By mid-1991 the Soviet Union had withdrawn its military forces from Hungary and Czechoslovakia and had agreed to withdraw forces from the territory of the former German Democratic Republic and Poland by 1994. The institutions of Soviet domination and influence in East-Central Europe have disappeared. The military command of the Warsaw Treaty Organization (WTO) was dissolved on April 1, 1991. The Council for Mutual Economic Assistance (COMECON) was terminated in late June 1991. The political structure of the WTO came to an end on July 1. With the dissolution of the Soviet Union in

December 1991 and the emergence of 15 independent states, the first objective of the Atlantic Charter (previously mentioned) was in the process of becoming a reality in Eastern Europe.

Progress also has been made toward further economic collaboration, at least on the European continent. Most former members of the WTO and the Soviet successor states forming the Commonwealth of Independent States (CIS) now have joined the International Monetary Fund (IMF) and the World Bank. The USSR was offered observer status at the G-7 summit in London in early July 1991. As the principal successor state to the USSR, Russia was granted full membership in 1992. The way is now paved for its full incorporation into the world's economic mainstream. Moreover, Hungary, Czechoslovakia, and Poland have associated themselves with the European Community (EC) and are looking forward to becoming full members during the 1990s. Thus, another of the principal objectives of the Atlantic Charter is coming closer to being realized.

The end of the East-West conflict also has facilitated progress on a third objective of the Atlantic Charter in the field of disarmament. The INF Treaty has eliminated an entire class of nuclear weapons from Europe. Remaining disputes about the treaty on Conventional Armed Forces in Europe (CFE) were resolved by former Soviet Union Foreign Minister Besmertnykh and U.S. Secretary of State Baker in Lisbon in late May 1991 and hammered out by negotiators in Vienna in June 1991, paving the way for a speedy ratification. Although the demise of the Soviet Union posed some questions as to just how the treaty would be implemented since the forces of the former Soviet Union were now distributed among a member of successor states, the newly formed North Atlantic Cooperation Council (NACC) has made the successful completion of the CFE one of its principal tasks. Indeed, all remaining obstacles were resolved in the NACC framework in Spring of 1992. This will result in a significant reduction of conventional military forces in Europe. On July 31, 1991, Presidents George Bush and Mikhail Gorbachev signed the START (strategic arms reduction talks) Treaty. After nine years of negotiations, the superpowers finally agreed to a major reduction of their strategic armaments. As with CFE, implementation of the Treaty, in the wake of the breakup of the Soviet Union, faced some difficulties. Today four states of the former Soviet Union have nuclear weapons—Belarus, Russia, Kazakhstan, and Ukraine. However, nothing yet appears to be an eminent block to an agreement among the four Soviet successor states and the U.S. Thus, the major reductions in strategic arms called for by the Treaty appear likely.

Needless to say, such changes have dramatic geostrategic implications for security and defense in Central Europe. The Soviet threat is gone. With the final withdrawal of all Russian troops from Germany in 1994, nuclear disengagement, a principal policy goal set in the late 1950s, will be a reality. By 1995, there will be a de facto nuclear weapons free zone covering Scandinavia, the three Baltic Republics, Belarus, the former East Germany, Poland, Czechoslovakia, Hungary, Romania, Bulgaria, and Ukraine, as well as a security "buffer" zone without the presence of foreign troops.

In 1989, Central Europe and specifically Germany had the world's highest concentration of both local and foreign conventional military forces and nuclear weapons. By 1994, about two-thirds of the troops will have been either demobilized or withdrawn. The equipment of an entire army (i.e., the former National People's Army of the former German Democratic Republic) will have been destroyed. Arms control, even disarmament (destruction of hardware, demobilization of manpower, conversion of defense industries) with its regional and structural economic implications will have become a political reality, not only for Russia, but also for a united Germany.

Furthermore, geostrategic changes in Europe have rendered NATO's strategy of "flexible response" and its "forward defense" concept for the central front obsolete. At the London Summit in 1990, the Allies agreed "to move away, where appropriate, from the concept of forward defense toward a reduced forward presence, and to modify the principle of flexible response to reflect a reduced alliance on nuclear weapons." At the Rome Summit in November 1991, NATO heads of state and government set guidelines for a new Alliance force posture more reflective of contemporary realities. Those guidelines identified a posture that no longer will be deployed in a linear fashion in the central region, will be reduced in size, and, in many cases, readiness, able to be rapidly augmented, yet increasingly flexible and highly mobile.

Now the question to be answered is what force postures are most appropriate, given the changed environment and the Alliance's avowed determination to reduce the numbers of troops deployed, yet increase their capacity for augmentation, flexibility, and mobility. At present, the threat of an attack on NATO by one or more of the Soviet successor states is remote, yet the possibility of conflicts that might threaten the security interests of the European states remains. Indeed, the absence of the harsh and sometimes brutal order imposed by communist regimes during the Cold War, ethnic and national conflicts that harbor the potential threat to European stability already has reemergenced in South-Central and Eastern Europe. Moreover, the broader security interests of European states could be threatened once again as they were with Iraq's attack on Kuwait.

Unlike the past where the forces of the Western states could be structured to deal with the unidimensional threat emanating from the Soviet Union and the Warsaw Pact, the potential security challenges of the future are likely to be multidimensional in nature. Thus, the tasks to be performed by military forces also will be multidimensional. Future force structures in the European theater must contribute to stability and continued confidence-building between the Western states and Russia. They also must contribute to a stabilized environment between and among the nations of Central and Eastern Europe. Moreover, they may need to be structured to respond to crises and conflicts within and among the newly emerging states of South-Central and Eastern Europe or even beyond Europe itself, as they were during the second Gulf War.

Thus, in a more specific way, the question arises: Are traditional approaches to defense, which include doctrines and tactics associated with firepower and maneuver (e.g., AirLand Battle), still appropriate, albeit at reduced force levels? Or, are other force structures, such as nonoffensive defense (NOD) or confidence-building defense (CBD), now more appropriate? Perhaps some combination of force structures might be necessary to meet the multidimensional nature of current and future challenges.

In the view of at least one of the editors, NOD or CBD philosophies and principles have much to offer in the search for security postures both for the post-Cold War environment in Europe and for the areas of continued high tension in the Middle East or in South Asia. Both editors agree that a thorough examination of alternatives is clearly warranted. Several NOD specific models have become obsolete with the disappearance of the central front in Germany. Others may have become obsolete with the dissolution of the Soviet Union. NOD principles, however, have won a degree of public acclaim since Gorbachev adopted the NOD philosophy in 1987–1988. References to NOD also can be found in NATO CFE position papers and in the German–Soviet and German–Polish treaties, partly reproduced in the appendices C and D of this volume. Thus, it seems appropriate to further explore NOD and CBD as potential alternatives for future Alliance force structures.

One thing is certain, new geopolitical and geostrategic factors have rendered old defense concepts obsolete. There is a clear need for new pragmatic approaches and conceptual thinking about Europe's future defense needs. NATO already has taken important first steps, yet more needs to be done. The editors hope that this volume contributes to the debate on security issues both in the peace research and strategic and security studies communities.

The editors and authors of this volume represent a diverse group of experts with frequently differing and competing views. They hope to stimulate a debate within and between schools of thought that during the period of the "Cold War" spoke past each other, seldom engaging in a real exchange of ideas.

A changed strategic landscape now yields a challenges of different nature than those that had to be confronted during the Cold War. The Gulf War and conflict between Serbs and Croats in Croatia, between Serbs and Croats and Muslims in Bosnia-Herzegovina, between Armenians and Azerbaijans in Nagorno-Karabakh and Nakhichevan, to name just a few, suggest the need for a collaborative search for peaceful solutions of conflicts, for mediation, economic sanctions, peacekeeping, and, as a last resort, for enforcement measures under Chapter VII and VIII of the UN Charter.

This third volume is organized into three parts. Part I provides a survey of the debate on force posture alternatives in the Federal Republic of Germany and in the United States. In Part II, six specific alternative force postures for Europe are explored by American and German authors. In Part III, the impact of the international and domestic changes on security planning in Germany and the future of European security and the new international order are addressed.

In Part I, Hans Günter Brauch and Robert Kennedy, respectively, survey the German and American debates on conventional alternatives for the defense of Central Europe. Given the changes that have taken place in Europe over the past three years and the interest in the former Soviet Union in "defensive defense" concepts, both authors believe that some of the analyses that have been done by those who have examined NOD force structure alternatives may be more applicable today than ever before and that a number of the conceptual elements of NOD may form the basis for a new European security system.

In Part II, six alternative force postures are examined. Manfred Hamm traces the evolution of AirLand Battle (ALB) doctrine, delineates the basic conceptual differences between ALB doctrine and the Follow-On Forces Attack (FOFA) concept, analyzes criticisms of ALB doctrine, and offers strong support for the Air-Land Battle doctrine and the FOFA concept. He further argues that both ALB doctrine and the FOFA concepts are compatible and complementary, while constituting no substantive obstacle to further arms control efforts. Although this chapter was completed before the momentus events since 1989, and the Gulf War, some defense specialists might argue that the Gulf War validated many of the AirLand

Battle concepts. Moreover, as both NATO and Soviet successor states reduce the density of their forces, ALB doctrine, which emphasizes firepower and maneuver, in the view of one editor, may prove to be more relevant than less for the forces that remain.

In Chapter 4, John Weinstein recognizes that the outbreak of war in Europe as a result of an adverse turn of events may not be likely today. However, U.S. and European security should not be mortgaged on the unsupportable promise that today's good times will continue indefinitely. It is upon this note of caution that he endorses the continued need for nuclear weapons, albeit at reduced levels, in Europe. Weinstein argues that while advanced conventional munitions (ACMs) have a number of desirable military and political advantages, it may be illusory to expect ACMs to eliminate completely NATO's reliance on nuclear weapons. Changes now underway in Europe, however, do support the cuts in NATO's current short-range nuclear forces that are being made. Nevertheless, Weinstein contends nuclear forces able to be projected from land, sea, and air to cover short and longer ranges with precision remain a prudent option for deterrence and defense in Europe. The acquisition of a nuclear tactical air-to-surface missile (TASM) and providing Harrier V/STOL aircraft with a nuclear capability are partial answers to NATO's potential future needs. Weinstein also suggests that the Follow-on-to-Lance (FOTL) be reconsidered as a flexible and all-weather replacement to the artillery-fired atomic projectile (AFAPS), which are being withdrawn from Western Europe. He also suggests that insertable nuclear component (INC) technology may be a politically acceptable way for the Atlantic Alliance to retain a short-range nuclear capability deployable to Europe should a future crisis so warrant.

In Chapter 5, Franz Uhle-Wettler contends that the debates on force improvements in NATO have concentrated heavily on weapons, equipment, and force structure. Seldom, if ever, have they concentrated on morale, motivation, tactics, and training. He believes that there is a clear danger of "high tech" with the consequent neglect of opportunities offered by the more traditional technologies and, especially, training. According to Uhle-Wettler, if NATO wishes to improve its military capabilities, it should focus on morale, training, tactics, and weaponry. He concludes that force improvements that concentrate on weaponry to the detriment of other factors will inevitably be deficient. Again, while this chapter was completed before both the Gulf War and the dissolution of the Soviet Union, Uhle-Wettler's concerns, cautions, and recommendations have a certain timelessness, which makes them worthy of consideration as we move to develop new force structures and postures to deal with the challenges ahead.

In Chapter 6, Horst Afheldt, one of the fathers of the contemporary German debate on alternative approaches to defense in Europe, identifies what he considers to be fundamental building blocks for a new security policy in Central Europe and outlines his own alternative force structure for a "Mutual Defensive Superiority" with conventional weapons. In his "ideal" case, Afheldt argues for a dispersed defense that provides no fixed targets and makes no effort to hold fortifications or fixed defensive lines. He contends that such a "hidden mode of battle" could be made possible by "autonomous technocommandos" employing weapons and tactics specialized for defense and supported by modern rocket artillery in the form of cheap, single use launch tubes and an operative command specialized for defense. Afheldt believes that if such forces were developed by all parties there would be no need for potentially offensive air and ground forces or a NATO nuclear first use strategy. According to Afheldt, such a model promises increased stability in Europe and a more credible deterrent and defense doctrine for NATO, given the changes taking place in Europe today.

In Chapter 7, Lutz Unterseher outlines the international Study Group for Alternative Security Policy (SAS) case for a "Confidence-Building Defense (CBD)." Unterseher notes that the concept of a CBD rests on four maxims: (1) military forces must be structurally unable to invade or bombard an adversary's territory; (2) force structure vulnerabilities should be minimized; (3) force structures should be designed to limit rather than extend damage or escalate conflict; and (4) the defender's inherent advantage of operating on familiar terrain should be optimally exploited. Unterseher sees the SAS "spider and web" concept as the key paradigm for such a defense. Unterseher's CBD model would include network infantry, mobile forces, and homeguard forces. *Network infantry* battalions would be assigned to fixed areas covering 7 to 10 interlinked zones of key strategic importance. Their tasks could include delaying, attriting, splitting up, and channeling attacking forces. *Mobile forces* would be composed of armor, cavalry, and light mechanized infantry capable of blocking, containing, counterattacking, and ultimately destroying intruding formations. Finally, *homeguard forces* would be designed to protect infrastructure against airborne, commando, and other lower-level threats. Since according to Unterseher, it is force structure that determines "defensivity" not the acquisition of "defensive" weapons, the SAS weapons mix is not fundamentally different from NATO's arsenal for conventional defense on friendly territory. There would be a shift of emphasis, however, in favor of such capabilities as more and denser underground communications, prefabricated elements for small-sized field fortifications, multisensor mines, and short-range combat drones.

Finally in Chapter 8, one of the United State's early thinkers on alternative approaches to conventional defense, Steven Canby offers a critique of the primarily European proposals for a nonprovocative defense from the vantagepoint of an American force designer. He also offers his own alternative model for European defense. Canby argues that for forty years NATO has deployed its forces mostly as a cordon defense. Only recently has this begun to change and operational reserves were formed. While Canby believes that NATO's cordon deterred Soviet aggression, he contends that had deterrence failed, defense also would have failed. To remedy the situation, he recommends a defense oriented to light infantry forward, and tank reserves rearward with technology and tactics fully integrated.

In Part III, Chapter 9, Hans Günter Brauch addresses NATO's emerging force structure and strategy readjustments, the Bundeswehr's implementation of the new multilateral and bilateral treaty obligations for manpower, force structure, deployment and procurement planning for 1984 and beyond, the constitutional and political self-restraint for the future role of German forces in international military conflicts and the continued relevance of nonoffensive or confidence-building defense concepts. Brauch suggests that the following tasks for NOD and CBD concepts are worthy of consideration in the post Cold-War environment:

- NOD concepts should become a *topic for future seminars on military doctrine* of the now expanded Conference on Security and Cooperation in Europe (CSCE).
- For CSCE member states, NOD principles should become the guiding princi-

ples for steering (1) the weapons process; (2) force structure planning; and (3) arms control policy.

- NOD principles also should become the guidelines for permitted arms exports into crises areas. Only those weapon systems that strengthen the defense but do not foster the capability for offensive operations should be permitted for export.

In the final chapter, Robert Kennedy examines European security, NATO, and the future of a new international cooperative system in light of the extraordinary events of the last several years. He contends that we are entering an age of epochal international systemic change. The end of the Cold War, the impending complete withdrawal of the forces of the former Soviet Union from Eastern Europe, and, perhaps more significantly, the Second Russian Revolution has set in motion sweeping changes of historic proportions. However, according to Kennedy, we have not reached the end of history. The world has not seen the end of conflict. Perhaps the greatest danger we now confront is not being able to perceive the dangers that lie ahead. Kennedy concludes that NATO, CSCE, EC, and the WEU can and should play complementary roles in meeting Europe's future security needs. He further concludes that if NATO is to prove useful in dealing with future, not past, crises and potential threats to western security interests, it will have to be structured to deal with future, not past, problems. He suggests the need for changes in the modalities within NATO, a broadening and a deepening of the Alliance, and the development of a significant capability to deal with out-of-area issues both at the political level and, if need be, at the military level.

Hans Günter Brauch
Robert Kennedy
Mosbach, Germany and Atlanta, Georgia
March 1992

I

SURVEYS OF FORCE POSTURE ALTERNATIVES

1

Debate on Alternative Conventional Military Force Structure Designs for the Defense of Central Europe in the Federal Republic of Germany

Hans Günter Brauch

INTRODUCTION: DEFINITIONS OF ALTERNATIVE DEFENSE

Alternative defense is a military concept[1] that has been described by many terms, such as territorial, nonoffensive, defensive, nonprovocative, nonaggressive, confidence-building, structural inability to attack, and defensive or mutual defensive superiority. These and many other terms describe a military concept that differs fundamentally from the force structures of Guderian, Fuller, and De Gaulle in World War II and those of both NATO and the former Warsaw Pact countries that have been optimized for counter-offensive or offensive operations.[2] In this chapter we use "nonoffensive defense" (NOD) as the generic term for this alternative school of thinking.

Björn Möller, editor of the *NOD Newsletter,* defined "nonoffensive defense" in this way: "The armed forces should be seen in their totality to be capable of a credible defense, yet incapable of offense."[3] The term "nonprovocative defense" has been defined as "A military posture in which the strategic and operational concepts, the deployment, organization, armaments, communications and command, logistics and training of the armed forces are such, that they are in their totality unambiguously capable of an adequate conventional defence, but as unambiguously incapable of a border crossing attack, be it an invasion or a destructive strike at the opponents territory."[4] According to Boserup and Neild, "defensive defense" is: ". . . to ease the military confrontation in Europe by restructuring conventional forces so as to minimize the capability to attack while maintaining intact their capabilities to defend. If that can be done, it will provide unambiguous evidence of peaceful intentions; it will be mutually reassuring; and it will enhance military stability."[5] Lutz Unterseher introduced the concept of "confidence-building defense" as a reaction to NATO's former nuclear posture and its then conventional force structure oriented at punishment rather than denial. As a defensive philosophy, it would rely on these measures:

1. Removal of nuclear assets from NATO's territory; separation of nuclear from conventional forces; and adoption of "no first use" (only if the demands on

the American nuclear umbrella are greatly reduced is there a chance for some form of extended deterrence to survive).

2. Creation of an inherently stable conventional deterrent, by tactically and organizationally emancipating it from nuclear weapons (which would no longer be counted upon as "trouble shooters") giving it the capability to restrict the battle zone; making it virtually safe from being overrun, bypassed, or "outmaneuvered," technically and tactically; and keeping it from presenting valuable targets to enemy fire, thus abolishing opportunities for the opponent making it structurally incapable of (and doctrinally not charged with) invading or bombarding the other side's territory, thereby removing the reason for preemption.

3. "Decoupling" from the arms race and consequently maintaining and improving the internal stability of the societies by doing away with the traditional concept of balance ("answering in kind") and by specializing on defense in a cost-effective manner.[6]

Since the 1950s, this alternative school to the traditional military and strategic thinking in NATO and the Warsaw Pact has been a specific reaction to nuclear deterrence and conventional defense concepts, and (in the case of Germany) also to the division of Germany. This school was influenced by Carl von Clausewitz, Sir Basil Liddell Hart, Bogislav von Bonin, Guy Brossollet, and Emmil Spannoc-chi.[7] From the mid-1970s to the early 1980s, the alternative school was primarily a German debate stimulated by the writings of Carl Friedrich von Weizsäcker and Horst Afheldt. Subsequently the debate spread to the Netherlands (Egbert Boeker, INSTEAD); to the United Kingdom (Alternative Defence Commission, Common Security Project, Just Defence); the United States (Randall Forsberg and Paul Walker); and since 1984, via the Conventional Weapons Working Group of Pugwash, to Eastern Europe—especially to Hungary and to the Soviet Union, where it was taken up and promoted by Mikhail Gorbachev as part of the new thinking and has thus become part of the international dialogue.[8] Since the 1970s, independently of Afheldt and the German debate, Stephen Canby, Ed Corcoran, and Robert Kennedy have initiated a similar debate in the United States (see Chapter 2). However, until the early 1980s, these two independent debates did not influence each other.

Most of the proposals were developed prior to unification by West German authors and a few independent thinkers in the GDR, such as Walter Romberg[9] who focused on the former central front between the NATO and Warsaw Pact nations, running down the divided Germany. They were conceived of as tools to reduce the reliance on nuclear weapons; to drop NATO's nuclear first-use option; to avoid an inadvertent nuclear attack by removing incentives for preemptive attacks; to enhance strategic and especially crisis stability; to exploit the terrain by increasing defense efficiency; to further detente and conventional disarmament; and to eliminate or drastically curtail the arms race by favoring the defense over the offense. However, the context in which these proposals were originally developed in Germany has disappeared since the winter of 1989. The question remains: Have the concepts themselves become obsolete as well.

This chapter first examines the old strategic context in central Europe, reviews the five stages of the German NOD debate, and identifies the major pure, add-on, and integrative and comprehensive proposals. It discusses the new international and domestic political context resulting from German unification and the potential implications for force restructuring.

NONOFFENSIVE DEFENSE AS AN ALTERNATIVE TO FORWARD DEFENSE?

During the 1980s, "conventionalization" and "alternative defense" were the catchwords of a debate on the military aspects of security policy in the Federal Republic of Germany. Geographic, strategic, historical, political, and economic reasons contributed to an intensive debate among government officials (the official debate), government advisers in research institutes close to or advising the Federal government (the semiofficial debate), retired officers, social scientists, and independent security experts (unofficial debate), and by peace researchers, peace activists, and the peace movement (the peace debate).[10]

The *geographic* reasons were self-evident: the territory of the Federal Republic of Germany would be the first battlefield in Europe if deterrence should fail and the East-West conflict escalate to the military level with the employment of both conventional and nuclear weapons. The *strategic* reasons were a reflection of the differing interpretations of NATO's doctrine of "flexible response" and of deterrence in general in Europe and the United States, most particularly in West Germany. Since the 1950s, NATO has been confronted with a "seemingly irreconcilable conflict of interests." Given the potential destruction of any war on their territory during the East-West conflict, Europeans, and particularly Germans, "have tended to advocate a strategy of absolute deterrence through the immediate threat of all-out nuclear war, and have looked with unease and suspicion at any development that appears to distract from this ultimate threat, or that threatens to 'decouple' Europe from the American strategic nuclear guarantee."[11]

Americans, in looking beyond deterrence, have "emphasized the need to deter conflict at all possible levels through the provision of a wide range of capabilities and options" and, if deterrence should fail, "to facilitate the termination of any conflict short of allout nuclear war," e.g., if a nuclear war should occur and if a conventional war should escalate to the nuclear level, to limit it and to prevent an allout nuclear war or a spillover into the continental U.S. As Americans called for flexibility and for as many steps as possible in the nuclear escalation ladder, many Europeans suspected that any increase in flexibility would lead to a strategic nightmare: the containment and limitation of any conflict to Europe. This dispute has lasted for three decades. It influenced the transatlantic multilateral force (MLF) debate in the 1960s, the intermediate-range nuclear forces (INF) controversy in the late 1970s and early 1980s, and the short-range nuclear forces (SNF) dispute in the late 1980s, as well as the debate on "conventionalization" (AirLand Battle and Follow-on Forces Attack (FOFA)) in the early 1980s.[12] Whereas the MLF debate took place primarily among governments and a few experts, the INF controversy led to a broad public debate that made the West German government far more sensitive to domestic concerns during the SNF dispute. As a consequence of the peaceful revolution in Eastern Europe, of German unification, and of the agreed Soviet troop withdrawals, the political, geographical, and strategic contexts have changed fundamentally.

FIVE STAGES OF THE DEBATE
ON ALTERNATIVE DEFENSE

Since its establishment in 1949, the Federal Republic of Germany was confronted with five fundamental debates on foreign and security policy:[13]

In the early 1950s: on rearmament and integration into NATO and the European Community institutions vs. national unification between the Adenauer government and the Social Democratic Party (SPD).[14]

In the late 1950s: on deployment of nuclear weapons or nuclear disengagement in Europe between the Adenauer government and the SPD and the first antinuclear movement.[15]

In the early 1960s: on the primacy of a transatlantic (U.S.) vs. a pro-European (France) orientation within the Christian Democratic Union and the Christian Social Union (CDU/CSU) parties.

In the early 1970s: on Brandt's Ostpolitik, the recognition of the borders, joining the Nonproliferation Treaty and on the participation in the CSCE between the Brandt government and the CDU/CSU opposition.[16]

In the early 1980s: on the deployment of Pershing II and cruise missiles and on the role of nuclear weapons in NATO strategy.[17]

With respect to the debate on military force structures and NOD concepts, five stages may also be distinguished (see Table 1-1).

In 1954–1955 (as the Bundeswehr was being established) among the military experts within and outside of the government.

In the 1970s when Carl Friedrich von Weizsäcker and Horst Afheldt published their studies on the implications and contradictions of nuclear deterrence (within the scientific community).

In the early 1980s on the background of the public INF controversy, a search for political alternatives to nuclear deterrence stimulated the development and proliferation of NOD concepts within the scientific community and the peace movement.

In the mid-1980s, NOD concepts for the first time had an impact on political parties, most particularly on the SPD after it lost power in 1982 and to a limited extent on the Greens.

In the early 1990s, the first historical opportunity to include NOD concepts in the review process of military force structures and military doctrines.

Only in the context of the fourth major debate did military force posture alternatives and NOD concepts come to play a significant role. Only then were NOD proposals intensively discussed and adopted in party resolutions and into the program of the SPD.

Stage 1: Establishment of the Bundeswehr; von Bonin, an Early Dissenter (1954–1955)

The unconditional surrender of 1945, the division of Germany, and the superpower confrontation during the cold war did not provoke a fundamental reassess-

Table 1-1   Five Stages of the Debate on Force Posture Alternatives in the Federal Republic of Germany

Stage ——— Years	Phase of East-West Conflict	NATO Strategic Context	FRG Political Context	Official, Semioffic., Traditional	Proponents of NOD Force Structure Proposals
1954– 1967	Cold war Limited Detente	Massive Retaliation Flexible Response MLF	Rearmament NATO, EEC Atlantic vs European orientation	Heusenberg[a] Kielmannsegg	von Bonin (1954) von Bonin (1967)
1971– 1978	Detente *Ostpolitik*	Flexible Response	NPT Treaty Moscow Tr. Warsaw Tr. CSCE (1975)	Defense White Papers 1970–1979[b]	v. Weizsäcker (1970) Afheldt u.a. (1973)[c] Afheldt (1976)
1979– 1984	Limited Detente, Second cold war	Flexible Response INF modern. FOFA/ALB	INF Dec. NOD Hearing (1983–1984)	Stratmann Nerlich K. Kaiser ESECS (1983)[d]	Uhle-Wettler (1980) J. Löser (1981) H. Afheldt (1983) v. Weizsäcker (1984) Hannig (1984) SAS (1984) Nolte/Nolte (1984) v. Müller (1984)
1984– 1989	Limited Detente	Flexible Response INF Treaty SNF Debate	SPD-Essen Party Cong.	Defense White Papers 1983 & 1985[e]	v. Bülow/Funk/ v. Müller (1988) SAS (1989) Gerber (1989)
1990–	Detente end of post- war period	Flexible Response Forward Defense Reassessm.	German unification	Official Statements Stoltenberg Eppelmann[f]	Afheldt (1991) SAS—Unterseher (1991)

[a]See Brill, op. cit. 1976 and op. cit., 1987.

[b]Bundesminister der Verteidigung, *Weißbuch zur Sicherheit der Bundesrepublik Deutschland 1970, 1971/72, 1973/74, 1975/76, 1979* (Bonn: BMVg, 1970, 1972, 1974, 1976, 1979).

[c]*Eine Andere Verteidigung? Alternativen zur atomaren Abschreckung. Aus der Arbeit der Vereinigung Deutscher Wissenschaftler (München: Hanser, 1973).*

[d]Peter K. Stratmann, *NATO-Strategie in der Krise?* (Baden-Baden: Nomos, 1981); Uwe Nerlich, "Missile Defense: Strategic and Tactical," Survival, 27, no. 3 (May/June 1985): 119–136; Karl Kaiser, Georg Leber, Alois Mertes, and Franz-Josef Schulze, "Nuclear Weapons and the Preservation of Peace: A Response to an American Proposal for Renouncing the First Use of Nuclear Weapons," *Foreign Affairs,* vol. 6, no. 5 (Summer 1982): 1157–1170; ESECS, *Strengthening Conventional Deterrence in Europe—Proposals for the 1980s* (London: Macmillan, 1983).

[e]Bundesminister der Verteidigung, *Weißbuch zur Sicherheit der Bundesrepublik Deutschland 1983, 1985* (Bonn: BMVg, 1983, 1985).

[f]See speeches and press conferences of the West German defense minister Stoltenberg, and the East German minister on disarmament and defense, Eppelmann.

ment of military force structures. Only Colonel Bogislav von Bonin[18] dissented from the mainstream represented by General Adolf Heusinger, Count Wolf von Baudissin, and Count Johann Adolf von Kielmannsegg in the Amt Blank (later to become the Federal Ministry of Defense).

Starting with reunification as the prevailing political objective, von Bonin designed a barrier zone along the demarcation line some 50 km wide that was to wear down and, if possible, to stop the armored thrusts of an invader. He believed that a small force of 150,000 to 200,000 soldiers could be built up within two years at relatively low cost. Von Bonin's force structure proposal consisted of a system of small, well-camouflaged field fortifications, distributed in depth with only small armored elements for tactical counterattack, to be manned by old *Wehrmacht* cadres still fit for service. Most of their equipment was to consist of relatively simple, state-of-the-art weapons, e.g., about 8000 antitank guns complemented by recoilless rifles and numerous hand-laid mines. Once von Bonin made his nonprovocative concept explicit, he was removed from his position in 1953 and portrayed as a dissident.

According to the von Bonin plan, nonprovocation was to be made operational through tactics and force structure, both designed for static warfare, for denial of attrition. Large-size mechanized all-purpose forces were thought of only in the context of allied reserves, coming to chop off enemy spearheads that might eventually pierce the proposed covering army. He was convinced that the allies' help could be counted on and that the delaying effect of the barrier zone would be welcomed by them. This purely German nonprovocative front layer was to avoid providing the Soviets with any incentive for a potential build-up of invasion forces in East Germany. No foreign mobile forces with offensive capabilities and armed with nuclear weapons that might create a climate of instability and confrontation and minimize the opportunity for German unification were to be stationed in central Europe. He proposed a virtual disappearance of military targets through camouflage and dispersion.[19]

Von Bonin's proposal was rejected both by military experts within the Amt Blank: by Heusinger, head of the military department of the Amt Blank, by the reformers, von Baudissin and von Kielmannsegg, and by the CDU/CSU, as well as by the defense experts of the SPD, Fritz Erler and Helmut Schmidt. Von Bonin's concept was supported by several retired generals, and his ideas were well received by some news media, most notably by the news magazine *Der Spiegel,* which published a long essay on "The Battle of Kursk—a Model for the Defense of the Federal Republic of Germany,"[20] in November 1966.

Von Bonin stated that the defense planners of NATO and of the Bundeswehr were still adhering to World War II concepts made obsolete by nuclear weapons. NATO's nuclear deterrence concept and the deployment of nuclear launchers on German territory would contradict its national interests. Strategy would require a removal of all provocative weapons systems and force structures and their replacement by a security system that would offer better protection and would not beg the opponent to preempt. He argued:

> As long as American nuclear weapons are deployed in the Federal Republic of Germany, the Soviet leadership would be forced to destroy this forward based U.S. atomic base. It must be the preeminent goal of the Federal Republic to remove its territory from the target list of Soviet nuclear weapons. A major Soviet attack has become unthinkable. The American nuclear weapons would make any Soviet aggression against Western Europe an incalculable risk.[21]

Von Bonin called for the following elements of an alternative mission for the Bundeswehr and for NATO:

Withdrawal of all nuclear weapons from West German territory.
Change of the structure of the Bundeswehr by replacing its offensive character with a nonprovocative structure.

A reduction and restructuring of the Bundeswehr to permit the withdrawal of several Soviet divisions from East Germany.

The prevailing mission of the Bundeswehr should be the defense of the border against a Soviet surprise attack.

This border defense would require about 250,000 regulars, of which 160,000 would serve in the army.

The first layer of defense would consist of eight border defense divisions of 15,000 men each for a territory of 100 km in depth.

A combination of sufficient mobility with strong attrition would have to wear down an aggressor in a system of several defensive layers.

This would require the introduction of multiple rocket launchers and of more potent ammunition and fire power.

The area defense force made up of conscripts would have to supplement the border defense force by exploiting the knowledge of the terrain for the defense. These forces could be trained in six months.

The tasks of the navy would be limited to the defense of the north German coast-line: 30,000 men would be sufficient for this task.

The air force would have to support the defensive battle of the army; 60,000 regulars for the air force and 12 air wings would be sufficient for this task.

The Federal Republic would require the support of NATO and of the United States. The restructured Bundeswehr could not prevent a massive Soviet attack. It would have to rely on the deterrence function of the U.S. strategic forces. However, it would be able to counter a more limited Soviet aggression and to stop it.[22]

Helmut Schmidt, then chairman of the SPD faction in the *Bundestag,* agreed to a large extent with von Bonin's analysis; nevertheless, he disagreed with his proposals. By preferring negotiated arms control agreements to unilateral efforts at restructuring of forces, Schmidt avoided any discussion of a nonprovocative force structure in his two books: *Defense or Retaliation* (1961) and *Strategy of Balance* (1969).[23] As the first Social Democratic defense minister (1969–1972), Schmidt initiated many reforms. He created a defense planning staff and partly reorganized the *Bundeswehr.* However, he avoided any change in the direction of von Bonin's concepts.[24] Von Bonin's proposals did not provoke a fundamental security debate within the tiny security political elite in the political parties, in societal groups, nor at universities.

Stage 2: Critique of Nuclear Deterrence; von Weizsäcker and Afheldt (1970s)

The second debate was stimulated by a decision in 1957 by 18 renowned nuclear physicists, among them Otto Hahn, Werner Heisenberg, and Carl Friedrich von Weizsäcker, not to cooperate in any nuclear project in the future. Since the late 1960s within the Federation of German Scientists (*Vereinigung deutscher Wissenschaftler*) and later within the framework of the Max Planck Institute for Research on the Living Conditions of the Scientific and Technical World, a small group of talented scientists under the chairmanship of the physicist and philosopher, Carl Friedrich von Weizsäcker, had analyzed the consequences of a limited nuclear war in central Europe on the economy, on stability, and on the environment.[25]

The group contended that no credible defense existed for the Federal Republic if deterrence should fail. Therefore war prevention was the primary goal for any rational security policy. However, they believed that the deterrence system was confronted with increasing challenges of destabilization due to new weapons developments. No permanent technical stabilization of a policy of war prevention by deterrence could be assumed. Thus political steps would be needed to maintain stability between two competing superpowers.

The social democratic government of Chancellor Willy Brandt and his defense ministers Helmut Schmidt and Georg Leber reacted with silence to this fundamental conceptual challenge, as did all parties in the parliament. However, the "Weizsäcker Study" influenced the political debate within the youth organizations of the SPD and the FDP—the Young Socialists and the Young Liberals[26]—and the debate within the tiny peace research community.

In 1976 in his major study, *Defense and Peace—Policy with Military Means,* Horst Afheldt presented a sharp critique of the contradictions of NATO's flexible response posture and military force structure. He also offered an alternative: the outline of an area defense force. This was the first radical and *purely military force structure alternative.*

In 1977, Afheldt set up a working group of retired military officers to work with him on military force structure alternatives that avoided the dilemmas of forward defense and flexible response. In the 1980s several of his collaborators, such as Jochen Löser and Norbert Hannig became proponents of pure force structure alternatives. Others, like Eckart Afheldt and Johannes Gerber, suggested adding NOD components to existing force structures, or dealt with specific aspects of NOD (add-on models).[27] Whereas all these models focused on the army, the SAS (Study Group on Alternative Security Policy) offered an *integrative* model for all three forces.

From 1978–1981, Alfred Mechtersheimer worked with Afheldt, and from 1983–1988, Albrecht von Müller was Afheldt's assistant and Lutz Unterseher acted as an outside adviser. All three were to play a major role in the alternative defense debate in the 1980s. Mechtersheimer later founded the Research Institute on Peace Policy.[28] Unterseher had already founded the SAS,[29] and von Müller played an active role in the Pugwash Workshop on Conventional Forces in Europe and as the coordinator of a research project under the guidance of Afheldt and Hans-Peter Dürr. In 1989 with Anders Boserup he founded the European Center for International Security (EUCIS).

Stage 3: INF and the Antinuclear Movement; Search for Alternatives and Proliferation of NOD Concepts (1980s)

During the INF debate in the early 1980s, several retired generals, active officers of the Bundeswehr, defense experts, members of parliament, and peace researchers offered their own alternative concepts after the peace movement and the media had created a substantial demand.[30] For the first time, the military and academic debate turned into a political one.

Stage 4: NOD Proposals as a Topic of the Political Debate and Their Impact on Political Parties

At the height of the missile debate, the Armed Forces Committee held a series of public hearings on "alternative strategies," from October 24, 1983, to February 6, 1984, for which the political parties designated 26 experts.[31] Not surprisingly, in its assessment, the CDU/CSU faction of the parliament supported NATO's existing military strategic concept, whereas the SPD called for a thorough reassessment of NATO's strategy of flexible response, rejected chemical warfare modernization plans, the forward deployment of nuclear artillery, and the AirLand Battle Doctrine of the U.S. Army. Instead the SPD called for the abandonment of nuclear artillery, a rearward deployment of nuclear battlefield systems, separation of the nuclear and conventional tasks of the air force, and a drastic reduction of nuclear weapons on either side. To raise the nuclear threshold, the SPD called for a strengthening of the conventional component through a better use of reservists, an improvement of the quality of conventional weapons, a strengthening of conventional forces with a visible defensive structure, an improvement of C^3 I systems, and an increase of cost efficiency as a result of standardization. The FDP proposed conventional improvements within the existing NATO strategy, whereas the Green Party supported nonviolent forms of defense, disengagement, and finally a dissolution of both military alliances.[32] However, the government of Chancellor Helmut Kohl and Defense Minister Wörner saw no need for a fundamental reassessment of NATO's defense posture.

Stage 5: German Unification; The Integration of the National People's Army into the Bundeswehr in 1991

As a consequence of the agreement between Kohl and Gorbachev at Zheleznovodosk on July 16, 1990,[33] within three to four years the armed forces of a united Germany will be reduced from an active strength of 578,000 (in July 1990: Bundeswehr 480,000 and NVA 98,000) to 370,000. In August 1990, the West German defense minister, Stoltenberg, announced an integration of some 50,000 soldiers from the NVA into the Bundeswehr, among them 25,000 to 30,000 officers and N.C.O.s and the rest conscripts.[34] For the first time, two armed forces trained in opposing military alliances and who attended military academies in the United States and in the Soviet Union will be united. This will require a reassessment of NATO strategy. With the reduction of the Bundeswehr and the creation of a territorial army outside of the integrated NATO commands, NOD concepts are likely to be seriously considered for the first time.[35] Undoubtedly a wide review of proposals will be considered.

A TYPOLOGY OF PURE, ADD-ON,
AND INTEGRATIVE NOD MODELS

Of the many NOD proposals, the 10 most significant are reviewed in three groups: the pure models of Horst Afheldt, J. Löser, and N. Hannig; the add-on models of F. Uhle-Wettler, E. Afheldt, R. Huber, H. Hoffmann, E. Schmähling, A. von Bülow, and A. von Müller; and the integrative model of the SAS. They share most of the following criticisms of NATO's defense posture:

Concern that NATO's defense doctrine of Flexible Response would be suicidal because it would destroy the territory to be defended.
Criticism of the nuclearization of NATO's defense and especially of the role of battlefield systems in the context of warfighting scenarios.
Concern that nuclear battlefield weapons or conventional forces would invite an opponent to preempt and thus reduce crisis stability.
A request for a more cost-effective use of scarce resources: manpower and money.

They also have the following conceptual features in common:[36]

An emphasis on a drastic reduction and total removal of all landbased nuclear INF, SNF, and battlefield systems in Europe.
A call for a conventional stabilization by avoiding deep strike concepts such as AirLand Battle and FOFA, building down offensive capabilities while retaining and improving defensive capabilities.
Elimination of the risks of rapid conventional attacks by increasing warning time and removing lucrative targets for preemptive strikes.
Emphasis on exploiting the terrain on the forward edge of the battlefield with both barriers and with highly mobile small infantry units.
Creation of defensive structures that would be unsuitable for the offense but sufficient for a conventional defense.
A force structure that would offer no targets for an aggressor and would break with answering in kind patterns that have legitimized the arms competition between East and West since the late 1940s.
A build-down of heavy conventional weaponry, especially of main battle tanks, self-propelled heavy artillery, fighter bombers, long-range missiles, and large surface ships.
An exploitation of conventional weaponry with short-range, limited tactical mobility, high accuracy on small weapons platforms (e.g., mines, rocket artillery etc.).
A close synchronization of efforts to achieve conventional stability with political steps to support detente and confidence building (CSBMs).

NOD proposals thus require an application of the announced arms control goals for the design of one's own military force structure and as a guiding principle for the selection of military R&D and procurement projects. Not all NOD proposals subscribe to all components. Some even attempt to combine NOD components with a call for a modernization of nuclear forces and for a conventional shallow strike concept.[37]

The Pure Models: Afheldt, Löser, Hannig

Horst Afheldt's techno-commandos

In 1976, Horst Afheldt offered a penetrating critique of NATO's Flexible Response doctrine and laid the theoretical foundations for what he considered to be a more rational security policy.[38] He emphasized several objective reasons for a review of NATO's security policy; mainly, the shift from United States nuclear superiority during the 1970s to a strategy of parity that had made any strategic strike of the United States against the USSR suicidal. For Afheldt, rational military planning was not to be limited to "pure deterrence"; it would have to include credible options if deterrence should fail. In 1978, Afheldt formulated a set of eight norms and 23 specific criteria that would have to be met by a rational defense policy for Europe that should fulfill these two tasks:

> *The first task would be to make an attack on Central Europe and an occupation of NATO territories as costly to any aggressor both politically and militarily and to prevent a fait accompli within hours or days in order to buy time for the U.S. nuclear forces. The second task would be to devise rational nuclear options for both the U.S. and its allies if deterrence should fail which will lead to a restoration of the status quo. Within the first task complex nuclear weapons could not be employed without destroying the rationality of the options while within the second task complex nuclear weapons could not be given any military task. They could be employed exclusively in accordance with political criteria.*[39]

Afheldt's alternative defense structure model was to develop rational options for the prevention of the fait d'accompli and for establishing a credible deterrence of restricted range with nonnuclear means and supplementary models for strategies of coercion for the nuclear forces of the United States.[40]

Afheldt's area defense model of 1976 would have set up a network of platoon-size infantry commandos, so-called techno-commandos, all across the Federal Republic of Germany, excluding only the highly populated urban areas. He called for a static light infantry of several thousand autonomous units, each made up of 20 to 30 men who are familiar with a territory of 10 to 15 square km that they are supposed to defend. In the forward area, these forces would be active permanently in order to provide protection against surprise. Further back, the reserve component would be recruited locally. The equipment would be suitable for blocking and destroying an aggressor (e.g., mines, antitank-guided weaponry—ATGW). The infantry component of the defensive network would neither be able to attack nor to mass forces.

Any possible effort by the aggressor to concentrate mechanized divisions would be countered by precise fire or artillery rockets directed at invading forces at the moment they tried to cross the demarcation line. These rockets (range: 20 to 80 km) would be based in the defender's hinterland. Just like the camouflaged positions of the techno-commandos, rocket launchers would be randomly distributed to avoid easy detection.

Afheldt's model did not require a highly vulnerable air force. In addition to his stationary units, he recommended mobile air defense squads armed with SAMs, man-portable antiaircraft systems, and antipersonnel weapons for use against paratroopers. Afheldt's peacetime personnel requirement was 390,000 in comparison to the then strength of the Bundeswehr of some 495,000 men.

In 1983, Horst Afheldt, influenced by his cousin, Eckart Afheldt, subscribed to a more pragmatic interim solution. His stationary *Jäger* units, protected by shelters, would exploit the terrain and fire with rather simple arms (including mortar) from alternative fighting positions. Afheldt, as in 1976, also proposed concentrations of long-range, highly dispersed, precision-guided rockets, firing from rear areas of defense, to protect his highly dispersed and static, terrain-oriented system from massed blows. The rockets would be simpler and cheaper than those currently under development for deep strike purposes. In his view, the danger of both nuclear and conventional war could be minimized by adopting such a conventional defense, which would (1) be immune to being overrun, (2) deny the enemy a premium for conventional, nuclear, or chemical fire concentrations (no-target philosophy), and (3) be nonprovocative as the result of a structural inability to attack.

Afheldt originally argued that the process of restructuring should be initiated and implemented unilaterally. In 1988/1989, however, he also discussed the prospects of a bilateral implementation of NOD concepts. Regarding the air component, he suggested a withdrawal of all NATO airfields to positions east of the Rhine and a simultaneous rearward deployment of all Warsaw Treaty Organization (WTO) airfields and range limitations for cruise missiles.[41]

Afheldt's "archetypal" model was criticized both from the Left and from military circles, who doubted the efficiency and the implementability of his radical alternative model.[42] During the 1970s, the SPD, the FDP, and the coalition governments of Brandt and Schmidt showed no interest in a detailed analysis of Afheldt's force structure model.[43] The Christian Democratic opposition party was not even interested in reviewing his alternative.

Löser's area covering defense model

Major General Jochen Löser was a member of Afheldt's working group before he published his own model in his book, *Neither Red nor Dead* (1981).[44] Assuming a Soviet surprise attack but influenced by Afheldt's criticisms of NATO's nuclear strategy, Löser called for an area covering defense (*raumdeckende Verteidigung*) that would consist of three zones:

Frontier area defense (*Grenzraumverteidigung*).
An area-covering defense web (*Raumverteidigungsnetz*).
Rear area (*Heimatschutz*).

Löser's area covering defense web was similar to Afheldt's *Jäger* brigades. These "shield forces" should be complemented by "sword forces" consisting of German and allied troops operating in the rear that would be comprised of armored vehicles capable of undertaking counterattacks. The home guard in the rear would consist primarily of volunteers who would fight against paratroopers, covert operations, and subversive activities. According to Löser, his model could be implemented gradually as part of an arms control strategy.

In 1984, Löser tried to merge his model with the AirLand Battle concept and supported the Rogers plan (FOFA concept), but he denounced SDI as fueling the arms race. However, he embraced elements of the common security concept and called for a gradual disengagement and a loosening of the military blocs. Löser suggested a doubling of the number of brigades in the Bundeswehr by relying more heavily on reserves in cadre-type organizations that would increase in numbers with the distance from the FLOT (forward line of troops). He proposed that during the early phase of implementation, shield forces consisting of light infantry should cooperate with traditional German and allied sword forces. During the process of transarmament, the shield forces would become preponderant, whereas the sword forces would become small, light units capable of exploiting the terrain, specializing in mine warfare, erecting fortifications, and fighting with light, easy-to-handle weapons.

Löser's efforts, however, to integrate into his model a variety of conflicting proposals (e.g., the Palme Commission's common security concept as well as NATO's FOFA concept) and his own model's inherent potential for stimulating an arms race did not advance its political attractiveness.

Hannig's forward fire barrier and defense wall

Norbert Hannig shared Afheldt's criticism both of nuclear deterrence and of conventional deep strike concepts (AirLand Battle and FOFA in his concepts of a forward fire barrier, 1984, or of a defense wall, 1986). He nevertheless drew completely different conclusions.[45] In 1984, Hannig suggested a tripwire defense along the demarcation line four km deep. This tripwire defense would be controlled permanently with electronic sensors. In case of conflict, a concentration of fire from the rear would make it impossible to cross the barrier. The essential components of this rearward concentration of fire would be ATGW, partly on elevated fighting platforms, mortars with terminally guided projectiles, artillery rockets of different calibers for projecting mines, and armor-piercing submunitions. They would be deployed primarily on light, highly mobile armored vehicles stationed in several echelons depending on their range. Antitank helicopters would also be employed. The fire power would be controlled by highly specialized units of about company size that would receive their orders from a relatively centralized command structure.

In 1986, Hannig merged his model with that of Brigadier General Johannes Gerber.[46] He introduced his new model, the DEWA (defense wall), as an alternative to the FOFA concept. The result was a nearly completely stationary defense with a high reliance on firepower that was to capitalize on the dispersal and concealment of the launchers and on a centralization of C^3 I structures. In addition to the rocket artillery, an infantry component would play a major role in antitank and air defense. The authors assumed that the DEWA would be impenetrable and that therefore no counteroffensive capabilities would be needed.[47]

Hannig's two concepts demonstrated a high degree of stopping power, provided that the sensors could not be fooled, the munitions supplies for the firing units could not be interrupted, and the centralized coordination and command remained intact. He assumed that his model would permit a reduction in NATO manpower in Central Europe down to 800,000 men. He calculated, based on cost estimates of the defense industry, that his initial proposal would require some $18–20 billion for transarmament in a 10–15-year period. That figure, however, appears to have been rather overoptimistic for the purchase of equipment not already in mass production.

Hannig's concepts were criticized for their vulnerability of the centralized C^3 I system, the overemphasis on technology, and the permissive use of long-range firepower. Moreover, some critics argued that if some technical components suggested by Hannig were added to existing structures, "the resultant mix may well have a significant offensive capability."[48] Nevertheless, Hannig's model has inspired several more pragmatic NOD designers such as von Müller's concept and the SAS Spider and Web model.

None of the three pure alternative force structure models, however, seems to provide an answer to the new emerging security environment of the 1990s. As a consequence of the changing environment, a major criticism of all NOD models will soon be gone: land-based nuclear battlefield weapons on the central European territory.

The Add-On-Models: Uhle-Wettler, E. Afheldt, Schmähling, Hoffmann/Huber, v. Müller, v. Bülow/Funk

Whereas the "pure models" called for a complete redesign of the present military force structure, this second group was less radical. It proposed changes in components of forces existing prior to German unification, e.g., an enhancement of the light infantry (Uhle-Wettler, E. Afheldt), better shield forces (von Bülow) combined with high-technology sword components for "shallow" strikes (von Müller).

Uhle-Wettler's light infantry

The most prominent "infantry advocate" within the German army has been Lieutenant General Franz Uhle-Wettler.[49] In 1966 he proposed a greater role for the light infantry to the detriment of the armored forces. In 1980 he criticized the overtechnification of the armed forces, which he contended reduced the teeth-to-tail ratio of fighters and supporters to 1:9. The resultant dramatic increase in logistics would hamper mobility, increase vulnerability, and incapacitate formations. Furthermore, the present defense structure was not adapted to the specifics of German geography: the industrial areas, the regions covered by forests, and the subalpine mountainous terrain. Uhle-Wettler called for a specialized utilization of fire power according to terrain. He believed that an overemphasis on heavy weaponry would hamper the infantry and thus increase armed forces procurement costs dramatically. Guderian's thinking and the preference for the offensive form of combat had, in his view, a major impact on the overmechanization of the Bundeswehr.

According to Uhle-Wettler, forested areas as well as population and industrial centers would be suitable for light infantry units armed with simpler and cheaper weapons, whereas mechanized divisions would be better suited for combat in open terrain. The tactics suggested by Uhle-Wettler would force the aggressor to protect the rear echelon with combat units and thus deplete his frontline strength. To improve mobility, the infantry should carry weapons that are as light as possible and should rely on transport vehicles and helicopters. His decentralized forces would be rather manpower intensive and would require long training. In 1980 he proposed a refocusing of the MBFR talks from manpower levels to armored forces. A reduction in heavy armored combat vehicles would impede the capability for aggression, whereas the defense component would be increased. Since March 1989, this idea has been included in the CFE I negotiations.

Eckart Afheldt's light infantry model[50]

After his retirement from the Bundeswehr, Eckart Afheldt became a close collaborator of his cousin Horst in his Starnberg working group. Eckart suggested a step-by-step substitution of light infantry for the armored forces, especially in the forward areas, in an effort to create an all-encompassing territorial defense. Although he shared the traditional threat diagnosis of a 3:1 Soviet conventional superiority, he disagreed with NATO's nuclear-prone strategic therapy, which he described as suicidal.

As an alternative, Afheldt proposed the creation of a 70–100-km-wide forward zone that would be defended by a web of about 100,000 *Jäger* troops deployed in-depth and greatly dispersed with an average of two *Jägers* per square km. All armored forces including tanks would be banned in the forward zone. *Jäger* troops would be armed with ordinary light infantry weapons, obstacle construction equipment, antitank missiles, and artillery rockets for the laying of land mines. In addition he suggested the use of both mobile and stationary multiple rocket launchers for close combat, and in the long run even laser weapons and a wide spectrum of electronic warfare would be employed.

Armored forces in mechanized divisions assisted by precision-guided ballistic missiles would remain in the rear. Afheldt employed the tactical principles suggested by his cousin Horst: dispersal of forces, no-target philosophy, and exploitation of the terrain by a stationary deployment of forces that would fight from full cover and avoid battles on unfavorable terms. His light infantry model could be implemented immediately. Foreign troops could be stationed as operational reserves in the rear. This pragmatic model was a response to the resource constraints as foreseen in the 1980s: its *Jäger* network would require a peacetime strength of 100,000 men, with an additional 35,000 reservists.

Huber's defense efficiency hypothesis[51]

From the perspective of operations research, Reiner K. Huber, director of the Institute for Applied Systems and Operations Research (IASFOR) of the University of the Bundeswehr in Munich, stressed the need for military efficiency based on both aspects of strategic stability: crisis and arms race stability. He contended that in the 1980s, on the nuclear level, crisis stability was achieved at the cost of arms race instability, whereas on the conventional level both alliances were structurally capable of offensive operations that contributed to crisis instability. From his analysis of stability considerations, Huber believed that the only escape from the security dilemma would be a systematic exploitation of the defender's advantages leading to defense superiority: "Even unilateral 'defensivity' might contribute to an increase in stability. If the other side would reciprocate in a similar manner, the area of mutually acceptable force states should increase further, until it might cover, after a sequence of defence enhancing actions by one, and reactions by the other, side the entire area of x,y > 0, which represents perfectly stable armaments states."[52]

According to Huber, in a unilateral conversion toward a "reactive" defense, several conditions would have to be met to avoid instability during the transition phase. In contrast, a bilateral implementation of a structural incapability of attack would result in armaments that would be decoupled from answering in kind patterns, thus contributing to arms race stability.

In several computerized simulation models, Huber and his colleagues[53] tested both traditional NATO force structures and several components of defensive models, including H. Afheldt's techno-commandos, Löser's area model, Hannig's fire belt, Gerber's antitank and SAM belt, the SAS model of 1984, and the SAS "cavalry batallions," as well as the author's own light infantry batallion. Based on a set of specific assumptions after approximately 500 simulation runs, the authors concluded that the currently deployed forces performed poorly in comparison with their own model of a selective fire barrier, the Swiss territorial defense concept and the SAS model of 1984.

Schmähling's alternative concept [54]

Rear Admiral Elmar Schmähling was the highest level active Bundeswehr officer who publicly criticized the official defense policy. In his assessment, the present views on warfare, organization of armed forces, and the armament policy were obsolete. He criticized duplication and the inadequate use of the civilian telephone, medical infrastructure, and the geographic and topological conditions that favor the defender.

He argued that the major surface ships were facing obsolescence due to their vulnerability to antiship munitions fired from land-based systems. He supported instead many small, possibly camouflaged mobile weapons carriers at the coast or offshore. With respect to land warfare, Admiral Schmähling pointed to several shortcomings: the lack of a modern barrier concept organized around light troops, the overdependence on weaponry that emphasizes the offense, deployment patterns that increase the need for early mobilization and are thus likely to be destabilizing in a crisis, and the integration of nuclear and conventional weapons that impeded the initial use of dual-capable systems. In his view, NATO's response to these deficiencies was counterproductive, e.g., its focus on deep interdiction. He supported the basic NOD concepts and principles of exploiting the friendly terrain:

> By the emplacement of optical fibre networks; by deployment of sensors etc. on tall buildings . . . ; by the integration of civilian radio transmitters and cable networks into the wartime communication network; by emplacement of seismic sensors below ground in the border areas, and plugged into the optical fibre network; by the construction of underground command posts; by the storage of mines, munitions, bridge-building equipment etc. In this manner a centralized, real-time combat management would become possible, and present plans for sub-delegation of command might thus be revised.[55]

Schmähling supported obstacle-creating systems such as dynamic mines that could saturate a large area, artificial tank barriers, and artillery systems fired from sheltered positions. Nuclear weapons should be drastically reduced and deprived of their war-fighting role. Such a territorially fixed (*raumgebunden*) defense would be incapable of offensive operations. Moreover, it could be accomplished unilaterally without requiring reciprocation of the other side.

Von Bülow's model [56]

Von Bülow, a former minister of research and technology and former parliamentary state secretary in the Defense Department, in his then capacity as chairman of the Security Commission of the SPD party board, was the only active politician to develop and propagate an alternative threat assessment and force structure. In 1984 he supported the development of defensive systems instead of structures suitable for wide-ranging offensives. According to von Bülow, NATO's no first use posture should be abandoned and all nuclear battlefield systems withdrawn. He supported greater European independence and closer Franco-German defense cooperation.

Following Afheldt's no-target philosophy, von Bülow gave high priority to artillery, aircraft-delivered mines, and antitank RPVs and PGMs. In his original proposal (1984), he maintained skeletonized heavy armored forces and follow-on forces with deep interdiction and offensive counterair missions with ranges of 100–150 km behind the infantry belt.

In the so-called Bülow paper of 1985, his main focus was on avoiding an inadvertent war by ruling out preemptive strikes. In addition to his previous demands, he called for an abandonment of FOFA and the AirLand Battle Doctrine while being ambiguous with respect to conventional deep interdiction missions by leaving open the option of a conditional offensive capability. He called for a defense structure that stressed antitank systems over tanks. Along the border on a 25–70-km deep belt, a dense network of dispersed antitank forces employing modern mines, drones, fire-and-forget antitank missiles, and antitank helicopters should wear down an aggressor. Allied forces could be integrated in the forward zone as could the French rapid employment force (FAR). He supported a unilateral as well as a bilateral negotiated restructuring of forces in Europe as part of an arms control concept.

In 1988, von Bülow, jointly with retired Colonel Helmut Funk, an engineer and policy adviser, proposed a bilateral scaling down of offensive capabilities with European ceilings of 5000 tanks, 2500 infantry fighting vehicles, and 2500 tank destroyers that would be combined with regional subceilings, e.g., no armored forces would be deployed in a zone extending to 60 km on both sides of the border (FRG, GDR, CSSR); 40% of the above ceiling should be limited to FRG, Denmark, Luxemburg, GDR, CSSR, and Hungary; the remaining 60% would be deployed in France, Belgium, the Netherlands, Poland, and the European part of the USSR. He suggested that the Bundeswehr could be reduced to 400,000 men by merging the territorial forces with the field army. He pleaded for a greater reliance on reserves, for a better use of the civilian infrastructure, and for a thinning out of the armored formations of the field army. By pushing forward with his own ideas, von Bülow's alternative model provoked many political and conceptual criticisms.[57] Having become politically rather controversial he was not reappointed as chairman of the Security Commission of the SPD Board. Instead he chaired a subgroup on NOD concepts that prepared a detailed paper in March 1990 on the "Bundeswehr in Transition."[58]

Von Müller's integrated forward defense model

Albrecht von Müller joined the security debate in 1982 as an assistant to a high level task force of the German Federation of Scientists (VDW) on European security, which prepared a statement on INF modernization.[59] In 1983 he was working with Horst Afheldt and since 1984 he has codirected a research project on "stability-oriented security policies" with Horst Afheldt and the physicist Hans-Peter Dürr.[60]

Von Müller's "integrated forward defense model" combined in an eclective mode ideas first presented by Horst and Eckart Afheldt, Löser, Hannig, von Bülow, and SAS. The model includes four zones:

1. A firebelt (5 km wide) resembling Hannig's proposals.
2. A network zone (75 km deep), inspired by both Afheldts, requiring infantry units armed with PGMs.
3. A maneuver zone (some 60 km deep) with streamlined armored units that integrates proposals by SAS.
4. A rear area without any restrictions for stationary and mobile units.

Whereas the first two zones would offer no lucrative targets, the firebelt was to have a close interdiction capability that could target enemy territory some 40–60 km deep. In 1988 he combined these two zones into a "web zone" (25 km deep) of light infantry and obstacle-building units that would require 40,000 men in peacetime and 120,000 in wartime. If the aggressor penetrated these two zones, he would feel worn down as a result of the defender's heavy attrition capability (defender's superiority) and would be confronted with an offensive counterattack by the defender. This last component provoked harsh criticisms from NOD proponents because it resembled in many respects the controversial proposal by Samuel Huntington for "conventional retaliation," which also envisaged offensive maneuver warfare, albeit merely for deterrence purposes.[61] Nevertheless, von Müller's model offered a greater diversification by combining several mutually complementable forms of defense. Moreover, it no longer required an in-depth defense. Defense could be implemented step-by-step. This model relied to a large extent on emerging technologies, such as sensor arrays that would be resistant to both EMP and ECMs, on "stochastic mines," and on reconnaissance drones, which made it attractive to Messerschmitt Bölkow Bloom (MBB), a major arms producer that collaborated in the project. Von Müller shifted from a unilateral to a bilateral implementation in the context of an arms control agreement. Jointly with A. Karkoszka, he presented a Modified Approach to Conventional Arms Control that aimed at a regime of mutual defensive superiority by "selectively cutting down platforms, deep strike capabilities, and other offense-prone components."[62] With respect to nuclear weapons, the two authors proposed a low ceiling of 500 warheads, with only 100 to be allowed on rockets.

Von Müller provoked severe criticism both from active officers and other NOD designers. Major K. A. Schreiner argued that his concept was not compatible with NATO; it violated the no-target philosophy and it lacked a structural inability to attack.[63] Lutz Unterseher stressed that this concept would enhance NATO's offensive capability by providing a shield while retaining a sword for a latent threat of intervention.[64]

Integrated Model for a Confidence-Building Defense: Study Group on Alternative Security Policy's Proposal

The most comprehensive, detailed, and sophisticated NOD model has been developed by the Study Group on Alternative Security Policy (SAS), which was cofounded and is headed by Lutz Unterseher.[65] In several reports, SAS criticized official threat assessments, the military planning of the West German Defense Ministry, and NATO's deep strike and emergent technology concepts.[66] The group's concept has been introduced as the Interactive Forward Defense Model

(1984), the Spider in the Web (1986), and as a Confidence-Building Defense Posture (1989) primarily with respect to West Germany. It relied on conceptual ideas from Horst and Eckart Afheldt, Norbert Hannig, Steven Canby, and Richard Simpkin. But SAS itself has been innovative and offered the only comprehensive design with specific proposals for a nonoffensive army, air force, and navy.

The Spider in the Web concept for the land forces consists of three basic components:

1. A static area defense (*Fangnetz*) that uses reactive "wait and see" tactics. This subsystem is in essence a decentralized infantry network, called the containment force.

2. Mechanized troops with a certain degree of operational mobility, capable of reactive and active missions. This element is called the rapid commitment force.

3. A rear protection force including light infantry for object defense and motorized/light armor units to deal with airborne assaults and large-scale diversion.[67]

The containment force, the static area defense (*Fangnetz*), would consist of current territorial forces that would be forward deployed and closely interlinked in a network structure. It would consist of about 80,000 active forward deployed troops, which would expand to 300,000 in times of crisis. They would be armed with light grenade launchers, antitank missiles, and mines.

To reinforce these stationary units, the rapid commitment force was conceived as the mobile and mechanized element that would consist of three different types of forces:

Infantry or *Jäger* batallions to fight in most cases on the ground in covered terrain. Cavalry regiments to cooperate with the stationary units and to act as advance guard for the shock units.

The heavier shock units were capable of fighting in open terrain under enemy fire.

The total manpower requirement for the rapid commitment force would be only 75,000 to 90,000 for the Bundeswehr. The rear protection force would be modeled similar to the home guard. After mobilization the total force strength would be 120,000 men.

Möller summarized the changes in the SAS model that have occurred between 1984 and 1989:

> *The role of the containment forces was made even more explicit: Due to their relative "lightness" they were not supposed to engage the armoured forces of the invader directly, but rather to "divide and channel" these forces, whereas the heavier "spider forces" were to be assigned the role of delivering the final blow of annihilation. In addition, the containment web was supposed to decimate any intruding airborne units or "spider" forces. Furthermore, they were to support the latter in terms of logistics and surveillance. In this way, the containment web would serve not merely as a "space multiplier" but also as a "time multiplier," hence as a true "force multiplier."*
>
> *As far as the weapons mix was concerned, the SAS further deemphasized the fairly long-range indirect fire systems, which have been preferred by most alternative models, in favor of distinctly short-range systems. The group had likewise abandoned its previous illusions about*

*the bright future of third generation "fire and forget" ATGM and of the persistent minefields.
. . . On the other hand, it was acknowledged that the tube artillery . . . would have important
roles, i.e., for the delivery of cheap "dumb" munitions. . . . In general, the trend in the
model's development could be seen as moving away from relatively few, highly sophisticated,
but fairly expensive systems towards a greater number of simple, but on the other hand more
robust and affordable, weaponry. What mattered most for the efficiency of the defense scheme
would not be certain magnificent technologies, but rather appropriate tactical principles which
would allow the defender to capitalize on the synergistic effects of a diversified defense system.[68]*

As a consequence of NATO's qualitative air superiority and to the sky-rocketing
procurement costs, Unterseher suggested that the air force's deep interdiction mission be abandoned and that the military concentrate on air defense and on air
support in NATO territory. He contended that the air defense mission should be the
joint task of ground-based air defense relying on mobile SAMs such as the HAWK/
Patriot (without giving it an ATM mission) and of a small number of remaining
fighting interceptors. The close air support mission could be performed by the
VSTOL (vertical short take-off landing) aircraft. To enhance aerial stability, SAS
proposed that aircraft be included in the CFE negotiations with the aim of reducing
the offensive air forces in the ATTU zone to about 1000 aircraft each.

With respect to the naval or maritime component, Bebermeyer and Unterseher
criticized both the high seas ambitions of the German navy and the U.S. maritime
strategy. They proposed that the tasks of the navy be limited to the defense of the
Baltic Sea and the southern part of the Northern Sea. Thus destroyers, frigates,
and submarines would be superfluous and corvettes and mine warfare ships would
be sufficient. The task of the naval component would be a defensively oriented
coastal defense, with ships, combat helicopters, and blocking equipment. In 1989
land-based antiship missiles were added. That same year Bebermeyer and Unterseher[69] suggested that 110 Tornados with antiship missiles be retained until the early
1990s; that the 19 antisubmarine and patrol aircraft be gradually replaced; that the
number of combat helicopters be increased to 40; that destroyers and frigates be
gradually phased out; that in the late 1990s six corvettes should be built; that the
submarines should serve in the Baltic until their withdrawal; that mine warfare
vessels be kept and modernized and the amphibious craft be considerably reduced;
that on-board air defense be improved; that antiship missiles be procured, and that
coastal artillery be deployed.

Furthermore, as a complement to a partial U.S. troop withdrawal, an American
SAS member proposed a restructuring of the U.S. 7th Army in the FRG that might
serve as "spider" or "rapid commitment forces."[70] Since spring 1990, the SAS
chairman has adapted the SAS model to the fundamentally changed political environment.[71] According to Unterseher, the SAS model could be implemented step by
step either unilaterally or as part of a gradualist strategy, but it should not be
dependent on reciprocal steps by the other side. However, within SAS different
positions exist on the specific role that disarmament in general and future conventional arms control, especially the CFE process, may play for a restructuring of
armed forces.

What then has been the impact of the four phases of the West German NOD
debate on the government and opposition parties and on the official defense policy
of the West German cabinet governments?

The Political Impact of NOD Concepts
in West Germany

Since the establishment of the Bundeswehr in 1956, alliance concerns and force planning dominated the security policy of the Federal Republic. Therefore, not surprisingly after von Bonin's conceptual ideas had been rejected in 1954, NOD concepts had no direct impact on government policy. However, the criticism of the nuclear component of NATO strategy was strong within both the Social Democrats and the Liberals in the late 1950s. A major shift occurred in the early 1980s, after the SPD reassessed its previous security policy at its Cologne party congress in 1983 by rejecting the INF decision. Already in April 1982 at its party congress in Munich, it established a Commission on New Strategies, headed by Egon Bahr. In June 1983 this commission submitted its interim report[72] and, in 1984, its final report.

The SPD in its resolutions at its party congresses in Essen (1984), Nuremberg (1986), and Münster (1988), and in a proposal for the "Bundeswehr in Transition" on March 23, 1990, adopted basic elements of the NOD-philosophy.[73] This debate in the SPD influenced the security debate of the British Labor party and in the social democratic parties of the Scandilux group.

In March 1990 the SPD called for both the adoption of a NOD doctrine and for a drastic reduction in the size of the Bundeswehr by half of its present strength to 240,000 men in peacetime, an abandonment of all nuclear missions, and the removal of all tactical nuclear weapons from Europe. The length of the military service obligation should be reduced from 18 to 12 months. All nuclear and chemical weapons should be withdrawn from the territory of a united Germany.[74] The central features of this proposal are:

> *The military protection of the Western Central region of Europe remains integrated into the alliance. With respect to the land forces, initially 13 restructured corps—7 German and 6 allied—with an average of 53,000 soldiers for each corps should be available. In support of these corps, NATO maintains integrated army groups and army reserves. The air defense relies on sufficiently strong ground and air based forces. The maritime flanks will be protected by allied naval forces. The forces should be structured in such a way that they could perform pan-European tasks also in cooperation with East European armed forces in case security agreements link both alliances should be agreed upon and a European peace order should be established.[75]*

The West German army should consist of seven corps whose tasks would be reconnaissance, protection of the rear, maintenance of the operative flexibility for the allies, integration of reserves, and civilian-military cooperation. Each corps would be structured in shield (denial brigades) and sword forces (tank and armored infantry brigades) for battle support, command, and logistics, as well as for the protection of the troops.

> *Our concept of the denial brigades that should make up for two thirds of the battle units of the army stresses the self defense without sending threatening signals to the other side. Armored mobile forces, that will also be available in our concept will not be as strong to give them an operative capability for attack. We would like to reduce the weapons systems conducive to the offense disproportionately: The number of the battle tanks of the Bundeswehr would be reduced from close to 5000 at present to about 1000.[76]*

With respect to the air force, the SPD concept for a restructured Bundeswehr assumes that no more air offensive forces (fighter bombers) will exist. However, fighter aircraft as part of the air defense mission would be needed against air offensive forces deployed outside of Europe. The new air force would rely on available equipment, e.g., for the reconnaissance mission the ECR Tornado would be used, whereas the air defense mission should rely on the Roland and the Patriot. However, the antitactical missile option would be canceled. The EFA (*Jäger* 90) project should be halted as soon as possible.

With respect to the future defensively oriented navy, the SPD concept calls for giving up submarines, navy fighter planes, fast rocket boats, and beach assault troops. The strict limitation of the employment of German naval forces to the North and Baltic seas would permit a 50% reduction of destroyers and frigates from sixteen to eight. The SPD proposal lacked any reference as to how the NVA should be integrated and what role the GDR should play in the defense of a united Germany.

The major goals of the suggested restructuring of the Bundeswehr in conjunction with the CFE mandate are to eliminate the capability for large offensive operations and to fashion in the longer term a new European security structure. How relevant are these 10 NOD models and one specific political proposal in the new political context of the 1990s?

THE NEW INTERNATIONAL AND DOMESTIC POLITICAL CONTEXT FOR NOD

The New Pan-European Context in the 1990s

By December 1990 the political division of Europe was over as was the postwar period that led to the division of Germany. The WTO is no longer an effective military alliance, only a forum for political consultation. NATO has already deemphasized its military and stressed its increasingly political functions. At the CSCE summit in November 1990, the first steps toward an institutionalization of the CSCE were approved. Both as a result of CFE I and of the 2 + 4 process, conventional and nuclear arms in Europe and Germany and foreign troops in a united Germany will be significantly reduced.[77]

Whereas NATO's military importance will decrease and the relevance of a collective European security system may increase, it is within this new security system and a gradual enlargement of the European Community that decisions will be made regarding the future military doctrine and force structure.

The New Domestic Context: Manpower and Equipment Surplus

One major domestic change has occurred since the opening of the Berlin Wall and the achievement of German unity: the manpower scarcity of the Bundeswehr that was a major problem until December 1989[78] has been replaced by a manpower surplus and the need to downsize the Bundeswehr by one-third to 320,000 by 1994 and the former National People's Army to 50,000 by 1991. The length of required military service of the Bundeswehr has already been reduced from 15 to 12 months, as of October 1, 1990. As a consequence, there will be a surplus of military equipment and a need to adjust the military budget downward. However, as a consequence of the end of the cold war and of German unification, the legitimization crisis of the Bundeswehr will further increase as the enemy disappears and cooperation with the Commonwealth of Independent States (CIS) develops.

The Need for Modifications of Existing Force Structures

As a consequence of the London Declaration, the need to readjust NATO's military doctrine and to work on force structure changes has been acknowledged. The U.S. Army AirLand Battle Doctrine and NATO's FOFA concept have become obsolete with respect to central Europe. Both NATO's force structure and that of the former Soviet Union must be reassessed as well as all NOD concepts and proposals in the context of the changed political environment.

Given the need to build down military manpower and to reduce hardware in the more cooperative environment that has emerged, there will be a unique opportunity for NOD concepts to be considered at three levels:

The national level, specially by the government of a united Germany, in anticipation of the departure of all Soviet troops.

The NATO level, especially when land-based nuclear weapons are removed.

The Pan-European level, as a topic for future seminars on military doctrines and force structures.

Thus nonoffensive defense concepts will not be obsolete if they are adapted to the new circumstances. Components of NOD concepts could be the ideal military force structure for national self-defense forces. However, they should be combined with a multinational professional component of a new European collective security system.

In 1990 in a uniting Germany, a new debate on the future military force structure emerged.[79] Given the speed of the unification process, it was not possible to include specific aspects of the future force structure of the territorial army in the East in the second (unification) state treaty that was ratified in September 1990.[80]

As a confidence-building measure, the united German government might invite military experts from Poland and Czechoslovakia to participate in the development of common principles and in the design of a nonoffensive confidence-building force structure for the territorial army in the eastern part of Germany. This new military force structure should become both a pilot project and a model for future nonoffensive conventional self-defense forces within the framework of a new Pan-European security system. There is a precedence. The bilateral cooperation between the Polish and the West German foreign ministries played a major role in the preparation of the first seminar on military doctrine that took place in the CSCE framework in January and February 1990. Such trilateral cooperation could also lead to the establishment of common military units on the bilateral level, e.g., between the German and the Polish navies with respect to common tasks of mine removal and ecological challenges in the Baltic Sea and between the German territorial army east and the Czechoslovak army with respect to conversion and environmental hazards created by acid rain.

On the NATO level, as part of the force structure adjustment process, both the political and the military committees, in cooperation with SHAPE, should set up a high-level force structure review board that should also include NOD proponents from different countries. This board should hold intensive hearings with experts of both the traditional school and the most original and competent proponents of nonoffensive defense proposals. As an advisory body, this review board should be free of political guidance and it should be tasked to make specific proposals with respect to the future NATO military force structure.

At the Pan-European level, NATO should enter into an intensive dialogue on force structure concepts in the CSCE framework by proposing as a confidence-building measure:

A follow-up to the seminars on military doctrine (Jan.-Feb. 1990 and October 1991) to deal with the doctrinal changes required due to the changed environment.

A seminar on the highest military level on present military force structures and on a review of available NOD proposals for Europe.

A high-level task force of military experts from the major European countries to develop common principles for military force restructuring.

In an optimistic political scenario for the 1990s, it is assumed in Chapter 1 of Volume 2 of this series[81] that by 1995 the EFTA countries of Austria, Sweden, and Finland will probably be in the European Community, and when the predicted additional 20, 40, or 60% military manpower reductions are implemented, Poland and Czechoslovakia will have joined as well. A military conflict among EC countries in central Europe will then be inconceivable. Given the new challenges that will confront Europe, military forces in central Europe should be given two missions: a territorial self-defense mission (80–50% of the manpower), and a common security mission (20–50% of the soldiers).

For the territorial self-defense mission, the forces should be structured in national contingents (with a strong conscript component) according to the principles of a nonoffensive or confidence-building defense (shield or web forces). For the common security mission, highly specialized professional forces (sword or spider) with a low or no conscript component should be trained together in multinational military academies for their specific common tasks: to act as peacekeeping forces in the context of the European or global collective security system, to deal with the implementation of disarmament: verification and conversion, environmental hazards, and border-crossing catastrophes. These common security forces should have a multinational command structure either on a subregional or a Pan-European level and multinational units.

As the process of political integration and of conventional disarmament in Europe proceeds and the potential threats to national security decrease, the manpower component for the territorial self-defense mission should be reduced from 80% by 1995 to 65% or even 50% after the year 2000, and the common security mission should be increased accordingly from 20 to 35% or even 50% of the soldiers. Thus highly professionalized and specialized forces would be available for collective security and peacekeeping operations both in Europe and outside to contain ag-

Table 1-2 Assumed Relationship of National Shield and Multinational Sword Forces in the 1990s for the United Germany

Size of assumed German forces	Size of assumed forces in central Europe	National shield or web forces (NOD)				Multinational sword or peacekeeping forces			
		slower		faster		slower		faster	
370,000	1,000,000	296,000	80%	296,000	80%	74,000	20%	74,000	20%
296,000	800,000	222,000	75%	207,000	70%	74,000	25%	88,800	30%
222,000	600,000	155,400	70%	133,200	60%	66,600	30%	88,800	40%
148,000	400,000	96,200	65%	74,000	50%	51,800	35%	74,000	50%

gression and violations to international peace and security, such as the invasion of Kuwait by Iraq. The national sword forces would be too weak and functionally too specialized for any independent offensive operation. They would only reach their military effectiveness as part of a multinational force (see Table 1-2).

CONCLUSIONS

The NOD concepts reviewed in this chapter have not been tested, and given the recent changes in the international environment, they will not be tested in their present form. However, the tactical principles and the NOD force components are not obsolete. They could form the vital conceptual elements for national territorial self-defense forces that would be unable to threaten any neighbor in a possible new European security system where no significant military threat among its members exists. However, these national self-defense forces could not deal with global violations to peace and security. Therefore, a gradually increasing force should be trained in a multinational framework for these global and Pan-European collective security functions. If one assumes by 1995 a total manpower strength for central Europe of 1 million, about 200,000 soldiers should be available for this multinational peacekeeping component and by the year 2000, of a total troop strength for central Europe of 400,000, about 200,000 soldiers could serve in the multilateral force. Moreover, the NOD concepts may have increasing relevance for areas with continuous political conflicts, e.g., between India and Pakistan. Such concepts offer the prospects of reducing the likelihood for military confrontation in Third World regions.

NOTES

1. See the bibliography by Björn Möller, *Non-Offensive Defence Bibliography,* and the *NOD Journal* (Copenhagen: Centre for Peace and Conflict Research).

2. Horst Afheldt, *Der Konsens—Argumente für eine Politik der Wiedervereinigung Europas* (Baden-Baden: Nomos, 1989).

3. Björn Möller, *Non-Offensive Defence as a Security Political Instrument, Vol. 1. Theoretical Analysis,* (Ph.D. dissertation, Institute of Political Studies, University of Copenhagen, Jan. 1990), p. 11.

4. Marlies ter Borg and Wim Smit, "Non-Provocative Defence, Conventional Stability and Reasonable Sufficiency," in Marlies ter Borg and Wim Smit, eds., *Non-Provocative Defence as a Principle of Arms Reduction and its Implications for Assessing Defence Technologies* (Amsterdam: Free University Press, 1989), p. 1.

5. Anders Boserup and Robert Neild, "Introduction," in Anders Boserup and Robert Neild, eds., *The Foundations of Defensive Defense* (London: Macmillan, 1990).

6. Lutz Unterseher, "Defending Europe: Toward a Stable Conventional Deterrent," in Henry Shue, ed., *Nuclear Deterrence and Moral Restraint* (Cambridge: Cambridge University Press, 1989), p. 311.

7. Carl von Clausewitz, in *Vom Kriege—Hinterlassenes Werk* (Frankfurt-Berlin: Ullstein-Materialien, 1980), argued in book 6, chap. 1 on the relationship between offense and defense: "die verteidigende Form des Kriegführens ist an sich stärker als die angreifende" (p. 361); Brian Bond, *Lidell Hart. A Study of his Military Thought* (London: Cassell, 1977); *Verteidigung ohne Schlacht: Emil Spannocchi, Verteidigung ohne Selbstzerstörung, Guy Brossollet, Das Ende der Schlacht* (München: Hanser, 1976).

8. Egbert Boeker, *Europese Veiligheid. Alternativen voor de huidige Veiligheidspolitik* (Amsterdam: VU Uiggiverij, 1986); Frank Barnaby and Marlies ter Borg, eds., *Emerging Technologies and Military Doctrine. A Political Assessment* (London: Macmillan, 1986); ter Borg and Smit, note 4; Alternative Defence Commission, *Defence Without the Bomb* (London: Taylor and Francis, 1983) and *The Politics of Alternative Defence—A Role for a Non-Nuclear Britain* (London: Paladin Grafton Books, 1987); Ken Booth and John Baylis, *Britain, NATO and Nuclear Weapons—Alternative Defence vs. Alliance Reform* (London: Macmillan, 1989); Michael Clarke, *The Alternative Defence Debate: Non-Nuclear Defence Policies for Europe*, ADIU Occasional Paper No. 3 (Brighton: ADIU, 1985); Robert Neild, Frank Barnaby, and Frank Blackaby, three former directors of SIPRI, are major proponents of the NOD concept in Great Britain. Randall Forsberg, *Nonprovocative defense—A New Approach to Arms Control* (Brookline: Institute for Defense and Disarmament Studies, 1986) and "Towards a Nonaggressive World," in *Bulletin of the Atomic Scientists*, 44, no. 7 (Sept. 1988): 49–54; see also the newsletter, *Defense and Disarmament News*, 1–3 (1985–1987) that was renamed *Defense & Disarmament Alternatives*, 1 (1988 ff) published by: Institute for Defense and Disarmament Studies, Brookline; Paul Walker, "Emerging Technologies and Conventional Defence," in Barnaby and ter Borg, pp. 27–43. For a documentation of the participants of the workshop, see *Pugwash Newsletter* (1984 ff). Selected papers have been published in Boserup and Neild, note 5, Stephan Tiedtke, *Abschreckung und ihre Alternativen. Die sowjetische Sicht einer westlichen Debatte* (Heidelberg: FEST Texte und Materialien, A/20, 1986); Kurt Baudisch, ed., *European Security and Non-Offensive Defence* (Berlin: World Federation of Scientific Workers, 1988). Laszlo Valki, "The Concept of Defensive Defence," in Pal Dunay, ed., *Studies on Peace Research* (Budapest: Centre for Peace Research Coordination of the Hungarian Academy of Sciences, 1986) and "Die Antwort Osteuropas auf das Konzept der defensiven Verteidigung," in Carl Friedrich von Weizsäcker, ed., *Die Zukunft des Friedens in Europa—Politische und militärische Voraussetzungen* (München: Hanser, 1990), pp. 264–273. See Chapter 3 in this volume and the contributions of Alexei Arbatov and Alexander Konovalov in Boserup and Neild, Foundations; and the chapters by A. Konovalov, Valeri Mazing, Gennedy Kochetkov, Victor Sergeev, Alexei Vasiliev, Vadim Makarevsky, Valeri Abarenkov in: ter Borg and Smit, note 4; In his speech to the UN General Assembly on December 7, 1988, Gorbachev announced besides a unilateral force reduction of 500,000 troops two of this series, "All Soviet divisions remaining, for the time being, in the territory of our allies will be reorganized. Their structure will be different from what is now; after a major cutback of their tanks it will become clearly defensive." Quoted from *Arms Control Reporter*, 7 (1988), 407.D.17.

9. Walter Romberg, "Ein gradualistischer Zugang zur militärischen Krisenstabilität in Mitteleuropa," in Studiengruppe Alternative Sicherheitspolitik, ed., *Vertrauensbildende Verteidigung—Reform deutscher Sicherheitspolitik* (Gerlingen: Bleicher Verlag, 1989), pp. 215–222, and "The relation between unilateral and bilateral steps" in ter Borg and Smit, *Non-Provocative Defence*, pp. 239–244, and "Towards non-offensive defence through unilateral limited and reciprocated reductions— on a gradualistic approach to military crisis stability in Central Europe," in Baudisch, *European Security*, pp. 62–67. Romberg became finance minister in the first democratically elected East German government in April 1990, and after unification, he became an observer of the European Parliament.

10. For details see Hans Günter Brauch, "Federal Republic of Germany: Searching for Alternatives," in Robert Rudney and Luc Reychler, eds., *European Security Beyond the Year 2000* (New York: Praeger, 1988), pp. 79–102, and "West German Alternatives for Reducing Reliance on Nuclear Weapons," in P. Terrence Hopmann and Frank Barnaby, eds., *Rethinking the Nuclear Weapons Dilemma in Europe* (London: Macmillan, 1988), pp. 146–182.

11. Hans Günter Brauch, "INF and the current NATO discussion on Alliance strategy: A German perspective," in Hans-Henrik Holm und Nikolaj Petersen, eds., *The European Missiles Crisis: Nuclear Weapons and Security Policy* (London: Francis Pinter, 1983), pp. 156–202 (157).

12. See Catherine McArdle Kelleher, *Germany and the Politics of Nuclear Weapons* (New York: Columbia University Press, 1975); Hans Günter Brauch, *Die Raketen kommen! Vom NATO-Doppelbeschluß bis zur Stationierung* (Köln: Bund, 1983); Thomas Risse-Kappen, *Null-Lösung. Entscheidungsprozesse zu den Mittelstreckenwaffen 1970–1987* (Frankfurt: Campus, 1988), an English translation has also been published by Westview Press; see Catherine M. Kelleher, "The debate over the modernization of NATO's short-range nuclear missiles," in *SIPRI Yearbook 1990—World Armaments and Disarmament* (Oxford: Oxford University Press, 1990), pp. 603–622.

13. One of the best monographs of West German foreign policy is Helga Haftendorn, *Sicherheit und Entspannung. Zur Außenpolitik der Bundesrepublik Deutschland 1955–1982* (Baden-Baden: Nomos, 1983). An abridged English version has been published by Praeger Publishers.

14. Klaus von Schubert, *Wiederbewaffnung und Westintegration—Die innere Auseinandersetzung um die militärische und außenpolitische Orientierung der Bundesrepublik 1950–1952* (Stuttgart: Deutsche Verlags-Anstalt, 1970); Charles Robert Naef, *The Politics of West German Rearmament, 1950–1956*, Ph.D. dissertation, Rutgers University, New Brunswick, 1979.

15. Hans Karl Rupp, *Außerparlamentarische Opposition in der Ära Adenauer. Der Kampf gegen die Atombewaffnung in den fünfziger Jahren. Eine Studie zur innenpolitischen Entwicklung der Bundesrepublik Deutschland* (Köln: Pahl-Rugenstein, 1970); Eugene Hinterhoff, *Disengagement* (London: Stevens & Sons, 1959).

16. Arnulf Baring, *Machtwechsel. Die Ära Brandt Scheel* (Stuttgart: Deutsche Verlags-Anstalt, 1982).

17. See Brauch, *Die Raketen,* and Risse-Kappen, *Null-Lösung.*

18. Bogislav von Bonin, *Opposition gegen Adenauers Sicherheitspolitik. Eine Dokumentation zusammengestellt von Heinz Brill* (Hamburg: Neue Politik, 1976); Heinz Brill, *Bogislav von Bonin im Spannungsfeld zwischen Wiederbewaffnung-Westintegration-Wiedervereinigung. Ein Beitrag zur Entstehungsgeschichte der Bundeswehr 1952–1955* (Baden-Baden: Nomos, 1987); Heinz Brill, ed., *Bogislav von Bonin im Spannungsfeld zwischen Wiederbewaffnung-Westintegration-Wiedervereinigung. Vol. II: Beiträge zur Entstehungsgeschichte der Bundeswehr—Dokumente und Materialien* (Baden-Baden: Nomos, 1989).

19. This section draws heavily on Egbert Boeker and Lutz Unterseher, "Emphasizing Defence," in Frank Barnaby and Marlies ter Borg, eds., *Emerging Technologies and Military Doctrine. A Political Assessment* (London: Macmillan, 1986).

20. Bogislav von Bonin, "Die Schlacht von Kursk—Ein Modell für die Verteidigung der Bundesrepublik," *Der Spiegel,* Nr. 48, Nov. 21, 1966: 42–53; reprinted in Brill, 1976, pp. 94–105, and 1987, p. 268–281 (see note 18).

21. See note 18 (Brill, 1987, p. 274).

22. Brill, 1987, pp. 277–280.

23. Helmut Schmidt, *Verteidigung oder Vergeltung* (Stuttgart: Seewald, 1961), and *Strategie des Gleichgewichts—Deutsche Friedenspolitik und die Weltmächte* (Stuttgart: Degerloch: Seewald, 1969); see also Schmidt's comment, in Brill, 1987, pp. 314–318 (note 18).

24. Reiner Steinweg, ed., *Unsere Bundeswehr? Zum 25 jährigen Bestehen einer umstrittenen Institution, Friedensanalysen No. 14,* (Frankfurt: Suhrkamp, 1981); Robert Hofmann, *Die Sicherheitspolitik der SPD 1966-1977. Innerparteiliche Willensbildung und praktizierte Regierungspolitik im nationalen und internationalen Bezugsrahmen* (Puchheim: Sozialwissenschaftlicher Verlag, 1987); Thomas Enders, *Die SPD und die äußere Sicherheit* (Melle: E. Knoth, 1987).

25. Carl Friedrich von Weizsäcker, ed., *Kriegsfolgen und Kriegsverhütung* (München: Hanser, 1971).

26. *Friedensanalysen, Für Theorie und Praxis 7, Sonderband: Jungsozialisten und Jungdemokraten zur Friedens—und Sicherheitspolitik* (Frankfurt: Suhrkamp, 1977).

27. Aspects of the work of this study group have been published by Carl Friedrich von Weizsäcker, ed., *Die Praxis der defensiven Verteidigung* (Hameln: Sponholtz, 1984). The recent military proposals of Uhle-Wettler, Löser, Unterseher, and Hannig are contained in the *Festschrift* for Afheldt's 65th birthday, C.F.v. Weizsäcker, ed., *Die Zukunft des Friedens in Europa—Politische und militärische Voraussetzungen* (München: Hanser, 1990), pp. 123–157.

28. Mechtersheimer was initially politically active in the Christian Social Union (CSU); since 1980 he was a spokesman of the independent peace movement and since 1987 he was an independent M.P. representing the Greens in the Bundestag. His major publications are: Alfred Mechtersheimer, *Rüstung und Politik in der Bundesrepublik—MRCA Tornado—Geschichte und Funktion des größten westeuropäischen Rüstungsprogramms* (Bad Honnef: Osang, 1977); *Rüstung und Frieden. Arguments für eine neue Friedenspolitik* (Reinbek: Rowohlt, 1984).

29. See Studiengruppe Alternative Sicherheitspolitik, ed., *Strukturwandel der Verteidigung. Entwürfe für eine konsequente Defensive* (Opladen: Westdeutscher Verlag, 1984); SAS, ed., *Vertrauensbildende Verteidigung;* see also Chapter 8 in this volume.

30. See the review in B. Möller, *Non-Offensive Defense As a Security Political Instrument Vol. II. Resolving the Security Dilemma in Europe. The Debate on Non-Offensive Defense in the German Federal Republic* (Ph.D. Dissertation, Institute of Political Studies, University of Copenhagen, January 1990), chap. 12, "The Men on Horseback," pp. 193–212; Brig. Gen. Ingo Günther and Maj. Gen. Günter Vollmer, *Verteidigung statt Vernichtung—Wege aus der atomaren Konfrontation* (Starnberg: ibf, 1983); Hans-Heinrich Nolte and Wilhelm Nolte, *Ziviler Widerstand und Autonome Abwehr* (Baden-Baden: Nomos, 1984); Andreas von Bülow, "Defensive Entanglement: An Alternative Strategy of NATO," in Andrew J. Pierre, ed., *Europe—America 5: The Conventional Defense of Europe: New Technologies and New Strategies* (New York: Council on Foreign Relations, 1986), pp. 112–151; Hermann Scheer, *Die Befreiung von der Bombe—Welfrieden, europäischer Weg und die Zukunft der Deutschen* (Köln: Bund, 1986); Karsten Voigt, "Konventionelle Stationierung und strukturelle Nichtangriffsfähigkeit. Ein systematischer Vergleich verschiedener Konzepte," in *Aus Politik und Zeitgeschichte. Beilage zur Wochenzeitung Das Parlament,* no. 18/88, Apr. 29, 1988, pp. 21–34; Dieter Senghaas, "Conventional Forces in Europe: Dismantle Offense, Strengthen Defense," in *Bulletin of the Atomic Scientists,* 44, no. 10 (Dec. 1987): 9–11; *Die Zukunft Europas, Probleme der Friedensgestaltung* (Frankfurt: Suhrkamp, 1986), and *Europa 2000. Ein Friedensplan* (Frankfurt: Suhrkamp, 1990); Johan Galtung, *Es gibt Alternativen! Vier Wege zu Frieden und Sicherheit* (Opladen: Westdeutscher Verlag, 1984); see the English translation published by Taylor and Francis; Hans Günter Brauch, *Perspektiven einer Europäischen Friedensordnung* (Berlin: Berlin-Verlag A. Spitz, 1983); Brauch, "Europa—Haus des Friedens—ein Fundament, drei Pfeiler und ein Baustein für eine europäische Friedensordnung," in Wolfgang R. Vogt, ed., *Mut zum Frieden. Über die Möglichkeiten einer Friedensentwicklung für das Jahr 2000* (Darmstadt: Wissenschaftliche Buchgemeinschaft, 1990), pp. 52–70; Egon Bahr/Dieter Lutz, eds., *Gemeinsame Sicherheit, Vol. 1: Zu den Ausgangsüberlegungen, Grundlagen und Strukturmerkmalen Gemeinsamer Sicherheit, Vol. 2: Zu rechtlichen, ökonomischen, psychologischen und militärischen Aspekten Gemeinsamer Sicherheit, Vol. 3: Zu den militärischen Aspekten Struktureller Nichtangriffsfähigkeit im Rahmen Gemeinsamer Sicherheit* (Baden-Baden: Nomos, 1986, 1987, 1988). A late-comer to this debate has been Dieter S. Lutz who contributed a new acronym: StruNA (Strukturelle Angriffsunfähigkeit). Dieter S. Lutz, *Zur Theorie Struktureller Angriffsunfähigkeit—Genesis, Definition und Kriterien Struktureller Angriffsunfähigkeit im Rahmen Defensiver Abhaltung und Gemeinsamer Sicherheit,* in *Hamburger Beiträge zur Friedensforschung und Sicherheitspolitik,* no. 22 (Hamburg: IFSH, Nov. 1987).

31. The CDU/CSU nominated only representatives of the traditionalist school: K. P. Stratmann, Gen. F. J. Schulze (Ret.), Adm. D. Wellerhoff, Lt. Gen. L. Domröse, Amb. R. Pauls, Adm. G. Poser (Ret.), M. S. Voslensky, G. Wettig, W. Seiffert, E. Wilkens, and R. Gramm. The FDP proposed: F. Bomsdorf and C. Bertram. The SPD invited these representatives of strategic studies: Brig. Gen. C. Krause, K. Kaiser, E. Lübkemeier, peace researchers: Count v. Baudissin, K. v. Schubert, G. Krell, D. Lutz, and proponents of NOD concepts: C. F. von Weizsäcker, L. Unterseher, H. Afheldt, E. Afheldt; the Greens proposed two peace researchers: J. Galtung and T. Ebert. The position of the government was presented by Amb. F. Ruth, disarmament adviser of the Federal government, Minister of Defense M. Wörner, under Secretary of Defense L. Rühl, Gen. W. Altenburg, and H. Rühle, then head of the defense planning staff.

32. Alfred Biehle, ed., *Alternative Strategien—Das Hearing im Verteidigungsausschuß des Deutschen Bundestages—Die schriftlichen Gutachten und Stellungnahmen* (Koblenz: Bernard & Graefe, 1986), pp. 22–44. A few papers of the hearing have also been published by Diethelm Schröder, ed., *Krieg oder was sonst? NATO: Strategie der Unsicherheit* (Reinbek: Rowohlt, 1984).

33. For details see the main points quoted in Chapter 1 in volume II of this series.

34. All former generals and high officers of the NVA were retired; younger officers and NCOs were given an opportunity to serve after a loyalty test for a certain time period in the new territorial army east of the Bundeswehr that will not be integrated into NATO command. No former East German officer would get an assignment in West Germany; Bundeswehr officers would command the new eastern territorial army. Sources: H. Schreitter-Schwarzenfeld, "Vom Verteidigungsminister zum Zirkusdirektor," in *Frankfurter Rundschau,* Aug. 3, 1990, p. 4; "Ein Teil der NVA soll als Territorialstreitkraft übernommen werden—50,000 bis 60,000 Mann/Bundeswehroffiziere auf wichtige Führungsposten/Vorstellungen Stoltenbergs," in *Frankfurter Allgemeine Zeitung,* Aug. 4, 1990, p. 1/2; *"Gesamtdeutsche Ärmee 370,000 Mann stark,"* in *Rhein-Neckar-Zeitung,* Aug. 4, 1990, p. 15; "Bonn

und Ost-Berlin ebnen 30,000 NVA-Zeitsoldaten Weg in deutsche Armee," in *Frankfurter Rundschau,* Aug. 4, 1990, p. 4.

35. See my proposal for a trilateral commission of German, Polish, and Czechoslovak officers and experts to form a territorial army east relying on NOD conceptual components (Chapter 1 of volume II).

36. See Boeker and Unterseher, "Emphasizing Defense," (note 19) pp. 89–109; Möller, Vol. II (note 30), pp. 29–31, 315–316.

37. See the critical analysis of the contradictory elements in the writings of Albrecht von Müller, in Möller, *Non-Offensive Defence,* Vol. II, pp. 149–161.

38. For a bibliography of Horst Afheldt's writings, see Carl Friedrich von Weizsäcker, ed., *Die Zukunft des Friedens in Europa—Politische und militärische Voraussetzungen* (München: Hanser, 1990), pp. 359–364. His major book publications are: *Analyse der Sicherheitspolitik,* unpublished Ph.D. dissertation, Technical University of Hannover, 1972; *Verteidigung und Frieden. Politik mit militärischen Mitteln* (München: Hanser, 1976); *Defensive Verteidigung* (Reinbek: Rowohlt, 1983); *Atomkrieg, Das Verhängnis einer Politik mit militärischen Mitteln* (München: Hanser, 1984); *Pour une defense non suicidaire en Europe* (Paris, 1985); *Der Konsens. Argumente für die Politik der Wiedervereinigung Europas* (Baden-Baden: Nomos, 1989).

39. Only a few of his articles have been published in English: Horst Afheldt, "Tactical nuclear weapons and European security," in SIPRI, ed., *Tactical Nuclear Weapons: European Perspectives* (London: Taylor and Francis, 1978), pp. 266–275 (quote on p. 280); "The Necessity, Preconditions and Consequences of a No-First-Use Policy," in Frank Blackaby, Jozef Goldblat, and Sverre Lodgaard, eds., *No-First-Use* (London: Taylor and Francis, 1984), pp. 57–66; "Conventional Defence Capabilities of NATO and WTO," in *Proceedings of the Thirty-Seventh Pugwash Conference on Science and World Affairs, Gmunden am Traunsee, Sept. 1–6, 1987* (London: Pugwash, 1988), pp. 89–96; "New policies, old fears," *Bulletin of the Atomic Scientists,* 44, no. 7 (Sept. 1988): 24–28.

40. For a very competent summary of Afheldt's first proposal of 1976 and of his predecessors Spannocchi and Brossolet, see Björn Möller, Ph.D. dissertation, Vol. II, Chap. 5 (note 30), pp. 75–102.

41. See Horst Afheldt, Chap. 6 in this volume and "Konventionelle Stabilität, Zivilschutz, Defensivüberlegenheit—Redebreiträge," in Bahr and Lutz, Vol. 3, (note 30), pp. 402–408.

42. See for a summary of the criticisms, see Möller, vol. II, pp. 99–102.

43. See Hofmann, note 24, pp. 344–347, 382–383.

44. Jochen Löser had been a member of the Wehrmacht from 1936 to 1945 and of the Bundeswehr from 1956 to 1974. His major publications are: *Weder rot noch tot. Überleben ohne Atomkrieg—Eine sicherheitspolitische Alternative* (München: Olzog, 1981); *Gegen den Dritten Weltkrieg. Strategie der Freien* (Herford: Mittler & Sohn, 1982); "Modern Defence Technologies for Non-Nuclear Border Defence," in Hylke Tromp, ed., *Non-Nuclear War in Europe. Alternatives for Nuclear Defence* (Groningen: Groningen University Press, 1986), pp. 195–200; Löser and Harald Anderson, *Antwort auf Genf. Sicherheit für West und Ost* (München: Olzog, 1984); *Löser and Ulrike Schilling, Neutralität für Mitteleuropa. Das Ende der Blöcke* (München: C. Bertelsmann Verlag, 1984).

45. Hannig is a retired air force officer and a former consultant with the German aircraft industry who has served both in World War II and in the Bundeswehr. His major publications are: *Abschreckung durch konventionelle Waffen. Das David-Goliath-Princip* (Berlin: Berlin Verlag A. Spitz, 1984); *Verteidigen ohne zu bedrohen. Die DEWA-Konzeption als Ersatz für NATO-FOFA* (Stuttgart: AFES, 1986; Mosbash: AFES Press, 1988); "Deterrence by Conventional Weapons: The David-Goliath Principle," in H. Tromp, ed., *Non-Nuclear War in Europe. Alternatives for Nuclear Defence* (Groningen: Groningen University, 1986), pp. 179–194; "NATO's Defense: Conventional Options Beyond FOFA," in *International Defense Review,* no. 7 (1986).

46. Johannes Gerber, *Die Bundeswehr im Nordatlantischen Bündnis* (Regensburg: Wahlhalla & Praetoria Verlag, 1985); "Fordert die Wirtschaftlichkeit eine neue Struktur des Heeeres," in Hans Adolf Jacobsen and Heinz Georg Lemm, eds., *Heere International,* vol. 3 (Herford: Verlag E.S. Mittler & Sohn, 1984), pp. 39–52, and *Beiträge zur Praxis der alternativen Verteidigung,* Reinhard Meyers, ed. (Münster: Hamburg: Lit, 1989), Studien zur Politik, Vol. 50.

47. For a detailed survey and critique see Möller, vol. II, chap. 6 (note 30), pp. 105–113.

48. B. Möller, vol. II, p. 113.

49. Franz Uhle-Wettler's last assignment was commandant of the NATO Defense College in Rome. Besides Chapter 5 in this volume, see his two major books: *Leichte Infanterie im Atomzeitalter* (Darmstadt: Wehr und Wissen, 1966); *Gefechtsfeld Mitteleuropa. Gefahr der Übertechnisierung der Streitkräfte* (München: Bernard & Graefe, 1980).

50. This summary follows closely B. Möller, Vol. II, (note 30) pp. 118–119; Eckart Afheldt, "Verteidigung ohne Selbstmord. Vorschlag für den Einsatz einer leichten Infanterie," in C. F. von Weizsäcker, ed., note 27, pp. 41–88; Eckart Afheldt, "Vorschlag für den Einsatz einer leichten Infanterie," in Horst Afheldt, "Defensive Verteidigung, 1983, pp. 66–127.

51. For a survey of Huber's writings see: B. Möller, vol. II, pp. 205–212; Reiner K. Huber, *Some Remarks on Structural Implications of Strategic Stability in Central Europe.* Working Paper No. 1 for the 5th workshop of the Pugwash Group on Conventional Forces in Europe, Castilionciello, Italy, Oct. 9–12, 1986; *The Defence Efficiency Hypothesis and Conventional Stability in Europe: Implications for Arms Control* (München: Universität der Bundeswehr, 1988), *Fakultät für Informatik, Bericht No.* SS-8801; Rainer K. Huber and Hans Hoffmann, *Some Thoughts on Unilaterally Reducing the Conventional Imbalance in Central Europe: Gradual Defensivity as a Force Design Principle* (München: Universität der Bundeswehr, 1984), Fakultät für Informatik, Bericht No. 8402.

52. Reiner K. Huber and Hans Hoffmann. "Gradual Defensivity: An Approach to a Stable Conventional Force Equilibrium in Europe," in J. P. Brams, ed., *Operational Research '84* (Amsterdam: Elsevier, 1984), pp. 197–211 (204).

53. Hans W. Hofmann, Reiner K. Huber, and Karl Steiger, "On Reactive Defense Options, A Comparative Systems Analysis of Alternatives for the Initial Defense against the First Strategic Echelon of the Warsaw Pact in Central Europe," in Reiner K. Huber, ed., *Modeling and Analysis of Conventional Defense in Europe. Assessment of Improved Options* (New York: Plenum, 1986), pp. 97–140; Hofmann, Huber, Steiger, "Some Remarks on the Costs of Reactive Defence Options," in Barnaby and ter Borg, note 19, pp. 303–314.

54. Rear Admiral Elmar Schmähling was one of the youngest admirals in the Bundeswehr. After heading its intelligene service (MAD), his last assignment was as commander of the Office for Studies and Exercises of the Bundeswehr. He was retired in 1990 after he had openly criticized the chancellor and the defense minister and the official defense policy, e.g., in his book, *Der unmögliche Krieg: Sicherheit und Verteidigung vor der Jahrtausendwende* (Düsseldorf: Econ, 1989). See for his earlier English publications: *The Survivability of Static and Large Weapons Systems Against Modern Stand-Off Weapons,* Working paper No. 3 of the 5th Workshop of the Pugwash Study Group on Conventional Forces in Europe, Castilioncello, Italy, Oct. 9–12, 1986; and *Thoughts on the Future of Surface Forces,* Working paper No. 2; "German Security Policy Beyond American Hegemony," in *World Policy Journal,* 6, no. 2 (Spring, 1989): 371–384.

55. This summary is taken from B. Möller, vol. II (note 30), p. 204.

56. Andreas von Bülow, *Alpträume West gegen Alpträume Ost. Ein Beitrag zur Bedrohungsanalyse* (München: C. H. Beck, 1984); Andreas von Bülow, "Gedanken zu einer Weiterentwicklung der Verteidigungsstrategie in West und Ost," in Hans Günter Brauch, ed., *Sicherheitspolitik am Ende? Eine Bestandssaunahme, Perspektiven und neue Ansätze* (Gerlingen: Bleicher, 1984), pp. 223–244; "Vorschlag für eine neue Bundeswehrstruktur der 90er Jahre. Einstieg in die strukturelle Nichtangriffsfähigkeit," in *Europäische Wehrkunde,* 35, no. 11 (Nov. 1986): 636–646; "Conventional Stability: An Overall Concept," in ter Borg and Smit, note 4, pp. 45–48; "Restructuring the Ground Forces," ibid., pp. 161–174; Andreas von Bülow, Helmut Funk, and Albrecht von Müller, *Sicherheit für Europa* (Koblenz: Bernard & Graefe, 1988). v. Bülow and Funk, "The Achievement of Mutual Conventional Forces Defender Superiority in Central Europe from the Urals to the Atlantic," in *Pugwash Newsletter,* 25, no. 3 (Jan. 1988): 108–110.

57. For a criticism of the manpower estimates of von Bülow and Funk, see: Christian Thimann et al., "Zum Personalmodell von H. Funk: Die Integrierte Vorneverteidigung Mitteleuropas," (Bonn: SAS, unpublished manuscript, 1988). Lutz Unterseher claims that the von Bülow/Funk model called for 56 mechanized and armored brigades that would imply a doubling of the Bundeswehr's sword to 8000 or 9000 tanks.

58. "Die Bundeswehr in Übergang," *Presseservice der SPD,* Mar. 23, 1990.

59. The conceptual ideas are contained in *Die Kunst des Friedens. Grundzüge einer europäischen Sicherheitspolitik für die 80er und 90er Jahre* (München: Hanser, 1984).

60. As a result of this well-funded research project, so far no final report and no book or reader are available and only a few articles by von Müller have been published (often several times in almost identical versions): "Confidence-Building by Hardware Measures," in Joseph Rotblat and Sven Hellman, eds., *The Annals of Pugwash 1984* (London: Macmillan, 1985), pp. 275–286; "Structural Stability at the Central Front," in Anders Boserup, L. Christensen, and O. Nathan, eds., *The Challenge of Nuclear Armaments, Essays Dedicated to Nils Bohr and His Appeal for an Open World* (Copenhagen: Rhodos International, 1986), pp. 239–256; "Integrated Forward Defence, Outline of a Modified Conventional Defense of Central Europe," in Hylke Tromp, ed., *Non-Nuclear War in Europe. Alterna-*

tives for Nuclear Defence (Groningen: Groningen University Press, 1986), pp. 201–224; *Conventional Stability in Europe. Outlines of the Military Hardware for a Second Detente* (Starnberg: manuscript, 1987). For a critical assessment of the available results, see B. Möller, vol. II (note 30), pp. 149–161.

61. Samuel Huntington, "Conventional Deterrence and Conventional Retaliation in Europe," in *International Security*, 8, no. 3 (Winter 1983–1984): 32–56.

62. Albrecht A.C. von Müller and Andrzj Karkoszka, "An East-West Negotiating Proposal," in *Bulletin of the Atomic Scientists*, vol. 44, no. 7 (Sept. 1988): 39–42. The proposal is based on these elements: a ceiling of 10,000 main battle tanks combined with density limits; a low ceiling for heavy artillery, rocket launchers with density limits; a low ceiling of 500 strike aircraft and 500 armored helicopters; a range limitation for conventional rocket of 50 km; no forward deployment (not closer than 150 km) of munitions stockpiles and prohibition of forward deployed mobile bridging equipment; logistical infrastructures that require a frequent backup by nonmobile service stations and other installations. However, this proposal addressed to the arms control community was contradicted by von Müller in December 1988 in a talk to a military audience in Bonn when he supported not only the Lance modernization but called for an additional shorter range nuclear launcher.

63. Karl H. Schreiner, "'Strukturelle Nichtangriffsfähigkeit' Eine Auseinandersetzung mit den Thesen von Albrecht A. C. von Müller,"in Hartmut Bühl, ed., *Strategiediskussion. NATO-Strategie im Wandel. Alternative Sicherheitskonzepte* (Herford: Mittler & Sohn, 1987), pp. 173–183.

64. Lutz Unterseher, "Fünf Thesen zur Vermeidung von Mißverständnissen um eine alternative Verteidigung," in Bahr and Lutz, vol. III, pp. 288–290. Unterseher, who had taught v. Müller NOD principles and force structure designs as a consultant to Afheldt in 1983/1984, described his former student as a "wolf in sheep's clothing" who offered different messages to different audiences. Similarly critical is B. Möller, vol. II (note 30), p. 161, who concluded: "On balance, it must be said that Albrecht von Müller has contributed only very few new ideas to the NOD debate. Rather he has skillfully couched old ideas in new conceptual garments, and hence with considerable success concealed their true origins."

65. For a perceptive presentation see B. Möller, vol. II, (note 30) pp. 163–182. SAS has so far published two books: Studiengruppe Alternative Sicherheitspolitik ed., *Strukturwandel der Verteidigung—Entwürfe für eine konsequente Defensive* (Opladen. Westdeutscher Verlag, 1984); Studiengruppe Alternative Sicherheitspolitik ed., *Vertrauensbildende Verteidigung—Reform deutscher Sicherheitspolitik* (Gerlingen: Bleicher Verlag, 1989), and many research reports. The international group consists of close to 50 researchers, military officers, and politicians from Germany, Europe, and North America. Several reports of members have been published in English by AFES Press Publishers, Alte-Bergsteige 47, 6950 Mosbach, FRG. Lutz Unterseher is a sociologist by training. For a decade he was working with the Institute for Applied Social Science (INFAS) before he cofounded a consulting firm SALSS in the early 1980s. For a bibliography of his writings and those of other SAS members, see SAS, 1989, pp. 271–298. See: Egbert Boeker and Lutz Unterseher, "Emphasizing Defence," in Barnaby and ter Borg, eds., note 8, pp. 89–109; "Emphasizing Defence: The Ongoing Non-debate in the Federal Republic of Germany," ibid., pp. 116–126; Charles J. Dick vs. Lutz Unterseher, "Dialogue on the Military Effectiveness of Nonprovocative Defence," ibid., pp. 239–250; John Grin and Lutz Unterseher, "The Spiderweb Defense," in *Bulletin of the Atomic Scientists*, 44, no. 7 (Sept. 1988): 28–32. His more recent unpublished reports in English are: *The Standard Batallion of Line Infantry: An Exercise in Force Design With Robust Technologies* (Bonn: SAS, 1987); *Spider and Web: The Case for a Pragmatic Defence Alternative* (Bonn: SAS, 1988); *Tactical Air Forces. For a Disarmament Initiative of the West* (Bonn: SAS, 1988).

66. SALSS, *Konventionelle Landstreitkräfte für Mitteleuropa: eine militärische Bedrohungsanalyse* (Bonn: SALSS, 1984); Malcolm Chalmers and Lutz Unterseher, "Is There a Tank Gap? Comparing NATO and Warsaw Pact Tank Fleets," in *International Security*, 13, no. 1 (Summer 1988): 5–49; Unterseher, "A Note on the Intricacies of Military Force Assessment," in Hans Günter Brauch and Robert Kennedy, eds., *Alternative Conventional Defense Postures in the European Theater, vol. 1: The Military Balance and Domestic Constraints* (New York: Crane Russak, 1990), pp. 69–75. See Hartmut Bebermeyer, "The Fiscal Crisis of the Bundeswehr," in Brauch and Kennedy, vol. I, pp. 128–147; Bernd Grass, "The Personnel Shortage in the Bundeswehr until the Year 2000," ibid., pp. 97–112; Wolfgang R. Vogt, "The Crisis of Acceptance of the Security Policy with Military Means in the Federal Republic of Germany," ibid., pp. 165–188. See, e.g., the two NATO reports by Hans Günter Brauch, *Evaluation of Antitactical Ballistic Missile Defense*, AFES Press Report No. 29 (Mosbach: AFES Press, 1989), Lutz Unterseher, *The Conventional Land Defence for Central Europe—Force Structure, Emerging Technology and Military Stability*, AFES Press Report No. 30 (Mosbach: AFES Press, 1989).

67. Lutz Unterseher, "Defending Europe: Toward a Stable Conventional Deterrent," in Henry Shue, ed., *Nuclear Deterrence and Moral Restraint* (Cambridge: Cambridge University Press, 1989), pp. 318–319.

68. Möller, vol. II (note 30), p. 173.

69. Hartmut Bebermeyer and Lutz Unterseher, *Eine künftige Bundesmarine im Rahmen einer defensiven Verteidigung konzeption* (Bonn: SAS, 1986); Bebermeyer and Unterseher, "Wider die Großmannsucht zur See: Das Profil einer defensiven Marine," in SAS (1989): 165–187.

70. Charles Knight, *New Realities. New Opportunities. A Proposal for Restructuring the U.S. Army in NATO* (Preliminary version) (Cambridge: Commonwealth Institute, 1988).

71. See Chapter 8 by Lutz Unterseher in this volume.

72. In its intermediate report in June 1983, the commission agreed on a set of criteria for a new defense strategy: "(1) Military strategies must aim at the political goal of war prevention. Military structures and weapons must therefore serve the strategic concept of defense. (2) Strategies of nuclear deterrence are only legitimate as an interim solution. (3) Nuclear weapons are strategic weapons of retaliation; they must not be made appear harmless in the disguise of battlefield weapons. (4) Military strategies, the structures of armed forces and armaments must be suitable for arms control, and compatible with military confidence-building. (5) Military strategies, the structures of armed forces and armaments must allow a self-conscious crisis management and must neither force the state to escalate, nor give the other side incentives or pretexts for escalation." See Egon Bahr, "Bericht der Arbeitsgruppe 'Neue Strategien' beim SPD-Parteivorstand vom Juli 1983," in Hans Günter Brauch, ed., *Sicherheitspolitik am Ende? Eine Bestandsaufnahme, Perspektiven und neue Ansätze* (Gerlingen: Bleicher, 1984), pp. 275–290 (p. 281).

73. For a detailed analysis of the debate till May 1989, see Unterseher in Barnaby and ter Borg, note 19, pp. 120–122; Unterseher, in Shue, note 70, pp. 328–331; Björn Möller, Vol. II, chap. 16 (note 30), pp. 269–292. For the most recent proposal: "Die Bundeswehr im Übergang," *Presseservice der SPD*, Mar. 23, 1990.

74. "Social Democrats Aim for Changes in NATO," in *International Herald Tribune*, Mar. 22, 1990; "SPD genügt halbe Bundeswehr—Regierungsprogramm fordert Abschied von NATO-Strategie," in *Frankfurter Rundschau*, Mar. 22, 1990; "SPD: Bundeswehr jetzt abrüsten," in *Frankfurter Allgemeine Zeitung*, Mar. 24, 1990, p. 2; Horst Schreiter-Schwarzenfeld, "'4000 Panzer verschrotten'— SPD legte Konzept zur Umstrukturierung der Bundeswehr vor," in *Frankfurter Rundschau*, Mar. 24, 1990. These reports were based on two press conferences with Ms. Heidemarie Wieczorek-Zeul on Mar. 21 (*Presseservice der SPD*, No. 126/90) and with Egon Bahr and Katrin Fuchs on Mar. 23, 1990 (*Presseservice der SPD*). In Apr. 1990, President Bush announced not to modernize the Lance, and in July 1990, NATO proposed a total withdrawal of all nuclear artillery shells from Europe. The military service in the FRG has already been reduced to 12 months. All U.S. chemical weapons were withdrawn by Sept. 1990. Thus many of these proposals have already been accepted or implemented.

75. "Die Bundeswehr im Übergang," *Presseservice der SPD*, Mar. 23, 1990: 14–15.

76. Ibid.

77. See for details Chapter 1, vol. II and the chronology at the end of vol. III.

78. See Bernd Grass, in Brauch and Kennedy, vol. 1, pp. 97–112.

79. See, e.g., Roland Kaestner, "Überlegungen zur künftigen Wehrstruktur deutscher Streitkräfte in einem Europa kooperativer Sicherheit," in *Sicherheit and Frieden*, Vol. 8, no. 2, 1990: 86–93.

80. In June and July 1990, this author suggested in conference and background papers to set up a trilateral force structure commission with experts from the GDR, Poland, and CSFR to develop principles for a nonoffensive territorial army and to make them a part of the unification treaty.

81. See Hans Günter Brauch, "German Unity, Conventional Disarmament, Confidence-Building Defense, and a New European Order of Peace and Security," in Hans Günter Brauch and Robert Kennedy, eds., *Alternative Conventional Defense Postures in the European Theater. Volume 2: The Impact of Political Change on Status of Technology and Arms Control* (New York: Crane Russak, 1991), p. 22.

2

The American Debate on Conventional Alternatives for the Defense of Europe

Robert Kennedy

Dramatic changes in Eastern Europe and the former Soviet Union since 1989 have forced NATO to consider what kinds of military forces and structures are likely to be appropriate for the emerging security environment in Europe. Moreover, the second Gulf War highlighted, once again, the clear fact that the long-term security of the nations of the North Atlantic Alliance can be threatened by events beyond Europe. While the debate over NATO's future role in "out of area" crises and conflicts is long from settled, the potential requirement to move highly mobile forces capable of confronting a powerful adversary and to move those forces rapidly will undoubtedly play a role in the thinking of some if not all the member nations of NATO as they turn to the problem of restructuring their forces in Europe. In its November 1991 meeting in Rome, NATO formally adopted a new force structure. However, the debate over appropriate force structures in Europe is far from over.

Of course, the search for military force postures capable of providing a comfortable measure of security to the nations of Western Europe is not new. At the close of World War II, the massive presence of Soviet troops in Eastern Europe following on the heels of Moscow's outright annexation of Latvia, Lithuania, Estonia, and areas of Finland, Poland, Romania, and eastern Czechoslovakia, which had occurred before the end of the war, raised concerns in Western Europe over Soviet intentions. The failure of the Moscow conference in March and April 1947, Soviet meddling in Iran, Turkey, and Greece, and the Soviet involvement in the "coup" in Czechoslovakia added measurably to fears of Soviet malevolence. Indeed, in a telegram to President Harry Truman on May 12, 1945, Winston Churchill expressed his concern over postwar Western force reductions and the possibility of a Soviet advance to the North Sea and the Atlantic.[1] Although most Europeans were not as concerned as Churchill over possible overt Soviet military aggression, the task as many saw it was to arrest the momentum of Soviet expansion, political or military, as exemplified by the presence of the Red Army in the heart of Europe.

By linking the United States and its strategic nuclear striking power to the defense of Europe through the formation of NATO, Europeans hoped to gain time to rebuild their economies to prevent collapse from within and to rebuild their military capabilities in order to deter any potential adventurism by the Soviet Union.[2] The explosion of an atomic device by the USSR in late 1949, however, presaged the end of America's monopoly on atomic might, and the outbreak of hostilities in Korea raised concerns that the Soviet Union might be willing to use force to achieve its objectives in Europe. French General Andre Beaufre, recalling Western anxiety, noted that " . . . as the Soviet nuclear threat developed, it became increasingly difficult to believe that recourse to a "nuclear exchange" would be made for any reason other than the defense of absolutely vital objectives. It seemed wise, therefore, to anticipate a more or less extended period of resistance before unleashing "massive retaliation."[3]

Under such circumstances, Western European security against conventional attack that had been presupposed by America's nuclear power now seemed to be in question. As a result, the West undertook its first serious attempt to create the forces necessary to bring balance to the European conventional military equation. In September 1950 the North Atlantic Council agreed to establish a unified command structure and to examine "methods by which Germany could most usefully make its contribution" to Western defense.[4]

The United States set the pattern for conventional rearmament by adopting a program that would require a quadrupling of its defense expenditures within three years. Britain followed suit by announcing plans to form three new divisions and promised to increase the British contingent in West Germany to five divisions by the end of 1951. France increased its defense budget by 30% and planned to add 15 new divisions in three years. All the other allies except Iceland, which had no armed forces, and Portugal announced plans to increase their military forces.[5]

Capstone of this new fervor was the decision by the North Atlantic Council in Lisbon in February 1952 to adopt the most ambitious conventional force goals in NATO history. NATO member states were to field 50 divisions, 4000 aircraft, and strong naval forces by the end of 1952; 75 divisions and 6500 aircraft by 1953; and 96 divisions and 9000 aircraft by the end of 1954. Not surprisingly, the forces to be fielded to meet the Soviet threat reflected traditional approaches to military power, which had matured with the great armored, air, and naval battles of World War II. Mindful of the costs of such heavy forces and the enormity of the task of balancing Soviet conventional power, not all defense specialists in the late 1940s and early 1950s held to traditional views.

EARLY ALTERNATIVES

Immediately after World War II, British Air Marshall, Sir John Slessor, strongly advocated supplementing active divisions with territorial forces. He proposed that the Federal Republic of Germany be covered with a network of highly trained, semistatic home guard units composed of local men whose primary armament would be antitank guns and automatic weapons. Slessor argued that such local men would know every inch of the ground to be defended, "every coppice and stream, land and street" in the town, village, or area they would be assigned. They would be inspired by the knowledge they were protecting their own homes and their own families and friends. In peacetime such a home guard would be responsible for the storage and defense of their weapons. In a crisis, their task would be to lay mine fields when so directed. In war, "their job would be to block every road and destroy every tank moving across country in their zone."[6]

Slessor's recommendations, however, were clearly out of the mainstream. Few defense specialists believed that such units would be any match for the Red Army. At best they could only expect to play a harassing role after territory or even the war had been lost.

Slessor, of course, was not alone. On the continent, as NATO turned to Germany as a means of increasing its conventional military deterrent, Colonel Bogislav von Bonin was searching for a nonprovocative defensive force structure that would wear down any enemy and thus deter aggression. He proposed a barrier zone some 50 km wide, manned by about 150,000 to 200,000 troops operating from simple fortifications and field emplacements and employing antitank weapons, recoilless rifles, and mines. Armored elements, characteristic of the traditional alternatives of the time, were to play only a minor role in von Bonin's plan as a means for tactical counterattack.[7]

Like Slessor, von Bonin did not reflect mainstream thinking in Germany, and he was removed from his position on the defense staff. Moreover, by the mid-1950s it was becoming increasingly apparent that NATO member states were either unwilling or unable to meet the conventional force goals set at Lisbon. As a result, NATO reversed its position and moved toward a nuclear emphasis strategy. In late 1953 President Dwight D. Eisenhower authorized the deployment of tactical nuclear weapons to Europe. In 1954 he announced his "new look" in defense, and American forces were in the process of being structured for an atomic battlefield. In an address in September 1954, General Alfred M. Guenther, supreme commander of allied forces in Europe, stated that "if we are able to use atomic weapons against an act of aggression, if it should take place, we will have a reasonably good chance of defending against an all-out act of Soviet aggression."[8] By 1957 NATO had approved Military Committee Document MC 14/2 and thus formally adopted a change in strategy. Efforts to develop conventional alternatives for deterrence and defense were officially dropped. Conventional forces would only serve as a thin "tripwire" that would trigger a massive U.S. nuclear response.

This change in strategy raised serious concerns among many on both sides of the Atlantic that if war did come the consequences would be devastating. As a result some defense specialists continued to search for promising conventional alternatives. George Kennan, in his Reith Lecture series aired over the British Broadcasting System in 1958, advocated territorial type forces as a potential core of resistance in areas that might be occupied by attacking forces.[9] In 1960 as Soviet nuclear capabilities were increasingly evident, Liddell Hart, in an attempt to answer the critical question of how to defend Europe without destroying it, said:

The answer—if we are honest, and brave enough to face the hard facts—can only be that, in the present conditions, effective defense is not possible.

For defense in a real sense of the word, as defined in dictionaries, means to "preserve, protect, keep safe, by resisting attack." At present if nuclear weapons . . . are actually used no country can hope to keep safe, or even to avoid fatal destruction.[10]

In the United States the new Kennedy administration, displaying a similar pessimism, began calling for a more flexible response in which conventional forces would play a much greater role in deterring aggression. Finally, NATO itself dropped its "tripwire" strategy in 1967 with the adoption of MC 14/3. Support for this move, however, was nowhere near unanimous in NATO countries. Many feared that the United States was attempting to decouple itself from a European war. Even among those who were seeking conventional alternatives, some remained concerned that NATO member states would be reluctant to take on the costly burden of increased defense expenditures to produce a credible conventional option. It took the 1973 Arab-Israeli war to stimulate widespread interest in and support for seriously exploring conventional alternatives.

IMPACT OF THE 1973 WAR
ON THE AMERICAN DEBATE

There can be little doubt that the American debate over options for improving the conventional defense of Europe received a boost as the result of the successful employment of "smart bombs" by the American military in Vietnam. However, the extensive use of precision-guided munitions (PGMs) during the 1973 Arab-Israeli war fired the imagination of Western, and particularly American, defense specialists. In 18 days of combat, the Arabs and the Israelis lost 590 aircraft and 2600 tanks. Malcolm Currie, director of defense research and engineering, in testimony before the U.S. Congress, stated that "a remarkable series of new technological developments has brought us to the threshold of what I believe will become a true revolution in conventional warfare."[11] Similarly, Amos A. Jordan, principal deputy assistant secretary of defense for international security affairs, noted that "as a result of major recent developments in conventional weapons technologies, we may be at the threshold of a new era in the conduct of warfare comparable in some respects to earlier periods in which new technologies rendered obsolete the tactics and concepts, even strategies, governing the conduct of war."[12] Articles proliferated on the impact of modern technology on defense. John W. Finney wrote "Guide Bombs Expected to Revolutionize Warfare," Gwynne Dyer questioned "Is Blitzkrieg as Passé as the Trenches," Edward B. Atkeson asked "Is the Soviet Army Obsolete?" and John Marriott captured the essence of the debate in an article titled "New Weapons for Defense in Europe."[13]

Perhaps one of the more far-reaching early conceptualizations of the impact of precision munitions on warfare was that of T. Finley Burke. In a presentation at the U.S. Army War College in early 1974, he foresaw a potential for a radical reorganization of the ground forces in order to maximize their defensive capabilities. Small teams of local men operating over familiar terrain, data linked to rearward positioned guided missiles capable of delivering a wide variety of munitions, including antitank and antipersonnel weapons, would be the heart of the defensive effort. These teams, operating in great depth, would be tasked to delay, disorganize, incrementally attrite, and ultimately destroy an aggressor.

Burke's ideas and those of others gave rise to serious discussions at the U.S. Army's Strategic Studies Institute (SSI) in which this author was frequently involved. One of the principal catalysts for these discussions was Stanley D. Fair, deputy director of the institute. Colonel Fair argued that modern precision technology would increase the conventional war-fighting capability of NATO forces, contribute to the achievement of a direct defense option, and thus permit the strategy of flexible response to become a reality, thereby enhancing their credibility as a deterrent to aggression.[14] Fair saw modern precision guidance technologies more as a supplement to current capabilities than offering an opportunity to explore a spectrum of nontraditional alternatives. Some at SSI saw the possibility of a wider range of alternatives. PGMs seemed to favor defense over offense. They forced the offense to avoid concentrations of the kind that gave the Soviet forces an advantage over the West. From the rugged country that sits astride the north-south approach routes in Norway to the mountain passes of Italy and the rough terrain of Greece and Turkey, PGMs seemed to offer an alternative to further procurements of costly, armor-ladened forces. Even in central Germany, topography seemed to favor a defense based on PGMs. Hills, forested areas, and urban sprawl all seemed to provide options for armies restructured to maximize defense using modern precision technologies.

THE AMERICAN DEBATE BEGINS

Structuring for Defensive Superiority

A far-reaching alternative was that of a civilian-based defense offered by Steven L. Canby in late 1974. In an Adelphi paper,[15] he provided two options that he believed would greatly alter the conventional balance in Europe. The first option involved a substantial restructuring of NATO forces. This restructuring would include the centralization and streamlining of logistics, the formation of cadre units and a corresponding organization in NATO countries for rapid mobilization to flesh out such units, the prepositioning of equipment of reinforcing American forces with parent units instead of in centralized supply depots like Kaiserslautern, and a replacement of heavy forward units with light antitank cavalry units armed with antitank guided munitions (ATGMs), light cannons, machine guns, and multi-barrelled antiaircraft guns. Canby believed such changes would enable NATO to achieve conventional equivalence with the Warsaw Pact.

To achieve "defensive superiority," he suggested a second option, which was even a clearer departure from the more traditional approaches. Canby argued that defensive dominance required defense in depth against enemy penetrations. To achieve such a defense in depth, he proposed a checkerboard defense composed of numerous half-company or company-size strong points positioned about 2.5 km apart. According to Canby, under NATO's present organization, a 40,000-man division slice could provide about 10 battalion strong points. With restructuring he maintained that 40,000 soldiers could be shaped into two division slices. Each slice could be organized into some 40 company-size strong points. Moreover, with some further restructuring to create extra divisions, the number of strong points could be increased by an additional 40%, making as many as 110 strong points for each 10 available under NATO's traditional structures.

These company-size forces would occupy a sector averaging 50 km wide and 8 km deep. They would be equipped with light armored vehicles, possibly wheeled, which would mount ATGMs and high/low pressure cannons. Accompanying infantry would be armed with short-range, compact ATGMs. Nightvision image-intensifiers would enable them to operate effectively in the dark as well as in daylight. Supported by artillery and heavy mortars delivering minelets and other weapons to their targets through laser and infrared guidance technologies, these units would embed attacking armor in a defensive grid, bogging down the penetrating forces until they are weakened and slowed sufficiently for a counterattack by local and general reserves employing new technologies to destroy and eject them.

Steven Canby has continued to develop and refine his ideas.[16] His most recent concepts on a 'light infantry forward" appear in Chapter 9 of this volume.

Civilian-Based Defense

At about the same time that Canby was fashioning his checkerboard defense, others were examining even more radical proposals. One such alternative, civilian-based defense (CBD), was outlined on the American side of the Atlantic by Gene Sharp.[17]

CBD is considered to be the application of a much more widely recognized phenomenon, nonviolent action, to the problem of national security and defense. It differs from traditional approaches to defense, as well as from those who would advocate pacifism, in several important dimensions. Where traditional approaches to defense call for armament, military preparedness, and violent action, if need be, and pacifists encourage disarmament, nonpreparedness, and nonaction, supporters of CBD hail transarmament, civilian preparedness, and nonviolent action as the operative means of deterrence and defense.

As Edward B. Atkeson has noted, transarmament is a fundamental concept in CBD. Transarmament retains the principal of preparedness but shifts it from military means by the armed forces of any given country to civilian means by the population as a whole. Transarmament envisions advanced preparations, possibly a trained directing elite and rehearsed plans for massive resistance. Thus disarmament, in the truest sense of the word, is rejected.[18] Moreover, as Gene Sharp maintains, "non-violent action is not an attempt to avoid or ignore conflict. . . . " Rather, it is a "technique by which people who reject passivity and submission, and who see struggle as essential, can wage their conflict without violence. . . . it is not passive. It is action that is nonviolent."[19]

According to Sharp, the methods of nonviolent action include protest, noncooperation, and intervention.[20] The threat of protest demonstrations, of the disruption of public services, of communications, of transportation, of the economic and social bases of the country, and the promise of the creation of a parallel system of government are to serve as a deterrent to aggression. Atkeson notes that "the objective would be to bring the potential opponent to a realization of the dimensions of the problem of attempting to manage the unmanageable, and hence to develop a significant sense of deterrence to aggression."[21] Moreover, according to some proponents of CBD, should deterrence fail, CBD could be used to coerce an aggressor to withdraw.

Among the more positive aspects of CBD, proponents contended that if defenses were based wholly or nearly entirely on such a concept, CBD would negate reasons for neighboring countries to have military forces. Furthermore, they believed that even the most totalitarian power could not ignore the enormous moral and psychological impact of a serious transarmament. During the years of the NATO/Warsaw Pact confrontation, this would have meant that stress would have been created within the Warsaw Pact if the Soviet Union forced countries to arm and maintain forces to "counter the Western threat." Grassroots efforts for peace would have emerged. As a result, the entire framework for the historic East-West struggle would have undergone a profound transformation.

Generally speaking, however, most who lent their support to the concept of a civilian-based defense saw it as additive to existing forms of defense rather than as a substitutable alternative. Thus they saw CBD as existing alongside other more "violent" forms of defense, as a means of resistance should deterrence and defense both fail.

A "Practical Low Cost" Alternative

Most defense specialists seeking ways to improve NATO's conventional posture in the early 1970s, however, sought alternatives that were clearly less radical than the approaches suggested either by Canby or by those who supported CBD. One such specialist was Robert Komer. Writing in the winter 1973–1974 edition of *Foreign Policy,* Komer suggested what he considered to be some "practical low cost ways to revamp NATO's conventional posture."[22] Among other things, he called for a restructuring of NATO's ground and air forces. Such a restructuring would include the tailoring of ground forces around a "smaller, leaner divisional 'slice'" with a higher combat-to-support troop ratio. It would also include the formation by our allies of five to eight similarly configured cadre divisions and a greater exploitation of "cheap territorial forces." Komer advocated providing all forces with much stronger anti-armor capabilities. According to him,

> Divisions should be given more AT missiles, mobile ground tank killer units could be formed, highly mobile AT-helicopter units could be used as "linebackers" to blunt any major penetrations, and light AT weapons could be widely distributed to reserve and territorial forces.[23]

Komer also recommended that NATO make more extensive use of mines, pre-planned demolitions, and even an extensive barrier system to slow down a Warsaw Pact offensive. He further maintained that through improved command and control and low cost measures to enhance survivability, NATO's air forces could achieve a clearcut air superiority over the critical central region. Finally, Komer underscored the need for NATO to rationalize its force structure in order to eliminate costly duplication, the product of 13 nations bent on maintaining separate national military forces, most of which had balanced triservice forces.[24]

THE LATE 1970s AND EARLY 1980s

In light of the seminal work done by James Digby and others, a wide variety of suggestions emerged in the late 1970s and early 1980s on how NATO might take advantage of new technologies to improve its defenses. The three services had examined the implications of the 1973 Arab-Israeli war for conflict at sea and in Europe. Among the less traditional approaches to improving European defenses were those that emerged at the Rand Corporation and from a series of discussions and office debates at the U.S. Army's Strategic Studies Institute (SSI) located at the Army War College in Carlisle, Pennsylvania.

Distributed Area Defense

At Rand, Paxton, Weiner, and Wise argued that Soviet superiority in armor demanded that NATO more fully utilize recent high technology developments in precision-guided munitions, sensors, communications, and combat vehicles in order to bring balance to the conventional equation in Europe.[25] They proposed a modification of NATO's initial forward defense. They recommended the use of numerous small units distributed throughout the battle area whose task would be to delay and attrite enemy forces rather than to defend territory. They suggested building a forward defensive system around an experimental squadron-size force of 900 men. The squadron would be divided into three troops, which would each be further divided into three platoons. The units would employ direct-fire, laser, beam-rider missiles and indirect-fire mortars guided by "hot spot" sensors, operated in conjunction with elevated imaging infrared sensors, for target location and acquisition. Units would be of two types: One type would be highly mobile motorcycle units, which would cover the main roads and trails and the forested areas; the other type would be responsible for the defense of specifically assigned areas with which they would have become thoroughly familiar through peacetime training exercises. The missions of both units would be the same: disrupt, disorganize, delay, and attrite forces attempting to penetrate the forward security zone in their area of responsibility.

The Army War College School

Building on studies undertaken by the services and by SSI[26] and on the ideas advanced by T. Finley Burke on reorganizing defense, as well as those expressed by Komer, Canby, and others, several of the institute's analysts began to focus on what they saw as a growing problem: conventionally defending in Europe in an environment of growing Soviet conventional and nuclear strength.

Area combat troops

In 1981 Lieutenant Colonel Edward A. Corcoran outlined an approach to redress the conventional imbalance in Europe. He believed that a crucial element in encouraging the Soviets to seek political solutions was a viable NATO military posture that neither foresaw a rapid resort to nuclear weapons nor would be susceptible to easy neutralization by Warsaw Pact nuclear weapons. He believed that such a defense could be constructed within the resources available to NATO member states and should include four main elements.[27]

The first major element in Corcoran's proposal was area combat troops (ACTs). According to Corcoran, if NATO countries in the central region utilized reserves to the same extent as Norway, there would be an additional 7 million troops at their disposal. These troops could be organized into small units that could be easily mobilized as ACTs. Armed with antiarmor weapons and supported by laser guided weapons, smart bombs, mines, and other stand-off munitions, and operating in dispersed formations in their home regions, ACTs could turn an attempted Warsaw Pact sweep across central Europe into a highly risky military maneuver. In forward areas ACTs would operate in conjunction with the second major element in Colonel Corcoran's proposal, regular combat maneuver units. These two elements would complement each other to inflict maximum casualties on invading forces.

> Artillery units, using the intelligence supplied by the pervasive net of Area Combat Troops and terminal homing modern munitions could place very effective fire on enemy units. . . . By taking advantage of the capabilities of Area Combat troops to soften up and disrupt Pact combat elements, NATO maneuver units could wage a much more effective mobile defense.[28]

In rear areas ACTs would provide a dense network of forces capable of neutralizing small Pact diversionary elements and locating and fixing larger Pact penetrations so that such penetrating Pact forces could be neutralized by other NATO combat elements.

The third major element of NATO's combat capability would be its support units. Corcoran maintained that each unit should be prepared to break down into an effective infantry fighting organization, trained to use a wide range of weapons. Should these units come under direct attack as the result of a successful penetration, they should be able to "exert an active presence similar to and in conjunction with the Area Combat Troops."[29]

The final element would be penetration units capable of taking the battle to Warsaw Pact territory. These forces would include long-range reconnaissance patrols and light infantry elements capable of creating maximum confusion and disorganization in the Pact tactical rear area, special forces units for similar operations in the Pact strategic rear, and combat forces prepared to carry out raids and diversionary attacks throughout the Soviet Union.

The heart of Corcoran's approach, however, was his area combat troops. He maintained that in addition to the obvious deterrent and defensive utility of such forces, ACTs, because of their dispersion, would decrease Pact incentives to use weapons of mass destruction. Perhaps more importantly, however, ACTs would pose a minimal external threat and thus provide maximum support to NATO political and diplomatic efforts.

A more flexible flexible response

This author had offered a more modest proposal four years earlier. Concerned with what I believed to be weaknesses in the arguments being made at the time by those who preferred that NATO adopt a nuclear emphasis strategy, as well as by those calling for a conventional emphasis strategy, I felt that what was needed was a more flexible response. I saw nothing inherently wrong in the NATO strategic concept of flexible response. Unfortunately the United States and its NATO allies, in my view, had simply failed to provide the conventional and nuclear forces required to offer a truly flexible response to all levels of aggression. Thus I argued for improvements in both areas.

In the area of conventional improvement, building on the ideas of Colonel Stanley Fair, I called for a heavy emphasis on precision-guided as well as area munitions. I did not view PGMs as a panacea for NATO's conventional weaknesses. However, I did believe that PGMs together with modern area munitions and coupled with appropriate organization offered the prospect of substantially improving NATO's conventional capabilities. In this regard I proposed that strong covering forces composed of numerous, highly mobile antiarmor (A-ARM) units supported by helicopter and airmobile A-ARM forces be deployed in NATO's forward area. Their task would be to attrite enemy forces. Main forces, also heavily equipped with antiarmor capability, would be assigned attrition zones to the rear of the covering force.

In addition I argued that territorial and reserve units could be organized to maximize the attrition of Warsaw Pact forces and support NATO counterattacks. In this regard, the German territorial army could have been reorganized so that in forward areas it would have an antiarmor role, with relatively few facilities protection units and almost no logistic support units. Forward area territorial A-ARM forces could be armed with inexpensive, easy to maintain and operate, lightweight, easily transportable antiarmor weapons. Because of the specialized nature and ease of training of these units, they could be maintained in a cadre status to be fleshed out by reserves within 24 hours. In other NATO countries, a sizable portion of reserves could be tasked as A-ARM forces for immediate mobilization (24 hours) and transportation to the battle area.

Looking toward the technology likely to be available during the next decade or so, I maintained that such a reorganization would provide NATO with a credible conventional defense capability. At the first sign of Pact aggression, NATO air forces would launch to counter Pact frontal aviation, suppress Pact air defenses, and in conjunction with ground rocket and missile forces would scatter mines and sensors along likely approach routes. Sensors, satellites, and remotely piloted vehicles would locate Pact forward and main force elements. Allied artillery, missile, and air forces would launch PGMs and area munitions to counter invading forces. As Pact armored forces closed with forward NATO covering elements, ground mobile regular, reserve, and territorial A-ARM units, supported by air and artillery delivered antiarmor PGMs and area munitions, would slow, attrite, and channel Pact forces into preselected killing zones. Backtracking radars and satellites linked to fire control systems could assist in neutralizing enemy artillery. Air forces, operating under the direction of allied ground control intercept radars, coupled with antiaircraft artillery, surface-to-air missiles, and infantry-fired antiaircraft missiles, would reduce the Pact aviation threat; mines and bomblets would be used to further attrite tank forces and decimate accompanying infantry. Stripped of large portions of their artillery, air force, and infantry support, the reduced numbers of Pact armored and mechanized forces could be successfully engaged by main force elements capable of slowing and/or halting the attacking force. NATO would thus gain the time needed to mobilize those forces needed to eject Pact troops from allied territories.[30]

Following the publication of this approach, I probed the Soviets during two visits to Moscow, once in 1977 and again in 1979, in an attempt to test their thinking on the idea of a mutually defensive disposition of forces in Europe based primarily on those principally equipped with ATGMs. I dropped further consideration of the idea, as the Soviets did not seem interested in such approaches at the time. The standard reply during those years was that the Soviet Union saw the tank as the best defense.

Territorial defense

In 1978, Lieutenant Colonel William O. Staudenmaier, adopting a similar approach, maintained that territorial defense is both a strategic and a force structure concept. As a strategic concept it is defensive in nature. It poses no threat to neighboring countries. It envisions a total integrated defense in depth, including areas that may be occupied by the invader. As a force concept it is relatively inexpensive and relies on locally recruited, locally assigned, and locally deployed citizen-soldiers that can be rapidly mobilized.

According to Staudenmaier, these citizen soldiers, armed with antitank and antiaircraft weapons, would operate in conjunction with regular forces. They would wait along the Soviet route of advance and attack Soviet forces as they approached. They could direct air strikes, perhaps using lasers to illuminate high-priority targets for air-delivered PGMs. They could lay mines. Their presence would turn cities into massive tank traps. They could sabotage the transportation, communication, and logistical network of the enemy. Moreover, territorial forces that had been organized into "antiaircraft killer teams" and armed with Stinger-type missiles could attack Soviet aircraft and helicopters.

Staudenmaier believed that if the passive concepts of civilian-based defense lent their weight to such an effort, "the potential of the enemy to achieve a lightning victory would be greatly diminished." More importantly, Staudenmaier argued " . . . if the Soviets cannot achieve a quick victory, they cannot win at all." Thus for Staudenmaier, territorial defense as part of a more comprehensive total defense, which would include offensive and defensive, strategic and tactical nuclear, and standing professional army, navy, and air forces—could provide a strong deterrent to aggression at any level.[31]

RECENT APPROACHES

By the mid-1980s a wide variety of proposals for improving NATO's conventional capabilities had emerged. Alternatives spanned the spectrum from increases in NATO's offensive capabilities, which would allow its forces to strike well into Warsaw Pact territory, to those that would curtail NATO's offensive capability and focus changes in force structure on creating forces optimized for defense. In the former category were such proposals as the one made by Samuel Huntington, the U.S. Army's AirLand Battle, and the Rogers plan, which became known as Follow-on Forces Attack (FOFA). In the latter category were proposals being made in Germany by Horst Afheldt and Hans-Jochen Löser and in the United States by James Garrett.

In April and July 1983 the U.S. Army War College hosted two workshops that brought together proponents from the various schools of thought. Among those who joined those discussions were Hans Günter Brauch, Samuel Huntington, General Hans-Jochem Löser, John Mearsheimer, Brigadier General Donald Morelli (one of the principal architects of the AirLand Battle Doctrine), Gene Sharp, William Staudenmaier, Lutz Unterseher, and Milton Weiner. During the second workshop Samuel Huntington expanded on a concept he had advanced in 1982.[32]

Conventional Retaliation

Huntington was concerned that as NATO attempted to fashion a new conventional strategy and force structure to strengthen deterrence and defense in the wake of what many perceived to be a declining credibility of NATO's nuclear forces, such efforts were being grounded on erroneous, generally unarticulated, assumptions. Principal among them was the notion that stronger conventional forces would mean a stronger conventional deterrent.

Huntington contended that to a limited degree such an assumption was justified. Indeed, stronger NATO forces would increase the investment the Soviets would have to make to overrun NATO. However, referring to Glenn Synder's seminal work on deterrence and defense, Huntington pointed out that deterrence may be pursued both through "denial capabilities—typically, conventional ground, sea and tactical air forces" and "punishment capability—typically, strategic nuclear power for either massive or limited retaliation."[33] By eliminating or drastically downgrading nuclear capabilities in favor of conventional capabilities, the retaliatory component of deterrence would be lost. This would leave only a denial strategy, which for Huntington is inherently a much weaker deterrent than one that combines both denial and retaliation.

According to Huntington, from the perspective of an aggressor the major difference between strategies that focus on denial and those that focus on retaliation "concerns the certainty and controlability of costs he may incur."[34] An aggressor faced with just a denial strategy can calculate his potential costs. He may decide to incur whatever costs are necessary to achieve his desired ends. He may decide to limit his costs and potential gains. He may choose no costs and no gains. The choice is his to make. In contrast, a potential aggressor confronted with a retaliatory deterrent cannot calculate the total costs he will have to pay. Thus the task, as Huntington saw it, for those attempting to fashion a credible conventional deterrent was to transpose the uncertainties of cost that had characterized the nuclear deterrent in earlier years to conventional deterrence.

Huntington's solution was straightforward. In the past NATO had relied on conventional and nuclear defense and nuclear retaliation. Now that the threat of nuclear use was losing its credibility, deterrence could be restored by relying on conventional defense and "a conventional retaliatory offensive directed against the Soviet empire in Eastern Europe."[35]

Huntington believed that such a strategy was credible and feasible. NATO could muster the forces for a prompt allied offensive in Eastern Europe. Moreover, he maintained that such a strategy had a number of additional advantages. First, it would force the Soviets to retain forces rearward to guard its flanks and rear areas. Second, it would encourage the Eastern European governments to avoid war. Third, it would threaten the Soviet Union with the liberation of Eastern Europe, thus raising the potential cost of aggression. Fourth, it would encourage Eastern European defections and thus threaten Warsaw Pact unity. Finally, it would increase the probability of a protracted war that would inevitably be to the West's advantage.

AirLand Battle Doctrine

As the Soviet threat evolved, the U.S. Army was not only concerned about what was perceived in some circles as the declining credibility of NATO's nuclear retaliatory threat, but more specifically with rapidly improving Soviet conventional capabilities as well. During the 1970s Soviet weapons and logistics improvements coupled with a growing doctrinal emphasis on rapid offensive action led many in the U.S. Army to criticize the doctrine of "active defense," which had been spelled out in the 1976 version of the army field manual FM 100-5.

Critics contended that "active defense" was too linear or positional for the modern European battlefield. Moreover, it emphasized attrition-style warfare based on massive firepower, rather than on maneuver. Thus it was seen as an inappropriate response to changes underway in Soviet doctrine and tactics. Furthermore, it did not seek to defeat the enemy. According to critics the main question was not when NATO forces might win but rather how long the defense could hold before succumbing to the weight of the onslaught.[36]

By 1982 the critics had won the day. A new FM 100-5 was published and the doctrine it espoused stressed initiative, agility, synchronization, and combat in depth. The unmistakable characteristics of this new army doctrine were mobility, maneuver, and offensive action. The objective was not just to avoid defeat. Rather, it was to win on an integrated battlefield where nuclear and chemical as well as conventional weapons might be present.

Of all combat factors, however, maneuver was clearly considered the critical factor. Maneuver permits surprise, momentum, and economy of force. Maneuver permits counteroffensive operations. Maneuver allows forces to operate against the enemy's flanks, to penetrate in depth to the enemy's rear, to disrupt and destroy his follow-on forces. In short, maneuver was seen as the key to fighting outnumbered and winning.

Under this new doctrine, the principal task of firepower no longer was the attrition and destruction of enemy forces. It was to support maneuver. Whereas the doctrine called for forward, direct defense, coordinate air/ground deep attacks became the hallmark of the new, offensively oriented army doctrine. The objectives of attacking deep were not to take and hold enemy territory per se, but to support the overall objective of the defense—to delay, disrupt, and destroy the enemy beyond the immediate forward edge of the battle area; to gain the psychological edge through surprise; to disrupt the adversary's battle plans; to limit his ability to maneuver and reinforce, to relieve pressure on allied defenses, and thus to set the stage for victory, not defeat.

The AirLand Battle Doctrine met with criticism in many quarters in Europe. Most of those who objected felt that it was too provocative for a defensive alliance, that it would exacerbate political tensions, foster reciprocal approaches by the Soviets, and contribute to the arms race. As a result, it remained exclusively an American doctrine. NATO, in contrast, adopted an alternative advanced by General Bernard Rogers, Supreme Allied Commander Europe (SACEUR).

The Rogers Plan

The Rogers plan, also known as deep strike or Follow-on Force Attack (FOFA), was, in some ways, similar to the AirLand Battle Doctrine that had been rejected by alliance members. It combined forward defense with deep attacks. Its principal characteristic was its focus on the enemy's rear area. Its principal objectives were to delay, disrupt, and destroy the enemy's follow-on, rear echelon forces in order to upset his battle plans, gain the psychological and strategic edge, and increase the probability of successfully defending against an aggression.

FOFA stressed taking maximum advantage of the West's advances in modern warfare technologies. In its deep strikes on enemy forces, it envisaged the use of modern surface-to-surface missiles, manned aircraft employing stand-off munitions, the latest technologies in target acquisition, identification, tracking, and precision homing and guidance, and in command and control. It differed from AirLand Battle in that it had no real "counteroffensive" operations by ground forces operating deep in enemy territory. As far as the deep battle in the enemy rear was concerned, FOFA was fundamentally an air offense, whereas AirLand Battle envisaged full-fledged air and ground offensives.

Area Defense

At the other end of the spectrum of alternative approaches to improving NATO's conventional posture was James Garrett's proposal for area defenses, first elaborated in 1984 and later considerably elaborated.[37] Garrett noted that active defense had six principal flaws: (1) despite its depth it was too linear and hence invited penetration, (2) with insufficient forces to cover the entire frontier area, NATO commanders were forced to guess where an attack might come, (3) a major portion of the defensive forces, the forward deployed U.S. mechanized cavalry screening units, was exposed to Warsaw Pact artillery and to isolation and defeat in detail, (4) territorial units in rear areas were much too weak to defend successfully against Soviet airborne divisions, (5) operational reserves were almost nonexistent, (6) the defense was a weak deterrent because its aim was only to prevent loss of territory, not to inflict disastrous losses on invaders.[38]

Garrett also faulted AirLand Battle Doctrine as violating the principle of economy of force by diverting major units to the secondary objective of disrupting the enemy's rear while depleting already inadequate defenses against a ground breakthrough. Operations would also have exposed the flanks of the adjacent German corps that were committed to active defense. Moreover, Garrett contended, the state of training of the U.S. Army in Europe has been too poor to conduct successfully the flexible actions called for. Instead of collapsing in chaos as the designers of AirLand Battle intended, Garrett believed that the Pact juggernaut would have advanced steadily through territory weakly defended by inadequately trained and prepared NATO forces.[39]

Garrett also saw flaws in territorial defense proposals such as those advanced by Steven Canby, Guy Brossollet, and Horst Afheldt. He noted that all territorial defense plans rely entirely or largely on militia or small local reserve units. Garrett maintained that it is unrealistic to expect such units to "stand up under the shock and terror that an invasion would create." Moreover, small units require joint training experience in order to develop sufficient cohesiveness to function effectively as teams under the stress of battle. Militia or reserve forces are unlikely to be so trained. Finally, a territorial defense alone is not likely to serve as a strong deterrent to a potential Soviet aggression. Indeed, according to Garrett, Horst Afheldt's proposal would have left NATO without further recourse, if his passive defenses failed, other than the use of nuclear weapons.[40]

As a solution to the conventional force dilemma that had plagued NATO for years, Garrett proposed an "area defense" based on several thousand small mobile defensive teams of active units or highly ready reserves armed with antitank and antipersonnel weapons and married to adequate fire support and operational reserve forces. These units would have been backed up by armor and mechanized infantry units that would be withdrawn from forward "frontier" missions and formed into operational reserves. He presented a detailed analysis of organization and fluid, guerrilla-like tactics to take maximum advantage of the defensive characteristics of West German terrain.[41]

In his most recent publication, Garrett argues that the current absence of any great power threat in Europe offers a unique opportunity for general adoption of area defenses that would provide all parties with adequate security without appearing to threaten any of them and would lay a foundation for lasting political and military stability in Europe.[42]

Middle Spectrum Approaches

During the 1980s as the gap between strategic and theater nuclear capabilities of the West and the Soviet Union narrowed and the Soviets continued to improve their conventional capabilities, there was a plethora of articles on what NATO might do to improve its conventional defenses. Many focused on how newly emerging technologies might be employed to enhance NATO's conventional defenses. For example, the European Security Study of the American Academy of Arts and Sciences (ESECS)[43] concluded that NATO's conventional capability could be improved through "(A) new advanced target acquisition and conventional weapons technologies that are realistically available; and (B) an improvement of conventional forces now in place and under procurement through new concepts and modes of operation." The study's steering group contended that

> New advanced technologies for target acquisition and conventional weapons can provide a far more effective conventional means than is now available for carrying out NATO's critical defensive missions. These include area impact and guided conventional submunitions; accurate delivery means for guided submunitions by surface-launched or air-launched non-nuclear missiles and by other stand-off weapons; and techniques for real-time surveillance and target acquisition.[44]

The steering group believed that such new technologies, if exploited in conjunction with an integrated and interoperable theaterwide information system, would be particularly useful in attriting Warsaw Pact air power, helping to counter the Pact's initial attack, and interdicting and disrupting Pact follow-on forces.

Similarly, Richard DeLauer, former U.S. undersecretary of defense for research and engineering, advocated that the West energetically pursue its advantage in high technology. With only modest changes in doctrine, roles, and missions, DeLauer encouraged the West to pursue

> . . . a comprehensive program that employs, wherever possible, a high degree of Stealth technology, that uses a highly accurate standoff capability with sufficient range so that the Air Force can interdict deep fixed targets, that has survivable command and control of weapons with increased kill probability systems for the Army's first echelon counterforces, and that seriously considers the utilization and exploitation of strengths of urban defense to blunt the Soviet's concept of surprise and rapid penetration.[45]

Neither the ESEC Study or DeLauer, however, saw such concepts as an alternative to existing approaches. ESECS saw "NATO's existing strategy of Flexible Response and Forward Defense . . . entirely adequate to meeting the challenge posed by the Warsaw Pact."[46] Similarly, DeLauer believed that his suggested approach would be consistent with FOFA and would also enhance the prospects of achieving the long-term AirLand Battle Doctrine.[47] DeLauer, however, did add an interesting twist to his approach. He noted that the Defense Science Board had found that the demographic development of Western Germany had resulted in a pattern of urban areas that, if internetted, could enhance defenses. According to DeLauer, by installing survivable communications beforehand and by planning for the rapid mobilization of troops that have been specially trained in such warfare, urban areas in Western Germany can be defended "with a degree of survivability against superior first-echelon forces." According to DeLauer this would considerably enhance the overall level of NATO's conventional deterrence.[48]

Operating within alliance political and economic constraints, the looming manpower shortage, and the "uncertainties about the military value of the West's technological edge," James A. Thompson advanced ideas for modestly improving NATO conventional defenses which he readily admitted would "work at the mar-

gin." Arguing that NATO had failed badly in setting priorities for force modernization and improvement and in overcoming inefficiencies in national and multinational force planning and weapons procurement, he advocated strengthening the
role of NATO's military authorities in operational planning, changing national and
multinational procedures for weapons acquisition, and setting the survivability of
NATO's air operations and increasing NATO's operational reserves as priority
programs.

Thompson considered these proposals as "essentially 'low tech' solutions" and
"consequently 'low risk,'" especially when compared to some of the 'high tech'
proposals to strike the Warsaw Pact's follow-on forces deep in enemy territory."
Differing from many of the proposals offered by those seeking more radical structural changes to NATO force posture, Thompson suggested that new operational
reserves, which might be cadre strength units in peacetime, be structured as heavy
combat divisions using "hand-me-down" equipment to reduce costs.[49]

A somewhat less conventional alternative was suggested by Robert B. Killebrew, who proposed a variety of potential ways of strengthening the conventional
defenses of the West, including the establishment of a French sector, new agreements with the French on the lines of communications (LOCs) throughout France,
the development of an in-depth barrier system, and the establishment of a SA-
CEUR reserve, possibly in northern Britain. Killebrew also saw great value in
deploying light divisions from the United States early in a potential conflict. Light
forces, armed with antitank weapons, could be useful in the mountainous terrain in
central Germany or on the highly urbanized northern plain. They could be deployed to take up defensive positions immediately behind forward-deployed armored or mobile units now stationed there. This would "thicken up" the defenses
and offer an opportunity for NATO to withdraw some of its heavy forward-
positioned armor units to be reconstituted as reserves, at the same time providing a
political signal to the Warsaw pact of the West's nonaggressive intent. According
to Killebrew, light forces, if provided with tactical mobility assets, could also be
used to assist in rear area security.[50]

CONCLUSIONS

Unquestionably, the startling changes in the European security equation fostered
by the revolutions of 1989, 1990, and 1991, as well as the long-term implications
of the Gulf War will stimulate a renewed interest in conventional alternatives for
deterrence and defense in the new Europe. Indeed, it appears more certain every
day that East-West relations have changed in a fundamental and profound way.
With the withdrawal of Soviet forces from Eastern Europe, a strategy that foresees
the flexible employment of vast quantities of nuclear weapons on eastern, much
less western, European soil no longer seems politically feasible nor likely in light
of matching unilateral withdrawals of nuclear weapons by the United States and
the USSR. With the signing of the CFE accords, the era of increasing conventional
military force capabilities has come to an end. Yet, the lessons of history instruct
that military power is a necessary instrument of statecraft if nations wish to protect
their interests. The nations of Europe will require military forces. And if the West
is wise, it will not dismantle an alliance that has enormously strengthened cooperation among its member states.

Yet, the question remains: How should alliance military forces be configured to reflect the changed landscape of tomorrow's Europe? Is the new structure adopted by NATO in November 1991 the best alternative? Or is it a temporary political response to present concerns? As the situation in Eastern Europe and the former USSR further clarifies itself and as the implications of the Gulf War and the consequences of any newly emerging world order become clearer, it is likely that the debate of military force structures for a new NATO will intensify rather than abate. It is also likely that none of the proposals surveyed here will be adopted by the alliance of the 1990s. However, the ideas advanced by those who have focused on this issue should help frame the debate. Should the nations of Western Europe and North America restructure their forces along less provocative lines? Should those forces reflect an inherent "defensive" posture? Is it possible to configure forces that are structurally unable to take the offense? Can such restructuring be done unilaterally? Must it be done in conjunction with the states of the former Warsaw Pact? If the forces of both Eastern, Central, and Western Europe were structured for, as Horst Afheldt would have it, mutual defensive superiority, would that, ipso facto, result in a more stable environment in Europe? If the Western European nations so structure their forces, will that limit their ability to join with other nations for the joint protection of mutual interests elsewhere in the world? Would a more satisfactory, long-term solution to Western, and indeed Russian, security be better based on fewer but more highly mobile forces, carefully balanced between heavy and light, to meet the potential demands of the future?

NOTES

1. Reprinted in Winston Churchill, *Triumph and Tragedy* (Cambridge: Riverside Press, 1953), pp. 572–573.

2. For example, in an address before Parliament in April 1949, Churchill, speaking about the power of the atomic bomb in American hands, said, "It is this, in my view, and this alone that has given us time to take measures of self-protection and to develop the units which make those measures possible." See Great Britain, Parliament, Parliament Debates (Commons), CDLXIV; 2030, quoted in Robert E. Osgood, *NATO: The Entangling Alliance* (Chicago: University of Chicago Press, 1962), p. 29.

3. Andre Beaufre, *NATO and Europe* (New York: Knopf, 1966), pp. 57–58.

4. "Communique of September 27, 1950," *Bulletin* (North Atlantic Assembly), XXIII (Oct. 9, 1950): 58.

5. See Osgood, NATO, p. 70.

6. See Horst Menderhausen, "Territorial Defense in NATO and non-NATO Europe, Report R-1184-ISA. (Santa Monica: Rand, 1973), p. 37.

7. For details see Hans Günter Brauch, Chapter 1 in this volume.

8. General Alfred M. Gruenther, "The Defense of Europe: A Progress Report," *Department of State Bulletin XXXI* (Oct. 18, 1954): 563.

9. See George F. Kennan et al., *Encounters with Kennan: The Great Debate* (Totowa, NJ: Frank Cass and Co., 1979), pp. 24, 66.

10. B. H. Liddell Hart, *Deterrence and Defense* (New York: Praeger, 1960), p. 47.

11. U.S. House, Department of Defense Appropriations for 1975, Hearings before a subcommittee of the Committee on Appropriations, 93rd Congress, 2nd session, Apr. 29, 1974, pt. 4, p. 450.

12. Amos A. Jordan, "Introduction: New Technologies and the U.S. Defense: Planning for Non-Nuclear Conflict," in Geoffrey Kemp, Robert L. Pfaltzgraff, Jr., and Uri Ra'anan, eds., *The Other Arms Race* (Lexington: D.C. Heath, 1975), p. xi.

13. John W. Finney, "Guided Bombs Expected to Revolutionize Warfare," *New York Times* (Mar. 18, 1974); Gwynne Dyer, "Is Blitzkrieg as Passé as the Trenches?" *Baltimore Sun* (Oct. 5, 1975); Edward B. Atkeson, "Is the Soviet Army Obsolete?" *Army* (May 1974): 10–16; John Marriott, "New Weapons for Defense in Europe," *NATO's Fifteen Nations* (Dec. 1973–Jan. 1974): 55–62. Also see,

e.g., John T. Burke, "The Changing Nature of Modern Warfare," *Army* (Mar. 1974): 12–16; G. H. Turley, "Time of Change in Modern Warfare," *Marine Corps Gazette* (Dec. 1974): 16–20.

14. Stanley D. Fair, Precision Weaponry in the Defense of Europe (Carlisle, Pa.: Strategic Studies Institute Strategic Research Memorandum, Dec. 15, 1974): 8.

15. Steven Canby, "The Alliance and Europe: Part IV Military Doctrine and Technology," *Adelphi Papers 109* (London: International Institute for Strategic Studies, Winter 1974/5).

16. For example, see Steven Canby, "NATO: Reassessing the Conventional Wisdoms," *Survival* (July–Aug. 1977): 164–168, and "General Purpose Forces," *International Security Review,* V/3 (Fall 1980): 317–346.

17. For example, see Gene Sharp, *Exploring Non-Violent Alternatives* (Boston: Porter Sargent, 1970); Gene Sharp, *The Politics of Nonviolent Action* (Boston: Porter Sargent, 1973). Europeans were contributing widely to the debate on civilian-based defense at this same time. For example, see the collection of articles by Adam Roberts in *The Strategy of Civilian Defence: Non-violent Resistance to Aggression* (London: Faber and Faber, 1967). Also, see Adam Roberts, *Nations in Arms: The Theory and Practice of Territorial Defense* (New York: Praeger, 1976).

18. Edward B. Atkeson, "The Relevance of Civilian Based Defense to U.S. Security Interests," in James A. Kuhlman, ed., *Strategies, Alliances, and Military Power: Changing Roles* (Leyden: A. W. Sijthoff, 1977), p. 321.

19. Sharp, Politics of Nonviolent Action, p. 64.

20. Sharp, "The Technique of Non-violent Action," in Roberts, *Strategy of Civilian Defense,* p. 88.

21. Atkeson, *Is the Soviet Army Obsolete?,* p. 322.

22. See R. W. Komer, "Treating NATO's Self-Inflicted Wound," *Foreign Policy,* 13 (Winter 1973–1974): 34–48.

23. Ibid.: 45.

24. Ibid.: 45–46.

25. E. W. Paxson, M. G. Weiner, and R. A. Wise, *Interactions Between Tactics and Technology in Ground Warfare,* R-2377-ARPA (Santa Monica: The Rand Corporation, Jan. 1979).

26. Colonel H. G. deMoya, Colonel S. D. Fair, Lt. Colonel R. F. Molinelli, L. Fischbach, and J. F. Scott, *The Impact of Precision Guided Munitions on Army Planning and Doctrine* (Carlisle, Pa.: Strategic Studies Institute, Feb. 28, 1974).

27. See Edward A. Corcoran, *Evolution of Europe's Defense in the 1980s* (Carlisle, Pa.: Strategic Studies Institute Strategic Studies Research Memorandum, Jan. 30, 1981).

28. Ibid.: 18.

29. Ibid.: 19.

30. See Robert Kennedy, *NATO Defense Posture in an Environment of Strategic Parity and Precision Weaponry* (Carlisle, Pa.: Strategic Studies Institute, Dec. 30, 1976).

31. Lt. Col. William O. Staudenmaier, "Territorial Defense: An Ace in the Hole for NATO," *Army* (Feb. 1978): 35–38.

32. See Samuel P. Huntington, "The Renewal of Strategy," in *The Strategic Imperative: New Policies for American Security* (Cambridge: Ballinger, 1982), pp. 21–32. Huntington's presentation at the War College was published as "Conventional Deterrence and Conventional Retaliation in Europe," *International Security,* 8, no. 3 (Winter 1983–1984): 32–56.

33. Glenn H. Snyder, *Deterrence and Defense: Toward a Theory of National Security* (Princeton, NJ: Princeton University Press, 1961, pp. 4, 14–16, cited in Huntington, "Conventional Deterrence," p. 6.

34. Huntington, "Conventional Deterrence," p. 37.

35. Ibid.: 40.

36. For example, see Manfred Hamm, Chapter 3 in this volume.

37. James M. Garrett, "Conventional Force Deterrence in the Presence of Theater Nuclear Weapons," *Armed Forces and Society,* 11 (Fall 1984): 59–83. Also, see his *The Tenuous Balance: Conventional Forces in Central Europe* (Boulder, Colo.: Westview Press, 1989).

38. See Garrett, *Tenuous Balance,* pp. 43–45.

39. Ibid., pp. 45–47.

40. Garrett, "Conventional Force Deterrence," pp. 71–72.

41. Garrett, *Tenuous Balance.*

42. James M. Garrett, "CFE II: A Quest for Stability," *Armed Forces and Society,* 18 (Fall 1991), pp. 51–79.

43. *Strengthening Conventional Deterrence in Europe. Proposals for the 1980s. A Report of the*

European Security Study of the American Academy of Arts and Sciences (New York: St. Martin's Press, 1983). Europeans and North Americans participated in this effort. Among the American participants were Robert R. Bowie, Harvey Brooks, McGeorge Bundy, Alton Frye, Andrew Goodpaster, Howard W. Johnson, Milton Katz, William W. Kaufmann, Catherine M. Kelleher, David Klein, Franklin A. Long, William J. Perry, Marshal Shulman, Richard H. Ullman, and Carroll L. Wilson.

44. Ibid.: 34.

45. Richard D. DeLauer, "Emerging Technologies and their Impact on the Conventional Deterrent," in Andrew J. Pierre, ed., *The Conventional Defense of Europe: New Technologies and New Strategies* (New York: Council on Foreign Relations, 1986), p. 69.

46. Strengthening Conventional Deterrence, p. 141.

47. DeLauer, "Emerging Technologies," p. 69.

48. Ibid.: 64.

49. James A. Thompson, *NATO's Strategic Choices: Defense Planning and Conventional Force Modernization* (Santa Monica: The Rand Corporation, Jan. 1986), p. 86.

50. Robert B. Killibrew, *Conventional Defense and Total Deterrence: Assessing NATO's Strategic Options* (Wilmington: Scholarly Resources, 1986).

II

FORCE POSTURE
ALTERNATIVES

3

Military Doctrine, Force Postures, and Arms Control in Europe: The AirLand Battle Doctrine and NATO's FOFA Concept[*]

Manfred R. Hamm

Since the mid-1970s and until the unification of Germany in 1990, numerous proposals were advanced to restructure the armed forces of NATO and the Warsaw Pact (WTO) so as to strip them of their capability to conduct large, offensive operations, especially with short warning. Conceptual studies of ways to strip military forces of invasion capability yielded a host of alternative defense concepts modulating the main armaments, dislocation, and organization of armed forces to give them a more unambiguously defensive character. Such a far-reaching restructuring of military forces and employment doctrines was to enhance military stability in Europe and, incidentally, also boost mutual confidence to further improved political relations.

It may be understandable that most of these alternative force posture proposals and defense strategies had their origin, or experienced their revival, in the Federal Republic. Given its exposed geographic position, the FRG provided the most likely battleground on which any future war in Europe would be fought. Accordingly, there was a genuine interest not only to prevent any war but also to reduce its destructiveness should deterrence fail. Many observers also viewed a demilitarization of relations with Warsaw Pact countries as a requisite for transcending the political division of Europe. In addition to contributing to this long-range goal, the FRG viewed arms control as a means to advance detente with the East, valued highly for its positive effect on intra-German relations. What is ironic, however, is the de facto repudiation by most alternative force structure proposals of two core principles of security policy defining and legitimizing the membership of the FRG in NATO: (1) forward defense of West German territory along its eastern border, and (2) a firm commitment to deliberate nuclear escalation by NATO to bring about an early end to a war, i.e., the centerpiece of NATO's former strategy of flexible response.

Both tenets were enshrined without exception at the insistence of past Federal governments in the strategy of flexible response for deterrence and defense. Most NATO force posture improvements, its arms control offers, and doctrinal innovations have been judged by their effects on them or justified in terms of them. The

---

[*]This chapter was completed prior to the events of 1988 and 1989.

readiness of alternative strategists to scuttle long-held axioms of West German security policy is evidence of both the breakup of the defense consensus in the country and the positive assessment of the utility of arms control for structuring a viable modus vivendi with the USSR that is more appropriate to specific West German security needs and, to some at least, its genuine national aspirations. Whatever their merits or shortcomings, the radicalism of these proposals constitutes their Achilles heel, placing them virtually a priori outside the agreed terms of reference of NATO security strategy.

Already in the 1970s, NATO was most concerned about the short-warning attack scenario and, at least implicitly, defined its own force requirements in terms of the principles of defensiveness and sufficiency. But these alternative security concepts evolved and helped popularize the terms now dominating the debate on arms control and security policy. Concepts, such as *defensive Verteidigung* and *strukturelle Angriffsunfähigkeit,* have thus become household worlds. Because these remain poorly defined, however, they tend rather to inflate public expectations than to aid in grafting specific arms control proposals. Without denigrating their actual contribution to focusing attention on the properties of certain weapon systems in terms of conventional arms control, their concepts have had only limited relevance in shaping the force structures or arms control proposals of both alliances.[1]

What distinguishes alternative strategists from mainstream NATO planners is that the former derive their minimum defense needs from force postures designed to maximize opportunities for arms control rather than to provide a reliable basis for security. It is precisely because—prior to 1990—established NATO military strategy and doctrine appeared to have left less room for grandiose arms reductions that it was being assailed as an obstacle to improving security at lower levels of armaments. Key aspects of this charge were its continued reliance on nuclear escalation and the purportedly offensive nature of NATO's force posture and military strategy and doctrine, especially, the U.S. Army's AirLand Battle (ALB) Doctrine and NATO's Follow-on Forces Attack (FOFA) concept. Most alternative strategists also accused NATO of exaggerating both the threat and the military capabilities of the Warsaw Pact.

Alternative strategists naturally rejected the accusation of seeking arms control at the expense of safeguarding security. There is no need to argue here again the case against a nuclear no first use posture or the denuclearization of Europe. This has been done comprehensively elsewhere[2] and is incidental to our basic contention that: (1) ALB Doctrine was—prior to 1990—compatible with NATO strategy, (2) NATO strategy, specifically the Follow-on Forces Attack (FOFA) concept, was inherently defensive and has hardly any strategical or operational offensive properties, (3) both were designed to support a politically mandated forward defense of NATO territory, and (4) conventional arms cuts to enhance stability in Europe that lead to CFE I (1990) could be accommodated by the ALB Doctrine and FOFA concept. In short, NATO's political strategy of war prevention and deterrence was congruent with the operational-technical dimensions of its military strategy. It did not suffer from the sharp disconnect between the defensiveness of the then Soviet/WTO official military doctrine and the offensive nature of its military-technical dimension. Only few took issue with this contention.[3]

In fact, this consensus on the fundamental characteristics of former Soviet/WTO military doctrine was underscored by the charge of some Western critics that both FOFA and AirLand Battle amounted to a "Sovietization" of NATO strategy. This false charge, however, was based: (1) on an improper reading of both concepts, specifically, the failure to distinguish between the tactical-operational and the operational-strategic dimensions of military strategy, and (2) on sheer ignorance of the political and structural restraints on NATO decisionmaking, ruling out either the initiation of hostilities or strategic offensive campaigns and the clear political guidelines governing NATO military planning for defense. These charges ignored, moreover, NATO's lack of resources for any sustained offensive operations against the former Warsaw Pact.[4]

The ALB Doctrine was merely responsive to developments of Soviet military strategy and force posture since the mid-1970s. In many respects it represented a routine evolution of the U.S. Army's military doctrine, adapting it to the changing conditions on the European battlefield. Much the same can be said about the FOFA concept that sought specifically to capitalize on advances in conventional weaponry and emerging technologies to tackle Soviet military doctrinal innovations and hardware improvements that have been undermining NATO deterrence and defense capabilities. The chief concern of the ALB Doctrine has been to remedy the glaring deficiencies of the attrition approach of the U.S. Army's active defense doctrine of the mid-1970s. It not only spells out how to fight on the modern "integrated battlefield"—a realistic description of conditions and not a policy prescription,[5] but with its focus on the operational level, it seeks to bridge the inhibiting gap between tactics and strategy and thus stipulates changes of the force structure and training methods at variance with past U.S. Army practices.

Because the ALB Doctrine and the FOFA concept were also responses to ominous ongoing and anticipated trends in Soviet military strategy during the 1980s which posed a threat to NATO, they stipulate neither unalterable weapons nor specific force structure needs. Being responsive measures, they can be assimilated within the context of an arms control regime affecting the size, structure, armaments, and disposition of military forces in Europe. Furthermore, the operational minimum and force composition of NATO for an effective defense is derived not only from a fixed force-to-space ratio but also from a host of assumptions about the dynamics of crises and war. Arms control agreements and political change in Europe will have an effect on these parameters and calculations and, in turn, have a bearing on future adjustments of the ALB Doctrine and the FOFA concept to the evolving European threat environment. Moreover, it will be contended that both probably will gain importance in a reduced-arms environment, although some of the weaponry to carry them out will be constrained by arms control agreements. Finally, some of its special assets might also be used in support of an arms control regime based on "reasonable sufficiency" and a defensive strategic orientation. There is thus no reason for either to impede the conventional arms control efforts that resulted in the CFE I Treaty of 1990 and subsequent negotiations.

The first part of this chapter traces the evolution of AirLand Battle and elucidates some reasons for confusion about its actual intentions. Next, some fundamental elements of the doctrine are described, emphasizing the radical departure from past U.S. thinking. The third section delineates basic conceptual differences between the ALB Doctrine and the FOFA concept to point out its essential compatability with NATO doctrine. Generic criticisms of the ALB Doctrine are analyzed next to set the stage for an examination of its implications for the new arms control regime in Europe.

WHY AIRLAND BATTLE: A RESPONSE
ADAPTATION TO A CHANGING THREAT

Since the late 1970s, NATO was embroiled in an acrimonious debate over nuclear strategy, the issue of intermediate-range nuclear force (INF) deployment, the improvement of conventional forces to raise the nuclear threshold, and the proper role of arms control in NATO security policy. This debate was sparked by: (1) the general deterioration of the overall nuclear strategic environment widely deemed to undermine the U.S. nuclear umbrella, (2) the steady improvement of Soviet conventional and nuclear forces in Europe, the emergence in the early 1980s of the Operational Maneuver Group (OMG), and other force structure and command and control innovations indicating Soviet interest in a conventional warfighting option in Europe, and (3) multiple sociopolitical changes calling into question continued reliance on nuclear deterrence.[6]

The ALB Doctrine published by the U.S. Army Training and Doctrine Command (TRADOC) in 1982 was a response to the first two concerns but totally oblivious to the third dimension, i.e., the critical and protracted public reappraisal of NATO defense policies that had sensitized and agitated publics, particularly in Europe. Its ignorance of political sensibilities accounts in part for the careless use of technical language and hyperbole in formulating the principles of the new doctrine as well as in describing the character of future combat. Further, the ALB Doctrine represented a radical departure from the 1976 "active defense" doctrine that, according to its critics: (1) was a doctrine for defeat; (2) had rigidly formalized an attrition-oriented forward defense devoid of maneuver and shaped by the linear and positional concept of warfighting; and (3) had already been totally inadequate and inappropriate to meet the Soviet threat at the time of its release.

The new doctrine claimed to fill the gap between tactics—the preoccupation of active defense—and strategy formulated at the political level and translated into specific missions in the superordinated FM-100-1. Although it is difficult to define the operational level of warfare in the abstract, it consists of more than the sum total of tactical engagements and reflects a "prevailing style of war in a given setting."[7] With its new focus on operational level activities, the U.S. Army tried to come to grips with the deficiencies of active defense while laying the foundation for successfully mastering the challenge of fighting outnumbered and winning. Its chief concern is the linkage between the tactical and strategic dimensions of warfare, i.e., the relationship of direct engagements and maneuver to the campaign and strategic objective.

Owing to its preoccupation with Vietnam and its intellectual and physical exhaustion thereafter, the U.S. Army had "not addressed itself to the question of what, if anything, was needed in terms of operational concepts, force structure, equipment, and training to break the political will of the WTO to pursue military actions should deterrence fail. Whereas nuclear weapons were integral to the concept of flexible response, automatic escalation to nuclear war was to be avoided. This called for improved conventional forces that the U.S. Army was unable to field. The army thus faced a twin challenge: to adapt its doctrine and to tailor its equipment modernization programs to meet the novel needs of the European environment. Both were reinforced by the institutional needs of the U.S. Army to rebuild morale, to provide a rationale for its weapons modernization programs, and to justify its overall budget share against the encroachments of its sister services.[8]

The active defense doctrine adopted by the U.S. Army to implement the forward defense of NATO territory had been equally an expression of political constraints, military considerations, and the cultural predilection for firepower and attrition engrained in U.S. military thought.[9] As regards NATO's flexible response strategy, the new concept conformed to the need of "holding a Warsaw Pact at bay while defending allied territory as far forward as possible to buy time—time to determine the intent and magnitude of the aggression, time for the Soviet elites to reassess both the strength of Western political resolve and the risk of continued hostilities, and time for careful consideration of its nuclear options."[10]

Within the context of forward defense, it was (1) to keep the Warsaw Pact from acquiring virtually unstoppable attack momentum; (2) to offer NATO more defensible terrain and increased tactical depth for defensive operations; (3) to respond to mounting concerns about the growing standing-start potential of the Warsaw Pact; and (4) to modify the modalities of nuclear weapons use to account for the specific concerns of the FRG by shortening the delaying zone. This made eminent sense from a military vantage point and was responsive to German political opposition against the "fallback" or the "tripwire" concepts that had involved relinquishing up to three-quarters of FRG territory.[11]

Yet, given NATO's limited resources, especially the lack of operational reserves, and the layer cake deployment of national corps along its defense perimeter, the positional attrition emphasis of active defense magnified the inherent shortcomings of forward defense rather than capitalizing on its strengths: (1) the principal direction of attack could not be identified in advance, leaving (2) the advantage of establishing favorable force ratios to the attacker, while (3) assigning most forces to shallow defensive positions deprived NATO of operational reserves to seal off a breakthrough of second-echelon forces, and (4) forced reserves to move laterally across national corps sectors behind the main line of defense, thus creating severe logistical problems.[12]

Given its emphasis on firepower, the active defense doctrine was heavily weapons-oriented, placing a premium on weapons management rather than leadership, tactical competence, operational thinking, and troop morale. It represented a managerial, if not to say a mechanistic approach to war fighting easily criticized as totally unimaginative micro-management not deserving of the appellation of doctrine at all. The doctrine was thus easy prey for intellectual leaders of the military reform movement in the United States. They took it as evidence of (1) U.S. Army failure to understand the fundamentals of military art and to draw the proper lessons of military history, (2) the lack of any theoretical foundation in U.S. military planning, (3) the utter disregard for the nature and dynamics of the threat, (4) the failure to link these changes to new imaginative operational concepts, despite (5) the serious mismatch of available resources and the forces needed to carry out the doctrine.[13]

These reforms contended that NATO's numerical inferiority in both material and men required a viable concept for winning when fighting outgunned and outnumbered. For them, the key to success was mobility and maneuver rather than the massive use of firepower to effect the physical destruction of the enemy through sheer attrition. Moreover, some proponents of new approaches to conventional defense attributed to conventional forces not only a denial capability but also a role in retaliatory deterrence consistent with ongoing efforts to lessen dependence on early recourse to nuclear weapons. The most prominent among them was Samuel Huntington, who advocated counterretaliatory employment of conventional forces.[14]

In view of these criticisms and the obvious inability of active defense to provide a coherent rationale and priority for the development and procurement of advanced weapon systems to modernize the army's obsolete weapons inventory, military theoreticians at TRADOC launched a reappraisal to mitigate its shortfalls and adapt it to the emerging European battlefield. Their main concern was to strike a better balance at the tactical and operational levels of warfare between the elements of firepower and maneuver, and to emphasize a timely disruption and destruction of second-echelon forces. In short, they laid the conceptual groundwork for the extended battlefield, stressing maneuver while at the same time deemphasizing the linear approach to defense because of steady lethality improvements of modern weaponry. TRADOC planners thus sought to exploit the force multiplier effects generated by the synergistic interplay among various "exotic" weapon systems, particularly those employing "emerging technologies" (ETs), and to effectively deter Soviet nuclear escalation by improving its own ability to transition from conventional combat to fighting under the stressing conditions of nuclear use.

The culmination of these efforts at the end of an arduous process of reexamination was termed ALB Doctrine. It was issued in 1982, revised in 1986, and validated most charges of the military reformers. Further, it met the institutional need of the army for some semblance of coherence in force structure planning, offered guidance in the application of emerging technologies to battlefield missions aimed at strengthening conventional forces, took account of Soviet military developments and the characteristics of future combat operations, and appreciated maneuver as a way to move quantitatively inferior firepower to reach local superiority to exploit enemy vulnerabilities rather than trying to wear down his strength through linear frontal engagements with numerically inferior forces.

THE AIRLAND BATTLE DOCTRINE:
KEY CONCEPTS

Since the late 1970s countless concepts had been advanced in response to political and military demands to "raise the nuclear threshold" in Europe. As part of this ongoing debate, preliminary findings of the TRADOC studies were published in the United States well in advance of the final version released in August 1982. The ALB Doctrine probably owes its name to TRADOC commander General Donn A. Starry who "selected 'AirLand Battle' to describe the emerging doctrine and characterize the whole concept of interaction . . . occurring between all air and ground assets in a firepower and maneuver context."[15] The confusion about its real meaning and relationship to NATO strategy stems from the concurrent parallel efforts within NATO and such precursor publications as Starry's.

It has already been pointed out that the ALB Doctrine sought to introduce the U.S. Army to the operational level of war. It postulates four essential principles to win the air-land battle within the strictures of a defensive strategy: initiative, depth, agility, and synchronization. The overriding theme of the manual is the "spirit of the offense" stressing centrality of initiative to successful operations, i.e., winning: "The purpose of military operations cannot simply be to avert defeat—it must be to gain victory" and, accordingly, the "concept is based on securing or retaining the initiative and exercising it aggressively to defeat enemy forces."[16]

To achieve this objective requires both agility and synchronization to enable the commander to select the optimal weapon for the right targets at the most opportune time. He must at all times be prepared to fight on an integrated battlefield because nuclear or chemical use is an inescapable eventuality during war in Europe. Despite the widely acknowledged practical problems of shifting smoothly from solely conventional to nuclear/chemical combat, the ALB Doctrine posits that this ability is needed to (1) ensure against a disruption of defense activities; (2) minimize the advantage hostile forces might gain from nuclear escalation; (3) dispense with extensive preparations for U.S. Army employment of nuclear weapons that might otherwise diminish surprise or even invite enemy preemption; and (4) to avoid weakening conventional defenses by reducing the responsiveness and flexibility of friendly troops. In sum, the immutable nuclear/chemical backdrop requires the U.S. Army to organize and conduct its combat operations to reduce the effect of enemy nuclear/chemical use while optimizing simultaneously its ability to exploit deliberate nuclear escalation after it has been authorized by the political authorities. From a purely doctrinal viewpoint, it thus really did not matter for the conduct of ALB operations whether NATO or the WTO initiated nuclear war.

The proponents of ALB contend that maneuver is needed to create favorable force ratios at points of engagement for a successful defense by inferior forces. Maneuver warfare requires initiative within the broad framework of mission orders (*Auftragstaktik*) implemented independently by subordinate commanders in support of the overall plan. This allows for tactical flexibility while ensuring that tactical engagements contribute to larger operational goals. As a holistic doctrine, ALB seeks to "bring the components of the triad of soldiers, weapons, and doctrine into harmony and avoids stereotyped patterns, calling instead for bold, flexible and offensively oriented defenses. Thus it is not an inflexible body of rules that prescribes routinized actions that apply regardless of the specific conditions of the battlefield but merely describes the future battlefield and posits general principles for managing operations to attain military objectives.

At the operational level of warfare, maneuver plays a critical role as it links strategy and tactics. Its purpose is to "place the enemy in a position of disadvantage through the flexible application of combat power."[17] Maneuver thus supports the need to fight and win outnumbered by furthering the attainment of tactical and operational objectives. It maximizes the effect of limited resources by concentrating them on exploiting the enemy's vulnerabilities at the *Schwerpunkt* of his operations. Based on good intelligence, a commander is tasked to anticipate his opponent's plans, to discern its weaknesses, and to "aggressively" exploit them through mass, mobility, flexibility, maneuver, and initiative. Movement in maneuver warfare is purposive and decisive at the same time, thus requiring superior leadership.

"Deep attack" is a specific form of maneuver. It relies primarily on firepower and represents "a coordinated effort to delay, destroy or disrupt enemy forces beyond the immediate battle area in order to gain tactical or operational advantage." Its goal is *not* to take or hold territory as part of a strategic offensive but is limited only to operations supportive of the operational defense. The principal goal of "deep attack" is to hinder enemy reinforcement of attacking forces, thus attenuating pressure on the local defense. The direct fire of maneuver forces is regarded as more efficient and effective than long-range fire support systems of linear defenses as it can be more quickly adjusted to respond to an evolving battlefield situation and the results of prompt kill assessments. Capitalizing on surprise, "deep attack" has a stronger psychological effect on enemy attacking forces, is more economical in terms of ordnance expended, and can be more disruptive of enemy offensive operations than long-range fire or aerial bombardment. Its payoffs are potentially so high that they are worth the attending to the defender. This is because if the attacker loses the initiative, this will jeopardize the success of the entire operation.

In view of its high dividends, the ALB Doctrine deems "the offense (as) . . . the decisive form of war, the commander's only means of attaining a positive goal or of destroying an enemy force."[18] Hence, offensive operations are no end in themselves but are designed to capture the initiative, to disorient the attacker and force him to shift to the defense. His attacker will thereby lose his momentum and the attending reconfiguration of his forces for defense will weaken his cohesion and combat power, thus offering the defending forces a chance to launch debilitating blows on his forces.

According to the ALB Doctrine, the close and deep battle will occur simultaneously on a multidimensional battlefield. This is in sharp contrast to the preoccupation of active defense with the direct battle. The operational depth of defending forces is not fixed but a function of time and space. Deep defensive operations seek to shape the attackers forces by disrupting his operational plans so as to enhance the efficacy of tactical defenses. The interplay of operational and tactical level defense defines the structure of the extended battlefield and demarcates the areas of responsibility for brigade, division, and corps level defense.[19] The hierarchical chain of command is thus being replicated on the extended battlefield.

In terms of forward defense, the mission of offensive operations beyond the main lines of engagement is broader than the function of covering or screening forces. They seek to harass, disrupt, delay, and attrite the attacking forces before they arrive at his main line of defense. Instead of performing these tasks on own terrain subject to all constraints that may impose, operational forward defense of the AirLand Battle seeks to soften the blow enemy formations can bring against defending forces before they reach the forward line of own troops (FLOT). It thereby mitigates some of the deficiencies that critics of the active defense doctrine had pointed out.

The new doctrine tries to come to grips with forward defense that is constrained by limited geographic depth against a reinforced attack with combined arms. It seeks to enhance the effectiveness of inferior forces by a mobile defense with heavy armored units and heliborne forces directed by superior C^3I assets and employing sophisticated conventional munitions. By linking defense at the tactical level with offense at the operational level, the new doctrine seeks to ensure that all engagements and battles contribute to strategic objectives formulated at the political level. It also assists in allocating limited resources effectively in terms of the priorities derived from an overall assessment of the battlefield situation in the theater. If managed properly in the NATO context, it could mount a true Clausewitzian defense of a "shield made up of defensive blows." Since the early 1980s, the U.S. Army has sought to acquire the hardware and to structure and train its forces to align them with the demands of the new doctrine for high mobility operational level warfare.[20]

In terms of hardware requirements, U.S. Army troops deployed in Europe are now equipped for high-speed maneuver warfare. Further, the U.S. Army has sought in recent years to inculcate the ALB mindset with new training methods, has optimized the command, and reconfigured the unit structure together with the associated equipment so as to be better able to implement ALB precepts in future combat. The new doctrine shares the thrust of the competitive strategy approach inaugurated by the Pentagon in the 1980s to guide U.S. R&D and procurement. Both aim at exploiting Soviet-WTO weaknesses. Despite substantial differences, the ALB Doctrine complements the objectives and hardware needs of the FOFA concept adopted by NATO in November 1985.

Although this discussion focuses on the European theater, it should be recalled that the ALB Doctrine instructs the U.S. Army "how to fight" worldwide in all potential theaters of war, encompassing defense and offense as well as all possible types of war.[21] Its universal character precludes both the prescription of rigid principles applicable under any and all circumstances and of specific combat rules for war in Europe. The FOFA concept was prompted by the similar concerns about the inherent deficiencies of forward defense, magnified by the vigorous moderni- zation and steady growth of then Soviet/WTO military power, as the ALB Doc- trine. In particular, FOFA responded to the diminishing credibility of nuclear inter- diction and perceived technological opportunities to perform this critical mission with conventional weapons.

THE AIRLAND BATTLE DOCTRINE AND FOFA: DIFFERENT MEANS TO THE SAME END

The principal concern that FOFA seeks to address is the creeping loss of credi- bility of extended deterrence and, hence, the diminishing ability of NATO to im- plement its strategy of flexible response. The concept is the centerpiece of a whole range of alliancewide initiatives to lessen reliance on the early employment of nuclear weapons by improving conventional defense capabilities. These were con- ceptualized by NATO councils independent of but parallel to the evolution of the ALB Doctrine in TRADOC. As they share very similar concerns, a certain con- ceptual affinity between both endeavors should not be surprising.

Like AirLand Battle, FOFA identified echeloned follow-on forces as a critical threat to NATO's defense posture. General Bernard Rogers recognized that inter- dicting second-echelon forces with nuclear weapons was impossible for political reasons, even if it had ever made sense from a military vantage point or had been feasible with the NATO's target engagement capabilities—two highly questionable propositions. Moreover, in terms of escalation uncertainty, the steady growth of Soviet theater nuclear capabilities meant NATO had lost theoretical ability to domi- nate and the escalatory process in the European theater. But delaying and disrupt- ing the timely arrival of these forces was imperative, if NATO's shallow defenses were to withstand unremitting attacks by WTO forces. With nuclear weapons no longer credible, the real challenge thus consisted of finding alternatives for per- forming this mission. Developments in surveillance C[3]I technology, the accuracy of long-range delivery systems, and sophisticated high lethality munitions held out the promise of being able to do the job with conventional weapons, thus promising a major qualitative breakthrough in warfare.

Contrary to allegations, the FOFA concept was neither a departure from the concept of forward defense nor was it offensive in the sense of stipulating large-scale conventional operations by NATO ground forces. In many respects it amounted to little more than a logical evolution of NATO's "deep interdiction" concept applying munitions (with all the necessary caveats). FOFA did not seek to conventionalize NATO's defense strategy; it rather tried to raise the nuclear threshold and, thereby, strengthen deterrence. Hence, efforts to delay, disrupt, and destroy second-echelon forces well before they could reinforce frontline units were meant to heighten the probability that NATO defenses could be reinforced in a timely manner while keeping the former WTO from piling up forces according to schedule in order to effect their rapid collapse.

Executing aerial strikes against second-echelon forces on the move is exceedingly difficult, even if coordinated by realtime surveillance and C^3I technologies. By themselves, these attacks would probably have been insufficient to buy time for NATO to bring up reinforcements. Recognizing these limitations, the FOFA target set thus included fixed installations, such as bridges, railheads, enemy C^3I, and logistics assets needed to move large forces from their peacetime locations in de facto competition with existing offensive counterair (OCA) missions. Air defense and offensive counterair suppression are also assigned a high priority to facilitate both NATO penetration of WTO airspace and to reduce the threat of WTO offensive airpower to NATO installations of vital significance to air superiority that, in turn, is critical to its conventional defense.[22]

As FOFA did not involve offensive operations by ground forces, it signified no shift from *Vorne- to Vorwaertsverteidigung* as its critics have repeatedly alleged. Other detractors of FOFA have questioned the prudence of devoting scarce resources to "deep strike" missions instead of boosting the direct defense assets of NATO ground forces where investments of similar financial scope would yield higher payoffs. Finally, some critics viewed FOFA as high technology gimmickry that would either not work in the fog of war or would be easily disabled by Warsaw Pact countermeasures. It might also prompt the then WTO to increase its forward deployed forces so as to improve their standing start attack potential. Such a measure would be both highly destabilizing and counterproductive from NATO's vantage point. Thus according to its critics, the FOFA concept would not raise the nuclear threshold. Instead, it might even expedite a conventional defeat, and hence, accelerate resort to nuclear weapons under conditions allowing for much less deliberate and controlled employment.[23]

Nonetheless, the FOFA concept was a useful planning emphasis to augment NATO's interdiction capabilities beyond the immediate engagement zone. It also reflected a realistic judgment of NATO's ability to effect the timely release of nuclear weapons given its cumbersome decisionmaking process and the diverse interests of its members. Moreover, it was a response to the changing nuclear balance at the strategic and theater levels and improved WTO capabilities to attain its objectives without recourse to nuclear weapons. This did not mean the former WTO could ever count on keeping a war conventional for NATO might still choose to escalate regardless of the costs of such a move. Alternatively, the former WTO might have chosen to preempt NATO nuclear escalation should it appear imminent.[24] Whereas there may be other measures to bolster NATO's conventional defenses more effectively, some of these could not have been implemented because of political constraints (e.g., barrier defenses in the FRG), whereas others were not directly responsive to WTO force posture developments. The chief advantage of FOFA is that it enhanced NATO's abilities to effect conventional denial and also signaled that WTO territory would not remain a sanctuary and thus be spared the destructive consequences of its decision to start hostilities.

Neither the ALB Doctrine nor the FOFA concept would have created a conventional deterrence posture that vitiated nuclear escalation, even if this had been actually desired. Yet both could have helped lessen reliance on the *early use* of nuclear weapons, thereby enhancing the credibility of their employment and their military and political utility. Neither FOFA nor ALB were offensive at the operational-strategic level of armed conflict. Being little more than an air force oriented targeting concept developed by SHAPE to interdict preferably with conventional weapons, FOFA addressed conceptually and tried to impact primarily a reinforced attack, whereas ALB was optimized to deal with a standing-start attack by the Warsaw Pact and developed from an army and corps perspective. In that respect, they actually reinforced each other in terms of enhancing deterrence by denying the Soviet Union the prospect of achieving a quick victory without recourse to nuclear weapons. However, the FOFA concept was not a NATO version of the ALB Doctrine for conceptual as well as political reasons.

AIRLAND BATTLE AND FOFA: GENERIC ARMS CONTROL CONSIDERATIONS

Critics in the West echoed the charges brought by the former Soviets and their allies about the "offensive" or "aggressive" nature of both concepts.[25] They considered the long-range weapon systems for second-echelon attack required by FOFA as destabilizing. Further, they portrayed AirLand Battle as the de facto operationalization of Samuel Huntington's controversial counterretaliatory strategy. Their assertion that both ALB and FOFA represented a sovietization of NATO strategy serves to qualify the veracity of Soviet charges about NATO's offensive orientation compared to the defensive outlook of their own military planning.

For instance, Soviet Colonel General M. A. Gareyev publicly stated that counterretaliatory capabilities were needed to crush the enemy on his own soil and Soviet forces were equipped and trained to perform this mission.[26] Thus even if ALB and FOFA possessed a strategic offensive thrust—they did not—this could not have been a legitimate criticism given the former WTO's own offensive orientation. Moscow appeared to be concerned instead with losing its arduously acquired conventional option and was worried that its inability to compete effectively in the area of "emerging technologies" might undermine its conventional edge in the long run. In the then Soviet view, the qualitative leap in conventional military technologies pushed by NATO was not merely an attempt to gain superiority but also designed to force the WTO into an economically ruinous arms race. Officials like Orgakov and Gareyev were referring publicly to a military-technological revolution and urged a new quality approach in allocating Soviet defense resources that emphasized more rapid technological innovation instead of large production runs of inferior equipment in order to meet its challenge.[27]

Finally, both officials drew attention to the imperative of adjusting the military-technical dimension of Soviet military doctrine to the implications of "emerging technologies" for a future war. They contended that these revolutionary changes in weapons technology and the concomitant NATO operational concepts are evidence of an aggressive turn from pure deterrence to compellence in NATO military planning akin to the greater emphasis given to nuclear war-fighting strategies in U.S. strategic nuclear thinking.[28] They were trying to fuel the controversies over defense policy in the West, hoping to at least slow technological progress. At the same time, they urged changes in Soviet R&D and procurement policies so as to enable the WTO to take advantage of new weapons technologies.

In the interim, Western critics, not confined to proponents of alternative strategies, debated the excessive dependence of ALB and FOFA on untested technologies, especially as regards their real potential for generating synergistic effects into which NATO force planners vested so much hope. They contended instead that the sheer complexity of these weapon systems render them extremely fragile and liable to breakdowns that, in turn, would exercise debilitating ripple effects that would unravel NATO defenses. In their view, the technology dependence of AirLand Battle and FOFA constituted a crucial Achilles heel.

Another criticism related to the scope and priority of FOFA. In its initial formulation, the FOFA concept stipulated extremely ambitious missions and, accordingly, called for excessive hardware requirements, in terms of both the level of technological sophistication and financial commitment. Especially with respect to projected costs, critics charged that scarce resources would needlessly be diverted from the more urgent task of strengthening forward defense capabilities, readiness, and sustainability. This fear was especially pervasive in the FRG and provided an additional impetus to carefully scrutinize the overall scope of FOFA with respect to the type of targets, their depths, and the kinds of weapon systems envisaged to engage them.

A more general criticism of alternative strategists relates to the effects that NATO's obsession with technological superiority had exercised on its approaches to arms control. This mindset accounted not only for NATO's failure to explore defense concepts that met criteria of strict "defensiveness," i.e., were compatible with arms control aiming at stable conventional structures. NATO's faith in technological superiority also ignored that these technologies are not neutral, i.e., can be applied to both offensive and defensive missions. Philip Karber, certainly no advocate of alternative strategies, drew attention to the double-edged quality of advances in weapons technology: " . . . although a given weapon or group of systems may be clearly defensive at the tactical level, when combined with surprise, quantity, and innovative doctrinal orchestration, the same technology can be decisively offensive at the operational or theater levels."[29]

In short, weapon systems or technological innovations such as "reactive armor" can favor equally the offense and defense. Such innocuous measures as the improvement of surveillance or command and control, usually billed as defensive improvements, can have offensive applications when embedded into an offensive doctrine. Since Western technological breakthroughs found their way into WTO arsenals within a few years, NATO's technological advantage was invariably emphemeral. Further, the penchant of the WTO for large production runs put NATO at a disadvantage, forcing yet another round of technological innovation. These built-in dynamics are not only excessively costly but add little in terms of new defense capabilities, impeding consideration of alternative approaches, and, most importantly, circumscribing politically opportunities for arms control by fostering mutual suspicion.

Thus as NATO looks to the future it must seek to balance technological feasibility for the sake of conventional force improvements with its interest to prevent the evolution of any potential adversary's forces from undermining its own gains that, in the long run, might result in even more formidable adversary offensive capabilities. To be sure, NATO has no monopoly on technological innovation and must hedge against an adversary's breakthroughs by maintaining robust research programs. However, doing so risks forfeiting opportunities while the transparency of NATO defense policymaking and research will shorten the time until potential adversaries will field comparable technologies. NATO's unilateral restraint in force modernization did not influenced the speed and direction of Warsaw Pact military developments. Rather, it has only tended to diminish the return on NATO investments over time. However, if sensibly pursued, arms control may offer an appropriate tool to shape the technological and strategic environment in a stabilizing way. Since AirLand Battle and FOFA are said to involve a quantum leap in weapons technology, critics deem both not only counterproductive and contrary to NATO's long-term interests, but also destabilizing impediments to constructive arms control initiatives that offer a chance to develop stable military structures in Europe.

Like most criticisms, these also contain a kernel of truth. First, all too often is technological innovation pursued for its own sake. Second, initial enthusiasm about accomplishing old missions more effectively and efficiently tends to give way to demands for additional missions as the full range of military opportunities of these new technologies is being explored. Third, doctrinal innovation to exploit fully technological advances tends to confirm latent suspicions of adversary intentions and raises anxieties about being left behind. Fourth, the proliferation of performance requirements adds to the complexity of weapon systems and tends to delay timely and mission-specific application of technologies to rectify existing force posture deficiencies. Fifth, the growing complexity of advanced systems heightens the risks of technical malfunctioning, the probability of breakdowns under stressing combat conditions, and may reduce system survivability. Sixth, the emergence of unduly fragile systems highly susceptible to disruption may tempt hostile preemption, hence diminishing crisis stability. Finally, a narrow research emphasis on new technologies to meet missions defined in terms of current operational-tactical principles and based on apparently immutable strategic-operational objectives tends to hinder the creative application of technological progress to explore alternative approaches to defense.

Soviet and WTO conventional arms control gambits of the mid 1980s have raised expectations of genuine opportunities for progress in conventional arms control. The 27th CPSU Congress seemed to have initiated a process of "rethinking" failed defense policies and a shift in Soviet arms control objectives away from gaining unilateral advantage to seeking equitable arms agreements. The novel emphasis on "war prevention" and "defensive sufficiency" that was articulated in February 1986 was amplified and fleshed out in numerous Soviet and WTO official pronouncements, such as the "Budapest Appeal" of April 1986 and the "Berlin Declaration" of May 1987 and its essential restatement at Sofia in March 1988. The Stockholm accord on confidence-building measures (CBMs) of 1986 and the INF-Treaty of December 1987 have contributed to more transparency in military affairs. Further, the surprise announcement of unilateral force reductions by Mikhail Gorbachev at the UN General Assembly in December 1988 and subsequent proportional cuts by some Eastern European countries, the release of the first official WTO force posture statement on January 30, 1989, admitting a substantial WTO edge in certain weapons categories, and the agreement on a mandate for the Vienna CFE talks that was based largely on NATO's conceptual approach to conventional arms control, all indicated then Soviet readiness to reconsider its traditional approaches to security.[30]

These unprecedented adjustments were probably conditioned mainly by pressing economic constraints. Whether they indeed signified a genuine reappraisal and long-term reorientation of Soviet foreign and security policy toward Western Europe was not clear at the time. In fact, a plausible argument can be made that, in the light of its past failures with military intimidation backed by frightening superiority, the Soviet Union had decided only on changing the methods to achieve unaltered objectives. Nonetheless, these initiatives offered some window of opportunity for a political breakthrough in conventional arms control based on conceptual approaches that either did not exist in the past or were not employed constructively owing to lack of political will.

NATO has historically pursued a two-pronged strategy to security assigning equal weight to its military and political dimensions. This approach was spelled out in the 1967 Harmel Report and most recently reaffirmed by the Comprehensive Concept of Arms Control and Disarmament adopted by NATO at its May 1989 Brussels summit. Thus the prevention of war has been NATO's paramount objective. To this effect, it sought to create a stable balance of forces based on the principles of defensiveness and sufficiency. Its own military policy and force posture reflected these precepts that, in addition to pluralistic decisionmaking, rendered NATO incapable of initiating or sustaining offensive actions.

Accordingly, NATO had insisted on asymmetrical reductions of then WTO conventional capabilities consistent with defense requirements leading to equal force ceilings somewhat below its own levels. Specifically, NATO exhorted the WTO to abolish its threatening standing-start and surprise attack potential and to cut its capabilities for large-scale strategic-operational offensive combat. Commenting on the "favorable evolution" that had taken place, the Alliance Comprehensive Concept acknowledged that much of its agenda had now been adopted by the WTO: "In particular, the concepts of stability, reasonable sufficiency, asymmetrical reductions, concentration on the most offensive equipment, rigorous verification, transparency, a single zone from the Atlantic to the Urals, and the balanced and comprehensive nature of the CSCE process, are Western aspired."[31]

The real issues in establishing a "stable" conventional balance in Europe, however, related not only to the "hardware" fielded by military forces but to the "software" guiding their employment in the event of war. These are shaped, in turn, by countless objective factors and subjective considerations, such as geostrategic conditions, alliance relations, domestic political constraints, national military traditions, historical experiences, and threat perceptions, to name but a few. On the one hand, these define the parameters of defense policy, i.e., they are the determinants of military hardware requirements, force structures, deployments, readiness as well as the logistics of military forces. On the other hand, based on general national strategic objectives, they give shape to the strategic-operational and operational-tactical concepts for the employment of military forces. Unfortunately, in the past the significance of the interaction between "hardware" and "software" has been largely ignored in conventional arms control approaches.

Strictly speaking, the software of military policy is called "military doctrine" only in WTO parlance, although the lax usage of the term in the West has contributed to obscuring this crucial fact. Western authors repeatedly called attention to the need to evolve "defensive" military doctrines and force postures. The Berlin Declaration proclaimed that the new WTO military doctrine was strictly "defensive" and called for consultations to compare the doctrines of both alliances. Conversely, some critics assailed the ALB Doctrine and the FOFA targeting concept for being "offensive." Given the confusion surrounding the notion of military doctrine and the terms "offensive" and "defensive," the imperative to agree on a common terminology and substantive comparability before commencing talks on ambitious schemes to restructure military forces was everywhere evident.

The WTO used the term "military doctrine" to describe both the sociopolitical and the military-technical dimensions of defense and security policy. Whereas the sociopolitical level of Soviet military doctrine was covered in Western terminology by concepts like security, defense, and military policy, the Western term "military strategy" referred exclusively to the military-technical level of Soviet military doctrine. By contrast, the Western term "doctrine" was clearly subordinated to military strategy, comparing in WTO vernacular to operational art and tactics.

The above distinctions, however, shed some light on the reasons for NATO's caution in taking WTO claims of a "new" defensive military doctrine at face value. For as long as this principle pertained only to the sociopolitical level of WTO doctrine while its military-technical remain permeated by an offensive spirit that found its expression in the actual structure, armaments, readiness, training, and logistics of WTO military forces, professions of "defensiveness" were more expression of intent than accurate descriptions of military capabilities. West German Foreign Minister Hans-Dietrich Genscher provided a cogent summary of the issue at a preparatory conference on military doctrines held in June 1989 at the Stiftung Wissenschaft und Politik (SWP) in Ebenhausen near Munich:

> *The defensive character of an alliance does not result already from a political-declaratory exclusion of military aggression. Affirmations of non-aggression and pledges of non-use alone offer no adequate assurance of security and stability. The defensive character of an alliance must be underscored by the defensive orientation of its military-strategic concepts. It must affect the operational, the strategic and the military-technical level of the armed forces . . . There must be no discrepancy between defense policy rhetoric . . . and the actual force structures and employment concepts . . .* [32]

In the case of the WTO, there existed a striking discrepancy between its public claims to defensiveness and the actual outlook of its military establishments. After some delay, this gap was admitted by Soviet officials who then announced far-reaching corrective measures aimed at resolving the obvious inconsistency. First Deputy USSR Defense Minister Colonel General M. A. Moiseyev contended recently:

> *A precise concept of restructuring has now been formulated . . . as the practical implementation of the requirements of a defensive military doctrine . . . Nearly all tenets of strategy, operational art and tactics are undergoing radical changes under the influence of not only military-technical, but also military-political factors. Basically a new theory of military art is being created.* [33]

Although changes take time to implement, it is important that the then WTO recognized that they had to be carried out unilaterally prior to conventional arms control talks.

The Soviets also seemed to recognize that even "defensive" force structures were still containing "offensive" components. But the scope of these offensive capabilities appeared to be at variance with Western notions of overall defensiveness. It still remains unclear whether the WTO had indeed abandoned the objective of dealing a "crushing defeat" to an aggressor on his own soil, rather than seeking an early termination of hostilities and the restoration of the status quo ante bellum as was NATO policy. NATO limited offensive operations to the operational-tactical level, whereas the WTO stipulated far more demanding requirements for counter-offensive operations in the strategic-operational sense. At least by Western standards, WTO concepts of defensiveness lacked essential qualities of inherent stability. The consultations on military doctrines could have been used by NATO to convince the WTO that "defensive sufficiency" is inherently incompatible with its maintenance of offensive capabilities for strategic-operational warfare. To this effect, however, the WTO had to accept NATO's far more limited notion of "victory," i.e., effective denial.

CONCLUSION

The widespread use of the vernacular introduced by alternative strategies in the mid-1970s fosters the impression that their conceptual principles have been adopted by mainstream military thought. Their new terminology, however, obscures the fact that concepts like "reasonable sufficiency" and "defensiveness" have long been integral elements of traditional Western thinking on military strategy and doctrine. This body of thought, however, has always assumed that arms control talks should rest on the firm foundation of nuclear deterrence backed by adequate conventional defense capabilities. The alternative strategists seem to have reversed this rank ordering of national security objectives.

They hold traditional thinking on deterrence, military strategy, and doctrine responsible for defense policies that fail to meet NATO's security needs and impede the evolution of more stable military structures by way of genuine arms control. Although they acknowledge the detrimental impact that former Soviet/WTO defense policy had exercised on NATO military planning, they tended to be apologetic about Soviet political motives and, instead, charged NATO with fueling historically rooted Soviet anxieties by emphasizing technological superiority and nuclear weaponry. The ALB Doctrine and the FOFA concept were allegedly only recent manifestations of this penchant to incessantly search for a competitive edge vis-a-vis the WTO by speeding technological innovation. In the case of the ALB Doctrine, they specifically assailed its "offensive" spirit that is supposedly part and parcel of an offensive shift in U.S. military planning and, by extension, in NATO security policy.

The examination of the genesis and precepts of the ALB Doctrine, however, does not bear out the serious charge that U.S. military planning has been "sovietized." In fact, it was demonstrated that the doctrinal innovation of the U.S. Army in the early 1980s was a direct response to four developments: (1) the inherent shortcomings and growing inadequacy of its active defense doctrine, (2) the evolving nature of the former Soviet threat in Europe and the expansion of the global missions of then Soviet military forces, (3) the institutional needs of the U.S. Army to rebuild its image and force structure after the Vietnam debacle, and (4) the anticipated availability of new technologies to broaden the scope and intensity of conventional warfare operations.

The charges brought against the ALB Doctrine may have resulted in part: (1) from a politically insensitive use of strictly technical terminology, (2) from the excessive use of hyperbole in advertising alternatives to nuclear escalation and the prospects of conventional defense by the U.S. Army, (3) the premature publication of still preliminary findings of studies conducted at TRADOC and the concurrent development of different as well as complementary concepts by sister services and NATO, and (4) from the overall deterioration of the political climate of East-West relations at the time of its promulgation. But major facets of the critique were mainly politically motivated and relied on either deliberate distortion of ALB precepts or plain ignorance of basic conceptual distinctions.

The basic conceptual flaw of the ALB critique stems from its obvious failure to distinguish between the strategic-operational and the operational-tactical levels of warfare. The ALB Doctrine addresses only the latter and, hence, terms like "offensive" or "aggressive" must not be interpreted as statements of policy but as expressions connoting a particular style of warfare conducted within the constraints imposed by national policy. These remain unchanged, whereas the ALB Doctrine spells out how the U.S. Army intends to fight successfully at the operational-tactical level in support of these U.S. strategic objectives.

Similarly, most criticism of the FOFA concept as the NATO-wide application of ALB Doctrine precepts derives from the failure to distinguish between "deep interdiction" by aircraft and ground forces. The FOFA concept stipulated only targeting requirements to delay, disrupt, and destroy former WTO second-echelon forces whose timely and unattrited injection into the direct battle is likely to ensure WTO breakthroughs and a collapse of NATO defenses. In its refined version, moreover, the FOFA concept was no more than a planning device for applying "emerging" conventional technologies to missions once assigned to both nuclear and conventional forces and spelled out the critical tasks that must be accomplished in order to execute these missions. But this involves neither an effort by ground forces to seize hostile terrain nor the dynamic maneuver defense as envisaged by the ALB Doctrine for conducting a flexible and effective operational-tactical defense.

Proponents of alternative strategies seem to have created strawmen that they can readily vilify to enhance the plausibility of their own proposals. They undoubtedly pursue the noble objective of fostering the evolution of stable military structures in Europe through the arms control process. Yet their methods are both objectionable and impermissible because they rely on misrepresentation and unwarranted inferences of political intentions backed by the scope of military doctrines or targeting concepts.

Perhaps even more detrimental than their equation of a doctrinal change at the operational level with a fundamental shift in NATO political strategy is their failure to recognize that the WTO emphasis on "defensive sufficiency" and the "prevention of war" had still to be followed by irreversible adjustments of WTO operational-tactical principles and force structure. Until these changes were implemented, WTO proclamations of "defensive" intentions at the policy level of their military doctrine could not have provided a basis for NATO force planning or arms control policy. Yet critics of ALB and FOFA should have recognized that NATO physically lacked the means to carry out the offensive strategy they alleged it had adopted when endorsing SHAPE's FOFA concept or acquiescing to the application of the ALB Doctrine to U.S. forces in Europe.

Finally, it was contended that both the ALB Doctrine and the FOFA concept were compatible and complementary while constituting no substantive obstacle to progress at the Vienna CFE talks. Both were supportive of NATO's forward defense strategy that, according to the West German minister of defense, Gerhard Stoltenberg, "for the foreseeable future requires a combination of conventional and nuclear forces at the lowest possible level."[34]

This then represented the basic frame of reference as well as the goal of NATO's arms control policy and could be achieved within the context of the ALB Doctrine and the FOFA concept and without fundamentally altering the force structures supporting both. Further, the lower the force levels negotiated at Vienna, the higher the premium on highly mobile maneuver forces. NATO's strategy of flexible response and forward defense could not have been upheld without conventional forces with technical capabilities and guided by operational concepts broadly resembling FOFA and ALB. Finally, until the demise of the USSR nuclear deterrence and commensurate nuclear forces in Europe remained necessary regardless of the extent of progress achieved in conventional arms control. Indeed, even today there is reason to expect nuclear deterrence and commensurate nuclear forces in Europe will be needed to shore up conventional stability at force levels significantly lower than NATO's current force posture. This point, which may well remain a truth today, was made by the secretary general of NATO in 1989, Manfred Woerner, at a conference on European security and defense policy: "Of course: no strategy is for eternity. And every strategy has to be adapted to changing circumstances. A conventional balance in Europe at minimum levels would have consequences for our strategy—without eliminating the need for a minimum nuclear deterrent."[35]

NOTES

1. Hans Günter Brauch, in this volume. The 1982 ALB doctrine was revised in 1986 to take account of some criticisms and to adapt it in light of the experience gained in the implementing the earlier version. The relevant documents are: FM-100-5 *Operations,* (Washington, DC: Dept. of the Army, Aug. 1982, and May 1986); see for discussion of the ALB doctrine, Manfred R. Hamm, "The AirLand Battle Doctrine: NATO Strategy and Arms Control in Europe," *Comparative Strategy,* 7, no. 2 (Summer 1988): 183–211; Herbert I. London, *Military Doctrine and the American Character—Reflections on AirLand Battle* (New York: National Strategy Information Center, Transaction Books, 1985); Richard Hart Sinnreich, "Strategic Implications of Doctrinal Change: A Case Analysis," in Keith A. Dunn and William O. Staudenmaier, eds., *Military Strategy in Transition: Defense and Deterrence in the 1980s* (Carlisle, Pa.: U.S. Army War College, 1984), pp. 42–59. For a discussion of the 1986 version of the ALB doctrine see: William R. Richardson, "FM-100-5—The AirLand Battle in 1986," *Military Review,* 66, no. 3 (March 1986): 4–11; Michael Forster, "AirLand Battle 1986—Das Ziel bleibt Abschreckung," *Europaeische Wehrkunde* (Dec. 1987): 670–674.

2. Karl Kaiser, "Der Nichterstgebrauch von Kernwaffen: Ein falscher Schritt in die richtige Richtung," in Holger Ehmke und Paul Lang, *Frieden und Sicherheit als Herausforderung,* 2nd ed. (Bonn: Bundeszentrale für Politische Bildung, 1985), pp. 210–217; Richard K. Betts, "Compound Deterrence vs. No-First Use: What's Wrong is What's Right," *Orbis,* 28 (Winter 1985): 697–718.

3. This distinction between the sociopolitical and military-technical level of Soviet military doctrine is often ignored but essential for the recent discussion on "defensiveness" and the attending need to shape military forces and employment concepts to reflect the new doctrinal emphasis. See: Ole Diehl

and Anton Krakau, *Die KRK-Initiativen des Warschauer Paktes im Lichte des sowjetischen Verstaendnisses von Paritaet und Defensivitaet* (Köln: Berichte des BI-Ost, Nr. 45, 1988).

4. Given the current force balance between both alliances in Europe, sustained offensive operations by NATO can be ruled out. Moreover, political constraints militate against NATO launching a strategic-operational offensive, not to mention initiating preemptive offensive operations against the WTO.

5. There has been a lot of discussion about the possibility of limiting a future European war to conventional engagements. See, e.g., John G. Hines and Phillip A. Peterson, "The Conventional Offensive in Soviet Theater Strategy," *Orbis,* 27, no. 3 (Fall 1983): 695–739. Nonetheless, there remains an "unavoidable nuclear backdrop" that combatants have to take into account. See Stephen J. Cimbala, "Conventional War in Europe: The Unavoidable Nuclear Backdrop," *Defense Analysis,* 4, no. 4 (1988): 361–376. Therefore, references to the "integrated battlefield" should be considered first as descriptive of likely conditions and only secondarily as prescriptive of a mode of fighting. It does not mean, however, that U.S. forces are free to escalate to nuclear or chemical warfare without prior political authorization, the latter being ruled out anyway by U.S. obligations pursuant to the 1925 Geneva Protocol.

6. John H. Maurer and Gordon H. McCormick, "Surprise Attack and the Conventional Defense in Europe," *Orbis,* 27, no. 1 (Spring 1983): 107–126; John G. Hines and Phillip A. Peterson, "The Warsaw Pact Strategic Offensive—the OMG in Context," *International Defense Review,* 16 (1983): 1391–1395; Richard Simpkin, "Countering the OMG," *Military Technology* (Mar. 1984): 82–103; Christopher N. Donnelly, "The Development of the Soviet Concept of Echelloning," *NATO Review,* 32, no. 6 (Dec. 1984): 9–17; Leon V. Sigal, ed., *Alliance Security: NATO and the No-First Use Question* (Washington, DC: Brookings, 1983).

7. Edward N. Luttwak, *Strategy—The Logic of War and Peace* (Cambridge: Harvard University Press, 1987), p. 92.

8. Donn A. Starry, "The Evolution of U.S. Army Operational Doctrine—Active Defense, AirLand Battle, and Future Trends," in Lars B. Wallin, ed., *Military Doctrines for Central Europe,* Proceedings FOA Symposium, Swedish National Defense Research Institute, Stockholm, June 5–6, 1984, pp. 47–61.

9. Starry observed: " . . . maneuver . . . is not the traditional U.S. Army way of war. With some notable exceptions we are essentially a country and an army wedded to the idea that mass wins in the end. For such was our experience in the dominant theaters in the American Civil War, in both World Wars in Europe, and in the Korean War . . . Of the great names in U.S. military history, but a handful understood and were masters of maneuvers." *The Evolution,* pp. 56.

10. Phillip A. Karber, "In defense of Forward Defense—The Frontline Europe," *Armed Forces Journal International* (May 1984): 27–50. A good review of the debate within the army and among its critics and defenders in the civilian defense community is contained in John L. Romjue, *From Active Defense to AirLand Battle: The Development of Army Doctrine 1973–1982,* TRADOC Historical Monograph Series (Fort Monroe, Va., 1984), Chap. 2.

11. Ibid, pp. 28–30.

12. For Lind's basic critique of active defense see his: "FM-100-5: Some Doctrinal Questions for the Army," *Military Review,* 57, no. 1 (Jan. 1977).

13. See Edward N. Luttwak, "The Operational Level of War," *International Security,* 5, no. 3 (Winter 1980–1981); Wm. S. Lind, "Defining Maneuver Warfare for the Marine Corps," *Marine Corps Gazette* (Mar. 1980).

14. Samuel P. Huntington, "Conventional Deterrence and Conventional Retaliation in Europe," *International Security,* 8, no. 3 (Winter 1983–1984): 32–56. For a succinct critique of this proposal see Keith A. Dunn, "The Retaliatory Offensive and Operational Realities in NATO," *Survival,* 27, no. 3 (May–June 1985): 108–118.

15. TRADOC Pamphlet No. 525-5, *Military Operations, Operational Concepts for the AirLand Battle and Corps Operations—1986,* released on Mar. 25, 1981. An abridged version was published the same month by General Donn A. Starry under the title "Extending the Battlefield," *Military Review,* 61 (Mar. 1981): 31–50.

16. FM-100-5 (1982), Chap. 2 "Combat Fundamentals," pp. 2-1–2-2; see also William Hanne, "The Integrated Battlefield," *Military Review,* 62, no. 6 (June 1982): 34–44.

17. FM-100-5 (1982): B-3.

18. FM-100-5 (1982): Chap. 8-5.

19. Boyd D. Sutton, "Deep Attack Concepts and the Defense of Central Europe," *Survival,* 59, no. 2 (Mar./Apr. 1984): 59.

20. Carl von Clausewitz, *On War*, Michael Howard and Peter Paret, eds. (Princeton, N.J.: Princeton University Press, 1984), p. 367.

21. For a more detailed analysis see Manfred R. Hamm, "The AirLand Battle Doctrine: NATO Strategy and Arms Control in Europe," *Comparative Strategy*, 7, no. 2 (Summer 1988): 183–211.

22. Karl-Heinz Kamp, "Die Diskussion um 'FOFA'," *Oesterreichische Militaerzeitschrift* (Mar. 1987): 220–225; Bernard W. Rogers, "NATO Strategie" Erfordernisse fuer eine glaubwuerdige Abschreckung und fuer Buendniszusammenhalt," *Europa Archiv* (1984): 52–60; Ibid., Follow-on Forces Attack (FOFA): Myths and Realities," *NATO Review* (Dec. 1984): 1–9.

23. See Eckhard Luebkemeier, "AirLand Battle und Rogers Plan," *Die Neue Gesellschaft*, no. 4 (1985): 340–345; Robert A. Gessert, "The AirLand Battle and NATO's New Doctrinal Debate," *RUSI-Journal* (July 1984): 52–60.

24. See Stephen J. Cimbala, *Extended Deterrence—The United States and NATO Europe*, (Lexington: Lexington Books, 1987), pp. 72–76.

25. General Lobow, "USA and NATO Continue to Strive for Military Superiority" (German language excerpts in *BPA Ostinformationen*, Nr. 83, May 2, 1989: 16–17). Die Gruenen im Bundestag, *Angriff als Verteidigung—AirLand Battle, AirLand Battle 2000, Rogers Plan*, 2nd ed. (Bonn, 1984) and "Die 'AirLand Battle'—Doktrin, Eine offensive Kriegsfuehrungsdoktrin fuer das Schlachtfeld Europa," *Militärpolitik, Dokumentation*, 34/35 (1983). For an excellent refutation of these charges see K. Peter Stratmann, "'Airland Battle'—Zerrbild und Wirklichkeit" (Ebenhausen/Isar: Stiftung Wissenschaft und Politik (SWP), 1984).

26. Col. Gen. M. A. Gareyev, *Svetskaya Voyennaya Nauka (Soviet Military Science)* (Moscow: Znaniya, 1987), p. 36; USSR Defense Minister D. T. Yazov, *On Guard over Socialism and Peace* (Moscow: Yoyenizdat, 1987), p. 33.

27. See Phillip A. Petersen and Notra Trulock III, *A 'New' Soviet Military Doctrine—Origins and Implications* (Sandhurst: Royal Military Academy, Soviet Studies Research Centre, Summer 1988, C68); William E. Odom, "Soviet Military Doctrine," *Foreign Affairs*, 67, no. 2 (Winter 1988/1989): 114–134.

28. The Soviets refer specifically to the 1974 Schlesinger doctrine stipulating the need for flexible options and the countervailing strategy formalized as Presidential Directive (PD-59) by Carter. For an analysis of PD-59 see Jeffrey Richelson, "PD-59, NSDD-13 and the Reagan Strategic Modernization Program," *Journal of Strategic Studies*, 6, no. 2 (June 1983): 125–146.

29. Phillip A. Karber, "In Defense of Forward Defense—The Frontline Europe," *Armed Forces Journal* (May 1984): 48–49. He reviews a number of weapon systems and surveillance technologies and points out how some of them might be even more effective when employed by the offense instead of the defense.

30. See Hartmut Pohlman, "Vergleichbares muss vergleichbar werden," *Sueddeutsche Zeitung*, Feb. 8, 1989: 9; Stuart White, "Military Glasnost and Force Comparisions," *International Defense Review* (May 1989): 559–566; Ole Diehl and Anton Krakau, *Das Militaerpotential des Warschauer Paktes in Europa* (Köln: BI-Ost, Nr. 36, 1989).

31. *A Comprehensive Concept on Arms Control and Disarmament*, A report adopted by the heads of state and government at the meeting of the North Atlantic Council in Brussels on May 29 and 30, 1989, *Atlantic News*, N. 2127 (Annex) June 1, 1989: 3.

32. Hans-Dietrich Genscher, no title, June 23, 1989; remarks at the SWP Conference on Military Doctrines (Bonn: Auswaertiges Amt, Mitteilungen fuer die Presse Nr. 1114/89), translated by the author.

33. Col. Gen. M. A. Moiseyev, "From a Defense Doctrine Position," *Kranaya Zvezda*, Feb. 8, 1989, excerpts in Leon Goure, "The Soviet Strategic View," *Strategic Review*, 17, no. 2 (Spring 1989): 82–83.

34. "Wir wollen die zu grosse Zahl von Atomwaffen in Europa deutlich verringern," SZ-Interview mit Verteidigungsminister Gerhard Stoltenberg, *Sueddeutsche Zeitung*, July 8, 1989: 12.

35. Manfred Woerner, "Does the West Need a New Strategy?" speech by the secretary general of NATO to International Conference on European Security and Defense Policy, Brussels, Belgium, July 7, 1989, *NATO Press Service:* 6; For a similar line of reasoning see Karl Kaiser, "Wozu Atomwaffen in Zeiten der Abruestung," *Europa Archiv*, 44, no. 9, May 10, 1989: 261–272.

4

Nuclear Forces and the Defense of Europe

John M. Weinstein

For almost four decades, nuclear forces have been the ultimate guarantor of NATO security. Ever since acknowledging its inability to field the 96 divisions and 9000 combat aircraft prescribed in the 1952 Lisbon goals, to meet the conventional threat posed by numerically superior Soviet and later Warsaw Pact forces, the Western alliance has incorporated tactical Short Range Nuclear Forces (SNF), theater Intermediate Range Nuclear Forces (INF), and, ultimately, U.S. and British strategic nuclear forces as a relatively inexpensive deterrent to the threat of Soviet aggression.

NATO nuclear strategy has rested upon the twin pillars of flexible response and forward defense. In flexible response, NATO reserved the right to initiate nuclear operations if conventional forces were about to be overrun. Furthermore, NATO would make its stand at the former inter-German border. This forward defense afforded NATO a chance to control escalation with relatively low-yield SNF, such as cannon and missile artillery, while signalling resolve to escalate, if necessary, to longer range and more lethal theater and strategic nuclear forces. While the West maintained its monopoly on tactical nuclear weapons and, later, theater and strategic superiority, NATO nuclear doctrine was uniformly endorsed by its members and presumably regarded by the Soviets as credible.

During the last two decades, however, the Soviet Union's attainment of strategic parity with the United States and its massive build-up of theater and tactical nuclear forces raised the specter of unrestrained nuclear conflict in Europe. It also undermined the credibility of a theater defense with nuclear weapons as well as the linkage of U.S. strategic forces to the defense of Europe. The West met these developments with what became known as the "dual track" approach: theater nuclear modernization coupled with efforts to reduce the threat from Soviet INF through an arms control regime.

Both efforts met with success. The deployment of 108 Pershing II ballistic and 464 Ground Launched Cruise Missiles (GLCMs); the modernization of the 8-inch and the planned modernization of the 155mm artillery fired atomic projectiles (AFAPs); and the planned Follow-on to Lance (a 100-plus km corps-support ballistic missile) confronted the Warsaw Pact with more accurate nuclear forces that had longer range, greater mobility, and survivability. At the same time, the 1987 INF Treaty, which eliminated all U.S. and Soviet missiles with ranges between 500 and 5000 km, as well as rejuvenated East-West talks on reducing short range nuclear and conventional forces in Europe occupied NATO and Warsaw Pact defense planners and politicians at the close of the 1980s.

WHITHER THE THREAT?

The momentous events of 1989 and 1990 radically transformed NATO's perception of the threat, resulting in serious questions about, and criticisms of, the Alliance's military strategy in general and nuclear strategy in particular.

Mikhail Gorbachev's domestic policy of perestroika had reduced military spending at home in an effort to transfuse resources into the former Soviet Union's moribund economy. To justify this shift in resources, he permitted unprecedented criticism of the military establishment. He also championed the policy of defensive sufficiency and, to further its implementation, replaced all marshals of the Soviet Union and many high ranking military officers and theater commanders with men who support his reformist views. In 1988, Gorbachev announced and immediately began to implement a unilateral Soviet withdrawal of 500,000 troops and 5000 tanks from selected Eastern European countries. The Conventional Forces-Europe (CFE) arms and forces reduction treaty, signed in 1990, has institutionalized, expanded, and accelerated the scope and rate of military withdrawals by the former Soviet Union from the territory of Eastern European countries. Consequently, NATO leaders no longer consider a surprise attack by overwhelming Soviet/Pact forces a credible scenario. Furthermore, given the amount of strategic warning now expected, NATO's conventional defenses are now considered sufficient for the task and the demand for prompt resort to nuclear forces in the early days of a conflict no longer appears inevitable. Finally, independence and separatist movements in the Baltic countries and throughout much of the former USSR; the increasingly demanding exigencies of open elections and parliamentary democratization; and an activist foreign policy aimed at securing technological, trade, and financial aid from the West were high on Gorbachev's agenda.

When coupled with the displacement of Eastern European communist regimes; the substantial reductions to East European military budgets and force structures; the dissolution of the Warsaw Pact and the ongoing removal of Soviet forces and armaments from East European soil; U.S. and Western European domestic economic problems, which have led to calls to reduce military spending on a massive scale; and finally, recent press reports of defects within the U.S. nuclear stockpile and weapons complex, it is hardly surprising that President Bush cancelled modernization of the new 155mm howitzer atomic projectile (W82) and the Follow-on to Lance (FOTL) corps-support surface-to-surface missile. Nor, in the absence of credible fixed targets in Eastern Europe or the urgent need to discourage the massing of Soviet forces on the now non-existent East-West German border, is it surprising that NATO is planning drastic cuts in its nuclear arsenal.

These developments raise two critical questions for the U.S. and its NATO allies: Is there a continued role for non-strategic nuclear forces (NSNF) in NATO and if so, what types and numbers of weapons are required?

A CONTINUING ROLE FOR NSNF WEAPONS

At its July 1990 summit in London, NATO reaffirmed its continuing need for an "appropriate mix of nuclear and conventional forces." However, the summit also noted the need for "far fewer nuclear weapons," particularly "systems of the shortest range."

NATO's insistence on retaining some short range theater nuclear forces as "weapons of last resort," rather than agreeing to the Soviet Union's call for a "third zero option" (which would immediately abolish all SNF in Europe), prudently acknowledged several important political and military factors: the dynamism within the former Soviet Union and the potential for regional destabilization; the emergence of increasingly lethal threats on NATO's periphery; and limitations with many of the Advanced Conventional Munitions (ACMs), touted by many as the high-tech military equivalent of and politically acceptable replacement for nuclear weapons.

The Soviet Factor

The self-congratulatory euphoria surrounding the end of the Cold War and the West's apparent victory overlooks several uncomfortable political and military realities. The most important political reality is that relations between states are dynamic; they are not necessarily unidirectional, cumulative, or predictable. The Gorbachev and now Yeltsin commitment to and ability to foster increasing democratization, civilianization of the massive and bureaucratically entrenched military-industrial complex, and reductions in strength of the Soviet military are by no means assured. The advocates of *glasnost* and *perestroika* still confront powerful conservative opponents who during the attempted coup in August 1991 failed to reverse what they consider to be the emasculation of the Soviet military, foreign policy retrenchment, and an overly conciliatory posture toward the West.

The failure to resolve the former Soviet Union's gargantuan economic problems has already accelerated the disintegration of the world's last great multi-national empire. Such developments could fan tendencies for a xenophobic Russian nationalism and ethnic and/or regional hostilities that could easily spill across national boundaries.

Looking beyond the immediate hopes for the democratization of Eastern Europe and the Soviet Union, one must recognize that rapid democratization itself is a potentially destabilizing process. Moreover, Europe in the 1990s bears many resemblances to the Europe of 1910 which tumbled headlong into a war nobody wanted or expected. A great empire (Austria-Hungary) was torn apart by the centrifugal force of nationalism. Germany became a unified country while the Balkans seethed with instability. While the outbreak of war resulting from such a turn of events may be unlikely today, consider how unlikely the unification of Germany seemed only ten years ago. Wars have occurred in more unlikely places and in spite of the desires and interests of national leaders. In short, U.S. and European security should not and cannot be mortgaged on the unsupportable promise that today's good times will continue indefinitely.

Peripheral and Out-of-Area Threats

The decisive victory of U.S.-led coalition forces in Desert Shield/Desert Storm did not put to rest a number of disquieting concerns. Despite vanquishing Saddam Hussein far more easily than many expected, we are reminded that the proliferation of nuclear weapons and ballistic missile technology throughout the Third World is not a development that the U.S., the Soviet Union, and others can forestall indefinitely. Nor should we expect other states to forego the development of chemical, biological, and nuclear weapons of mass destruction or the increasingly lethal conventional implements of modern warfare so readily available in international arms markets.

The prospect of anti-Western powers, armed with such weaponry, on Europe's periphery or within striking range of Europe provides an additional rationale for the alliance's maintenance of a nuclear deterrent.[2]

The Promise of Advanced Conventional Munitions (ACMs)

The promise of ACMs, demonstrated quite spectacularly in the Gulf War, grows out of the development of new targeting and munitions technologies. Long-range, survivable sensors such as the AWACs electro-optical image and signal sensors, and motion detector radars have begun to generate the capability to acquire and track tactical mobile targets. Advances in low-cost digital information processing and distribution now allow realtime processing of significant information which can then be fed into grid systems that integrate the information and display the location of target arrays.

Non-nuclear terminally guided submunitions (TGSMs), accurate short-range (e.g., multiple launch rocket system-MLRS), and long-range surface-to-surface or air-delivered stand-off missiles could then be used against a range of hard-point and area targets. Some argue that these munitions approach the effectiveness of low-yield nuclear weapons and, therefore, can be used with marked success to engage air defenses, airfields, hardened command posts, logistics bases, and second echelon armor.

The widespread acquisition and deployment of such weapons could have, according to proponents, several desirable military and political effects that could hedge against a reemergent Soviet threat. First, NATO's conventional deterrent forces would become far more formidable. The long-range targeting and strike capabilities of ACMs would place an adversary's follow-on and reserve forces at risk, bolstering deterrence by increasing an adversary's military uncertainty and reducing prospects for conventional victory. Second, ACMs would not be encumbered by restraints associated with nuclear weapons and could be used at the force commander's discretion. As a result, NATO responses could be more timely, flexible, and supportive of NATO political-military objectives. Third, these forces would necessitate a thorough reappraisal by an adversary's political and military leaders of their forces, doctrine, and strategy to cope with NATO's new capabilities. Indeed, there was already ample evidence that the former Soviet military had begun such a reassessment in light of the performance of Soviet equipment and the rather dismal application of Soviet doctrine by the Iraqis in the Gulf War.

At the very least, NATO's ability to see and strike deep with highly accurate conventional forces would require an adversary to concentrate more on force dispersal and defensive operations, orientations less threatening to NATO's interests. Additionally, ACMs should be able to generate increased domestic support throughout Europe for NATO's military strategy by raising the nuclear threshold and eliminating the prospect of raining nuclear warheads on individual members or the emerging democracies in Eastern Europe. Finally, the significant procurement of ACMs could reduce the substantial logistics burden associated with "dumb" munitions.[3] Some analysts suggest the ACMs could result in a six- to sevenfold increase in ammunition tonnage carried and to be resupplied, thereby improving maneuverability, force survivability, and endurance. Additional benefits include reduced sortie and massed artillery requirements, consequently enhancing operational availability by reducing component replacements.

ACM Limitations

The difficulty in locating and destroying Iraq's mobile Scuds is a notable reminder that there are limits to what we can realistically expect from ACMs and supporting high-tech acquisition and targeting systems. While ACMs are certain to play a critical role in future European defenses and should, for many of the reasons cited above, be acquired, it may be illusory to expect high technology ACMs to completely eliminate NATO's reliance on nuclear weapons. First, quite a gap exists between the identification of a technological concept on the drawing board, that concept's development into a viable weapons system, and its subsequent deployment. Problems with the fire-and-forget Advanced Medium Range Air-to-Air Missile (AMRAAM) and the Army-Air Force Joint Surveillance and Target Acquisition Radar System (JSTARS) illustrate this difficulty. One cannot underestimate the scope and complexity of significant problems in the development of high tech weapons. For instance, the Copperhead anti-armor projectile was the first laser-guided projectile and is the forerunner of ACMs. Despite the fact that the Copperhead has nowhere near the level of sophistication of multiple mode sensors technology, that system has had serious technical problems in engaging moving and obscured targets. The development of new technologies often results in unanticipated delays and may ultimately fail to provide increased effectiveness over existing systems. Such was the case with the Army's Division Air Defense (DIVAD) gun. The reliability estimates of high technology warheads may also be lower in the punishing environment of field operations than in the more benign projections associated with engineering development. At the same time, one cannot expect one's adversaries to stand still, given the mutual suspicious and potentially disastrous consequences for deterrence of a significant military breakthrough that results in an imbalance. Irrespective of the potential sophistication of one side's arsenal, an adversary's ability to develop effective technological and tactical countermeasures must be considered. Marshal Ogarkov's call for the intensive development of ACMs by the former Soviet Union makes it likely that a new generation of offensive and defensive countermeasures will be pursued once the political and economic situation has been stabilized in Russia. But less expensive and possibly equally effective tactical solutions may exist to counter ACMs. For instance, the deployment of enemy armor in forests, while visible to ACM supporting sensors, may markedly reduce ACM effectiveness due to foliage shielding. Also, the deployment of obscurants and electronic defenses could further reduce effectiveness. The question, then, becomes one of cost effectiveness at the margin. Can a potential adversary with sizable military budgets and the motivation to field formidable armed forces develop effective countermeasures more cheaply than NATO can develop its new antitank and deep interdiction weapons? And can we assume that the next time and place for U.S. and Western military operations will be in a hospitable environment for high-tech weapons or against a military leader as inept as Saddam Hussein?

Cost is a second factor that must temper the enthusiasm for *deus ex machina* solutions. Europe's current domestic political-economic priorities and the disinclination to expend large sums of money on military hardware make it unlikely that NATO will foot the bill for ACMs whose total costs have been estimated from $10 to $200 billion. As a result, NATO commanders may not have enough of these capable rounds to end their reliance upon nuclear weapons. NATO's need to replace and modernize traditional weapons such as tanks, ships, and planes; improve communications; and deploy strategic lift and mobility assets will compete for scarce funds needed for ACM development and acquisition. Such an argument becomes more convincing when one considers that due to technology costs, higher personnel requirements, and greater numbers of ACMs required to achieve damage levels comparable to SNF, acquisition and logistical costs of the former are projected to be substantially greater than for the latter. Moreover, nuclear force modernization by the allies may be pursued at no cost to them. Existing delivery systems do not change and nuclear research, development and procurement costs are borne by the U.S. ACMs will offer the allies no such low-cost force multiplier.

Third, ACMs may be inappropriate for engaging certain types of targets such as hardened positions and highly mobile second echelon armor moving under smoke screens or fog, hugging tree lines or exploiting other natural cover. In military scenarios before the demise of the Soviet Union, the praises of ACMs most often associated with the deep attack against second echelon follow-on forces, made possible by the development of "look deep" target acquisition sensors. There is little doubt that the commitment of follow-on/reserve forces could have been decisive and Soviet tactics and doctrine extolled adroit ability to exploit reserve and follow-on forces in the great patriotic war. The development of the Operational Maneuver Group (OMG) was a partial response to NATO's improving deep attack capabilities. Its employment concept is centered on extreme mobility and fluidity, making these forces a difficult target for any long-range system. NATO's best chance of engaging such bands of forces would be as they massed for a breakthrough operation. In this situation and upon the authorization by appropriate U.S. and NATO officials to use nuclear weapons in response to a commander's request, the delivery of decisive fire must be effected within abbreviated time windows. Such firepower may only be achievable through the use of nuclear forces since hundreds of ACMs may be required to achieve the effect of even a few low yield weapons. This seeming contradiction of the previously suggested ACM-SNF coverage comparison is due to the fact that ACM dispenser area coverage cannot be equated with the lethal area of a nuclear weapon. Specifically, while ACMs may be countered with active and passive means, sheltering (i.e., digging in and shielding) is the only effective countermeasure for nuclear weapon damage attenuation. However, sheltering reduces the enemy's mobility and thus his offensive capabilities.

However, the most notable deficiency of ACMs vis-á-vis the use of nuclear forces on the battlefield may be their inability to signal NATO political resolve to escalate the conflict to defend its interests. In the event of hostilities and the failure of NATO's conventional defenses, SNF may provide the only alternative to capitulation, as well as the last resort for meaningful escalation control, before the employment of longer-range theater and strategic forces. Those who focus too exclusively upon the military attrition characteristics of weapons often overlook the potential escalation control/intrawar deterrence contributions of SNF.

The Future Force: Types and Numbers of Weapons

The demise of the Warsaw Pact, the withdrawal of Soviet forces from Eastern Europe, and reductions to the size and infrastructure of the Red Army itself have undercut the rationale of many Western arguments for continued SNF deployment. The disappearance of overwhelming Soviet-Warsaw Pact superiority undermines the need for offsetting nuclear forces. Unilateral and CFE-driven troop withdrawals have eliminated many of the fixed targets which generated large weapons requirements in nuclear warplans. And the return of former Soviet forces to Russian territory means that in the event of a future Russian attack, NATO's principal nuclear targets would be on the Russian borders, far beyond the range of SNF forces. Furthermore, the expectation of many months of strategic warning preceding actual hostilities would give NATO as well as East European forces time to mobilize sufficient forces and equipment and to prepare adequate defensive positions to defend the aggression with conventional forces.[4]

While NATO at its November 1991 Rome meeting has reaffirmed a continuing role for nuclear weapons in its defensive posture and doctrine, the arguments above provide the rationale for making deep cuts to its SNF forces, especially the shortest range systems. NATO may retain less than a thousand nuclear weapons, drawn largely from modern gravity bombs and/or a new stand-off tactical air-to-surface missile (TASM).[5] This smaller, more modern force is deemed sufficient to fulfill traditional SNF political-military missions: to demonstrate U.S. commitment to NATO's defense; to link that defense to U.S. strategic forces; and to assure NATO's non-nuclear states that they need not develop their own nuclear forces to guarantee their security.

Contributions of Land-Based Airpower and Sea-Based Forces

Traditionally, land-based airpower has involved five problems and risks: the vulnerability of fixed operating bases; extremely capable Soviet air defenses which threatened aircraft penetration probabilities; the burden of withdrawing dual-capable aircraft from the conventional battle when their role is perhaps most critical; the difficulty, due to long lead times for mission planning, of aviation assets to mount a timely attack against mobile targets (such as Scuds); and weather-darkness factors that could cause mission cancellation or, at a minimum, mission degradation.

In the post Warsaw Pact-CFE world, some of these problems are less daunting. Elimination of offensive air assets of the former Soviet Union as well as air defenses in Eastern Europe translate into higher NATO facility and aircraft survivability and mission accomplishment. Also, the planned installation of more survivable nuclear weapons storage sites on U.S. airbases complicates adversary targeting of U.S. nuclear assets in Europe and insures higher weapons survivability.

Additionally, the development of the Short-Range Attack Missile-Tactical (SRAM-T) with a 250 mile range, a tactical air-to-surface missile (TASM) which might be deployed in Europe on the F-15E fighter toward the end of the decade, is designed to fulfill NATO nuclear requirements into the next century. In his July 1991 testimony to the Senate Foreign Relations Committee, NATO's Supreme

Allied Commander, General John Galvin, strongly supported the SRAM-T, noting "I think we have to . . . have something that is technologically more accurate (than old nuclear bombs) and has the range and penetrability that the TASM would have."

Nevertheless, there are several difficult problems associated with increasing NATO's reliance on land-based airpower. The first is programmatic. The Air Force has not identified the SRAM-T program with sufficient priority to assure its survival in a constrained budget environment. The second is political. In light of past problems for the missile's two-pulse rocket motor system and the elimination of Warsaw Pact targets that legitimized its mission, continued congressional support for the TASM is doubtful. Third, substantial political opposition in Europe makes European deployment of the system unlikely. Finally, some of the problems (e.g., targeting mobile assets) and vulnerabilities associated with airpower still exist. To the extent that NATO abandons its Army systems, these remaining vulnerabilities become more significant.

The Navy is likely to assume increased nuclear responsibilities as Army nuclear modernization programs are cancelled and forces are withdrawn from the theater. Naval assets face some of the same problems noted above and some unique ones too. Naval tactical aviation units will confront the same weather-darkness and air defense challenges as land-based units. Also, carrier battle group commanders are rarely enthusiastic about jeopardizing the integrity of the group for land-support missions if they are confronted with any substantial maritime aviation threat. Even assuming that U.S. naval and NATO nuclear command and control nets, procedures and targeting can be integrated, the problem of how to achieve a unified allied response must be addressed. An essential element of NATO's nuclear strategy is based on incorporating as many alliance members as possible in a nuclear response. This broad participation demonstrates NATO resolution and solidarity. However, unlike the case with artillery and aviation assets, nuclear execution from U.S. naval platforms would be unilateral.

The employment of SLCMs involves additional specific problems. The first is the trade-off between committing naval weapons to the defense of Europe and the operational flexibility (i.e., maneuverability) required to protect U.S. maritime interests worldwide. And this tradeoff becomes even more crucial in the face of the potential reduction from 14 carrier battle groups to 12 or fewer. Second, SLCM support of Europe will require substantial terrain mapping of Eastern Europe and the territories of the former Soviet Union to support the missile's accurate guidance system. Finally, SLCM employment may be viewed as escalatory by an adversary that has repeatedly characterized SLCMs as strategic weapons and has sought to capture them within the START regime.

Nuclear Artillery: Still Able to Contribute?

These are hard times for the U.S. Army and Marine Corps nuclear artillery communities. The disappearance of the Soviet threat on the former East-West German border and even the disappearance of that border itself have undermined traditional SNF artillery missions. With fewer requirements and the availability of air and naval forces to perform future nuclear missions, President Bush cancelled the new 155mm AFAP program and the Follow-on to Lance and U.S. officials have hinted at the withdrawal of all U.S. nuclear artillery forces from Europe.

The expiration of the Lance's System Life Extension Program in the middle of this decade and the Army's cancellation of the 8-inch howitzer improvement program leaves U.S. ground forces ill-prepared to conduct nuclear operations. Despite the much-needed replacement of the old 8-inch AFAP (W33) with a more modern and safer AFAP (W79), the Army and Marines will still be required to use increasingly obsolete howitzers that lack crew protection and are not easily transported. The 155mm self-propelled howitzer is highly accurate—its rocket-assisted nuclear round has the same range as the 8-inch gun—and is easily transportable. However, the current 155mm AFAP (W48) is not considered to be militarily effective. Finally, the Marines are relegating their nuclear artillery to their reserves, the same destination as the Army's 8-inch howitzers.

Though no longer attractive from a political perspective, artillery SNF weapons can make important contributions to continued European security. Should this continent be thrown again into turmoil, whether due to ferment in the Balkans, a resurgent Russia, or some unforeseeable development, the West will require weapons that are survivable, responsive, accurate, flexible and capable of all-weather employment to hold mobile and other targets at risk on the integrated battlefield. Given the limitations of land-based air and naval forces discussed above, the potential contributions of artillery SNF should be viewed more favorably.

Cannon and missile artillery are flexible and responsive all-weather systems. Employed near the forward edge of the battle area in a future conflict against a superior force (perhaps with nuclear arms) or in some out of area contingency, they discourage an adversary from massing troops for high-tempo breakthrough operations. By discouraging massing, the presence of nuclear-capable artillery serves as a conventional force multiplier. If conventional defenses fail and these weapons must be used as weapons of "last resort," they can demonstrate Western resolve, link the defense of Europe to the U.S. strategic arsenal and play a decisive tactical role while limiting destruction and encouraging the cessation of conflict at the lowest possible level of violence.

SNF Redeployment

Once stored in the U.S., how easily could U.S. nuclear artillery be redeployed in Europe in an emergency? Assuming that NATO would respond in a timely fashion to strategic warning and the existence of sufficient lift during a crisis that would stress our logistics system to return U.S. nuclear assets and supporting equipment to the theater, serious challenges remain to executing this operation. The first is that the very act of returning these weapons to Europe would be a very serious step, one that an adversary would undoubtedly perceive as threatening. Redeployment would be a NATO rather than a unilateral U.S. decision. NATO-approved, automatic redeployment criteria might circumvent the political problems attending crisis redeployment. Such criteria that would remove allied governments from the nuclear decision process during crisis are, however, most unlikely. In their absence, it is questionable whether NATO governments would undertake an action that might heighten tensions in the pre-conflict stage at the very time when a premium was being placed on crisis management and stability. After the outbreak of hostilities, redeployment would be difficult and uncertain. Arriving weapons would have to transit a few coastal chokepoints or vulnerable airfields and then be dispersed to field storage locations and eventually rendezvous with remote firing units.

The diminution or complete elimination of Army nuclear capabilities from Europe could reduce future capabilities to execute these weapons in an integrated manner with ongoing conventional operations. The maintenance of a credible nuclear capability relies on far more than having weapons in place; it depends upon specialized training as well as unique procedures, expertise, and equipment. First, the army may find it difficult to motivate its most capable artillery and ordnance personnel to become nuclear specialists. The many officers and non-commissioned officers who became nuclear missile (i.e., Pershing and Lance) artillerymen are witnessing the disappearance of their systems due to arms control or obsolescence. For those unable to be reclassified and trained in a new occupational specialty, upward mobility is threatened. While some missile artillerymen will make the move to the Multiple Launch Rocket System (MLRS) or other occupational specialty areas, others risk being passed over for promotion because their skills are no longer in demand. In the event that the U.S. and its allies decide in the future that a nuclear missile artillery capability is required, the reestablishment of skilled personnel will have to be achieved. This undertaking will take time and money. It will also have to overcome natural suspicions among the troops about career field stability and security.

Apart from recruitment and retention problems, readiness is likely to suffer as well. Fewer or no army nuclear weapons could result in fewer nuclear alerts, exercises and inspections. Reduced training opportunities throughout the chain of command will dull the skills of those already proficient in nuclear operations and impede the development of new specialists. While individual, nuclear-certified units will remain proficient in their specific operational requirements, special nuclear command and control (NC2) channels are likely to atrophy. NC2 equipment will not be acquired as Congress looks for ways to reduce the defense budget. Army forces will also decline in their ability to conduct combined and joint nuclear operations.

Future Issues and Possibilities

NATO's continuing endorsement of a nuclear capability recognizes that a requirement remains for the maintenance of all-weather, survivable, and responsive nuclear forces that can be tactically decisive in diverse scenarios while minimizing the threat of rapid and uncontrolled escalation. As such, flexible nuclear forces remain a prudent option for the defense of NATO should deterrence fail and as a hedge against shortfalls in ACM procurement or of ACMs to perform as expected. The challenge for Western defense planners is to fashion a nuclear force that can meet NATO's future needs while simultaneously recognizing new European political realities and likely arms control eventualities.

A future NATO nuclear force should be able to be projected from land, sea, and air. Land-based forces should be able to cover short and longer ranges with precision. The Follow-on to Lance (FOTL), whose development was halted by President Bush, should be reconsidered as a flexible replacement to AFAPs being withdrawn from the Central Region and because the U.S. may face contingencies in other parts of the world in which the employment of easily transportable, all-weather employable nuclear weapons is in the national interest. The planned

FOTL could be effectively employed at close-in ranges (currently covered by howitzers) as well as 200–300 km and with high assurance of penetration against air defense artillery assets. Furthermore, technology could be developed to produce a conventional warhead that could be converted into a nuclear warhead by an insertable nuclear component (INC). The development of INCs, coupled with continued training in targeting, emergency action procedures, and other tasks associated with nuclear operations, might retain a nuclear capability for selected flexible conventional systems. At the same time, INCs could be stored in the U.S. and, because of their reduced size, be more easily and quickly deployed to Europe in a crisis. While INCs would undoubtedly create verifiability problems for arms control negotiations, such a capability might satisfactorily address European sensitivities to the presence of land-based nuclear forces on European soil and relieve battlefield commanders of many of the logistic, training, and personnel rigors associated with nuclear weapons. The recently modernized AFAPs, when withdrawn from Europe, should be stored in the United States as a hedge against a reversal of current favorable trends on the Continent as well as a potent response to contingencies elsewhere in the world.

Providing the Harrier/VSTOL aircraft with a nuclear capability would be a wise move for the Western alliance. First, the aircraft's ability to disperse to virtually any level site solves the problem of relying upon vulnerable fixed airports. Second, the Harrier's relatively limited range and slow speed make it appear less threatening to any future adversary as an offensive weapon than current faster and more sophisticated nuclear-capable aircraft. Third, the Harrier can be deployed from sea as well as land, further increasing the possible axes of attack. This characteristic makes it a potentially attractive weapon for the defense of NATO's northern tier. Fourth, the aircraft is relatively inexpensive and could be produced by a number of the European allies, thereby providing powerful economic and political incentives for support.

The essential point of the foregoing is that NATO strategists and weapons planners must look beyond the projected requirements of the next few years. Even if preserved on U.S. bases, today's modernized nuclear artillery may be ill-suited to confront threats and scenarios in the year 2010. Now is the time to begin thinking of new types of weapons that can continue to serve as a bulwark for NATO's security. To accomplish this, the alliance needs to establish a long-range planning group which includes policy experts, planners, and weapons developers. No such long-range requirements group, similar to the Senior Level Weapons Protection Group (whose mission is nuclear security), now exists in NATO.

In addition to U.S. submarine-launched ballistic missiles, carrier-based tactical aviation assets as well as Tomahawk nuclear cruise missiles are also available to support the alliance. The survivability, flexibility, and off-shore deployment of these weapons make them attractive components of or complements to NATO's nuclear arsenal. However, employment problems discussed earlier must be addressed to balance the optimum effectiveness of these forces with the competing conventional missions of their platforms.

The issue of nuclear weapons in Europe also raises questions about the role of the French nuclear arsenal. Deterrence has been well-served by the independence of France from NATO's military structure and the unpredictability of French nuclear employment in a crisis. However, France's long-standing desire to play a leading role in the European alliance, that country's obvious interest in the course of German unification, and the drawdown of U.S. forces on the continent portend a more central and influential role for the French. And the recent and ongoing modernization of its sea-based and land-based nuclear forces provides a sufficiently flexible military capability that can balance future withdrawal of U.S. nuclear forces from Europe. An increased nuclear role for the French, either individually or in concert with Great Britain (with which France is developing a longer range version of the Air-Sol Moyenre Portee stand-off TASM called the Air-Sol Longue Portee), in the defense of Europe will require a radical change in French defense doctrine. However, the momentous and unanticipated changes to the European defense equation that have occurred in the last few years make such a French transformation indeed plausible.

A related issue attending a more central role of French and/or British nuclear forces in the defense of Europe is the rationale for the SACEUR (Supreme Allied Commander-Europe) remaining an American general. Traditionally, it was argued that an American SACEUR linked the defense of Europe to U.S. strategic forces. It may be that in light of reduced nuclear assets deployed in the European theater in the coming years, the link to U.S. strategic forces embodied by an American general as the SACEUR may become even more important. However, an American SACEUR may be increasingly hard to justify given the heightened nuclear role of the French and the British. This is but one of the many political issues associated with the evolving nature of NATO and its nuclear strategy that U.S. and European leaders will confront in the coming decade.

A FINAL NOTE

Sergei Karaganov, Deputy Director of Russia's Institute of Europe, recently observed that if we fail to create a just Europe, the transitional period will lead

> . . . to realignments, prolonged instability or even to a complete reversal—not to the relatively stable two-camp system, but rather to something again transitional, such as the Versailles system. [6]

Current developments in Europe hold great promise for a more tranquil and prosperous future. As much as the West may desire such a vision, its military strategy and resulting role for nuclear weapons must also recognize the real possibility of a darker and more sinister course of events.

NOTES

1. The views and opinions contained in this essay are those of the author and should not be considered as an official U.S. Nuclear Command and Control System Support Staff or Department of Defense position.

2. The execution of a retaliatory nuclear option against a Third World nation would raise uniquely interesting issues. Hypothetically, while, during conventional hostilities, a Soviet strike with weapons of mass destruction against a NATO member, such as Turkey, would have resulted in a retaliatory strike with broad NATO participation, can one assume the same response against other aggressors? Had Iraq attacked Turkish airbases with persistent chemical weapons to interrupt the coalition's air attack, would Turkey have requested a NATO nuclear retaliatory strike against such weapons of mass destruction? Would such a strike have been authorized? Would the alliance refuse a Turkish request and jeopardize its southern flank? Would Turks be authorized to carry out? If so, how would the Greek government react?

3. Let us consider specific contributions of ACMs against some potential missions: a 400 meter-long column of tanks engaged at the FLOT and a 3,000-vehicle armored division, a difficult area target for contemporary conventional ordnance. In engaging the tank column, one salvo of Skeet-like munitions from a 12-tube MLRS dispenses 72 delivery vehicles, each with four terminally guided submunitions (TGSM).

Each TGSM searches for a "hot spot" such as a tank engine or exhaust system or senses electromagnetic radiation (EMR) reflectivity. The composite search patterns of the 288 TGSMs cover an area covered by a 0.1-kt fission artillery fired nuclear projectile and about one-quarter the area covered by a 1-kt enhanced-radiation device.

Against an armored division, consisting of about 400 tanks and armored carriers, 2,500 trucks, and assorted air defense vehicles and artillery pieces, more than 2,200 successful sorties of Tornados and/or F-111's delivering unguided iron bombs would be required. Using unguided submunitions such as the U.S. Air Force's Low Altitude Dispenser (LADS) or the German MW-1/Tornado System, the number of required successful sorties drops to 300 to achieve the 60 percent kill which was the Soviet criterion for annihilation. Using Skeet or other suitable TGSMs, the requirement falls to 50–60 sorties.

4. It is interesting that as NATO seems able, for the first time since its formation, to defeat aggression without early resort to nuclear weapons, the threat of an adversary's use of nuclear weapons may become more credible. The Soviet Union's past overwhelming conventional superiority and forward positions within sight of NATO territory afforded the now dissolved Pact the luxury of eschewing the first use of nuclear weapons. In the event of a future conflict deemed sufficiently crucial by Moscow to necessitate war against NATO, Russia would face mobilized forces in well-prepared defensive positions throughout the depth of East and West Europe. That country's resort to nuclear weapons may appear to be the only means to achieve victory while avoiding a lengthy war of attrition. The nuclear option might appear more attractive if the Russians perceived the linkage of U.S. strategic forces to the defense of Europe, either due to troop reductions and base closings or strategic force reductions, to be less certain.

5. Catherine M. Kelleher, "Short-Range Nuclear Weapons: What Future in Europe?", *Arms Control Today*, Vol. 21, no. 1, January/February 1991, p. 19.

6. S. A. Karaganov, "The Year of Europe: A Soviet View," *Survival*, Vol. XXXII, no. 2, March/April 1990, p. 126.

5

Improving NATO's Defense

Franz Uhle-Wettler

Throughout NATO's history, debates on force improvement have concentrated heavily on weapons, equipment, and force structures. The reason has been obvious: NATO is an alliance of nations that guard their sovereignty and national pride jealously. Seldom, if ever, will a NATO commander criticize the morale, discipline, or training of the national forces that, in time of tension, will come under his command. High-sounding eulogy is much more frequent. Likewise tactics, generally formulated at the national level, are seldom commented on, although they may be discussed in one of the innumerable working groups at NATO offices. Supervision of training by nonnational NATO officers is restricted to nuclear assets. Discussions on such intangibles and unquantifiables as morale, discipline, and professionalism are more or less taboo.

One might ask: Is this the right order of priorities? When Napoleon tried to educate his brother, Joseph, he told him that "The moral is to the physical what three is to one." A similar message comes to us by way of an anecdote from World War II. A week after the beginning of the German offensive in France in 1940, the French prime minister asked his chief of defense for the reasons behind the apparent German qualitative superiority over the French and British troops. On May 19, General Gamelin responded. He was honest. He admitted that the forces under his command were defeated by an enemy inferior in numbers and equipment. He mentioned those mistakes for which he bore at least some responsibility, especially the obsolete armor tactics of the allied armies. Then he concluded:

> Finally, and first of all, the German success is the result of physical training and of the high morale of the masses. The French soldier, yesterday's citizen, did not believe that war was possible. Often, his interest did not extend beyond his workshop, his office, his fields. He liked to criticize incessantly everyone who had some authority and he had been persuaded to use civilization as a pretext for an easy life from one day to the next. Thus, between the wars, the conscript had not received the moral and patriotic education that would have prepared him for the drama in which the fate of his country would be at stake.

Obviously, in those days, a debate on force improvement that failed to concentrate on morale, motivation, tactics, and training missed its mark. Equally, a debate that concentrated on weaponry and equipment was certain to lead to faulty conclusions, because it would have predicted an easy victory for the French and British armies. The importance of immaterial factors like morale and training is corroborated by Sir William Slimm, a British field marshall of World War II. He argued that soldiering "depends on three things: spiritual, intellectual, and material. And that is the order of their importance. Spiritual belief and steadfastness must come first because it is only a strong spiritual foundation that can stand up under real strain. Then comes the intellectual factor because free men are moved by reason as well as by feeling. The material side comes last.''

THE FACTOR OF MORALE

Thus it seems that any discussion on the improvement of NATO's defense must first of all examine the status and improvement of the most important factor: morale. To do so, however, is actually difficult. Innumerable are the instances when commanders misjudged the morale even of their own forces with whom they had served for many years. But NATO has 16 nations, if France be included, 15 of which have armed forces (Iceland has none). Who could possibly have the expertise to reliably assess the morale of these forces and to recommend whatever improvement might be needed? It seems that there is an impasse. An analysis is required for which no single person has the expertise. However, a beginning should nevertheless be made by exposing some of the salient problem areas, and for a short essay this may perhaps be sufficient.

The Importance of Military Values

The industrial and the scientific revolutions have changed human society drastically. They have weakened the influence of the landmarks and signposts that have guided humans through millennia: religion, tradition, the advice of elders. In addition, they have created what is known as the nuclear family in which the young often chose their own way with little advice or even without the presence of the elders. This is bound to influence the transmission of those values that formerly had been transmitted by tribes, clans, families, and elders. Yet the military seem to assume tacitly that in all the changes, their own values and their transmission to the young remained unaffected: courage, self-sacrifice, leadership, the readiness to lead and the readiness to follow, patriotism, and comradeship—values that depend so much on the cultural environment, which obviously has changed. This raises the question if the values of the military profession remained essentially unaffected or if they have changed in the way that General Gamelin's comment in 1940 would suggest.

Balancing the Rights of the Individual and Those of the State

Do we balance the rights of the state with those of the individual? The modern society has been described as strongly influenced, if not dominated, by the rights of the individual. Clearly, this befits a democracy. Thus it is not surprising that even high military leaders declare that the rights and the well-being of the individual are at the center of all their thoughts. Nor is it surprising that such statements are usually received with satisfaction by the public. However, the basis for an effective military is not the well-being of the individual. Rather it is the fighting efficiency of the armed forces, and in war this may even demand the individual's supreme sacrifice. The best the military can do for the individual's well-being may not be ease and comfort, but the hard training that enables the individual to survive the psychological and physical hardships of the fire-swept modern battlefield.

To illustrate the point by an example, it has become widely accepted that the individual has the right to determine his or her sex life without government interference. But several NATO countries apply this rule to the military also and consider interference of officers with the wives or daughters of subordinates their private affair—despite the obvious dangerous consequences for unit cohesion and for the confidence of subordinates in their superior's personality. Thus the question appears justified: Do we still strike the right balance between the rights and desires of the individual and the necessities of training men for war?

Has the Military Remained a Redoubt for Traditional Military Values?

In some NATO countries, the values and behavior patterns of a highly individualistic society (some call it a permissive society) are widely acclaimed. Since the military is integrated into this society and is part thereof, their thinking is affected also. This raises the question of whether military values and requirements are still sufficiently upheld by the military itself.

As an example, in the West German armed forces, officer cadets are forced to study at a Bundeswehr university up to the equivalent of a master's degree. Almost all subjects offered are hardly related to the daily activity of an officer: economics, education, civil engineering, computer sciences, etc. The professors are civilians; the students are military in theory only (they don't even wear uniforms while attending classes).

When this scheme was introduced, the public was unanimously delighted. There even was widespread support in the upper echelons of the military. The question, however, is whether this scheme attracts those whom the military requires. The answer is simple: Those who offer peanuts will attract monkeys, and those who offer, even require, a master's degree will attract academics. However, Einstein probably could not have done what Rommel did. Nor could Rommel most probably have performed Einstein's job.

Even more important, between three and four years are devoted to the study of the subjects noted above. Unfortunately, since the time available for the training of officer cadets is limited, all those subjects have vanished from the cadet's curriculum, which once broadened one's military perspective: the study of Sun Tsu, of Clausewitz, of Napoleon (i.e., of military history, of the roots of the military profession). Military sociology, military psychology, and strategy all have been sacrificed. As a result, military professionalism has also been sacrificed. Numerous are the officers with a master's degree in education who do not know all the men of their company by their names. In summary, the emphasis on civilian subjects has had the inevitable effect of reducing expertise on subjects traditionally considered imperative for the military. Thus we are brought back to the question of whether NATO forces are striking the right balance between the requirements of the civilian society they are part of and the requirements of their military profession. If NATO's nations fail to strike the proper balance, they will find themselves one day in the same situation in which the allied forces found themselves in 1940— with all the wonderful paraphernalia of armed forces, but without fighting forces; with parades, medals, uniforms, with bands playing, flags flying high, and military ceremonies reflecting the glory of old and of yore, but with scant devotion, discipline, chivalry, sacrifice, and readiness to face danger and death. In short, they will find themselves with many managers and many men in uniform, but with few leaders and few warriors.

TRAINING

The emphasis of NATO's force improvement studies on weaponry was and still is justified. There is little doubt that several NATO countries do not devote enough financial resources to their armed forces. Illustrative are those rich countries that still field tanks like the M41 or the Centurion, wholly dated and unable to fight the armor of any of their likely opponents.

But the emphasis on weaponry has been one-sided and has led to a dangerous neglect of training. Procurement of modern and even ultramodern equipment frequently silences the critics. However, too often such procurement results in a facade only. Illustrative are those nations that purchased such modern planes as the F16 and then funded only 100 or 120 flying training hours per year for their pilots instead of the 180 or 200 considered by all experts as the minimum to attain and preserve combat efficiency and to exploit the capability of the plane.

Some years ago, one of the leading American military historians and military scholars, Trevor N. Dupuy, published the results of his analysis of hundreds of battles fought in the U.S. Civil War, in the world wars, and the Middle East wars. He arrived at the conclusion that battle results (in terms of casualties inflicted) are determined far more by quality of manpower (morale, training, tactics) than by quality of weaponry.[1] In fact, Dupuy demonstrated that quality of manpower pays off in an *exponential* fashion, whereas quality of weaponry pays off in a linear way only. For in order to contain 10 enemy tanks, five friendly tanks have to be twice as good ($5 \times 2 = 10$). If equality is sought not by equipment but by quality of personnel, another calculation applies. The tank crews have to be better by a factor of 1.41 only ($5 \times 1.41^2 = 10$).

We need not concern ourselves with the mathematics involved nor with the extensive study effort that led to this view. The gist of the argument is in its essence self-evident. High-quality, well-trained personnel can exploit fully the capability of their (mediocre) equipment and can conduct sophisticated tactics, whereas mediocre personnel will fail to capitalize on the full potential of their top-quality weaponry and will be less able to employ effective tactics. The British-French forces in France in 1940, the British army in Malaya 1941/1942, the Russian army in 1941/1942, and the Arabs in several Middle East wars all were defeated in battle after battle by an enemy inferior in numbers and, in most cases, in quality of equipment also.

Moreover, Dupuy's view is well illustrated by the bi-annual tank gunnery competition of NATO Central Region nations, which is called the Canadian Army Trophy. The competition has been criticized because it is among NATO crews that have been carefully trained and groomed for several months. Thus it suggests that NATO forces are much more proficient than is actually the case with average NATO crews. In fact, however, the competition bears witness to the incredible gap between NATO's average crews and those who have received optimum training. This raises the question of whether we should continue to buy high-quality equipment for personnel that we fail to train adequately for want of training grounds, flying hours, ammunition, and time.

There are 15 NATO nations with armed forces. Almost all of them have three or even four services. Those 45 different services have several and sometimes many different branches, from those tasked to launch intercontinental ballistic missiles through forces tasked to conduct naval minesweeping to infantry. Training concerns the individual, the units from the lowest to the highest level, the staffs, and the commanders. Therefore, it is impossible to generalize as to whether the training of "the" armed forces of the NATO alliance is sufficient or insufficient. However, even without analysis it is evident that training in vast and important areas is indeed insufficient: as mentioned above, there are nations whose pilots fly less than experts considered necessary. There are nations whose conscripts serve for 12 months or even less, producing uniformed men which would have had poor chances in duels against soldiers of former Warsaw Pact countries who served 18 and often 24 months or longer. There are nations that, in addition to having short conscription terms, restrict the working hours of their military to 40 hours per week in order to coincide with the working hours of their civilian work force, whereas their potential adversaries in the former Warsaw Pact worked and trained longer hours in order to meet the needs of the modern battle. There are nations whose reservists undergo hardly any refresher training worth speaking of. This list of training deficiencies is certainly not complete. It may suffice to illustrate the salient point that any attempt to improve NATO forces must also focus on improvements in training. Almost certainly there are NATO forces whose combat capability could more easily be enhanced by better training than by better weaponry. Indeed, it may be counterproductive to modernize military forces and thus provide high-capability weapon systems to soldiers who already have difficulty exploiting the capabilities of their present, less complex weaponry and whose current level of training will not allow them to exploit the additional capability of new weapon systems.

WEAPONS AND EQUIPMENT

There is a strange, even amusing or disquieting dichotomy. On the one hand, NATO countries claimed that their technologies, including military, were and remain far advanced over those of the former Warsaw Pact. Moreover, NATO outspent the Warsaw Pact. On the other hand, NATO was far inferior in numbers, and many of its weapons were and are dated. How is this possible?

The reasons for this situation are many. The first, most obvious, and frequently studied reason is that too many nations develop their own weapon systems. For example, the United States, Britain, France, Germany, and Italy each have developed their own main battle tanks. The result is not only small numbers and problems of interoperability, but a tremendous waste of research and development funds. The remedy is widely believed to be joint development undertaken by several nations. However, it is important to note that almost all major weapon systems that have been successful on the international market have been developed nationally, e.g., the M113 personnel carrier, the M60, and the Leopard 1, the F15, F16, and F18 aircraft, the Hawk and Bloodhound, etc. It seems that products developed jointly generally have a built drawback that makes it difficult for them to compete with nationally developed systems. They frequently are encumbered by demands made by the nations involved in the project that multiple capabilities be built into the weapon systems. Since there is no powerful umpire to decide which capabilities should have priority, the result is a final product that, all too often, has the national requirements added on, making the weapons system large, expensive, difficult to handle, and difficult to maintain. The failures of the first joint U.S.-German tank development program (MB 70) and of the British-German-Italian development of a 155mm SP howitzer are illustrative.

One potential way to solve the problem may be illustrated by approaches to missile development. Most NATO nations rely on one nation's products, from Honest John, Hawk, and Patriot to Sidewinder, Aim, and Lance. Of course, it is unthinkable that all nations would buy all their weaponry from one country. But the problem could be solved if nations agreed to buy the missiles from one nation, tanks from a second, infantry fighting vehicles (IFVs) from a third, artillery pieces from a fourth, and radios from a fifth, and so on. Nonmilitary influences, however, render this solution unrealistic also. Thus the problem remains. Nations will continue trying to solve it through bilateral development and some will even believe if they tried hard enough the problem could be solved thereby. However, this hope is vain. NATO nations unfortunately are destined to live with the tremendous waste and major logistic and interoperability difficulties that result from the fact that the alliance is composed of 16 sovereign nations.

The second reason for the dichotomy besetting NATO's armory may be illustrated by a look at NATO's tanks. They rank among the proudest products of Western technology, and many believe our tanks were superior to Russian tanks in all important aspects. But:

According to the doctrine of most Western nations, when tanks move into battle and are not yet actually engaging an enemy, commanders and the loader/radio operators are to scan the battlefield from open hatches. Both, of course, do have helmets and earphones. But, unfortunately, the two do not fit together. Thus in the age of proximity fuses and in view of the powerful Pact artillery, the two have their head protected by a utility cap only; 4,500 years ago, army commanders did better. Egyptian soldiers had their heads protected by metal helmets.

When it rains and the wind blows from the front, the rain obscures vision from inside tanks and sights of many Western tanks. In 1908, Prince Heinrich of Prussia, the kaiser's brother, had invented the windshield wiper and obtained a patent for it. Today, even the tiniest motor car has windshield wipes, and all Russian tanks have them.

On soft ground, tracks throw up so much dirt that it often blocks the driver's vision. But few of our armored vehicles allow their driver and gunner to wash their vison blocks and optics.

On a dark night, our tanks and IFVs have difficulty keeping their position relative to tanks traveling on their left and right because the commander, observing from the turret, may find it difficult to see his neighbors against the dark ground. Russian tanks have the very tiniest of "position lamps," which shine dimly to the side and rear, allowing neighboring vehicles to keep their position.

Many older Western tanks still carry a big box somewhere at the front of the turret. It houses the infrared searchlight. But normally neither the box nor the cables serving it are protected by armor. Their chances of surviving enemy artillery fire are poor, thus increasing the probability that our tanks will be blind at night. Russian tanks have their searchlights protected by armor plating.

Western tanks are much taller and bulkier than Russian tanks. They are generally more exposed to counterfires. They cannot easily hide or seek the protection of rolling terrain. A low profile is important and none of our tanks can quickly construct its own hull-down position. Unless by chance a sunken road or a stone wall is close at hand, our tanks must await enemy attack sitting high and dry on the ground, exposing their proud size to enemy sensors, observation, and fire. In contrast, many Russian tanks do have bulldozer blades. These provide extra protection for their lower front armor plate and, in particular, enable the tank to construct rapidly a hull-down position.

On a dark night, and especially in a forest, it is sometimes difficult to follow another tank. Often it happens that the lead tank turns off, whereas the following tank misses the turn and rolls off into the wilderness with the rest of the unit following behind. Nature gave hares, rabbits, deer, and elk a white behind—guess why? At the rear side of Russian tank turrets, a tiny lamp is burning inside a small metal case with a perforated symbol in its back through which a dim light is shining.

At night it is often almost impossible for a commander to find a way to identify a specific tank, say, the tank of a company commander with whom he wishes to talk. This is particularly true if the tanks are buttoned up and if radio silence must be observed. But Russian commanders are much better off—as noted earlier.

There is hardly an exercise of NATO troops without a powerful counterattack by NATO's armored reserve. But according to Russian tactics, the flanks of Russian penetrating forces are to be rapidly protected by minefields. Moreover, the Russians have the means to implement such tactics. Unfortunately, the mine clearing equipment available to NATO's armor formations is not worth speaking of. In contrast, Russian tanks can fix two primitive "ploughs" in front of their tracks that clear the ground while a chain sets off the fuses of mines laid between the tracks. Again, it is the Russians who have acquired a much-needed capability by simple, even "primitive," means. The use of cheap, unsophisticated approaches to battlefield problems seems to be beyond the imagination of NATO's engineers.

The above, of course, is not the complete story. It is, however, sufficient to illustrate the point that NATO tanks have everything that is expensive and that requires costly research and development. In short, NATO has the high technology. Its equipment, however, may not meet the needs of the modern battlefield in some very important areas mentioned above. What is frequently missing is equipment that is inexpensive and that could sometimes be produced by any village blacksmith for a few dollars. Only one diagnosis of this problem seems possible: NATO countries are infatuated with high tech. They are also blind to the capability of traditional technology.

To develop the argument further, one need only cast a glance at the terrain and the lines of sight (LOS) that exist in NATO's central region (formerly West Germany). Most of NATO's antiarmor weaponry and armor have been developed with this terrain in mind. Statistics provided by the West German Office of Military Geography show that 55% of the LOS are shorter than 500 m, 17% are longer than 1500 m, 10% longer than 2000 m, and 6% longer than 2500 m. These distances are clearly shorter than NATO's constant clamor for long range weaponry would suggest. Furthermore, the figures are not the whole story. They take account of terrain coverage (woods, built-up areas) only. However, other terrain features (hills, valleys) will certainly further reduce the LOS, which will also be adversely affected by night, rain, fog, and snowfall. Moreover, once battle has been joined, in densely populated central Europe, the smoke of burning villages and vehicles, the smoke fired by vehicles in distress and by artillery as well as the dust raised by tracks and by artillery barrages will even further reduce visibility and will add to what has been frequently called the "dirty battlefield" or the "fog of war."

Thus there is a strong argument in favor of the view that NATO should prepare for an antiarmor battle fought at rather short ranges—if not in built-up areas and forests then at ranges below 1000 m and certainly below 1500 m. Clearly the emphasis should not be on longer and longer ranges. Such a continued emphasis illustrates the degree to which the technological challenge, even technological enthusiasm drives weapon development to the detriment of tactical performance. A typical case in point is the history of hand-held antiarmor weapons: in World War II, the German *Panzerfaust* could be issued to every soldier; the launcher was discardable. True, the range left something to be desired. However, the weapon meant a tremendous proliferation of antiarmor weapons, not only at the front but in far rear areas also. Equally important was the morale boost that the *Panzerfaust* provided to all units facing armored attack at the front or in rear areas where enemy armor had broken through. No soldier on the battlefield needed to feel hopeless and forsaken. Equally important, enemy armor faced a threat wherever they attacked and wherever they broke through.

Unfortunately, after World War II, the *Panzerfaust* and the British PIAT were "improved." More range was added. The result was that the launcher became so heavy and so expensive that what had been a discardable weapon now became standard equipment, issued to a few selected soldiers only. Despite the numerous villages and towns to be defended, the excellent defense positions available in those towns and villages, the weapon could no longer be fired from an enclosed room—the soldier had to run out into the yard or onto the street to fire the weapon. The result was that most soldiers were forced back to a World War I environment. They had to face tanks and IFV with their rifles. A responsible commander could only advise them to take cover (and curse those responsible for weapons development). Of course, in the late 1980s and early 1990s, nations have been busy correcting a number of glaring deficiencies. But that is not the point. What is important is the fact that an infatuation with long ranges pervades NATO's weapon development even at the price of operational effectiveness.

The emphasis on long range also illustrates a second danger to which NATO's weaponry often falls victim. That is, the law of diminishing returns. Engineers frequently note that it is often the last 10% of given technological advance that is the most difficult and the most costly to attain. At the same time, this last 10% of capability can seldom be employed on the battlefield. In other words, we pay more and more for what we can utilize less and less. For instance, the percentage of occasions in which a direct-fire weapon can take advantage of increases in range falls progressively, whereas the cost of developing weapons that can operate effectively at long ranges increases dramatically.

Furthermore, neglect of the law of diminishing returns has consequences. Time and again, NATO ministers confirmed their policy of offsetting the Warsaw Pact's numerical advantage through superior quality. This can be a very sound policy, but it also can be a very dangerous one. For instance, it can mean that all three basic capabilities of any fighting vehicle (protection, mobility, firepower) may be technologically overdeveloped to a point where a very high price must be paid for a relatively small, seldom used additional capability. Small wonder that NATO devoted such large sums to defense and yet was far inferior to former Pact forces in numbers.

TACTICS

Goliath was an expert in close combat, well armed with spear, sword, and body armor. David did not try to match him where he was strong. When David prepared for battle, he tried and then discarded sword and body armor, the weapons of Goliath. He preferred to rely on a sling. This illustrates one of the basic laws of tactics: Do not try to match the enemy's strengths. Seek his weak points. Unhinge the enemy's defense not by breaking through where the enemy does best, but by doing as David did.

Of course, all NATO countries try to emulate David and many pundits claim they succeed. But, do they really? In this regard, it may be valuable to look at a potentially decisive factor, the antiarmor battle both past and present. Many are the statements by British authors confirming the tactical superiority of their opponents during World War II in 1940 in France, in Greece, in Crete, and most notably in the North African desert. When analyzing armor battles, they almost invariably attribute this superiority to the integrated use of *panzer* (tanks) and *pak* (antitank gun or *Panzerabwehrkanone*). In the attack, panzers led, with IFVs and *pak* following behind. In defense and when an enemy counterattack developed, the panzers immediately withdrew behind the *pak* screen, ready to fill gaps or to return to their primary role: attack and counterattack. Such tactics were also masterly implemented by the Russian army in the battle against the German offensive at Kursk in the summer of 1943 (Operation Zitadelle) in which the Germans lost whatever offensive capability was left or rebuilt after Stalingrad.[2]

The success of these tactics is remarkable indeed, especially since the weapons used were poor, certainly low-technology, in comparison to today's antitank guided weapons (ATGW):

Only relatively few *paks* were available.
The *pak* guns had the same caliber and often were even identical with the tank guns, i.e., they were superior neither in range nor effect on target.
They were heavy and difficult to handle, to camouflage, and to dig-in.
Their conspicuous signature gave their position away at the first round fired.
Their crews were very vulnerable to artillery or mortar fire.

Despite these handicaps, the tactics were successful. Their objective at first sight was to save the panzers for offensive action and to base the antiarmor battle on antiarmor weapons and to base defense on weapons optimized for defense. Underlying this concept was the intention not to smash the enemy where he is strongest by brute force, but to out-trick him by exploiting his weakness. In short, firepower bashing was avoided, tactics were utilized.

Thus a clear message was left by the Russian army at Kursk and by the German army in North Africa. However, the message was soon forgotten. Perhaps this happened because in both world wars, in the Korean War, and in Vietnam the armed forces of the United States and those of its allies invariably had the means to achieve and to sustain firepower superiority enabling them to opt for fixed position, attrition-style warfare over an emphasis on tactics and maneuver.

The result for NATO has been strong reliance on firepower. The tendency has been accentuated through a by-product of forward defense: ground must be held as far forward as possible and by all means reasonable. Such an approach has tended to restrict movement and enhance the importance of firepower. The development was capped by the effect of long-range weapons on tactics. HOT and TOW or indirect-fire weapons such as MLRS do not deny tactics. But they tend to emphasize frontal firepower exchange.

A development that occurred in the West German army is illustrative of this point. Upon its foundation in 1956, with successful World War II tactics in mind, *Panzerjäger* (antiarmor) became a branch of the army, parallel to infantry, armor, artillery, etc. A few years later, however, the branch was disbanded. Even chiefs of army staffs had stated "The best weapons against enemy tanks are friendly tanks." *Pak* was dead.

Today even a fleeting glance at the table of equipment (TOE) of any Western armored division and that of their former Warsaw Pact counterpart reveals startling differences:

Western nations have very few dedicated antiarmor systems and units; they are used almost solely for support of their (mechanized) infantry.

Therefore, when a division deploys for battle and, of necessity, deploys its infantry into the close terrain, the antiarmor battle in open terrain is left to the tanks operating independently or nearly independently. This leads to a straight duel: friendly tanks against enemy tanks. It is the opposite of what brought success in World War II.

Also, it is as if David had opposed Goliath not by a sling, but by trying to outdo Goliath "whose height was six cubits and a span, and he had a helmet of brass . . . and he was armed with a coat of mail . . . and he had greaves of brass upon his legs, and a target of brass between his shoulders, and the staff of his spear was like a weaver's beam and his spear's head weighted six hundred shekels of iron." Surely, David would have lost if he would have done as NATO armies do today.

Clearly, this is not the occasion to analyze the tactics of a specific branch in detail. The story of NATO's antiarmor philosophy is told only to illustrate one point: NATO's armies are in danger of emphasizing firepower at the expense of tactics and of trying to "solve" tactical problems not through better tactics but through additional firepower, i.e., more technology.

It may be useful to illustrate this point by a further example. During the last 200 or 300 years, the firepower of armies has increased dramatically. But human vulnerability has remained constant. Therefore, whoever will survive on the modern, fire-dominated battlefield, has only two options: either he must dig in or he must maneuver in an armored vehicle.

Obviously, the attacker cannot seek protection by digging in. Therefore, he needs armored vehicles for his combat troops (armor, cavalry, infantry) and for his combat support troops (artillery, antiaircraft, combat engineers) also. The organization of former Warsaw Pact divisions shows the consequences: there is no foot infantry whatsoever.

The situation of the strategic defender is different. Of course, he does need mechanized forces for counterattacks and for the defense of open terrain. But wherever the terrain permits, one would expect to see at least some foot infantry. Clearly it is nonsense to defend a wooded or built-up area with Leopard 2 and Abrams tanks or with Marders or Bradleys. Thus the defender can save the tremendous cost of mechanized forces and can considerably improve his tooth-to-tail ratio. But seldom do NATO armies adopt this solution. Why is this the case?

In NATO armies, the view is widespread that mechanized forces, i.e., tanks and IFVs have great firepower and excellent mobility. This view is certainly true as regards open terrain. But in a swampy forest or in wooded hills, such vehicles are essentially road-bound. Their off-road mobility is next to nil. Their firepower, especially at long ranges, cannot be utilized and quite possibly the gunner cannot even turn his turret. This illustrates that fire power and mobility are not absolute values. They are determined by the terrain over which they must operate: 30% of the central region is covered by woods, 10% are built-up areas, and much of the remaining 60% open terrain exists in small patches between forests and villages. Thus there are large areas that call for the mobility and the short-range weapons of infantry, foot infantry, which unfortunately is nowhere available in NATO and which at best are considered a concession to financial shortages. Therefore, such areas must be defended by mechanized forces who in close terrain are likely to resemble a beached whale: immense, once powerful, but wholly out of place and defenseless. Again, the infatuation of some army planners with high-tech, large machines, and long range at the expense of tactics is obvious.

SUMMARY

What conclusions can thus be drawn from the above analyses? Should one conclude that NATO forces are weak, are in dire need of improvement, are poorly trained, poorly equipped, have poor tactics, and probably even poor morale? Certainly not. There are many powerful reasons that suggest that many of the NATO nations' armed forces are of excellent quality in many and possibly even in every respect. But even those forces must develop further to meet the requirements of the future. Thus the call for further improvement of NATO' forces is a valid one and is applicable to the forces of all NATO nations, big and small, good and less good.

It would be prudent to seek such improvements keeping the following considerations in mind:

1. Of those factors that determine the combat capability of military forces—morale, training, weaponry, and tactics—weaponry is not number one and possibly it is number four only. Force improvement efforts that concentrate on weaponry to the detriment of the other factors are clearly deficient.

2. Concerning morale, the military are well advised to take note that in a highly individualistic society, a number of traditional military values must be jealously guarded.

3. The armed forces of some NATO nations are simply not well trained and in the absence of additional, intensive training are and will remain incapable of adequately using whatever high-capability equipment they might receive.

4. There is a clear danger of overemphasizing high tech, of NATO military leaders falling prey to the lure and lore of high tech with consequent neglect of opportunities offered by the more traditional technologies and especially of tactics.

NOTES

1. T. N. Dupuy, *Numbers, Predictions and War. Using History to Evaluate Combat Factors and Predict the Outcome of Battles* (Indianapolis: Bobbs-Merril, 1979), and *The Evolution of Weapons and Warfare* (London: Jane's, 1980).

2. See Bogislav von Bonin, "Die Schlacht von Kursk-Ein Modell für die Verteidigung der Bundesrepublik," in *Der Spiegel,* no. 48, Nov. 21, 1966: 42–53.

6

Mutual Structural Defensive Superiority: A New Security Philosophy and Elements of a New Force Structure Design

Horst Afheldt

This chapter identifies building blocs for a new security policy for central Europe. I develop my own alternative of a "Mutual Defensive Superiority" with conventional weapons as the focal point of a security doctrine for a new Europe that is in the process of overcoming post-World War II divisions.[1]

BUILDING BLOCS FOR A NEW SECURITY POLICY

On Developing a Criteria for Security Policy

Is Superiority the only Guarantor of Survival?

For centuries of human evolution, a general attitude has developed that the stronger one's own group is, the better and the more secure one will be. A security policy devoid of illusions must satisfy this basic human belief: security requires superiority. However, the simple call for superiority fails to provide an acceptable criterion for the security of Germany, of Europe, and of the NATO alliance. If there are two opposing countries or alliances, only one can be superior. In a bipolar world, the striving for superiority was therefore the equivalent of an arms race.

Thus, the experience of the postwar period shall be used to demonstrate the general problems of military security. This period has been characterized by both qualitative and quantitative arms races. Moreover, the qualitative arms race in which the West sought to balance superior Soviet conventional forces on the continent of Europe by developing and deploying nuclear weapons has led to the major dilemma of a nuclear-based security policy.

A Way Out of the Unsolvable Dilemma

Until the fall of 1989, the first cause for the dilemma of our security policy was probably the then adequate assumption that the Warsaw Pact could capture large parts of Western Europe if it attacked with conventionally armed troops and the

This chapter was completed in June 1990, just prior to Dr. Afheldt's retirement.

[1] This chapter has been translated into English by Hans Günter Brauch, language edited by Robert Kennedy and approved by the author. It is based on a condensed, revised, and updated version of the following sections in my book: *Der Konsens—Argumente für die Politik der Wiedervereinigung Europas* (Baden-Baden: Nomos, 1989), pp. 89–176.

West defended itself using only conventional weapons. This traditional threat perception was based both on the numerical superiority of Warsaw Pact forces and on historical experience that suggested that, given the present troop structure in East and West Europe, an attacker would have good chances for success, even if he were numerically inferior.

The second cause for the dilemma is the recognition that the industrial societies in central and in western Europe would be extremely vulnerable given their densely populated areas, their centralized supply systems for food, water, sewage, electricity, and gas, their chemical industry, and their nuclear reactors. So, even a conventional war of longer duration would destroy the European countries as industrial nations. Hence, it is and has been necessary to prevent any war, not just nuclear war. Such considerations resulted in a preference for nuclear escalation deterrent strategies, which, in contrast, created the unsolvable dilemma of NATO's current security policy.

In the early 1970s, it became obvious that this precarious dependence in Europe on nuclear escalation strategies had become much more persistent than originally predicted or promised. As a result, some defense analysts recognized a need to completely rethink Western defense strategies and enlarge the scope of alternatives beyond those that relied on nuclear weapons or on more and more modern conventional armaments.[2]

By the mid 1970s, the first studies were published that called for comprehensive revisions of defense policy in Europe.[3] Very rapidly it became evident to those involved in these studies that new approaches would require a complete scrapping of strategies that relied on old formulas for conventional defense and on nuclear escalation. In 1976 in my book *Defense and Peace,* I offered some answers to the problem. A multitude of proposals followed quickly in the area of security policy, military strategy, military tactics, and armament—proposals that have been largely ignored because they would not fit the military structure of the day. However, taken together these ideas did shed some new light and could be further developed to make up a new conceptual design. Most of these building blocs came from active and retired officers of the Bundeswehr.[4] Fundamentally new approaches had been developed in France and in Austria.[5] This independent development of similar concepts supported our basic assumptions. A few critical journalists helped to spread the message.[6] The traditional arms control school and its institutions[7] did not make any contribution.

Criteria for a Military Means of Security

From the many efforts identified above, the problems of NATO security policy were identified and the following criteria for a stable, effective Western security policy were derived:

Criterion 1. Stability in peace against (a) unprovoked attacks and (b) arms race.
Criterion 2. Stability in a crisis against: (a) military incentives for a preemptive attack and (b) war resulting from military escalation.
Criterion 3. Stability in war against escalation in a war that would destroy what is to be protected. This criterion demands the implementation of the following.
Criterion 4. Defense strategies and means must be selected that if employed would

not destroy our social and economic structure (which in turn demands the following criterion).

Criterion 5. An effective defense capability with conventional means against any conventional attack of the Warsaw Pact, even given its potential numerical superiority. (Based on this criterion, a further criterion may be deduced.)

Criterion 6. NATO's nuclear weapons may not be given a military task. No targets whose destruction would make military sense or could be decisive should be offered for the nuclear weapons of the opponent.

If one accepts the above criteria, one is opting for defense measures that, in fact, could actually be implemented (unlike those measures associated with nuclear weapons) if war prevention should fail and the worst should happen. Indeed acceptance of the above criteria is predicated on the belief that weapons should never be employed that would destroy the countries to be defended. Equally important, acceptance of the criteria is predicated on the belief that the threat to employ self-destroying options will have no, or only a very limited, war-preventing deterrence effect. A better war-preventing option would be to prepare for defense measures that could be implemented in the worst case.

To the above, however, a final criterion must be added if stability in Europe and a lasting peace is to be established. The capability to fight a war without a prior aggression by the Warsaw Pact has to be excluded. Criterion 7 clarifies this point:

Criterion 7. Military capabilities should be so structured that they can only be employed if an attack of the Warsaw Pact on our territory has taken place. This criterion calls exclusively for such military options that are reactive and defensive in nature. In essence it is a demand for a no first shoot army.

The Concert of a Criteria

One who attempts to formulate such criteria recognizes that any major reformulation is likely to yield criteria that partly contradict each other. Moreover, one who tries to optimize outcomes over a broad array of criteria often finds solutions that are not optimal for each individual criterion. However, it can be demonstrated that such limitations do not apply to the above criteria, even though certain criteria will limit the number of possible alternative solutions available for consideration.

The key factor for such a surprising result is criterion 5: defensive capability even if the aggressor is numerically superior. Such a defensive capability presupposes a strong superiority of the defense over the offense. A strong defensive superiority is not only compatible with most other criteria, necessarily it even combines many criteria. In our historical example: With a strong conventional defensive superiority, NATO no longer had required nuclear weapons for direct defense (criterion 6 is satisfied). This, in turn, would have made it possible to defend the Federal Republic of Germany without destroying it through the use of nuclear weapons (criteria 3 and 5 are thus automatically satisfied). In crises, a strong defense superiority removes any incentive to initiate a war because the aggressor is confronted with the probability of defeat through denial (criterion 2 is satisfied). However, it must be noted that the criterion of crisis stability reduces the number of defense options that can be employed. For example, time-consuming excavation work on tank barriers or for the preparation of defensive positions could give the attacker a premium for surprise attack and is therefore excluded.

Moreover, the two criteria of neither selecting a defensive option that would destroy what should be defended (criterion 5) nor offering any militarily significant and decisive targets the opponent could destroy with nuclear weapons (criterion 6) further limit the number of conceivable strategies for defensive superiority. This excludes, for example, the defense of villages and cities as fortresses against attacking tank forces. This also excludes purely defensive chains of nuclear mines at the frontier or other defensive nuclear concepts.

Different opinions may exist on the extent that the concept of the defensive superiority can reliably safeguard peace (criterion 1a: war prevention). In contrast, the criterion of preventing an arms race (criterion 1b) and of effective defensive superiority reinforce each other. The reason for this relationship is one of the most important characteristics of the defensive principle. This connection becomes obvious on closer examination.[8]

If an offensive capability can be obtained more cheaply than the defensive superiority, one may never expect to be able to establish a defensive superiority. If, in contrast, an attacker can only restore his offensive capability by investing much higher financial resources in new offensive equipment (e.g., new generations of tanks) that would be required of the defender to maintain or rebuild its defensive superiority, a further build-up of offensive armament would be economically foolish, and the threat to do so would no longer even be a good bargaining chip for arms control negotiations. As a consequence, defense superiority necessarily leads to arms limitations, if the cost-efficiency of such a specialized defense is so high that the conditions allow the establishment of defense superiority.

DEFENSE WINS

But How?

Given the structures of the armed forces of the Warsaw Pact and NATO at that time, defense does not win. Based on historical experience, both NATO and the Warsaw Pact correctly assumed that an aggressor who takes the initiative will obtain an advantage over the defender, even if the aggressor is numerically inferior.[9] This raises the question: What kind of defense would result in a superiority over the aggressor?

In the 1970s several authors who believed that an alternative defense was possible and who had tabled specific proposals predicted that some form of alternative defense could be realized in the 1990s. "Defense wins," Colonel Goblirsch concluded in 1977 in an article in which he argued that modern technology would make it possible in the 1990s, to locate, track, and destroy large military forces.[10] Based on such a perceived advance in weapons technologies specialized for the defense, a new doctrine based on defensive superiority could be seen as a realistic objective.

Initially it was only a plausible assumption that specialization for defense enhances its efficiency. It was based on the general experience of daily and of economic life that specialization allows a maximum payoff with respect to inputs and efficiency. No doubt, NATO's mission has never been to initiate conflict. NATO has not had a first-shoot mission. Indeed, its mission has been to avoid shooting first. But a no first shoot mission also requires a special force structure that permits waiting, but at the same time denies the aggressor success on the battlefield. Unfortunately, NATO's forces have not been effectively structured for this mission. Thus the question remains: How can a defense specialized structure be realized? What we do know is that corrections in one sector alone, e.g., the development of "defensive weapons systems," cannot solve the problem. In order to achieve defensive superiority, tactics, operative command, and military strategy all the way up to the grand strategy must be specialized for such a new mission also.

Weapons Specialized for the Defender?

Whereas the combination of tanks, mechanized infantry, and air support is the backbone of the modern offense, weapons systems that endanger such categories of offensive armament are fundamentally suited for the defense. During the Yom Kippur War, it became evident that tanks could be destroyed by infantry men employing modern antitank weapons from a distance of 1 to 2 km. At that time, one could foresee that more efficient antiaircraft missiles would be developed that also could be employed by infantry. Indeed, the war in Afghanistan demonstrated that an extremely efficient antiaircraft missile (Stinger) built by the Americans could be employed as a defense against attacks by sophisticated Soviet aircraft by reasonably unsophisticated Afghani infantry. Likewise, mine technology, always an important means for the defense, made major progress during the 1970s. Moreover, according to weapons manufacturers, precision munitions for mortars, cannons, and missiles will soon be available. Even if some capabilities have been oversold by industry, it is probably safe to assume that a decade from now many such weapons systems will be available if we give them a high priority for development now.

Today, many weapons systems similar to those mentioned above are being developed for today's armies as currently structured. However, they must fill requirements specified under present, primarily offensive, tactics and operative command. A specialization for the defense might remove a variety of systems requirements that constrain their efficient development and employment for a strictly defensive mission.

Tactics—Optimized for Defense?

Tactics of the Infantry in the Battle Against a Mechanized Aggressor

On a battlefield, the foxhole or similar shelter is the most secure place as long as one does not disclose one's location by shooting. To leave the foxhole or to shoot from it, to aim an antitank weapon and to direct it toward an attacking tank requires a heroic act. An effective defense concept should not be based on the fiction that a large number of heroes will be at hand for any length of time on the modern battlefield. This is true both for tactical military and primarily for human reasons. Ideal defensive tactics are realized by that soldier that counters the opponent from the protection of a *hidden* foxhole without disclosing his position by shooting. This ideal may never be fully realized. One should, however, attempt to come as close to it as is possible if one wishes to optimize one's defensive capabilities.

Fortified lines like the Maginot Line and "fortresses" constructed in peace with concrete and steel cannot be defended in this way. For such permanent locations will be known to the enemy and, of necessity, will inevitably disclose themselves through persistent fire. Hence, they can be easily and effectively attacked with the artillery and modern precision-guided munitions.[11] Even worse, field fortifications, fortified and defended cities, or Maginot Line type of defenses would provide targets that could be eliminated easily with nuclear or chemical weapons. Indeed, it could be argued that such defenses enhance the danger that the enemy might use nuclear weapons (a violation of criterion 6). As a result, the defense of fortresses plays no role in concepts that are seeking defensive superiority.

The primary goal of defensive defense concepts is to make the aggressor fail with his offense. For that aim, it is of much less importance exactly where his attack disintegrates. Dispersed defense that does not offer fixed targets and makes no effort to hold fortifications or fixed defensive lines is suited to the task. Such a defense concept has often been called "area defense." An extreme example of this concept is the proposal for an area defense by then French Major Brossollet who proposed an impenetrable and deep defense from the dividing line between East and West to the Alsace and the Benelux countries.[12]

By foregoing the requirement to defend fortified locations and fixed lines, a hidden mode of battle (what I called in 1976 autonomous techno-commandos) is made possible. Such a tactic for battle offers a defender new defense options. With a hidden defense, one can defend oneself not only against the first echelon of the aggressor, but also against his follow-on forces. Under artillery fire, for example, the defender may wait until the enemy's spearheads have passed by and attack the first echelon from behind or attack follow-on echelons.

To conduct an effective offensive against such a widely dispersed, hidden infantry is not an easy task. NATO standards, for example, assume that to obtain a 25% casualty rate against entrenched infantry, 12,000 artillery rounds per square km must be fired. If one assumes that on a dispersed battlefield, only 4 to 10 soldiers will operate in a square km, artillery becomes a very inefficient instrument.

Moreover, there is an unequal division of psychological burdens between the defender and the aggressor under such conditions. Whereas the defender is fighting from his shelter without revealing his position, the aggressor is permanently confronted with the paralyzing feeling that he is facing an invisible opponent with sudden fire, without knowing when and where he will be attacked and possibly killed, and without being able to defend against the assault.[13] The problem, of course, is how can a soldier fulfill his battle mission if he seldom leaves his shelter and if he cannot use direct fire in defense for fear of disclosing his position?

One approach would be to assign him the task of detonating prepared mine barriers. An additional, very effective option is the Milan tower,[14] which has been available since the late 1970s. The Milan tower includes a Milan missile mounted on a tripod, which is stationed some 100 m from the shooter who then can guide the missile by wire control. The tripod carries a TV camera that can be aimed at the target. On the monitor in his shelter, the shooter observes the target area of the Milan missile. If he sights a target on his screen for which he has a good shooting position, he can guide the missile using his monitor to the target. A single infantry man can, of course, direct several missiles of this kind hidden at different locations. It does not require much fantasy to extend these basic concepts to wireless, guided mortars stationed 10 to 15 km to the rear that could be directed by hidden artillery observers in the battle area to fight attacking enemy forces.[15] Today, artillery missiles may even be employed over distances that are greater than 40 km and that fire intelligent munitions that can effectively function against tank units. Indeed, the jumping mine (AT2) is already available for such a use. Moreover, better and more intelligent munitions will soon go into production.[16]

For some defensive tasks, observers may be replaced by sensors. For example, sensors might be used widely to protect the battle stations of the hidden defenders from surprise attacks. These sensors could be linked to other defensive means, such as to wireless guided machine guns that could be employed in such a way that they could control certain areas. The same tasks could also be performed by missiles and mortars delivering unsophisticated mines.

In general, the emerging picture is in some ways similar to the automated battlefield the United States designed in the 1960s for the protection of the demarcation line between North and South Vietnam. Even though those attempts failed, the principle remains valid. The automated battlefield envisaged by the United States for Vietnam was designed to hold off guerilla fighters by mechanized units of the U.S. Army. In the context of a defensive Western European defense, the task would be completely different: Guerillalike defenders would be protected against easily recognizable motorized aggressors. In addition, during the past 20 years, specifically designed technologies have been developed rather fast for this purpose.

Which Tactic Against the Air Force?

NATO relied on widely dispersed, highly mobile motorized units that must be concentrated for defense and for counterthrusts. As a result of the need to move and concentrate masses of tanks and motorized troops for defense, NATO was forced to maintain air superiority over the battlefield area in order to protect its forces from direct air attack. This involves a costly air effort. The need for air superiority dictates early attacks on enemy airfields to cripple enemy air forces and render his airfields unusable. Unfortunately, as both sides seek air superiority in an effort to protect their forces on the ground, an unstable situation is dramatically intensified by the introduction of missiles able to destroy airfields and even airplanes in shelters.

Instability in a crisis, high armament efforts (e.g., with the new European fighter aircraft (EFA) *Jäger* 90 and equivalent aircraft on the other side), more efficient attack missiles and low altitude flight exercises are inevitably required by such configurations. As long as one sticks to the basic concepts of employing fast-moving mechanized troops, which were developed before and during World War II, aircraft will remain necessary in order to protect tanks and to prepare their way. In turn, an opponent will need an air defense in order to protect his tanks and to guarantee their movements. Moreover, one needs an air defense to protect airfields and aircraft on those fields. Very soon, countermeasures against rockets will be needed to protect air defenses, and so on.

The best solution to that problem will be to use tactics for defense that offer no targets for enemy air forces. Troops that do not assemble in large units are not greatly endangered by the air forces of the opponent when they move to their defensive positions. Moreover, air power is nearly useless against a hidden and well-dispersed opponent. Moreover, an air enemy that overflies a wide area of hidden defenses never knows when he is really in danger because he cannot identify the defensive positions. Consequently, an attacking air formation cannot fly low without high losses. The high rate of losses of the Soviet air force in Afghanistan was partly due to this development. Moreover, since a well-hidden defender does not require the protection of his own air force, the problem of preserving that air force and its air fields is of reduced importance. However, the problem that must be solved is how to replace the firepower of the air force with another kind of firepower that can be employed as effectively, as fast, and across large distances in a concentrated manner.

Rocket Artillery

Modern technology offers a simple alternative: destroy the attacker directly with precision munition that can be launched by rockets from hidden locations. Such a defense would require artillery rockets with ranges of 40, 60, and 80 km that can be guided by observers from hidden shelters in the zone of combat against an identified enemy. Batteries that have fired once, however, can be located and identified and thus will invariably become the target of enemy fire. Therefore large rocket launchers, like the multiple rocket launcher system (MRLS), would contradict the logic of hidden defenses. Small packages of one to four cheap launch tubes armed with precision rockets to be used only once better serve this principle.

Such a system would offer an opportunity for a surprising concentration of fire within minutes against any point in a wide area of responsibility without any visible movement of launching pads. If one assumes, for example, that NATO's defense forces would have deployed in a depth of 80 km parallel to Warsaw Pact borders and in each square km five missiles each with a 40-km range are deployed, an aggressor that attacks along a 50-km front would find his forces crippled by 40,000 high precision rockets before he had advanced 50 km into the territory of the defender.[17]

Operative Command Specialized for the Defense: Everything That Can Go Wrong, Will (Murphy's Law)

Whereas Murphy's law has often been validated in civil life, it is even more relevant in war, "the area of the uncertain." This is what Clausewitz called the "frictions" of war. The history of war offers thousands of examples that raise serious questions as to whether the right decision will be made at the right moment. Even a correct decision that may lead to a particular military success may in the long run lead to a catastrophe. Nevertheless, NATO always believed that nuclear weapons will successfully deter, and, if deterrence fails, NATO would choose exactly the right nuclear option to force an opponent to end the war.

An opponent probably errs if he remains unpersuaded by a NATO threatened use of nuclear weapons and fails to withdraw or even to capitulate. But mistakes are not permitted to happen on either side under any circumstances when nuclear weapons are involved in what Clausewitz referred to as the "battle of wills." A single error could be deadly. If nuclear weapons remain the main pillar of security policy, the fate of the world depends on faultless decisionmaking on both sides. However, the history of war suggests that errors in decisions will be made.

Miscalculations can also be made that could lead to a long or intensive conventional war even if nuclear weapons were completely eliminated. The task, therefore, is to develop a strategy that increases the probability of defensive victory and that the probability of defeat can be demonstrated to a potential attacker beforehand.

It is the thesis of this author that such a strategy can be fashioned. The proposed strategy of defensive superiority relies on the same fundamental military considerations as the offensive superiority of World War II relied on but exploits them in reverse. In order to develop an effective strategy of defensive superiority, one must therefore examine the successful offensive strategies that were developed by Liddell Hart, Guderian, de Gaulle, and others prior to World War II and that made the deep striking attacks of World War II possible.

Whoever tries, as NATO has done, to defend a line successfully against an assumed Russian attack, whoever wants to win what was called "forward defense" must succeed in the following tasks:

• Recognize where the enemy is about the break through one's defense.
• Assess properly whether breakthroughs in other areas are probable in order not to spend remaining reserves too early.
• Correctly predict the direction of the enemy thrusts.
• Develop a concept for counterattack for one's own armed forces.
• Translate counterattack tasks into proper commands. These commands must follow these lines: brigade - division - brigade or: brigade - division - corps - division - brigade. On each level they must be correctly processed.
• Units that are to initiate counterattacks must be ready at the right time at the proper place.
• Units must correctly understand their orders.
• Units must not be interrupted by the activities of the enemy (e.g., by air strikes during their movement) in order to implement their orders at the right time.
• Forces for counterthrusts must arrive at the planned time, which is hopefully the correct time.
• Forces must arrive at the planned and (hopefully correct) place.

All such required actions for an effective forward defense may go well. However, if one assumes each of the above 10 requirements for an effective defense has, for example, an optimistic 90% probability of success (a utopian assumption in a war), the resultant overall probability of success would be only 35%. That means that there would be a 65% probability of failure. There may be one, two, or ten critical situations during a conflict, one failure is enough, and the thin and mobile defense will move in the direction of chaos.

With respect to the attacker, of course, everything will go wrong that can go wrong, too. But there are fewer activities and events on which the success of an attack depends. His decision chains are shorter. Historical experience on the superiority of modern mechanized armies is based on that statistical foundation. In other words, today the aggressor exploits Murphy's law in his favor while the defender fights the uncertainties of war, the mischances of Murphy's law. By exploiting Murphy's law in war, the offensive strategy of Guderian, de Gaulle, and Liddell Hart could overcome the traditional argument that "defense is stronger than the offense if one presupposes the same means." Thus it becomes understandable why small offensive mobile forces can beat larger mobile forces.

The Basic Paradigm of Defense With
the Second Shot

Whereas the offensive strategy in World War II deliberately reduced the chain of actions and decisions for the aggressor, the concepts of defensive superiority hold out the promise of reducing the decision chain for the defense. To achieve that effect, a net of defensive forces must be stationed in a territory soldiers know. Thus both in peace and in a conflict, the defender can prepare his defense. He is equipped with mines, antitank rockets, precision mortars, and air defense systems. The net of defensive forces is assisted by a net of wide-ranging artillery that is ready on request to concentrate fire in any selected area.

Such a network will require only short chains of command. Each unit, each module of this net, from the very beginning of the crisis has the same order: harm the attacker as much as possible, smash as much of his warfighting machinery as possible while minimizing your own losses. In such a defense, a fiasco in one engagement does not reduce the chances of success elsewhere. Even a complete disaster in one "module" does not lead to a breakdown of the whole system. Under such circumstances, the offense will fight against Murphy's law, not the defense. Indeed, such a network defense may obtain a maximal defense effectiveness of 90% compared with 35% or less for forces structured as NATO forces in the Cold War period (and even today). Breakthroughs would not be possible if the defensive net has adequate depth. Moreover, the incentive, frequently strong, to force success through the employment of one's remaining reserve forces and means will be denied the enemy from the very beginning. As a result, one factor that might contribute significantly to the rigor of the offense would be eliminated.

In sum, what is being offered here is a military strategy that relies on modern weapons technologies, is based on tactics that take advantage of a soldier's natural instinct for self-preservation, give that soldier and his unit more leverage for independent activities, and whose principles of operative command statistically optimize the probability of defeating offensive forces. Such a defense will inevitably demotivate the attacker from the tactical to the strategic level and limit collateral damage of one's own territory. Indeed, today it is possible to make defense the strongest form of battle again. The political and strategic goal of NATO remains unchanged: defense against eventual Russian or other infringements and pressures. This new doctrine, however, will do what the old doctrine of flexible response could never do. Indeed, one could say in the old NATO terminology that defensive defense, structural defensive superiority in Europe, is not only the appropriate response, it is the flexible reaction to the disappearance of the old Soviet threat.

MUTUAL CONVENTIONAL DEFENSE
SUPERIORITY

The Ideal of Structural Defensive Superiority
and Political Reality

New doctrines and "models" for security offer the promise of increased stability, only if the result is new relationships between adversaries on a potential battlefield. If new proposals and reality cannot be combined in a way that will lead to better security than what has been offered by the old thinking, the "new thinking" will remain an intellectual game without any relevance.

The proposals for the armament, tactics, operative command, logistics, etc., of the "ideal" military force for the maintenance of peace in central Europe that have been developed above are completely opposite to Guderian's ideals of an offensive army. Thus they were in complete contrast to NATO reality as well. As Guderian was never able to realize his ideal army, none of the proponents of alternative defense models believe that an optimal structurally defense and superior army can be realized quickly. However, both the offensive armies of Fuller, de Gaulle, and Guderian and the models of armies with defensive superiority have a specific task: to serve as a guide for the development of new military means of politics that corresponded with the political objectives of the time. In reality, both politics and the military leadership have to live with transition models. Thus the realization of the new concepts is confronted with the constraints of the existing political and military reality. But that reality has fundamentally changed since 1989. The concept of defensive superiority has been devised as a way out of the cold war confrontation. So it is as much a child of that confrontation as nuclear deterrence theories have been. Concrete proposals were developed in the framework of the defense of western Europe at the former border between the two German states prior to unification. Yet as of July 1, 1990, that border disappeared. No military concept can be judged outside the political context. But today a very different political context is developing in Europe. There is, on the one hand, the development of a "European house" with all its variants for a distribution of rooms between the Europeans and the superpowers. On the other hand, there is the risk that the cold war confrontation could be revived through a adverse turn of events, especially in the Commonwealth of Independent States. Moreover, military concepts themselves may have a serious effect on the developing political environment.

As a result, very different outlines from those that have characterized the "cold war" period should be considered. Nevertheless, since the concept of "defense superiority" was developed during the cold war, it is not difficult to present a concrete proposal for a fallback position should developments in Europe force a return to cold warlike confrontations. So I start with the worst prospect, the revival of confrontations in Europe under the assumption that in spite of the unification of Germany, the division into two competing camps in Europe endures. I also outline a posture for the defense in Europe that will be effective in such a worst case, but at the same time promotes the process of the future unification of Europe.

Structural Defensive Superiority in a Divided Europe: Denial Instead of Deterrence

At What Cost?

The procurement of new conventional precision-guided munitions to support defensive concepts is likely to involve additional costs. Moreover, new weapons systems are only one part of what would be needed for a transition from old structures to new ones. If defense is to be effective against a potential surprise attack, if it is to contribute to crisis stability, then both the troops and equipment must be located close to their site of employment. Such a deployment would be consonant with the principle of engaging defenders in war within the same area in which they exercise during peace time. Needless to say this increases their advantage over an aggressor who would be less familiar with the terrain. It would also require a redeployment of troops and new barracks. This implies additional cost.

In contrast, defensive concepts do not need the very costly weapons systems that were required to support deep strike concepts or the Rogers plan (Follow-on Forces Attack—FOFA). Furthermore, the high procurement costs for air defense sites and defense systems to defend air forces and airfields against missiles no longer would be required. Likewise, the multibillion-dollar EFA project would become superfluous. Thus the principal constraints to adopting such a concept are not financial, but rather political.

A Tribute to the Traditional Political Views

For 40 years, the defense of Europe with conventional means appeared to be impossible. For 40 years, we became accustomed to the surrogate for effective defense: nuclear deterrence with all its advantages and disadvantages. No wonder that it is now difficult to relinquish this surrogate for defense. Proponents of the traditional view still dispute the notion that conventional denial can replace nuclear deterrence. As long as the belief is strongly held that the threat of mutual suicide cannot be renounced and as long as it determines political and military decisions, new thinking, new military strategies, and new weapons procurements will be constrained by old approaches.

Frontal Battle or Forward Defense?

Another obstacle for the introduction of a new defense-strategy is the myth of forward defense. The closer forces are positioned to the border, the less depth they have to contain a possible breakthrough by an aggressor. Therefore, the farther forward the defense, the greater is the advantage of the aggressor. As a result, the likelihood that the forward defense will become a true defense and thus be able to stop the enemy is slim. The result has been threats that any attack by an aggressor would lead to a nuclear catastrophe.

Only a deeply structured defensive defense net can provide an effective forward defense by denying the territory to an aggressor, at the same time limiting the potential destruction of a defensive battle. Such a defensive net should begin at the border. The only form of attack that might offer some promise of success against such a defensive net would be a highly concentrated attack in small corridors. Only in such a way could an aggressor choose to be confronted with fewer barrier and defensive weapons. If an aggressor selected such a strategy, destruction would be limited to the small corridors. Moreover, the defender could further reduce collateral damage in these corridors by choosing the areas where he wishes to fight and where he would prefer not to fight in order to minimize noncombatant casualties and damage to civilian facilities. A highly mobile, mechanized "forward defense" concept does not offer such an option.

"To Restore Territory"—or War Termination?

Prior to NATO's "Rome Declaration" of November 1991, both NATO and the German defense ministry supported the impression that it would be the NATO strategy to restore all territory that was lost as the result of an attack by the former Warsaw Pact and nothing more. However, this suggested objective is the least likely of all. Why? First, how would NATO have restored lost territory when it claimed to be so conventionally inferior that it needed nuclear weapons not only for deterrence but also for "direct defense?" Nuclear weapons were hardly suitable for restoring lost territory. Second, cities could hardly be defended by NATO nor could they be reconquered. NATO lacked the needed infantry divisions. Yet, it was a special aspect of NATO strategy not to defend cities nor to try to reconquer them, since that would have killed the civilian population and destroyed what was to be protected.

Whereas defensive concepts would contribute more effectively to the protection of territory, they would not contribute to a restoration of the territory. However, the restoration of territory is no end in itself, but a means to terminate the war according to conditions that are acceptable to the defender. If the means for a restoration of the territory are not available, other means have to be found. In the nuclear age, the task of military forces on the battlefield can only be to provide the time needed for a political termination of the conflict. In this regard, concepts of defensive defense do have an advantage over concepts that build on nuclear force components, simply because defensive concepts are nonescalatory in nature. Once an attack has been stopped, defensive defense concepts allow time for negotiations that would not occur if more dramatic military approaches were employed. War termination remains a problem for all thinkable strategies. However, unrealistic demands for a military reconquering of territory implies a catastrophic lack of realistic preparations for war termination and is likely to have negative consequences for the optimization of military forces for defense. The problem of war termination requires much more work both for the theorists and for the practitioners. Such work should no longer be postponed.

NOTES

1. In the view of this author, an ideal security and political context of the unification of Germany and for the realization of defensive superiority would have been a membership of a united Germany in both alliances. This proposal has been overtaken by events after the agreement between Chancellor Kohl and President Gorbachev of Shelevedosk of July 16, 1990 in which the Soviet Union accepted the NATO membership of a united Germany. See for the rationale of this proposal, developed in Feb. 1990, Horst Afheldt, "European Security and German Unity," in Horst Afheldt, Hans Günter Brauch, Malcolm Chalmers, Jonathan Dean, eds., *German Unity and the Future European Order of Peace and Security* (Mosbach: AFES Press, 1990).

2. See H. Afheldt, Ch. Potyka, U. P. Reich, Ph. Sonntag, and C. F. von Weizsäcker, *Durch Kriegsverhütung zum Krieg* (Munich: Hanser, 1972), pp. 131–135.

3. See, e.g., Max Himmelheber's "deterring defense" concept, in *Eine andere Verteidigung?* (Munich: Hanser, 1973).

4. Especially from Brig. Gen. Eckard Afheldt, Colonel J. Goblirsch, Maj. Gen. Jochen Löser, the Belgian General R. Close, Lt. Col. Norbert Hannig (Ret.), Maj. Gen. J. Gerber (Ret.), Lt. Col. A. Mechtersheimer. Also see the fundamental critique of the then Col. Franz Uhle-Wettler, *Gefechtsfeld Mitteleuropa—Gefahr der Übertechnisierung von Streitkäften* (Koblenz: Bernard & Graefe, 1980). See also the previous chapter by Lt. Gen. Uhle Wettler (Ret.), former commander of the NATO Defense College.

5. Emil Spannocchi and Guy Brossollet, *Verteidigung ohne Schlacht* (München: Hanser, 1976); see also the original version of Guy Brossollet, *Essai sur la non-bataille* (Paris: Editions Berlin, 1975).

6. See especially the former security correspondent of the Süddeutsche Zeitung, Christian Potyka, "Gesucht: Eine Drohung Ohne Bluff," in *Süddeutsche Zeitung,* Nov. 17, 1976: 9.

7. See especially the International Institute for Strategic Studies in London, the Stiftung Wissenschaft und Politik in Ebenhausen or the German Society for Foreign Policy (DGAP) in Bonn. Initially, there were no conceptual inputs from German universities and from peace research institutes.

8. The following section is based on my book *Defensive Verteidugung* (Reinbek: Rowohlt, 1983), p. 43.

9. See Chapter 5 in volume II of this series.

10. Joseph Goblirsch: "Technotaktik—90" in *Europäische Wehrkunde,* 26, no. 6 (1977): 283–228.

11. This point should not be overstressed. For example, towers of dismantled tanks on a small concrete socket are very difficult to destroy, even if the position is known in theory (one element of the Austrian defense). Since modern tank towers are fully automatized, one soldier can direct some such towers from a foxhole, distant of the towers, with a good chance of survival.

12. Brossollet, *Essai sur la non-bataille,* p. 80.

13. J. F. C. Fuller described the fear of the British troops in the war with the Boers in his book *Die entartete Kunst Krieg zu führen* (Cologne: Verlag Wissenschaft und Politik, 1964), p. 152.

14. This has been developed and demonstrated by the German armament company Messerschmidt-Bölkow-Blohm (MBB).

15. This system is called Bussard and it is being developed by the German armament company Diehl.

16. See an article on the Sadarm-Missile-System and on the wide area mine in *New Scientist,* Jan. 7, 1989: 34.

17. See for further details my book, *Defensive Verteidigung,* pp. 89–90; for other examples see Norbert Hannig, *Abschreckung durch konventionelle Waffen. Das David-Goliath Prinzip* (Berlin: Berlin Verlag Arno Spitz, 1984); Norbert Hannig, *Verteidigen ohne zu bedrohen—Die DEWA Konzeption als Ersatz der NATO-FOFA* (Mosbach: AFES-Press, 1988).

7

In Support of Stability in Central Europe: The SAS Proposal and Its Implications

Lutz Unterseher

This chapter concentrates on the future military protection of central Europe.[1] NATO's conventional defense of central Europe has been criticized for its many problems and failings. Increasingly, there is the impression that the Western posture comprises force elements that can be perceived as provocative, and that these components (for example, armored divisions, "air cavalry," and fighter-bomber wings) dominate NATO's defense structure, especially in Germany.

Since the early 1980s, NATO has developed forces for operational counterattack in order to neutralize the perceived threat from the East. In the eyes of many conservative military analysts in the West, the then Soviet concept of operational thrusts required as an adequate response the stimulation of operational thinking within NATO, and, as a consequence, the creation of a relatively large maneuvering mass. Dieter Senghaas, a German peace researcher, has called this kind of imitation the "sovietization" of the Western alliance.

Currently, NATO continues to develop its operational potential. However, the concept of operational and, now, strategic mobility has been provided with a new rationale. *Conventional disarmament,* it is said, could undermine the defender's stand because it would lead to force-to-space ratios insufficient for holding terrain. The solution to this problem is seen in enhancing the agility and offensive capabilities of virtually all remaining forces. To such a frame of mind, aggressive mobility is the key to defensive area control.

If all parties were developing their postures along these lines, the resulting provocation, embedded in the respective military structures, could turn out to be quite problematic. Assuming relative stability of detente as a major political trend, there may not be the danger of an armed clash. Yet a halt in the further process of disarmament could well occur if new concerns about military stability were arising.

Unfortunately, the Western posture not only has provocative aspects, but it also exhibits considerable vulnerabilities such as extreme force concentrations and overcentralized mobilization procedures. Moreover, the high demands of an all-mobile, all-purpose structure with its unfavorable teeth-to-tail ratio (combat vs. support) raise grave problems of long-term sustainability. Even if the process of disarmament leads to a substantial reduction in troop strength and the quantity of main weapon systems, new qualitative arms dynamics, resulting from technologically very demanding operational concepts, can consume most of the savings the arms controllers hope for.

These and other inconsistencies at the conventional level have led to a reliance on atomic weapons. Today, however, given the changes in the former Soviet Union and in Eastern Europe, as well as flagging public support for a full-blown nuclear deterrent with all its war-fighting implications, continued reliance on such weapons to deter war in Europe must be questioned.

Obviously there is a need for an alternative more compatible with the process of detente and disarmament. This chapter presents a detailed concept, proposed by the International Study Group on Alternative Security Policy (SAS),[2] and demonstrates that such an alternative is not unrealistic and should be regarded as a legitimate choice.

ON THE MEANING
OF CONFIDENCE-BUILDING DEFENSE

The proposed new scheme has been called the *"confidence-building defense."* Indeed, such a scheme promises to create trust in a double sense in that it offers to one's neighbors a minimal offensive potential while ensuring effective protection of one's own population.

Definition

The idea of confidence-building defense can be condensed into the following four maxims:

1. Military forces should be made structurally unable (and have no doctrinal foundation) to invade or bombard an adversary's territory. This principle of non-provocation can be seen as stabilizing in an international crisis because there would be no immediate reason for the other side to launch a preemptive strike.

In this context it is noteworthy that not only invasion potentials but also capacities for deep-reaching (air) strikes are to be abolished or substantially restricted. Typically, the military effectiveness of deep strike assets very much depends on their early use, before the other side has dispersed its forces for combat. This rationale of an early use would bring political decisionmaking under time pressure, which could prove counterproductive in times of crisis.

2. Structural vulnerabilities should be minimized. This demands: (a) military capabilities that restrict rather than extend the battlezone; (b) defenses that are virtually safe from being overrun, bypassed, or "outmaneuvered" technically and tactically; (c) mobilization procedures that are robust; and (d) more generally, force structures that do not present ripe targets for enemy fire. The minimization of vulnerabilities, and in particular the no target principle, eliminates military opportunities for a potential opponent and so reduces the likelihood of preemption in the course of a crisis (again: crisis stability is enhanced).

3. Even in times of detente, any responsible defense policy must take into consideration that the mechanisms of war avoidance, dealt with above, might fail. Consequently, there is a clear case for force structures that limit rather than extend damage. The requirement of damage limitation suggests the need for a practically feasible defense and rules out options that might permit a minor skirmish to develop into a doomsday scenario. Such an approach increases the credibility of the defender. This is a quality that, after all, can be regarded as the most important

precondition for averting open military conflict. Damage limitation is one's ability to minimize the structural vulnerabilities of the defensive posture. But, in this context, it is equally important to avoid escalation. This means that offensive capabilities should be extremely restricted. It is also quite evident that nuclear weapons for war-fighting purposes do not meet the requirements of preventing escalation. (Nuclear strategists must still answer the question of how the use of atomic weapons can be limited or controlled if an adversary can respond in kind.)

4. The defender's inherent advantage of operating on familiar terrain should be optimally exploited. This implies the adoption of specialized defensive force structures with tailored weapons mixes. The defender would no longer need to "answer in kind" by matching his opponent's formations of armor or fighter bombers with similar elements in greater number or quality or both. Rather, he would develop different, less expensive structures that are effective only as long as they are used to defend one's own territory.

It should be added here that other important steps may be taken that could contribute to a decoupling from the arms race. NATO could undertake a bold rationalization of national forces in conjunction with improved schemes of burden-sharing by seeking a better "division of labor." National forces could become more complementary rather than remaining all-round military machines.

Such a policy would ease the strain on public expenditure budgets, given that long-term economic growth expectations for most Western partners are moderate and that other competing demands on the governments' resources can count on continuing or even increasing political support. Social welfare, programs to promote the competitiveness of national industries, environmental protection, etc., are likely to increase. Already quite a few NATO countries have confined their defense expenditures to a constant, or even declining, share in overall public spending. This, however, has occurred before any significant changes have been made in the direction of a confidence-building defense. As a consequence, the conflict between budgetary constraints and the traditional cost dynamics of arms procurement for current force structures tends to paralyze long-term defense planning.

Argumentation

The definition given for a confidence-building defense concurs with the idea of war avoidance through denial. Its rationale is supported by historical evidence, in particular in a study conducted by the American analyst John J. Mearsheimer.[3] This study suggests that the outbreak of war, or the beginning of strategic offensives, can be best explained in the context of structural conditions prevailing at the time of the respective historical incident.

The more concentration for the offense on the one side, the more fears are raised on the other. Moreover, by concentrating for offense, one weakens the coverage of other sectors of home territory. This results in greatly improving the adversary's chances, provoked as he feels, of successfully exploiting one's less protected flanks by striking preemptively.

There is an opposing school of thought that could be called "deterrence through conventional retaliation." The advocates of conventional retaliation have concluded from two-person-zero-sum games that a potential aggressor can be induced to abstain from attacking by putting his home territory at risk. This approach has best been illustrated by Samuel Huntington:

> For a prospective attacker, the major difference between denial and retaliation concerns the certainty and controllability of the costs he may incur. If faced simply with a denial deterrent, he can estimate how much effort he will have to make and what his probable losses will be in order to defeat the enemy forces and achieve his objective. He can then balance these costs against the gains he will achieve . . . the choice is his. If, however, he is confronted with a retaliatory deterrent, he may well be able to secure the gains he wants with relatively little effort, but he does not know the total costs he will have to pay and those costs are in large measure beyond his control.[4]

The argument that the costs of denial can be calculated by an aggressor, whereas the potential costs of conventional punishment cannot, appears to be badly flawed. Indeed, if the risk of an aggressor consisted "only" in a good chance of being defeated in the course of a conventional assault on Western Europe, that would be sufficient. No further punishment options would be needed. An initial defeat caused by a strong denial-type defense would leave the aggressor in a situation of utter incalculability.

Besides that, the concept of deterrence through conventional retaliatory capabilities should be criticized for not sufficiently taking into account the danger of a crisis getting out of hand. Worse, it may even contribute to such a development. This is particularly important as a large and increasing proportion of independent political and military analysts in Europe consider intentional war far less likely than the danger of an "ordinary" political conflict developing into an open clash (although, for the time being, it is hoped that the process of detente remains strong enough to prevent such a disaster).

Finally, one should not ignore the fact that the advocates of conventional retaliation have based their reasoning on experimental games whose results are not really transposable to the macro-world of nation states and political alliances. Nonetheless these advocates see themselves in line with "long-standing traditions in strategic thought."[5] It can be demonstrated, however, that their use of historical evidence is irritatingly selective.[6]

Design

Early concrete concepts of non-offensive or alternative defense have envisaged a military posture that looked quite bizarre and, in any case, very different. Let us take, for example, Horst Afheldt, the German peace researcher, and his model, which provides a picture of strictly defensive land forces while totally leaving out air and naval assets.[7]

Afheldt's proposal of a "pure" alternative consists of nothing but numerous small techno-commandos in virtually total dispersion. These little infantry teams basically rely on just one type of line-of-sight weaponry, namely antitank guided weapons. Via network communication, they can call upon fire support from numerous, dispersed launchers of rocket artillery. There is no counterconcentration of defending troops because this could, according to Afheldt, develop into provocative, offensive capabilities. Generally, movement of troops is substituted for by mobility of fire.

Afheldt's idea of a radical dispersal of forces, getting a multitude of unimportant targets instead of relatively few important ones, has been very attractive to other alternative force designers. Moreover, the proposal to solve the problem of counterconcentration by the flexible application of precision-guided fire, rather than moving around clumsy, noisy, and frightening armor, appeared to be quite charming to some of the community of defense experts.

However, a sober net assessment of this concept suggests a number of problems. A technical and tactical monoculture is created. The structure of such a defense is too simple, and its array of sophisticated weapons far too homogeneous. Such a posture lacks that particular kind of complexity that puts an intruder on the "horns of a dilemma"[8] and therefore invites the optimization of countermeasures. Although Afheldt, in his personal presentations, has tried to make it quite clear that "defensivity" does not just mean buying the right kind of weapons, he has been frequently misunderstood in this respect. Some authors have drawn profit from this misunderstanding. They have portrayed themselves as champions of alternative defense through emphasizing "advanced, light, defensive" technology, at the same time ventilating the idea of conventional punishment.[9]

Since Afheldt's early works, more advanced proposals for a confidence-building defense have evolved, which put more emphasis on the development of defensive yet flexible structures as the basis for tailoring an adequate weapons mix. In selecting weapons and other equipment for such a mix, cautious pragmatism appears to be appropriate. So-called defensive technologies (particularly if highly sophisticated) often are not as cost-effective as their proponents claim.

In the debate about more advanced proposals, Spider and the Web is a key paradigm. The concept, as developed by SAS,[10] envisages the close cooperation of a network of relatively light forces committed to particular areas with highly agile elements for quick reinforcement. Through area control and attrition, the former "prepares the ground" for the latter. As a result, the allocation of mobile forces is greatly optimized. This is why they can be rather small. Along with the covering potential of the dispersed web forces, this very feature guarantees a relatively low target profile of the defense.

Moreover, the smallness of the mobile element and the fact that its effectiveness very much depends on the shelter of the network, minimizes the provocative potential, which is inherent in any flexible defensive posture. Such an approach has been called a case of synergism in which two structural elements of robust simplicity are combined in such a manner as to present a potential invader with deadly complexity ("the horns of a dilemma"). He would have to move in an environment against the resistance of network forces or the flanking threat of heavier mobile elements, or both. He would thus lose the initiative, being unable to adjust adequately to actual battle conditions.

Interestingly, Spider and the Web seems to be a more universally accepted principle among those seeking alternative approaches to defense in Europe. With equal plausibility one could conceive of:

A maritime defense based on a network of coastal monitoring stations, and land-to-sea missile batteries, guarding minefields in the immediately adjacent waters, with fast-attack craft forming the interventionary element.

An air defense consisting of a network of radar stations and observation posts, interconnected "clusters" of surface-to-air-missile (SAM) positions, and a force of interceptors controlling the unprotected areas as well as the air space above the missile shield.

A ground defense comprising light, dispersed, but interconnected infantry forces, possibly backed up by (or consisting of) some kind of "home guard," with small components of armor, mechanized infantry or cavalry loitering nearby, to be able to quickly exploit the trapping function of the underlying web structure.

All this sounds familiar to the military mind. And, indeed, some of the above mentioned features already exist in some countries (e.g., Austria, Finland, Sweden, Norway, and Denmark), and even in central Europe as reflected at least partially in NATO's air defenses.

Quantitative Dimensions

As of June 1992, the Federal German armed forces (Bundeswehr) had roughly 450,000 soldiers under arms. The Bundeswehr's wartime strength would be 900,000 men. There also were some 300,000 foreign allied troops stationed on West German territory. In the event of a crisis or war, these forces could nearly be doubled within a matter of weeks.

It is claimed that through defensive specialization alone, the SAS concept would permit significant reductions in active as well as reserve personnel. This means that, even without further reductions in the military potential of the CIS, in other words: without going beyond the CFE results, confidence-building defense opens the road to unilateral cuts in NATO forces. In this context, a reduction of the Bundeswehr's active strength to 300,000 soldiers appears to be militarily justified. Likewise, the number of active allied troops could be brought down to about 100,000 soldiers or less. The size of the respective reserve potentials would be reduced accordingly.

Such independent measures of disarmament through defense-oriented "transarmament" could stimulate bilateral processes of arms reductions. These could be based on continued formal negotiations on Conventional Forces in Europe (CFE), or on a "gradualist" approach (a "downward spiral" of actions and reactions aiming at disarmament), or on a combination of both of these policies.

Assuming that the process of detente remains stable and that bilateral action proves to be productive, even more drastic cuts in NATO's military potential in central Europe can be envisaged. Within the next 8–9 years, a build-down of Germany's standing forces to 200,000 soldiers and the shrinking of the respective allied element to 50,000 soldiers appears to be technically feasible.

THE SERVICES IN THE SAS MODEL

Land Forces

Structure

The defense of central Europe should be based on three main elements:[11]

1. Network infantry composed of 250 (150) battalions, each assigned to a fixed area, 7–10 interlinked zones of key, stralegic importance. All battalions of network

infantry are skeletonized with 25% active personnel. The mobilization mode is decentralized, simple, and robust.

2. A mobile force under armor protection of about 100 (75) combat battalions is partly positioned on the western side of the former demarcation line, but principally deployed within the area-covering infantry scheme. For high effectiveness (through optimal exploitation of terrain conditions), this mobile element breaks down into three structurally different components: armor, cavalry, and light mechanized infantry. These are more streamlined and handier than current equivalents. Unlike the area-covering infantry scheme, which relies on lateral communication, the mobile element is organized hierarchically, with a somewhat straightened chain of command. This element's personnel is about 90% active, which means that the mobile units can protect the network infantry during mobilization.

3. The homeguard serves to protect infrastructure (logistics, roads, bridges, etc.) against airborne, commando, and other lower level threats. It is a light, interconnected object defense with a few mobile formations (motorized/ mechanized) for flexibility. The homeguard is skeletonized to a high degree and has relatively old equipment. It is omitted in the discussion below.

Operations

The network infantry (or web) is well protected against concentrated artillery barrages, able to disappear in dispersed shelters, which could be rapidly constructed from prefab parts, and has an organic extrication capacity. Network infantry can be expected to fulfill the following tasks:

Combat function. This comprises delaying action, gradual attrition, and the splitting up and canalizing of intruding forces. These purposes mainly require randomized obstacle systems (barriers) and a flexible component of indirect fire.

Covering function. This implies that network infantry is able to block or decimate rapid avantgardes (including heliborne assaults) to such a degree that one's own mobile counterattack forces could march virtually unhindered and undetected. This can be even better accomplished by making extensive use of electronic countermeasures and dummy targets.

Supportive function. This includes a diversity of tasks such as the continuous collection and provision of information (particularly to defending mobile forces), and the protection as well as operation of a decentralized system of stationary depots in the network area. This latter task could lighten the logistical burden of the mobile forces.

Military-political function. This refers to the web's capacity to maintain coherent area control along with a clear picture of where one's own and the adversary's forces are. Given the fact that the web, with its delaying and covering potential, buys time, the overview of the situation may serve as a basis for rational political decisionmaking.

The mobile element interacts with the web like a spider. Whereas the web forces are of a low density (even if their assets of indirect fire permit considerable concentration), the spider forces are capable of massing for certain, preferably short, periods of time. They block, contain, counterattack, and ultimately destroy intruding formations. It is not only that the mobile element profits from the web.

Conversely, the web also benefits from the support of the spider formations. The latter either extricate exposed network infantry or help in "repairing the meshes," depending on the situation. Generally speaking, spider and web form a deep and flexible, coherent defense, one that is extremely difficult or impossible to bypass, outmaneuver, or leap over.

Technology

It is structure that determines defensivity, not the acquisition of "defensive" weapons as such. Antitank guided weapons, for instance, would take on quite an offensive meaning if given to light motorcycle infantry, trained and organized for deep infiltration, rather than to a network of forces structurally confined to the protection of given areas of land. Consequently, the SAS weapons mix is not fundamentally different from NATO's arsenal for the conventional defense on friendly territory. There is a shift of emphasis, however, in favor of more and denser underground communications, more prefab elements for small-size field fortifications, plenty of (multisensor) mines, remote control of light direct-fire weapons (less exposure of infantrymen), more rapid-fire mortars, more shoulder-fired SAMs, and the introduction of fiber-optically guided missiles (Fog-M). In contrast, other, generally more expensive, categories of equipment would be present in substantially reduced quantities: tracked and wheeled armored vehicles with high-velocity cannon, mechanized tube and rocket artillery (ranges up to near 50 km) and multipurpose helicopters with antitank capability.

Weapons for deep strike purposes are rejected not only because of their destabilizing characteristics, but also for their high-tech exoticism. Disquiet has in any case been expressed over the cost-effectiveness of such assets, and the benefits of very sophisticated weaponry for the defense have yet to be demonstrated.[12]

In the course of a continued thinning-out of military manpower, the technological emphasis would have to shift further, namely, to fiber-optical network communications, integrated sensor fields, and modern means of "shallow"-range indirect fire (such as advanced mortars and FOG-Ms).

Air Defense

In principle, a ground force posture with a much reduced target profile facilitates the air defense task of protecting friendly troops from enemy fighter bombers. As a result, the accent can be shifted to the protection of civilian infrastructure with the object of neutralizing the potential threat of terror attack.

The air defense itself should have a low target profile, thereby contributing to the tactical frustration of an opponent's fighter bomber and missile forces. Offensive counter-air (OCA) capabilities should be given up, not only because successful operations against the other side's fighter bombers still on the ground demand surprise (which could mean preemption or putting political decisionmaking under time pressure), but also because there is an aggravating problem of effectiveness.[13] OCA does not enjoy the particular advantages of defensive counter-air over friendly territory; namely, a close association with a ground-based monitoring and missile organization.

In view of these considerations, a future air defense in central Europe would comprise the following elements:

A surface-to-air missile organization with clustered positions for the protection of military and civilian infrastructure. This ground-based air defense scheme, almost the same size as NATO's current system, should be continuously modernized, upgraded technologically, hardened, better dispersed, and well camouflaged.

A force of 500 (300) light air defense fighters that would operate in the space between the ground-based missile clusters as a means of flexible concentration within a static pattern. These planes, derivatives of existing models, should have STOL (short take-off and landing) capability and be supported by a mobile base infrastructure that could, as a matter of course, make use of makeshift runways (stretches of roads).

Such an air defense posture, as already indicated, could dispose of all fighter bombers for deep penetration. If these cannot all be scrapped unilaterally, their destruction may be offered at the conference table for something in return. If negotiations are nonproductive, some current aircraft may be transformed into air defense patrol planes (with different avionics and a much different weapons mix).

This posture might, however, comprise some close air support (CAS) elements to back up the ground forces' defense flexibly and directly. In central Europe there should be 300 (200) CAS planes ready at hand: preferably Harrier-type craft with VSTOL (vertical short take-off and landing) capability and/or highly agile propjets of recent British design, which could operate from almost unprepared fields and deal with anything from attack helicopters to armored/mechanized intrusions. Once Western air forces were, as a whole, genuinely specialized to defend and only intervene over friendly ground, it would not be destabilizing if rearward and transatlantic reserves were available to double the central European complement in a few days.

Protection of the Baltic Coasts and Exits

In order to minimize their vulnerability, to reduce their offensive qualities, and to enhance their cost-effectiveness, the Baltic defenses should be more closely integrated with the land defenses on the Danish isles, in Jutland, and in Schleswig-Holstein. The following recommendations should be adopted:

A sizeable complement of mine warfare vessels (with a good capacity to lay semi-intelligent minefields in straits and vital coastal areas).

For surveillance and flexible defensive concentration: 30 (20) medium helicopters and 40 (20) fast patrol boats with antiship missiles or guns operating from dispersed (heli)ports.

No fighter bombers for missions against another side's coast, no submarines for deep interdiction.

Again , we see the interaction between area-covering structures and elements for mobile counterconcentration. Such a coastal defense in the western Baltic would not need any heavy back-up forces from far behind.

ALLIED INTEGRATION AND BURDEN-SHARING

With respect to ground forces, it should be noted that those 250 (150) battalions of network infantry are mainly to be recruited regionally from German personnel. (The light homeguard forces are exclusively German and recruited from the region.) The 100 (75) combat battalions of the mobile spider element break down into 40 (40) German and 60 (35) other allied formations. This implies a reduction by about two-thirds (75%) of NATO's current armored or mechanized forces in central Europe.

Obviously, Germany's partners would benefit from this shift of emphasis, namely, a greater German specialization in ground defense, and could save resources for other military and nonmilitary purposes. In this context it is remarkable that even the German part of SAS-type land forces would not be very demanding, certainly needing less active manpower and fewer financial resources than current official planning. The main reasons for this are to be found in a more cost-effective weapons mix, the good teeth-to-tail ratio of network infantry, and an optimized use of reserves.[14]

The Luftwaffe could assume considerably more responsibilities in the ground-based missile shield against air threat. This shield would, in any case, have to be integrated with the German infantry network's antiair component. In return for this, and for accepting a larger share in the land forces, Germany could expect its allies to maintain a much increased proportion of their air forces (light fighters and CAS planes). Increasing their proportion, however, does not mean that these countries would have to enlarge their air fleets, for through defensive specialization, plus bilateral disarmament, overall reductions in the number of airplanes seem possible.

The proposed concept for an improved protection of the Baltic coasts and exits requires even closer Danish-German cooperation, affecting, for instance, more aspects of arms procurement than today. For example, the Danish navy is currently building a series of multipurpose boat hulls of a type that may meet the Federal German Navy's demands for cost-effective mine warfare and antiship missile platforms.

The concentration of the German navy on coastal defenses should be combined with its gradual withdrawal from aspirations in the northern North Sea, the Norwegian Sea, and the eastern parts of the Atlantic. This implies a step-by-step reduction of the German frigate and destroyer force. Assuming a more prominent role of the Germans in the land defense of central Europe, it is only fair to expect the traditional blue-water navies of the Netherlands, Britain, and the United States to take over more responsibilities for sea control missions, a task for which they are in any case specialized. Such increased specialization also would complement the economic and political structures now emerging in the new, more integrated Europe while preserving the cross-Atlantic link.

TWO SERIOUS OBJECTIONS

Defense without Strong Operational Reserves?

Some military critics argue that this kind of alternative defense is too light. It concentrates only on the improvement of tactical resistance, but virtually neglects the threat of large-scale operational attacks that would require massive operational counterattack capabilities. In other words, the SAS model is not capable of answering in kind!

However, the accumulation of strong operational reserves, which normally means several armored divisions not committed to the initial defense, is very expensive and highly ambiguous (because of the inherent provocative potential). Moreover, the following nine points strongly suggest that defense is possible without answering in kind.

1. The very existence of a protective web, which cannot be circumvented or knocked out quickly, would frustrate any Blitzkrieg attempts. (Blitzkrieg scenarios are what operational assaults are designed for in the first place.)

2. Spider and the Web, in combination, confront an intruder with an incalculable environment wherever he moves. This is of more than tactical importance.

3. Spider forces, supported by the web, have significantly increased combat value (the web is a space, time, and force multiplier).

4. Small crises can be solved before developing into disaster (spider forces are able to intervene quickly because they hide just around the corner).

5. An enemy's operational thrusts need a series of tactical successes. Thanks to the depth and the consistency of the defense, such successes can be denied again and again.

6. Marches to support a hard-pressed neighbor are facilitated. The web enhances the mobility of spider elements, and these are quite compact and relatively free from clumsy logistical tails.

7. Cross-corps coordination, another current weakness, is greatly improved through stable network communication. Simple bilateral (corps-to-network) exchanges could replace complicated multilateral (corps-to-corps-to-corps) communication.

8. The very existence of an underlying web structure, with which mobile elements have to coordinate their actions, could encourage the standardization of field manuals. Doctrinal patchwork is reported to be yet another problem faced by allied commanders as things are now.

9. Last but not least, the pin-down effect of the web, along with much improved intelligence conditions (no longer the potential confusion of an all-mobile structure), is a sound basis for the optimal use of close air support.

Confidence-Building Defense and the New European Peace Order

It has been said that the concept of confidence-building defense is a bit old-fashioned. Some critics believe that it still places too much emphasis on the military aspects of security. They argue that its "frontal orientation" is reminiscent of the confrontational politics that we now have a good chance to overcome.

Indeed, the concept of confidence-building defense has, for pragmatic reasons, accepted the frontal orientation, which so far has characterized Western defense, as a point of departure. However, through an alternative orchestration of defense; namely, by taking away threat and fear, the SAS model contributes to a demilitarization of political conflict and thus permits both East and West to move beyond the cleavages of the past.

Moreover, the paradigm of Spider and the Web is well suited for a military defense that, ultimately, would have no frontal orientation at all. This is why it recommends itself for the organization of those military elements that remain in a future European peace order. Imagine a situation by the year 2005 in which most European countries maintain only some light national forces of local nature that are structurally incapable of offensive operations beyond the lowest possible tactical level. These troops would be part of an international network (web). They would control areas and provide intelligence as well as logistical support for relatively small European rapid deployment forces (spiders). These would be an integrated multinational organization of air mobile and mechanized troops, that could, assisted by local web elements, prevent or contain future nationalistic confrontations. Such a posture of Spider and the Web at the European level could also avoid turning the old continent into a power vacuum and thereby prevent the neighboring power centers of the future from indulging in dirty speculations.

Last but not least, an integrated body of interventionary forces, organized and directed by all-European authorities, could serve as a means to make tolerable and acceptable the political weight that naturally would stem from a unified Germany.

NOTES

1. This chapter does not deal with the issue of armed intervention in areas outside of NATO territory, which, in the wake of the war against Iraq, has attracted considerable attention. Instead, the reader is referred to a recent in-depth study that explores factors of regional military stability and potential role of intervention from outside, C. Conetta, C. Knight, and L. Unterseher, "Toward Defensive Restructuring in the Middle East," *Bulletin of Peace Proposals,"* 22, no. 3 (June 1991): 115–134. This study argues that, in the interest of long-term effective crisis resolution, top priority should be given to the development of regimes of nonoffensive, confidence-building defense also for Third World nations and alliances. Indeed, the concept of nonoffensive defense appears to be at least as applicable to a Third World environment as it is to a European context. Parallel to such a development, First World intervention capabilities should be minimized, with the objective of a productive demilitarization of North-South relations.

2. The SAS, founded in 1980, is an independent, nonprofit association of defense analysts, social and natural scientists, active military personnel, and politicians. The group has members in Austria, Denmark, France, Germany, Italy, the Netherlands, the United Kingdom, and the United States. Central research facilities are located in Bonn.

3. J. J. Mearsheimer, *Conventional Deterrence* (Ithaca, N.Y.: Cornell University Press, 1983), pp. 203–212.

4. S. P. Huntington, "Conventional Deterrence and Conventional Retaliation in Europe," *International Security,* 8, no. 3 (Winter 1983–1984): p. 37.

5. Huntington, "Conventional Deterrence": p. 38.

6. L. Unterseher, *The Conventional Land Defense in Central Europe: Force Structure, Emerging Technology and Military Stability* (Mosbach: AFES-Press, 1990), p. 16 (study commissioned by NATO).

7. H. Afheldt, *Defensive Verteidigung* (Reinbek bei Hamburg: Rowohlt, 1983).

8. This expression was coined by W. T. Sherman, the greatest captain of the American Civil War. See also J. Grin, L. Unterseher, "Spezialisierung auf die Defensive: Einige Zusammenhänge," in Studiengruppe Alternative Sicherheitspolitik, ed., *Vertrauensbildende Verteidigung* (Gerlingen: Bleicher, 1989), pp. 139–148.

9. See, e.g., A. A. C. v. Müller, "Conventional Stability in Europe. Outlines of the Military Hardware for a Second Détente" (Starnberg: Max Planck Society, 1987).

10. Studiengruppe Alternative Sicherheitspolitik, ed.; L. Unterseher, "Defending Europe: Toward a stable conventional deterrent," in H. Shue, ed., *Nuclear Deterrence and Moral Restraint* (Cambridge: Cambridge University Press, 1989), pp. 293–342.

11. Figures first refer to the unilateral concept; figures in brackets to a scenario of cumulated (independent and bilateral) cuts.

12. S. L. Canby, "The Operational Limits of Emerging Technology," *International Defense Review,* 6 (1985): 875–880.

13. "NATO's Central Front," *The Economist,* 30 (Aug. 1986): 49.

14. L. Unterseher, "Ein anderes Heer: Wesentliche Einzelheiten," in *Studiengruppe Alternative Sicherheitspolitik,* ed., pp. 240–270; see also H. Bebermeyer, "The Fiscal Crisis of the Bundeswehr," in H. G. Brauch and R. Kennedy, eds., *Alternative Conventional Defense Postures in the European Theater, Vol. 1: The Military Balance and Domestic Constraints* (New York: Crane Russak, 1990), pp. 128–147.

8

Nonprovocative Defense: A Conceptual Critique and an Alternative Approach

Steven L. Canby

Nonprovocative defense (NPD) is a concept born of frustration with a Western defense that was costly, yet weak, destabilizing, and overly reliant on nuclear weapons. NPD seemingly offered an alternative. But its presumptions and desirability could be questioned at every level from grand strategy to infantry tactics. Nonetheless, its ideas offered a creative and refreshing contrast to the stodgy thinking of the NATO alliance.

This chapter argues that NPD has been inappropriate. In the new context of a united Germany, NPD does have its attractions in reassuring neighbors all around. But the question of its military utility (beyond an initial screen for Germany's eastern region) for the defense of Germany remains. Parity in equipment and manpower for NATO and the former Warsaw Pact as a whole does not equate to military equality where it counts the most—on the Paris-Berlin-Moscow axis.

NONPROVOCATIVE DEFENSE: A GRAND STRATEGY

NPD has a messianic appeal: if soldiers had only shields and no swords, aggression and war would disappear. This may follow from the perspective of a single state, but not for the world as a whole. In Europe primacy of defense over offense led to feudalism and the breakdown of central authority. In today's world, who keeps the Qaddafis in line? Defensive primacy and the removal of force as a sanction facilitates state terrorism. Without world government or projective power, would there be chaos or order?

A country such as the former Yugoslavia could base its security on the difficulties of attacking a territorial beehive in the mountains; the rest of Europe cannot. Nor can a Europe that has dominated the globe for a half millennium and remains the leading economic power escape the responsibilities and burdens of prominence. Nor can Germany itself. Since Charlemagne, Germany has been the fulcrum of European power, either too strong or too weak and rarely just right. The NPD does not change this geopolitical reality.

Militarily, defensive primacy has been Europe's curse. Clausewitz railed against the bloodless wars of maneuver, those stale chessboard wars of the monarchs conducted by trained professionals. Nor were Napoleon's lightning campaigns conducted by motivated citizen soldiers particularly destructive. Defensive dominance beginning with the American Civil War and culminating in World War I has, in contrast, been disastrous in terms of blood, treasure, and public emotion.

The belief in defensive superiority led to the timid attitudes of France and Great Britain in the interwar years. This operationally passive defensive doctrine made intervening against Nazi transgressions of the Versailles Treaty militarily difficult. Nor could France honor its treaty commitment to Poland and Czechoslovakia.

When France did defend itself, its defensive doctrine proved brittle and inflexible. France lacked the mobile forces to make good local failures against a German army that espoused the offense but was itself more organized for defense than offense. The Wehrmacht of 1940 was not an armored army; 90% of its formations were horse-drawn infantry divisions more suitable for defense than attack and little different from the French. The attack was conducted by high-quality precursing reconnaissance formations (mostly motorcyclists) followed by tanks bypassing points of resistance. The (echeloned) infantry "merely" followed and consolidated. This highlights the dilemma posed by a structural inability to attack. Adhered to formally, all is lost as defeat in detail ensues. Yet even a small (counter) attack capability provides the potential for a "Wehrmacht."

Advocates argue that NPD removes NATO's dangerous proclivity toward nuclear escalation, Follow-on Force Attack (FOFA/deep strike), and air bombardment. They are apparently unaware that these manifestations of a vengeful sword are the Anglo-American derivatives of French defensive doctrine. Armies, as the air enthusiasts in England and America argued, are to hold "lines" while airpower strikes the home front directly. This "Douhet" approach to war presumed defensive superiority and sought to minimize one's own casualties. As articulated by SACEUR in the mid-1970s, NATO's ground forces are the protective shield and its air forces the avenging sword.[1]

Neither can NPD be justified by reference to strategy. NPD may be good for Germany, but what about Norway and Turkey? Norway remains vulnerable to a *coup de main;* its north cannot be defended by NPD-like schemes. How is Norway to be defended? The Persian Gulf? With the West's structural inability to attack, Russia, as did Hitler's Germany, could readily defend in the west while it attacks south, east, and north.

Defensive sufficiency suggests that Russia, too, may forgo mobile warfare and adopt defensive primacy. But how? As one moves farther east into the spatial expanses of Eurasia, how practical are NPD-like defenses? Could the USSR have defended its Iranian or Chinese borders with such defenses? However Mikhail Gorbachev might personally have preferred defensive "sufficiency," could he have adopted a force structure that clearly was impractical for Russian geopolitical circumstances? Would his marshalls have let him?

Warfare in the Asian steppes has always been fluid, unlike that in western and central Europe. Russia could reestablish its World War II-style machine gun divisions west of the Urals with few Conventional Forces in Europe (CFE) Treaty Limited Equipments (TLE). Yet Russia's legitimate need for tank divisions east of the Urals undercuts any posture of defensive sufficiency facing west.

At the still higher level of grand strategy, NPD has displayed a similar lack of perspective for the needs of a superpower. Whereas this may no longer be the case in the wake of the dissolution of the USSR and Russia is now bent on economic reconstruction, the argument nevertheless retains some content besides revealing degrees of strategic naivity. Had the USSR desired to remain a full playing superpower, how would it respond horizontally against American maritime power if its tanks could no longer have held Europe hostage? If it could no longer have leaned politically on Europe, how would it have responded horizontally and avoided vertical escalation to nuclear weapons? By attacking China or Japan? A third country on its periphery? "Leaning" appears aggressive; its absence might actually require aggression. Thus what might appear stabilizing from a "little" Europe perspective might not be so stabilizing from a "big" Europe view.

FROM IDEALISM TO REALISM

NPD has in a decade mirror-imaged the evolution of defensive tactics in this century. NPD began as an attrition and linear scheme of war dependent upon emerging technology for sensing targets and delivering firepower. Its initial forms were Norbert Hannig's firewall and Horst Afheldt's dispersed groupings of "techno-commandos."[2] The first was obviously too brittle. The second was the antithesis of forward defense and the very conditions that the Federal Republic contracted with its NATO allies. Proponents themselves have perhaps provided the best critique of NPD's initial formulations and the dilemma posed in rectifying their weaknesses. In answering the central question of sufficiency to deter a Soviet attack, the former director of SIPRI has noted that the Afheldt and Hannig models could be too monistic to be invulnerable to enemy adaptation, in tactics or technological counter-measures.

> *The barrier defense is vulnerable to overrunning or circumvention, and once that happens all seems lost. The static infantry network on the other hand, offers no protection against a slow offensive, nibbling away at Western Germany, owing to its lack of mobile armoured forces, and is also vulnerable to intense enemy concentrations. The SAS proposal, with its rapid commitment force, does offer the possibility of rolling back the offensive, but then the non-provocative character of these armoured forces must be carefully guarded.[3]*

To avoid this pitfall, later models and Afheldt himself have added tank reserves. These are most prominent in von Bülow's second version. Whereas his first version contained no armored reserves, his second contains as many as 42 *German* armored brigades. Exactly how these are to be formed or how they square with the SPD's proclaimed desire for structural inability to attack are never quite explained.[4]

Lutz Unterseher's interactive forward defense (SAS) and Albrecht von Müller's integrated defense models share this contradiction.[5] Their models have done most to square NPD with the requirements of the real world. They recognize the need for armored counterattack forces but fence them by bolstering the attrition components of NPD and by restricting their logistical reach. The SAS model downplays hi-tech and emerging technology and seeks to emphasize the tactical quality of its light infantry and its interaction with supporting armor in a larger operational scheme.

Von Müller's model, by contrast, adds a fourth element—Hannig's firewall—to SAS's three elements of dispersed static infantry in-depth, rearward mobile, and fire support units, and rear area security zones. Müller places less emphasis on tactics and more upon technology. His is a hi-tech play, albeit one without the many cost, technical, and operational complications of FOFA. His demands upon technology call for short-range systems. Within this framework, he and his MBB sponsor have developed innovative technology for support of the immediate battle.

Armored reserves in these later models provide the link to Atlantic alliance strategy and forces that was missing in the early formative models. With this link, NPD can operate within the overall framework of accepted alliance strategy. Whereas the forward zone may be mostly German, the British and American armored reconnaissance screens along the border are not excluded, and the mechanism is in place for alliance operational reserves to reinforce and interact with forward nonprovocative defenses.

Tank reserves make the more recent NPD formulations militarily viable. Yet it is apparent that with them NPD has come full circle and become little different in concept or practice (though not rhetoric) from recent NATO practice. Yet in the circling process NPD has facilitated three important changes. The political Left has been brought back to military realism. The financially pressed Bundeswehr has for its part used the new realism to break the stylized NATO mold and begin restructuring itself to incorporate more reservists and to adopt more specialized "shield" (and sword) formations in lieu of the costly and encumbered all-purpose units favored by NATO.

MILITARY EFFECTIVENESS

NPD in all formulations assumes a capability for lightly armed and loosely arrayed forces against tanks that heavy forces and regularly organized infantry more densely arrayed lack. Some day the technology of firepower will outstrip the technology of protection and tanks will face the same dilemma as the armored knight in the fifteenth century. As new munitions for bottom and top attack proliferate and old direct-fire weapons improve, armor protection will require too much bulk and weight for effective use on the battlefield. Armor will be shed for acceleration and mobility and its shielding effect will be about as effective as the shirt was for the infantry in World War I. Obstacles and fire will stop the tank and maneuver. War will again become static. Defense will undoubtedly assume the form of small, disposed groups of in-depth infantry with vast amounts of direct and indirect firepower at their disposal. But that day is still many years away. Defenses prematurely presuming nonexistent capabilities are likely to be roundly defeated in the interim.

A second assumption concerns the quality and steadfastness of the light infantry. Operating in small isolated squad-size groupings without visible mutual support is psychologically demanding, especially at night, as is withstanding the stresses of mass attack and artillery bombardment. There is no question that elite light infantry like the Royal marines, French paras, and Wehrmacht *Jägers* could perform the most demanding roles these models require. Moreover, only some must posses light infantry (stealth and stalking) skills to protect the more numerous static component against infiltrating enemy infantry as the static groupings focus upon blocking and destroying enemy main efforts with firepower. But there is a real question whether any militia could stand up to even these lesser battlefield stresses and tactical demands without having first gone through regular military service both to develop these qualities as well as to generate the required small unit leadership. Without them the defensive belt collapses. If active service is required, why not stick with regular formations, active and reserve, in the first instance? The tactics and procedures, as in the Hoffman/Huber model, can be similar.[6]

LIMITATIONS OF METHOD

Acquiring the requisite technologies and infantry skills that preoccupy regular establishments is no mean achievement. If NPD requires technologies and combat skills only approaching regular force standards and yet is militarily superior as alleged, its advantage has to be due to either (1) better tactical and operational methods or (2) greater (combat) numbers (as, e.g., better organization so as to obtain a higher "teeth-to-tail" ratio).

Regular forces necessarily are better trained and superior in technique, but their tactics may not be. In NATO's particular case, Unterseher's Spider and the Web model is probably tactically and certainly operationally superior to NATO's linear ("layer cake") battle of compartmented corps. The latter NPD models all place a substantial light infantry screen forward and all armor is pulled back into operational reserve. This idea is neither mystical nor new, just good military practice.[7] If regular forces do this, too, as NORTHAG has in the last half decade, the two become functionally similar and differ only in degree: the relative emphasis placed on the forward screen versus the rearward operational reserves. For NPD the forward screen mainly attrits, whereas for regulars it is the vehicle for setting up decisive counterattacks.

Functional similarity suggests a contradiction in claimed personnel needs. If a viable NPD defense requires in wartime the same ground strength as NATO fields forward in peacetime (796,000) and little in the air, NATO should have no security problem in the first instance. NATO need simply imitate NPD practice. In contrast, NPD personnel requirements may be misspecified. Unterseher's model, for example, requires 200,000 mobile troops (90,000 German and 110,000 allied) and 550,000 German infantry (200,000 active and 350,000 reservists). Viability with such modest numbers reflects either superior organization (from force-multiplying tactical effects of an interacting layered defense and better use of personnel) or misestimated effectiveness and personnel requirements. One suspects that whereas NP defenses are more stringently organized, the "iceberg" phenomenon may also be present: the count focuses upon the (teeth) ice above the waterline when most (tail) is below. In modern militaries, actual fighters are in a distinct minority. In divisions their numbers amount to only 25%. For the U.S. army in Vietnam, "bayonet" (tank and infantry platoon) strength was 8%. Surely some armies may have far too much "tail"; but even with drastic restructuring and multifold improvement, fighters remain a minority.

NPD advocates may well have discovered organizational shortcuts, but as long as they too remain keyed to obstacles, indirect firepower, and armor, the numbers of support personnel cannot be as small as their schemes imply. Moreover, if cleverer means of support have been found, their application to regular forces is not precluded and solves the problem of European security in a more orthodox manner. That is, if the teeth ratio is doubled from 10 to 20%, NATO would have twice as many division equivalents. That gives NATO an unambiguous defensive capability if the additional units are placed in operational reserve and not to beef up the line as has been NATO's defensive proclivity.

Should NATO obtain added strength in this low cost manner, the resulting posture gives both alliances reasons and incentives for mutual build-downs. It does not, of course, solve the problem of preemptive attack and crisis stability. It does remove the West's driving concerns in conventional arms control negotiations.

NPD advocates attempt to resolve these concerns by structural inability to attack; this has failed. But it is still possible to hobble offensive capabilities without prejudicing the defense by structural devices limiting force projection like severe restrictions on mobile air defense, bridging, and light reconnaissance.

The argument that NATO need not adopt the NPD posture but merely some of its methods is reinforced by the resource reallocations implied by the small role NPD accords outside forces and its minor regard for the air and naval arms. These arms and U.S.-based reinforcements amount to three-fifths of the alliance's military budget! NPD proponents have limited their scope to the battlefield. They should expand their scope, and political leaders should assess the implications. If a military balance or near balance in central Europe can be obtained by their organizational techniques, why is so much being spent upon tactical airpower for delivering firepower deep? Why so much to protect unnecessary reinforcements crossing the North Atlantic?

Thus, whereas it may well be that NPD itself does not offer a solution and may be trying to do too much with its idea of "structural inability to attack," it does nevertheless offer fresh ways to think about conventional defense, crisis stability, and arms control options. Its goals are unexceptional. What it seeks can be done more comprehensively by other techniques once its operational, organizational, and tactical ideas are appreciated and adopted.

AN ALTERNATIVE APPROACH: LIGHT INFANTRY FORWARD

The tank has dominated European warfare for the last half-century. In the next fifty years, warfare, in Europe and elsewhere, is likely to be increasingly influenced and finally dominated by light infantry. To be sure, the notion of an infantry-based defense is popular politically and financially. An infantry forward defense disengages armor, decreases the opportunities for surprise attack, and saves money by reducing the need for so many tanks. These considerations are likely to be imposed upon militaries in the near future. Still, should war break out, they will be discarded.

The basis for asserting the eminent rise of light infantry and the relative demise of the tank are due to a convergence of several new and different technologies. This is indeed ironic for the public debate, blessed by such prestigious institutions as the Pentagon's Defense Science Board, is oriented toward the immediate problem of combat today: the apparent invincibility of the tank due to improved composite and reactive armor, making penetration ever more difficult, and to behind the armor technologies, reducing the effects of penetrations that do occur. Yet by the year 2000, the tank may well be relieved of frontline combat duties due to its vulnerabilities, and combat will have increasingly shifted to combat in close terrain, with profound implications for the nature of war and arms control in the first half of the twenty-first century.

NATO in its first 20 years fielded mostly infantry, albeit of an old style of little value in Europe (or elsewhere). Static infantry deployed along linear cordons (as in Korea today) have no place in modern warfare. They are readily smashed by artillery or enveloped by armor in open terrain and high quality light infantry in close terrain. In the 1960s, infantry divisions were converted into mechanized divisions with their nearly equal split between tank and mechanized infantry battalions. NATO's firepower score increased immensely. It was only belatedly recognized that NATO had created an Achilles heel: insufficient dismounted infantry to control the vast amounts of close terrain interspersed everywhere along the front in the Federal Republic.

The German army was, of course, cognizant of the problem, even as it drifted along the mainstream of alliance practice. The Bundeswehr experimented with an ill-fated *Jäger* division and did assign several mobilized infantry battalions to its heavy divisions. The British also experimented with infantry operating in close terrain, but they seemed to be mostly motivated toward finding useful roles for home-based infantry brigades that Britain could not afford to mechanize and needed as well for out-of-area contingencies in former colonial domains.

A decade ago the notion that light infantry could be the basis for the forward defense of the Federal Republic was considered laughable. Today, most officers may discount it, but few dismiss it completely. Everyone seems to recognize that more infantry is needed. Most envisage infantry battalions as complements to armor. Infantry is to be assigned various mundane tasks so that the elite may maneuver about the open terrain.

The American army mostly holds a more regressive view: light infantry divisions and brigades buttressed with tank and antitank reinforcement "plugs" are to be assigned sectors. This inappropriate deployment is based on internal institutional pressures and incomplete appreciation that the infantry divisions still constituting a significant fraction of its active and reserve formations are anachronistic.

Much of the new appreciation too can be credited to the efforts of Carl Friedrich von Weizsäcker, Horst Afheldt, Lutz Unterseher, and others who have placed nonprovocative defense on the political map and made it militarily respectable as well. Still, it can be argued that what they propose with militia forces can be done still better with regularized forces. Regular forces too are more amenable to an alliance stressing deterrence, even if it should discover a way to field a real conventional defense.

For 40 years NATO has deployed its forces mostly as a cordon defense. Only recently has this begun to change and operational reserves been formed. NATO's cordon has effectively deterred Soviet aggression. However, it is also true that had deterrence failed, defense too would have failed. As Clausewitz, citing Napoleon, said, a cordon is among the weakest forms of defense.

For these 40 years, a defense oriented to light infantry forward and tank reserves rearward would have been militarily more effective than NATO's stance. As most of the East-West border (70%) happens to be forested, mountainous terrain, a light infantry forward defense would have allowed an earlier defense of the Federal Republic instead of the NATO practice of drawing up defending forces in the open terrain after this easy-to-defend close terrain had been traversed. Nor would deterrence have been weakened.

During this period, the purpose of light infantry forward would have amounted to a strong screen. Its principal purposes were (1) to conserve forces so that large operational reserves could be formed, and (2) to draw in, overstretch, and ultimately annihilate the attacker by counterattack/stroke.

This tactic would not, of course, have been appropriate for the third of the border, which before unification had wide open corridors leading into West Germany. Some light infantry could have been usefully employed, but mostly this battle would have had to been conducted with standard heavy forces. Still the overall strategy of light infantry forward would have facilitated this battle as well for reasons (1) and (2) above. A corridor is simply a tactical channel widened into an operational channel.

Operationally an initial light infantry defense (or strong screen) contributes to the overall battle in five ways:

1. Screens the front and sidesteps main thrusts.
2. Relieves armored forces for concentration into operational reserves.
3. Strips out the precursing reconnaissance and breaks down the synergism of the attacking enemy's combined arms team.
4. Channelizes the attack into thrust vectors.
5. Sets up and masks the tank counterattack into the deep flank of the enemy thrust vector.

Light infantry holds its ground in urban areas. Its protection from tanks and artillery is masonry and rubble. In forests, light infantry fights spatially and in small groupings. Tanks are not a threat. Artillery is. Elusiveness is the way light infantry protects itself from artillery firepower and the assault of motorized infantry, which lacks the infantry skills to fight in a similar, elusive manner.

This concept forms the basis for light infantry in armored warfare. In the screening scheme outlined above, light infantry was the foil for the armor. Heavy forces remained the dominant element. Emerging technology will soon reverse these roles. Light infantry itself becomes the main destroying mechanism.

The major payoff from new technology is not from marginal improvements in familiar weapons systems. Major payoffs require integrating technology, tactics, and terrain (T3) in new ways. Occasionally these are significant enough, as in this case, to form a tactical discontinuity on the battlefield. The tactical irruption dominating warfare for the last half-century can now be contained in much the same manner that Wellington stopped Napoleon's columns. Equilibrium, long overdue from a historical perspective, is once again returning to European warfare and the age-old struggle between the defense and offense, firepower and maneuver, stability and irruption.

Emerging technology will soon be forcing the tank out of the open into the close terrain. A defender oriented toward long-range hypervelocity direct fire gunnery will be soundly defeated by an attacker stressing (1) multispectral smoke, movement freezing mines, and heavy top attack munitions against defiladed defending tanks, and (2) close terrain maneuver for his own tanks.

Conversely, new technology leads to a tactical discontinuity unambiguously favoring the defense. New technology allows defenders in close terrain to dominate adjacent open terrain with concealed and sheltered antitank weapons while holding armor out of close terrain and allowing infantry to fight only within close terrain. Antitank fire in this system is rapid and indirect and controlled by a tight firing loop with elevated sensors. Firing platforms with telescopic masts hug buildings for shelter or fire from small openings in forests. Escorting light infantry fighting only within the close terrain protects these platforms from assault from enemy infantry and tanks. Techno-engineers establish monitoring sensors, on-call minefields, and automated unmanned first lines of defense along the edges of the village/forest. The latter can be smashed but not suppressed.

This defense poses a triple threat to any offensive against NATO. First, it completely overthrows an aggressor's tempo of operations. Second, whereas an aggressor can with great concentrations of effort and cost systematically clear the first layering of villages in thrust areas, an aggressor cannot provide the requisite artillery support for such attacks when drawn into depths of 10 km or more. Nor is an aggressor's motorized infantry suitable for clearing forests defended by amorphous *Jäger*-style light infantry. Third, the new defense is not readily finessed by surprise attack nor collapsed from breakouts by Operational Maneuver Groups.

This tactical discontinuity, termed "framework defense," because close terrain is organized as a frame around which armor in open terrain is held and destroyed, has global applicability. Wherever close terrain is common, this system applies in full force. Whenever close terrain is rare, the systems nevertheless remains distinctly superior to defenses keyed to tanks, hypervelocity missiles, and ATGMs.

Light infantry in this scheme forms half the forward strength and is deployed in depth as circumstances develop. Other elements in the overall defensive system, noted in Table 8-1, include shallow FOFA attacks on the attacker's reinforcing echelons and narrow tanks suitable for movement through close terrain for initial covering and subsequent counterattack.

The next section addresses the difficulties of present-style defenses. The chapter then addresses how new technology could be used innovatively to create a new and better defensive system. The last section details the new operational approach.

Table 8-1 ALB 2004 vs. Infantry Framework Defense

	ALB 2004	Framework Defense
Overall purpose	Attrit block & shift plan	Draw-in and annihilate
	By fire and counterattack	By fire and counterstroke
Extended battle (similar shallow FOFA tech)	Attrit Disrupt plan	Begin drawing in process Attrition secondary
Frontline battle	Seeks PSTNS for L-R direct fire Successive PSTNS Exposed	Indirect fire from W/I close terrain Defensive depth Concealed and sheltered
(comparable range)	LOS Mechanized	LOS and NLOS Light Infantry techno-engineers specialized IDF AT wpns
4×4 km space	Battalion	Reinforced company
Counterattack/stroke	MBTs	Narrow, light tanks (operational masking principal concern)
	Modest reserve	Large operational reserve
Considerations	Front line battle questionable by 2004	Tact. and tech. robust Cheaper Lighter equipment Suitable for most global contingencies

Problems of Present Defenses

Present antitank defense is based on (long-range) direct fire by tanks and ATGMs from suitable positions. Its logic is that the defender putatively has a kill rate advantage of as much as 4:1 at opening ranges of 3 km, but this falls to 1:1 at an opening range fire of 1 km. This logic induces the defender to seek terrain positions suitable for long-range stand-off fire. It also leads the technological and armor communities to seek ever longer ranges for tank gunnery even though the evidence shows that ATGMs with their longer ranges have substantially identical "tank engagement percent distributions" as current tanks in the Federal Republic because of terrain.

Technologically, this approach to defense fuels a continuous frontal arc "armor/ antiarmor" (A3) contest. This contest leads to better armor, on the one hand, and better glacis penetration, on the other, accompanied by an ongoing debate on who is on top at any particular moment. For example, declaring the tank dead was a popular notion a decade ago; today the official establishment is concerned that fielded (and projected) kinetic and chemical energy warheads cannot penetrate current (and projected) Russian frontal armor.

The real problem is quite different. Long-range, direct-fire defense, no matter how good the weapon system, is already difficult and will become even more difficult due to applications of new technology.

Positions for direct-fire weaponry are readily discernible. Such positions have for years been easy to suppress, mask by smoke, and maneuver against. In the Federal Republic with its 45% close terrain and elaborate road net, low intervisibility ranges often enable enemy vehicles to approach these positions closely so that only the final approach need be covered by massive artillery barrage (if indeed, positions are not simply bypassed or enveloped). Early disclosure and confirmation of the outline of the defense by long-range gunnery allow the attacker time to devise countering options.

In most circumstances in the Federal Republic, the probability of line of sight (LOS) gunnery over 2000 m is only 15%. In addition, there is the complication of terrain folds everywhere temporarily blocking LOS fire as the tank approaches. These considerations challenge the logic of a direct-fire defense in its own terms. What is the point of long-range direct fire if targets are few and avoidable by the enemy in any case? Why emphasize ever greater range and accuracy? For tanks, it is costly; for ATGMs, all illusions for man-portability are removed.

By the turn of the century, new technology in the forms of surveillance, indirect fire, and rapidly dispersed mines will make the situation worse and untenable for direct fire defense. Defilade cannot protect against top attack by large (i.e., more than about 120 mm) indirect fire warheads. Nor can tank tops be sufficiently armored. (Even if they could, they remain vulnerable to blast effects from HE shells of this size.) Rapidly dispersed mines will freeze the defense in place. Moving about and changing positions will become difficult, slow, and costly. Already some commanders are shifting their positions from the open to forest/ village edges in order to obtain cover while still obtaining the requisite direct fire. In avoiding one problem, they create others.

The Potential of Indirect Fire

Precision indirect fire overcomes terrain and destroys advancing enemy vehicles without being threatened by them or by their supporting artillery. Tanks and artillery cannot hit or suppress indirect-fire platforms concealed and sheltered entirely within close terrain. These platforms (breech-loaded heavy mortars and vertical launch missiles in frontline positions and reinforcing FOG-Ms rearward) too can be rapidly placed in depth and along the flanks of developing enemy thrusts and breakouts. Enemy units thrusting themselves into a framework defense and held in open terrain are vulnerable to all-azimuth fire from many close terrain firing weapons. This defeats too the multispectral smoke countermeasure.

In essence, the vulnerable direct-fire strip now characterizing present-day defenses is replaced by a robust, yet amorphous in-depth defense characterized by indirect fire from many close terrain locations firing guided warheads onto enemy vehicles located in open terrain. Such a defense assures high exchange ratios between the defense and the offense. Open terrain becomes a firetrap for the attacker while movement is foreclosed through close terrain by defending artillery, infantry, and techno-engineers.

At the same time, there is no longer the interspersion of forces that in the past has hampered the use of indirect precision weaponry during dynamic encounters, specifically the critical chaotic circumstances of surprise attack and defense-collapsing breakouts. Friendly forces move to close terrain to hold attacking forces in the open terrain. This technique too simplifies the IFF (identification friend or foe) demands upon target acquisition sensors.

The New Operational Approach

Overview

The new approach hinges on the tactical discontinuity made possible by new technology, tactical change, and physical use of German terrain features. Tactical discontinuity per se applies only to the defensive framework of the frontline battle. Nevertheless, this discontinuity implies corresponding, if less dramatic, change for the other elements of the overall defensive battle; namely, FOFA-like fire into the enemy depths, covering force operations and the counterattack. It also implies a major change in air defense weaponry and in the use of attack helicopters and close air support.

In this chapter, however, we discuss only the simultaneous battle, as outlined in the U.S. Army's *AirLand Battle—Future (Heavy) 2004* (Jan. 1989). By contrast, the new framework defense operational approach (1) completely revises the frontline battle from an open to a closed terrain orientation and (2) changes the emphasis in the extended battle from attrition and force ratio management to shaping the battle operationally. As indicated in Table 8-1, ALB 2004's extended battle implies blocking and attriting as opposed to drawing the attacker in and allowing him to overextend and entrap himself. The latter is the defensive-offensive method used by Wellington. It is the method implied in *Bundeswehrplan 2000.* The principal components of the new operational approach are:

Frontline Battle—Framework Defense

Control of the open terrain from closed terrain.
Defense of the closed terrain.
Resilience under crisis situations.

Extended Battle

Extending the battlefield depth forward.
Shaping the battle operationally.
Creating operational reserves.
Killing the right targets at the right time.
Primacy of the target intelligence battle.

The Frontline Battle

Former Soviet military doctrine was based on high tempo operations to collapse NATO's front, envelop its forward forces, and preempt operational and nuclear responses. The framework defense forecloses high tempo operations. Rapid, if not all, movement through open terrain is foreclosed. Closed terrain must first be cleared. The Soviets lacked the infantry numbers and artillery resupply for re-peated built-up area assaults. They particularly lacked the infantry for clearing forests against a *Jäger*-style infantry. Former Soviet motorized infantry can smash and envelope positional infantry in forests, but it is not suited for clearing forests against (hi-grade) amorphous infantry. Nor was their airborne and air assault in-fantry much better for this task.

Defense of closed terrain has until now required much infantry and infantry deployments along dangerous and obvious edges of village and forest. "Tree line deployment" was the only way infantry could both be relevant to the on-going open terrain battle and prevent cheap entry into the close terrain during assaults. This is no longer the case. Now a few infantry aided by simple, static unmanned devices can defend the closed terrain from within, while the indirect-fire antitank systems within mount too deadly an antivehicular fire to be ignored and by-passed.

The unmanned devices include remotely armed or activated obstacles and an unmanned perimeter network of sensors and direct-fire weapons. The perimeter network is intended to deal mostly with assaulting dismounted infantry. Approach-ing vehicles are stopped or crippled by activated minefields and the techno-engineers launching dual-moded mines directly onto approaching vehicles. Ap-proaching vehicles are killed mostly by indirect fire from platforms located inside the attacked village and from mutually supporting adjacent villages/forests.

Artillery support with autonomous guided warheads and remotely delivered mines is also available. While interspersion of forces is no longer a primary con-cern, precision fire artillery should be mainly oriented to the extended battle. Their fire will not generally be needed for a set framework defense. Their fire will be needed to help stabilize the battle and provide time for setting the framework should surprise or a breakout occur.

The Extended Battle

Extended fire is a new capability popularized by the FOFA concept. Whereas deep attack FOFA is a highly questionable proposition, shallow FOFA oriented to

Schwerpunkte (= centers of gravity) is a valued capability. Shallow FOFA can be used to block or to channel. The first is oriented to attrition; the second, maneuver. The second purpose is preferred for the framework defense.

Whereas the framework defense is a battlefield tactic, its layering in depth creates an operational method. In this case, it is desirable to minimize the initial profile and fire of units in forward layers to pure self-defense so as to allow (and induce) the attacker to pursue the "successes" of his lead detachments. This stretches out the attacker and prepares the conditions for a subsequent firetrap, counterstroke, and annihilation of erstwhile penetrators.

Correspondingly, as in the German method, it is desirable to extend this stretching process into the enemy's depth, rather than have it begin only at the FLOT. Thus in Figure 8.1, rather than blocking and shifting the focus of the enemy's thrust as in ALB 2004, FOFA weapons should be mainly oriented to holding the attacker within the confines of the "funnel." This stretches attacking flanks farther and allows defending forces in non-*Schwerpunkte* areas to be reduced to screening so as to add to the depth of the framework defense (if infantry) and to the size of operational reserves (if armor).

Of course, it will also be desirable to attack forces transiting within the funnel. It is a "target-rich" environment. Yet attrition is secondary. Moreover, the preferred targets for discriminating weapons like FOG-M are air defense weapons, bridging, artillery, etc. Supporting arms should be peeled from the tank. For it is

COMBINED ARMS ARMY CONDUCTING
A BREAKTHROUGH

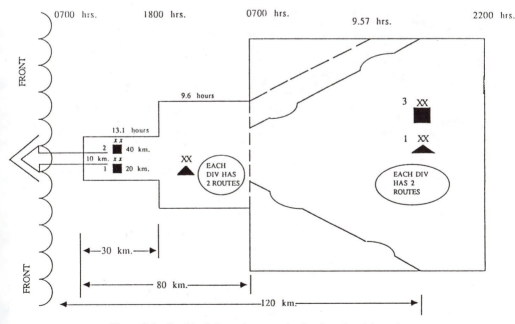

Figure 8-1 Combined Arms Army conducting front breakthrough.

these arms that later have the potential for threatening the integrity of the framework defense. The tank itself does not.

Timely and reliable target data are vital for the extended battle. Success hinges on target intelligence. This requires a variety of many target acquisition sources within tight, rapid firing loops. Such loops minimize confusion and enemy countermeasures and are in any case necessary for precision fire against moving targets.

CONCLUSION

The evolution of technology suggests that tanks will soon have too low an exchange ratio in the defense to warrant their continued participation in forward defenses. Their role will be limited to covering and counterattacking. (And the tank itself will be narrower, lighter, and possibly wheeled. The ability to hide and move through close terrain takes precedence over glacis-busting with high-powered gunnery, a function now assumed by the omnipresent, telescopic-mast heavy mortar tank.) The new operational approach developed here removes the tank from the direct defense and substitutes specialized antitank weapons escorted by light infantry and techno-engineers.

All the technologies broached in this chapter are out of the laboratory. Some first-generation primitives like the German Panther are already fielded. Thus the new defense can be deployed concurrently with the withdrawal of the tank from forward defenses. This will be necessary around the turn of the century.

NOTES

1. Andrew Goodpaster, "NATO Strategy and Requirements 1975–1985," *Survival* (Sept./Oct. 1975): 212.

2. For a discussion of several of the main NPD models, see Egbert Boeker and Lutz Unterseher, "Emphasising Defense," in Barnaby and ter Borg, eds., *Emerging Technologies and Military Doctrine* (Basingstoke-London: Mac Millan 1986): 89–109.

3. Marlies ter Borg and Frank Barnaby, "Paving the Way to European Security," in ibid., p. 273.

4. Andreas von Bülow, "Voschlag für eine Bundeswehrstruktur in den 90er Jahre," *Europäische Wehrkunde* (Nov. 1986).

5. Abbreviated versions of these schemes are outlined by the respective authors in *Bulletin of Atomic Scientists* (Sept. 1988).

6. Hans Hofmann and Reiner Huber, "The Land Defense of Europe—Ways Forward," *Common Security in Europe: Defense of Europe,* Vol. I (Oxfordshire, Foundation for International Security, 1987).

7. See, e.g., Michael Howard and Peter Paret (eds. and transls.), Carl von Clausewitz, *On War,* (Princeton: Princeton University Press, 1976) Books Six and Seven.

III

INTERNATIONAL AND
DOMESTIC CHANGES:
FUTURE ROLES OF
GERMANY AND THE
UNITED STATES IN THE
NEW INTERNATIONAL
ORDER

9

Germany's Political Role and Military Force Planning in the Post Cold War Order in Europe and Continued Relevance of Non-Offensive Defense

Hans Günter Brauch

The dramatic political change in Europe, the unification of Germany, the dissolution of the Soviet sphere of domination in Eastern Europe and the USSR, as well as the emerging reunification of the old continent have changed fundamentally the security context in and outside of Europe. After a brief review of major political developments in Europe from September 1990 to March 1992,[1] this chapter addresses (1) NATO's emerging force structure and strategy readjustments; (2) the Bundeswehr's implementation of the new multilateral and bilateral treaty obligations for manpower, force structure, deployment and procurement planning for 1994 and beyond; (3) the constitutional and political self-restraint for the future role of German forces in international military conflicts; (4) the continued relevance of non-offensive or confidence building defense concepts; and (5) several conclusions which can be derived from the recent changes in Europe, for the future security architecture in Europe.

POLITICAL CHANGE IN EUROPE: NEW CONTEXT FOR DEFENSE POLICY IN THE 1990s

Four factors have changed the international context for NATO and German defense planning: the end of the East-West conflict, German unification, the new European and global challenges and the second Gulf War (1990-1). Each have had an impact on the newly emerging European and global security structure, on NATO's strategy and force structure concepts, and on German defense planning.

End of the East-West Conflict and Charter for a New Europe

The East-West conflict has come to an end in the peaceful revolutions of 1989 and 1990.[2] The postwar Yalta system that divided Europe into two rival social, political, economic, and military camps disappeared with German unification on October 3, 1990[3] and with the Paris Conference on Security and Cooperation

(CSCE) summit, November 19–21, 1990.[4] In the *Charter for a New Europe,* the CSCE member states resolved:

> *The era of confrontation and division in Europe has ended. We declare that henceforth our relations will be founded on respect and co-operation. Europe is liberating itself from the legacy of the past. The courage of men and women, the strength of the will of the peoples and the power of the ideas of the Helsinki Final Act have opened a new era of democracy, peace and unity in Europe.[5]*

The 34 CSCE members overcame their past controversies and agreed on fundamental human rights; on a set of principles for economic freedom and responsibility; on friendly relations among member states; on security, unity, the CSCE and the world; and on a set of guidelines for the future dealing with all three baskets of the Helsinki Final Act. In the security realm, they stressed:

the freedom of states to choose their own security arrangements (alliances);
the establishment of new negotiations on disarmament and confidence- and security building measures combining the Conventional Forces in Europe (CFE) and Confidence and Security Building Measures (CSBM) talks by 1992;
the creation of a *Council* of Foreign Ministers and of a *Committee of Senior Government Officials*;
the establishment of a *CSCE Secretariat* in Prague for administrative support, a *Conflict Prevention Center* in Vienna initially for the implementation of the CSBMs; and on an *Office for Free Elections* in Warsaw.[6]

The *Conflict Prevention Center* (CPC) was tasked to support the Council in the reduction of the danger of conflicts. In the second stage this center is to support the implementation of the CSBMs, such as the mechanism for consultations and cooperation with respect to military activities, the annual exchange of military information, the communication net, the annual meeting on the assessment of the CSBM implementation, and the cooperation in dangerous military incidents. A Consultative Committee of the CPC was formed in late January 1991 on which many of the delegates of the CSBM talks were represented.[7] On June 20, 1991 at the first meeting of the Council of Foreign Ministers in Berlin a mechanism for consultation and cooperation in urgent situations was approved. Within two weeks, the crisis in Yugoslavia provoked the first test: On July 2, 1991 the CPC met in Vienna and on July 3–4, 1991 *Committee of Senior Government Officials* met in Prague to implement the new crisis mechanism by sending an observer mission to Yugoslavia in cooperation with the initiatives launched by the EC.[8]

The CPC could well become the nucleus for a functionally oriented security institution within the CSCE framework that could deal with conflict prevention, crisis management, peaceful settlement of disputes and further conventional disarmament in Europe.[9] Thus, the CPC in Vienna, by facilitating the work of delegations to the CFE IA and to CSBM and after March 1992 to the combined CFE II talks, could take up the functions of consultation, policy coordination, and monitoring of treaty compliance in the security realm. For the political and security field the CPC could gradually evolve as the secretariat, planning and implementation body of the existing *Council* of Foreign Ministers, and of a possible *European*

Security Council, representing also the Defense Ministers, and a potential *Military Council* for the national chiefs of staff.[10]

While all new CSCE institutions under the Paris Charter were set up in 1991, the institutions of Soviet domination of Eastern Europe have been dissolved: the Council for Mutual Economic Assistance (COMECON) in late June 1991 in Budapest, the military arm of the Warsaw Treaty Organization (WTO) in April 1991, and the political consultative committee of the WTO on July 1, 1991 in Prague.[11] In the dissolution protocol, the former WTO member states advocate "the transition to pan-European structures of security" through the CSCE. Thus, the framework for a military bloc-to-bloc "balance" oriented arms control policy has disappeared.

By end of September 1990, with the withdrawal of all American chemical weapons from West Germany, Europe from Portugal to Poland became a chemical weapons free zone. By May 1991, the INF Treaty was implemented with the destruction of all SS-20, SS-4, SS-22, Soviet owned SS-23 as well as Pershing II and GLCMs. By June 1991, all Soviet troops and nuclear weapons were withdrawn from Hungary and Czechoslovakia. Furthermore, all Soviet forces and nuclear weapons will be withdrawn from Poland between 1992 and 1994 and from the former German Democratic Republic (GDR) by end of 1994.

By 1995, 50 years after the end of World War II, *nuclear disengagement* will be a reality for large parts in Europe: a de facto nuclear free zone will exist covering Sweden, Finland, Poland, the former GDR, Czechoslovakia, Hungary, Romania, and Bulgaria, as well as the successor states of the former USSR: Estonia, Latvia, Lithuania, Belarus, Ukraine, Moldavia, Georgia, Armenia, and Azerbaijan. Moreover, either as a result of unilateral actions or of a bilateral U.S.–Soviet treaty on short-range nuclear forces (SNF), all land based short-range nuclear forces in Europe (e.g. SCUD, Lance, nuclear artillery) are likely to be withdrawn by the mid 1990s. Furthermore, despite of the insistence of several NATO countries on a modernization of air-based ballistic and cruise missiles, their future deployment in European non-nuclear countries appears unlikely. Indeed by the year 2000, most likely nuclear weapons in Europe will be deployed only in peacetime on the territory of three nuclear CSCE member countries: Russia, Great Britain, and France.[12]

Since early 1991, the 1990 Vienna Agreement on Confidence and Security Building Measures has been implemented. On May 31, 1991, the U.S. and Soviet Foreign Ministers Baker and Bessmertnykh resolved existing controversies of interpretation of the Conventional Forces Treaty (CFE I) and thus eased the way for its ratification. By early 1992, the CFE treaty will most likely be ratified and by 1994 fully implemented (see Table 10.1). This treaty requires the successor states of the former USSR to reduce some 18,670 [19,670] hardware items, united Germany to reduce about 11,273 [10,275] weapons systems while the United States must destroy only 2,063 [2,074] weapons, France some 372 [427], and Britain some 126 [126] systems. Several NATO countries will even be permitted to increase their forces if they so choose to higher overall national ceilings. On November 26, 1990, the CFE IA talks resumed in Vienna to include personnel reductions and aerial inspection. An agreement was signed at the start of the fourth CSCE Review Conference in Helsinki on 24 March 1992.[13]

After this CSCE follow-up conference in Helsinki, the conventional disarmament process must be fully reframed from a bloc-to-bloc undertaking aiming at a

Table 9-1   Reductions Under CFE I for NATO and Former WTO Countries[14]

	Ceilings for NATO/former WTO						Reductions			
	Alliance total	Centr. Region	Region Center	Ex.Re. Center	Flanks	Depot	NATO		Warsaw Treaty Organization	
Tanks	20,000	7,500	10,300	11,800	4,700	3,500	6,400 [−5,183]ᵃ	(24%)	17,700 [−11,713]	(47%)
ACVs	30,000	11,250	19,260	21,400	5,900	2,700	5,300 [−4,408]	(15%)	14,400 [−11,832]	(32%)
Artillery	20,000	5,000	9,100	11,000	6,000	3,000	800 [−2,157]	(4%)	6,000 [−4,754]	(25%)
Helicopters	2,000	—	—	—	—	—	no [+281]		1,700 [+338]	(45%)
Aircraft	6,800	—	—	—	—	—	no [+954]		3,200 [−1,568]	(32%)
Total NATO excluding ex-GDR							[−10,675] [+161]		[−29,529]	

ᵃThe figures of [February 1991] include holdings of the former GDR on the NATO side.

conventional balance, to pan-European process aiming at force reductions and restructuring. Both in the context of the second CSCE seminar on military doctrine in October 8–18, 1991 and in the post-CFE disarmament process the basic non-offensive or confidence-building defense (NOD or CBD) concepts and three NOD principles: no-target philosophy, structural inability to attack, and decoupling from arms competition should be considered.

In the political realm, the reunification of Europe has begun. Hungary and Czechoslovakia have already become members of the Council of Europe and of the European Human Rights Convention (1990). Poland will join in 1991 and Bulgaria, Romania, and Albania may become members once they fully abide with the Council's democratic requirements. Prior to the civil war in Yugoslavia, Italy, Yugoslavia, Austria, Hungary, Czechoslovakia, and Poland cooperated in a new subregional grouping, the "Hexagonal," that was renamed "Central European Initiative" in 1992.

In the economic area the 12 members of the European community (EC), and the seven members of European Free Trade Association (EFTA) agreed on a European Economic Space (EES) whose rules will apply for the Common European Market in 1993.[15] At the London summit of the G-7 (U.S., Canada, Japan, France, Germany, Italy, UK) in mid-July 1991, the USSR was invited to become an observer to the International Monetary Fund and the World Bank. Gorbachev in a letter dated July 15, 1991 applied for full membership in both institutions.[16] Thus, also the economic division of the postwar world is coming to an end.

German Unification[17]

For the Soviet leadership both the permanent adherence of a united Germany to the nonproliferation treaty (non-nuclear status) and significant German troop reductions were a precondition for accepting its full NATO membership.[18] On July 17, 1990, Chancellor Kohl and President Gorbachev agreed that the future size of the armed forces of united Germany should be 370,000. On August 30, 1990, this agreement was introduced to the CFE negotiations in Vienna by Foreign Minister Genscher and subsequently incorporated as a self-restraint in Article 3 of the *Treaty on the Final Settlement with Respect to Germany* that was signed by the two German states and the four allied powers U.S., USSR, France and UK (2 + 4 Treaty):

> *The Government of the Federal Republic of Germany undertakes to reduce the personnel strength of the armed forces of the united Germany to 370,000 (ground, air, and naval forces) within three to four years. . . . Within the scope of this overall ceiling no more than 345,000 will belong to the ground and air forces.*[19]

While united Germany must reduce some 11,273 weapons systems under the CFE Agreement, the manpower reductions under the 2 + 4 Treaty necessitate the most drastic reduction, restructuring, and territorial expansion of the Bundeswehr since it was set up in 1955 and 1956. In addition, unilaterally, more than 1 million small arms and 294,000 metric tons of munition[20] from the arsenals of the National People's Army (NPA) will be removed.

Under Article 4 of the 2 + 4 Treaty all 380,000 troops of the former USSR (more than 500,000 citizens from the Commonwealth of Independent States (CIS)) must leave the territory of the former GDR and of East Berlin by 1994. The U.S. government has indicated it will reduce its forces in Germany from 245,800 in 1989 to 50,000–70,000,[21] whereas the UK will reduce its forces from 66,190 in 1989 to 55,000 by June 1991 and to 23,000 by 1994 or 1995.[22] France has already reduced its troop presence from 50,000 in 1989 to 44,000 by May 1991 and plans to complete a full troop withdrawal by 1993 or 1994 with the exception of the German-French Brigade in Böblingen.[23] Belgium and the Netherlands, in the context of the new NATO force structure, will limit their presence of Germany to one brigade each.[24] Canada announced in February 1992 its intention to withdraw all troops from Europe. Thus, between 1991 and 1994, a major demilitarization process will occur in Germany. The military density which in 1989 was 18.6 soldiers per 1,000 civilians in both Germany will be reduced to 6.1 soldiers by December 1994, when about two thirds or some 300,000 German troops will be reduced and 660,000 allied soldiers (both Western and Soviet) will be withdrawn from the territory of the united Germany.[25]

New European and Global Challenges

With the disappearance of the East-West conflict, the risk of a global nuclear war has practically disappeared. NATO planners now assume that a nuclear first strike or a conventional surprise attack by the CIS is inconceivable. With the progressing disengagement from competitive involvements in Third World conflicts (e.g., the Angola peace settlement, late May 1991), a deliberate or unintentional horizontal escalation appears impossible and an unintentional nuclear war has become unlikely. Thus, in the 1990s, Europe will be confronted with new and different challenges.[26]

the disintegration, secessionist domestic conflicts and decline in the CIS;
a revival of ethnic conflicts in the Balkans. In Yugoslavia after the declaration of

independence by Slowenia and Croatia, a civil war erupted. In Romania conflicts may occur between the Romanians and the Hungarian minority;
military conflicts in the Third World, such as the two Gulf wars;
new non-military challenges of the environment, climate, catastrophes and a migration from the East and the South.

Such challenges, however, cannot be countered any longer in a competitive
confrontational mode by military alliances but only through cooperative common
efforts. Nuclear deterrence cannot solve ethnic conflicts nor could it prevent new
military confrontations in the Middle East. A fundamental shift is required from
competitive to cooperative efforts, from military to political concepts, from military instruments to political and economic tools, from deterrence to conflict avoidance, to mediation and peaceful settlement of disputes. These new opportunities
and challenges require a different security system, changed military doctrines and
force structures. The framework of European security policy has fundamentally
changed.

Future military conflicts in the Middle East, in Asia, Africa and in Latin America also depend on the continued uninhibited transfer of the most modern weapons.
However, once the extension of the East-West conflict to the peripheries is gone,
military exports are no longer political tools of influence in the Third World. Thus,
major arms export restrictions by the arms suppliers among the CSCE states will
be required. However, without a drastic reduction of the military industrial infrastructure in CSCE countries, the pressures for exports will increase as domestic
procurement requirements decline. What will be required is both a common policy
of non-intervention and arms export constraints and controls.

In sum, the new non-military threats to human survival will be of an economic
and ecological nature. Catastrophes like Chernobyl, oil spills, global warming,
and migration from the poor to the rich countries cannot be prevented with military rationales and means. These new challenges require cooperative responses: a
short-term containment of catastrophes and a longer-term common approach to
overcome their causes. In the first seven months of 1991, the most intensive
military conflicts have been the second Gulf War, the civil wars in Ethiopia, Su-
dan, and Somalia. However, only the Gulf War and the internal conflict in Yugoslavia caught much public attention in the U.S. and in Europe.

The Second Gulf War (1990-1991): A New
Global Challenge?

The differing reactions of the international community and of the Security
Council to two major acts of aggression by Iraq within a decade is revealing.
When Iraq attacked Iran in the fall of 1980 and thus started a war that lasted for
eight years and cost the lives of 1 million people, not a single resolution on
sanctions was adopted by the U.N. Security Council. Rather, the three permanent
members of the Security Council: the former Soviet Union ($20.2 bn), France
($6.7 bn) and China ($3.9 bn) supplied the aggressor from 1980–1987 with more
than 70 percent of all its arms imports. The United States and many European
countries helped otherwise.[27]

Iraq had violated the Geneva Protocol repeatedly from 1984 to 1988 by using mustard and nerve gas against Iran and the Kurds. However, it took the Security Council until 1986 to condemn the violator.[28] Again no sanctions were adopted by the Security Council or by the U.S., French, British, or German governments. Iraq could purchase without difficulties equipment for the buildup of its war industry from most industrial countries.

When Iraq took over Kuwait on August 2, 1990, the international community led by the United States reacted differently. For the first time, all permanent members of the Security Council in several resolutions adopted measures under Chapter VII of the U.N. Charter and approved the use of force by a coalition of countries to expel Iraq from Kuwait.[29] The United Nations, its Secretary General, its Secretariat and its Military Staff Committee were not involved either in planning or in conducting operation Desert Storm. However, the conditions of the ceasefire and of the destruction of Iraq's weapons of mass destruction as well as the reparations were approved by the Security Council. For the first time since 1945, the end of the East-West conflict permitted the United Nations to act in accordance with Chapter VII of the UN Charter. This very action and the military implementation of U.N. resolutions (concerning the Iraqi invasion and occupation of Kuwait) by a U.S. led coalition of nations may deter future aggressors and thus contribute to the maintenance of regional peace.

However, the war outcome did not yet create the foundation for a lasting peace in the region. Neither could the first major ecological war started by Iraq be deterred nor the genocide against the Shiites and the Kurds in Iraq be stopped. By keeping Saddam Hussein in power and reinstalling the oligarchic family rule in Kuwait, no improvement could be observed in terms of respect for human rights and democratic principles in the region.

Contradictory lessons have been drawn from this second Gulf War. The U.S. and the European defense industries called for increases in funding for military research and development into high technology weapons systems and for the procurement of enlarged air transport capabilities. Since March 1991, the U.S. defense industry and the Pentagon started a new marketing effort to sell new military hardware to the states of the coalition: Israel, Egypt, Saudi Arabia, Kuwait, and the other Gulf Sheikdoms, at the same time when President Bush had launched a major disarmament proposal for the Middle East.[30] Both new conceptual proposals for a new peace order in the Middle East and hardware proposals reflecting the interests of the defense industry dominated the security debate in Western Europe between March and July 1991.[31] How has NATO reacted to the political change in Europe and to the Gulf War?

IMPLEMENTATION OF THE POLITICAL CHANGE AND NATO PLANNING

The European security debate since NATO's London declaration of July and the Paris CSCE Charter for a New Europe in November 1990 has focused on (1) the relationship between EC, WEU and NATO; (2) the development of a new NATO strategy and force structure; and (3) the future role of the CSCE with respect to conflict prevention and the creation of a new lasting order of peace and security in Europe.

Common European Security Policy: The Role of the WEU and the EC

In the political debate since the Paris summit in November 1990, various proposals were made for a European defense identity inside and outside of NATO. By July 1991, in the transatlantic debate two alternatives could be distinguished: (1) the French and German proposal for a linkup between the European Community and the Western European Union, and (2) American opposition to strengthen European institutions outside of NATO.

In December 1990, the European Council, the major organ of the European Community, compiled a list of vital security issues: arms control and disarmament, security matters covered by the CSCE and the UN and cooperation on the production, exportation and, non-proliferation of arms. In the same month and again in February 1991, France and Germany proposed the development of a regional foreign and security policy within the European Community through the gradual transformation of the Western European Union into the defense arm of the European Council.[32] In March 1991, Jacques Delors, the President of the EC commission, suggested in his Buchan Memorial Lecture:

> *If we are to create a European union, a lengthy process must be set in train to allow integration of the WEU and its acquis into the Community. . . . The new treaty should allow for common defense issues to be dealt with by the European Council and by joint councils of foreign and defense ministers. Little by little a framework for decision-making and action would be set up between the Community and the Alliance with redefined aims and new resources would come into being.[33]*

Inspired by Delors' proposal, in fall of 1991, the debate on the WEU's future role was dominated by two proposals:

> *a* British-Italian proposal *of October 4, 1991, to keep the WEU independent and to task it subsidiary to NATO with "out of area" operations;*

> *a* Franco-German initiative *of October 14, 1991, to create a joint corps in the WEU framework and to submit the WEU to the European Council.*

After intensive negotiations, the WEU members of the EC agreed at Maastricht in an appendix to the Treaty on the European Political Union that the WEU would be both the defense component of the European Union and a means of strengthening NATO. In 1996, two years prior to its 50th anniversary, the WEU members will review this new arrangement. Furthermore, the WEU members agreed to create a joint planning staff, to achieve a closer cooperation in logistics, transport, training and strategic reconnaissance, to hold meetings of its chiefs of staff, and to create forces assigned to the WEU. In a second declaration, the WEU offered the other European NATO states associate membership. Thus, at Maastricht, the gradual transition of the WEU from an independent organization under Article 51 of the UN Charter to an organ of a common defense policy of the EC was approved.[34]

In the Treaty on a European Political Union that was signed in early February 1992 in Maastricht, the 12 EC members agreed to gradually move ahead from an intergovernmental European Political Cooperation (EPC) to a Common European Foreign and Security Policy. This movement was long in the making. After the federalist approach to establish a European Defense Community and a European

Political Community failed in the French National Assembly in 1954, it took another 15 years until the Hague summit (1969), when the European Political Cooperation was established. At its Stuttgart meeting (1983), it was approved to include the political and economic aspects of security policy, and in the Single European Act (1986), the EPC was institutionalized and a EPC secretariat was established in the EC Commission.

After trhe initial Franco-German irritation on unification, both Mitterrand and Kohl agreed in spring 1990 on two parallel government conferences to develop the framework of a Common European Foreign and Defense Policy and an Economic and Currency Union. At the Maastricht summit of the European Council in December 1991, a common EC foreign and security policy was adopted. The goal is a closer harmonization on all important foreign and security questions and a representation of the common view in international organizations, e.g., by France and UK as permanent members of the Security Council. Under certain conditions a majority vote will be permitted. On defense issues, the EC requests the WEU to prepare and implement those actions in accordance with the WEU organs. The European Council develops the principles and guidelines of the common foreign and defense policy with the active participation of the Commission and in consultation with the Parliament.[34a]

Changes in the North-Atlantic
Political-Military Context

There is general agreement that NATO will continue to play (for a longer transition period until a new stable security has evolved) an active role in defense planning and policy consultation, it will provide military reinsurance against unforeseen changes in the Soviet Union as well as the legal framework for continued U.S. presence in Europe and the full military integration of 320,000 of the 370,000 German troops into an alliance structure. Since the London Declaration of July 6, 1990, in which NATO had announced a fundamental change in its strategy,[35] the work for a new alliance strategy, for fundamentally revised resource and force goals has been rather intensive in the national defense departments, at NATO and SHAPE.

In March 1991, General Colin S. Powell, Chairman of the U.S. Joint Chiefs of Staff, stressed an increase in U.S. contingency forces while the military size would shrink from 2.0 to 1.6 million by 1995.[36] In the JCS Military Net Assessment report of March 1991, the focus shifted from the Soviet threat to "major regional contingencies." Vital military strategic concepts were: crisis response through power projection, forward presence, reconstitution, collective security, maritime and aerospace, and technological superiority. "Reconstitution" as a new *military strategy concept* "requires us to maintain the capacity to reconstitute a large, competent defense capability in the aftermath of reductions from relatively high force levels."[37] SHAPE based its planning on the assumption that allied forces in Europe would be reduced by half within a few years. NATO force planning assumed that regional troops will be strengthened first by the multinational "NATO fire brigade". If this warning to a potential aggressor would be insufficient, these forces should be further strengthened by national contingents of a rapid deployment force.[38] At the joint ministerial meeting on May 28–29, 1991 in Brussels,

NATO's Defense Planning Committee and its Nuclear Planning Group welcomed the withdrawal of Soviet troops, the dissolution of the WTO, and the success of the coalition forces in the Gulf War. They also pointed out the uncertainties and risks associated with the domestic change in the Soviet Union. The Defense Ministers agreed on the Ministerial Guidance 1991 with policy guidelines for national and alliance defense planning through 1998 and on the essentials of a new alliance force structure:

> We have agreed the basis of a new force structure consisting of Main Defense Forces, Reaction Forces and Augmentation Forces *(emphasis added), including multinational forces of all types: land, air, and maritime. In particular we have agreed various national contributions to the multinational corps of Main Defense Forces for which detailed planning will now proceed. With regard to Reaction Forces, we have agreed that these consist of immediate and rapid reaction forces, comprising contributions from most NATO nations and including national as well as multinational formations. As part of the rapid reaction forces, we have agreed the creation of a* Rapid Reaction Corps *(emphasis added) for Allied Command Europe, under United Kingdom command with a multinational headquarters. These forces, together with our future air and maritime force structures, will provide the basis for the flexible deployment of a range of forces depending on the situation. In this context we have agreed the establishment of multinational* Reaction Force Planning Staff at SHAPE *(emphasis added) for development and coordination of plans for all Allied Command Europe Reaction Forces. . . . Finally, we have agreed that a study of NATO's command structure should be pursued as a matter or urgency with the aim of streamlining and adapting it to the new situation.*[39]

According to Defense Secretary Cheney, the U.S. places:

> *greater emphasis on a force structure that is based on mobility and flexibility, not static defense. We will make extensive use of multinational forces, which give concrete evidence of the collective nature of our common defense. . . .* Reaction forces *(emphasis added) will add an additional element of flexibility to what will already be a more flexible force. As for U.S. force contribution to NATO, . . . by the mid 1990s, we expect to have a corps headquarters and two Army divisions, and corps support elements in Europe. We will also continue to provide significant air and naval forces.*[40]

The new *Main Defense Forces* in Central Europe are to be based on 16 (8 of which are German) instead of 23 to 28 divisions (18 of which were German). They will be grouped in six multinational corps of which two are under German; one each of which are under American, Dutch, and Belgian command; and one of which (Landjut) is under joint Danish and German command to cover NATO's northern flank.[41] The seventh corps deployed in the former GDR will consist of two German divisions in conjunction with the provisions of the 2 + 4 Treaty. To achieve this new corps structure an American, a British, and a Dutch division have been associated with two corps. Of the 28 German brigades in the new structure, 13 will be under the command of another nation. Bundeswehr brigades will be represented in all seven corps. This force structure was adopted without any preliminary decision on the future command structure.[42]

Before a new military strategy and doctrine of the alliance was adopted and detailed studies were launched and without any prior political consultations on the tasks, strength, composition and command of the *Rapid Reaction Forces,* NATO's Defense Ministers approved proposals of SACEUR, General Galvin, that as part of NATO's *Rapid Reaction Force* a *Rapid Reaction Corps* would be established under British leadership with a multinational headquarters. The corps, with a total between 50,000 and 70,000 European troops and U.S. attack helicopters and ground attack warplanes, will consist of two British divisions, one of them deployed in the UK, and two multinational divisions for which the Bundeswehr will contribute two or three brigades. These forces, in conjunction with restructured naval and air forces, will provide the basis for high flexibility and transportability.[43] A multinational planning staff, with a rotating chairman, will be established at SHAPE to develop the contingency plans for all allied rapid deployment forces in Europe and to consult with the allies.[44] The defense ministers also agreed on a fundamental review of its military command structure including whether or not a U.S. general should continue to have overall control of NATO's forces in Europe.[45]

Before and after the NATO meeting, the *Rapid Reaction Corps* caused much friction between the Americans and the French and obviously also within the Kohl cabinet between Defense Minister Stoltenberg and Foreign Minister Genscher. While France had favored a rapid deployment troop of the WEU and later of the EC, the U.S. backed by the British, had opposed any independent purely European force.[46]

At the spring meeting of the NATO Council in Copenhagen on June 6 and 7, 1991, the foreign ministers of the 16 NATO countries in a declaration on Central and Eastern Europe stressed the need for a close liaison and for a further development of the CSCE institutions.[47] While the foreign ministers conceded the right to the WEU and the EC to develop a common European defense identity they failed to specify the coordination with NATO. The foreign ministers recognized the CSCE as the political roof of a new security structure for the whole European continent. In a separate declaration on the key security functions of NATO in the new Europe, the foreign ministers stressed that NATO should remain the essential forum for consultations and defense cooperation among the allies as the means of achieving four key objectives: (1) to guarantee a stable security environment in Europe; (2) to provide a transatlantic forum for consultations; (3) to deter any attack on its members; and (4) to keep a strategic balance in Europe. In a second declaration on Central and Eastern Europe, the 16 foreign ministers promised to intensify the political cooperation and security consultations with the new democracies in East Central Europe and to contribute to the realization of the goals of the CSCE process by implementing a wide array of new initiatives, such as:

meetings of officers and experts on the exchange of opinions and information on security questions, on military strategies and doctrines, on arms control, non-proliferation and conversion issues;

intensified military contacts between NATO and SHAPE and officers of the new democracies;

participation of experts from these countries at specific NATO colloquia, especially on environmental issues;

gradual expansion of NATO's information programs to this region;

support for intensified contacts between the parliaments of these countries and the North Atlantic Assembly.[48]

Christoph Bertram, a former director of IISS and diplomatic correspondent of the liberal German weekly *Die Zeit,* interpreted the evolving NATO force structure and the American coup which gained an endorsement of a NATO RRF in order to block a similar European initiative as remnants of old cold war thinking.[49]

Defense Minister Stoltenberg opted for the American and against the French and German initiative favored by Foreign Minister Genscher and the chancellor's office. Developments during the NATO spring meetings once again highlighted the primacy of military over political thinking. the defense ministers adopted vital elements of a new force structure before the new NATO strategy was even completed, debated and approved by the heads of governments.

Between June and November 1991, several political developments occurred with an impact on the strategy debate in NATO:

The signing of the START treaty on July 31, 1991 in Moscow;

The failed military coup in the USSR that resulted in a rapid disintegration of the Soviet Union and granting full independence for Lithuania, Latvia, and Estonia in August 1991;

The acceptance of Lithuania, Latvia, and Estonia as independent states in the CSCE and in the United Nations in September 1991;

The unilateral initiatives for drastic reductions of tactical nuclear weapons of President Bush of September 27 and former President Gorbachev of October 4, 1991 that will result in a total elimination of all nuclear artillery shells and landbased SNF systems. These proposals were approved by NATO's NPG in Taormina in October and the NATO summit in Rome in November 1991.

The rapidly escalating civil war in Yugoslavia, primarily between Serbia and Croatia and the failure of all attempts by the CSCE and EC countries to reach a lasting settlement.

The political debate on the future European security architecture in general and on the European security identity was influenced by the different political perspectives with respect to the specific role of the European political union in foreign and security policy, the relationship of the EC to the WEU and NATO. At least six initiatives were undertaken in fall of 1991, besides the Franco-German and Anglo-Italian proposals on the future role of the Western European union:

The draft proposal of the Dutch European Community (EC) presidency for a European Political Union (EPU) statement tabled in September and subsequently withdrawn;

The Baker-Genscher proposal for a North Atlantic Cooperation Council between NATO and former WTO countries;

The agreement on a European Economic Space for the 12 EC and the seven EFTA member states in October 1991.

The agreement on a joint European foreign and defense policy in the EPU document approved by the EC summit in Maastricht on December 9–10, 1991.

Both the developments in Eastern and Western Europe[50] were reflected in the two policy documents that were adopted at NATO's Rome summit on November 7–8, 1991, replacing the two major NATO documents of 1967: the Harmel plan and its strategy of flexible response: NATO's New Strategic Concept and the Rome Declaration on Peace and Cooperation.[51] NATO's New Strategic Concept applauded the political changes in Europe, which had overcome the political division as "the source of military confrontation of the Cold War period", it noted that "the monolithic, massive and potentially immediate threat which was the principal concern of the alliance in its first forty years has disappeared," and it stressed, "The threat of a simultaneous, full-scale attack on all of NATO's European fronts has effectively been removed and thus no longer provides the focus for Allied strategy."

The new risks for Allied security are described as "multi-faceted" and "multi-directional" and difficult to predict being less the result from calculated aggression but rather a consequence of instabilities arising from economic, social, and political difficulties, ethnic rivalries and territorial disputes. They may erupt from the uncertainties in the Soviet Union, from the Southern Mediterranean and the Middle East, from the proliferation of weapons of mass destruction and from terrorism and sabotage.

Given the common values of its members, NATO's objective remains unchanged as the "transatlantic link by which the security of North America is permanently tied to the security of Europe." Its fundamental security tasks remain:

to provide an indispensable foundation for a stable security in Europe;
to serve as a transatlantic forum for Allied consultations;
to deter and defend against any threat for the territory of any member;
to preserve the strategic balance within Europe.

While the document notes that "other European institutions such as the EC, WEU and CSCE also have roles to play" and the creation of a European security identity "will reinforce transatlantic solidarity", nevertheless it emphasized that "NATO is the essential forum for consultation among the Allies". Based on a broad definition of security with its economic, social and environmental dimensions, the new NATO strategy is based on three reinforcing elements: dialogue, cooperation, and maintenance of a collective defense capability. NATO will promote the diplomatic liaison and military contacts with the countries of Central and Eastern Europe. Thus it proposed an annual meeting of the North-Atlantic Council and a North Atlantic Cooperation Council of NATO and former WTO member states "to start a new era of partnership". Based on the principles of the Charter of Paris for a New Europe, NATO will broaden "bilateral and multilateral cooperation in all relevant fields of European security" to prevent crises and ensure their effective management. The strategy document contains also guidelines for defense; on the principles of alliance strategy, on the alliance's new force posture, its missions and guidelines for the alliance's Force Posture with the characteristics of conventional and nuclear forces. However, NATO stressed that it "will maintain for the foreseeable future an appropriate mix of nuclear and conventional forces based in Europe and kept up to date where necessary, although at a significantly reduced level." The document stresses that NATO's force posture moves away "from the concept of forward defense towards a reduced forward presence, and to modify the principle of flexible response to reflect a reduced reliance on nuclear weapons". The future force posture will require a smaller manpower size but enhanced flexibility and mobility combined with an assured capability for augmentation. The conventional forces will include immediate and rapid reaction forces, main defense forces as agreed upon in Brussels in May 1991.

In the Rome Declaration, the heads of State and Government participating in the North Atlantic Council meeting on November 7–8, 1991 agreed that the challenges facing the new Europe require "a framework of interlocking institutions tying together . . . Europe and North America. Consequently, we are working toward a new European security architecture in which NATO, the CSCE, the European Community, the WEU and the Council of Europe complement each other." With respect to the European security identity, the dispute between the Atlanticists and Europeanists was resolved by this compromise that "the further strengthening of the European pillar within the alliance, will reinforce the integrity and effectiveness of the Atlantic alliance" and that "the result will contribute to a strong new transatlantic partnership by strengthening the European component in a transformed alliance." On the relations with the Soviet Union and other central and eastern European countries, NATO welcomed the political change, offered its assistance and called for closer cooperation in the framework of a North Atlantic Cooperation Council to contribute to the achievement of the CSCE both on security related, but also on scientific and environmental issues. With respect to the CSCE, the Rome Declaration called for a gradual strengthening of the new institutions created by the Paris Charter; the CSCE Council, the committee of Senior Officials, the Conflict Prevention Center and the Office for Free Elections. In addition it was proposed that the CSCE's capability "to safeguard, through peaceful means, human rights, democracy and the rule of law in cases of clear, gross and uncorrected violations of relevant CSCE commitments, if necessary in the absence of the consent of the state concerned" and "that further political impetus be given to economic, scientific and environmental cooperation so as to promote the basis of prosperity for stable, democratic development."

If compared with the Harmel Report of 1967 and the Paris Charter of 1990, both the new strategy document and the Rome declaration fail to offer a clear longer term vision on the specific security role the CSCE is to play in the new Europe in relationship with NATO, the EC, and the WEU (e.g., there is no discussion on a potential future regional system of collective security under Chapter VIII of the UN charter).

The modesty of the document reflects the lowest common denominator of NATO governments, the still unresolved competition between Atlanticist and European perspectives most particularly on the scope of the European political union in the area of defense, security, and foreign policy cooperation.

The security environment changed dramatically in December 1991 when the Soviet Union was replaced by a Commonwealth of 11 Independent States (CIS), President Gorbachev formally resigned as president of the USSR on December 25, 1991, and after Russia took over the position of the former USSR as a permanent member of the Security Council.

During this state succession from the USSR to the CIS, the North Atlantic Cooperation Council (NACC) held its first meeting on December 20, 1991, in Brussels between NATO's 16 nations, the former WTO members, and the three Baltic Republics. At a second meeting on January 10, 1992 of the same group with representatives from all 11 CIS member states, the participants agreed that the CFE should soon be fully implemented after all CIS members had ratified the treaty. At a second formal NACC meeting on March 10, 1992, this consultative body welcomed the 11 CIS representatives as new members. The consultative body of 22 states that had signed the CFE Treaty in November 1990 had expanded in the NACC framework to 35 states. Thus, the NACC has already become the major pan-European body for the implementation of the CFE I Treaty and for security consultations.

The same group of nations had negotiated the Open Sky Treaty that was signed on March 24, 1992, at the opening day of the fourth CSCE Follow-up Conference in Helsinki by 25 NACC members (all 16 NATO countries, Poland, CSFR, Hungary, Bulgaria, Romania, Russia, Belarus, Ukraine, and Georgia). In a CSCE declaration of this treaty that was approved by all 51 CSCE states, the remaining neutral CSCE states may join this Open Sky Treaty within six months. Once the CFE I Treaty has been fully implemented, it is possible that the NACC membership might be further expanded to include all 51 or—after Bosnia-Hercegovina and Macedonia have been accepted as full members—all 53 CSCE member states. However, this would imply that the NACC may well become the security organ of CSCE members and may function as a European Security Council in the CSCE framework, or as the nucleus for a pan-European collective security system under Chapter VIII of the UN Charter.

The CSCE: The New Roof for a European Security System

The institutional setting for European security policy changed drastically between NATO's London Declaration of July 6, 1990, the CSCE Charter of Paris of November 21, 1990 and the first meeting of the Council of Foreign Ministers of CSCE states on June 19 and 20, 1991 in Berlin where the Council adopted the following decisions on security matters:

1. Albania was accepted as the 35th CSCE member.
2. The use of the communication network set up in the CPC framework in Vienna for the mechanism for urgent situations was approved.
3. The creation of a Parliamentary Assembly of the CSCE states was endorsed.
4. The Committee of Senior Government Officials was requested to submit proposals on the future development of CSCE institutions and structures to its next meeting in Prague on January 30 and 31, 1992.
5. Their representatives in the consultative committee of the CPC were mandated to initiate preliminary talks on disarmament issues in September 1991 and the second seminar on military doctrines organized by the CPC from October 8 to 18, 1991 was welcomed.
6. More constraints and transparency on arms transfers to crises areas were requested.

The major achievement was the adoption of a *mechanism for consultations and cooperation in urgent situations*. Each state can initiate the mechanism by requesting within 48 hours information on developments that are of concern. If the situation remains unresolved each state can request an urgent meeting. Whenever twelve nations support the request within 48 hours, an urgent meeting must be held within three days at the CSCE Secretariat in Prague. This meeting of the Committee of High Government Officials may approve on recommendations and conclusions for the solution of the crisis.

Based on the proposals of an expert meeting in La Valetta the Council of Foreign Ministers adopted guidelines for the *peaceful settlement of disputes*. The Council invited all members to nominate up to four persons for a list of qualified mediators by August 30, 1991. The director of the CPC in Vienna was requested to act on its behalf as the nominating institution. As soon as forty nominations were received the mechanism would be inaugurated. The Council recommended that both the mechanism, the facilities, and the international bureau of the Permanent Court of Arbitration in The Hague should be fully utilized for CSCE purposes.[52]

During the Berlin meeting, modest steps toward an institutionalization of the CSCE process were approved. Within ten days, the new mechanism for urgent situations had to pass its first test with the crisis in Yugoslavia. Neither the Pentagonale, NATO, or the WEU were called. At the third human rights meeting in September 1991, procedures for the implementation of human rights decisions were adopted.

At the second Council meeting in Prague on January 30 and 31, the *Prague Document on the future development of CSCE institutions and structures*[52a] was approved. The Committee of Senior Officials was asked to intensify the coordination and political consultations and to set up a CSCE communication network. Specific proposals were made on the implementation of the decisions on the human dimension: on human rights, on democracy and the rule of law, on economic cooperation, and on the parliamentary assembly, as well as on the relationship with International Organizations, foreign states and NGOs, and on improved instruments for crisis management and prevention.

The Council requested the CSCE Follow-up Conference in Helsinki that started on March 24, 1992 to review the following instruments: a) factfinding and reporting missions, b) observer missions, c) good offices, and d) advice, mediation and settlement of disputes. Furthermore, the possibility of peacekeeping measures by the CSCE or its role in such measures should be carefully evaluated. In addition, the functions of the Conflict Prevention Centre were to be strengthened: its consultative committee will serve as the forum for comprehensive and regular consultations on security issues, for cooperation on conflict prevention, and factfinding and survey missions in the framework of the Paris Charter. The CPC will invite NATO, the WEU and relevant UNO bodies to contribute to future seminars on security problems.

Given the limited impact the CSCE mechanisms have had so far (e.g., in Yugoslavia) on conflict management and the peaceful settlement of disputes, major advances in the institutionalization of the CSCE in this area are urgently needed.

The CSCE membership increased in September 1991 at the third CSCE meeting on human rights, when Lithuania, Latvia and Estonia became members. At the Prague meeting all 11 members of the CIS joined the CSCE and on March 24, 1992, Slowenia, Croatia and Georgia enlarged the CSCE membership to 51 states. During 1992, Bosnia-Herzegovina and Macedonia most likely will be approved as full members, bringing the total to 53 members.

Simultaneously with the CSCE meeting in Prague, the heads of states and governments of the 15 members of the Security Council met in New York, emphasizing the importance of the UN collective security system. They invited the Secretary General to submit specific recommendations up through July 1, 1992, to strengthen the effectiveness of the UN, especially on preventive diplomacy, to the creation and maintenance of peace. The Security General was specifically asked to analyze the possible contribution of regional organizations for the work of the Security Council in agreement with chapter VIII.[52b] While there is still a long way to go until the CSCE can function as an effective regional collective security system under Article VIII of the U.N. Charter, nevertheless the *functionalist* approach (form follows function) appears to be most promising.

With the disappearance of the WTO and COMECON, the role and function of neutrality and of the neutral and nonaligned (N&N) states must also be redefined. What should be the future institutional framework of former WTO states that will be a denuclearized political and military buffer zone between NATO and the CIS? Should they strengthen the N&N caucus; should they join NATO or the WEU, or should they form a new "Prague Pact?"[53] Proposals for new East-Central European political and security organizations and new "buffer alliances" ignore the political interests of these former WTO states: (1) to become associated and full members of the EC (and possibly also of the WEU); and (2) to develop the CSCE as the unique framework for a future pan-European collective security system. Three former WTO and COMECON countries: Hungary, Czechoslovakia, and Poland, joined a new subregional forum for political and functional cooperation called the "Hexagonale" in July 1991 which, due to the civil war in Yugoslavia, was renamed "Initiative for Central Europe."[54]

In summary, I conclude that a significant change in the role of security institutions after the end of the East-West conflict can be observed:

> *the* North Atlantic Cooperative Council *may be the first step to an enlargement of NATO's membership and territory to cover the northern hemisphere from Vancouver to Vladivostock;*

> *the* WEU *is becoming the security organ of the EPU, whose common foreign and defense policy will be gradually developed until 1996; and*

> *at the* Helsinki conference, *the* CSCE *may emerge as an institutional predecessor of a new regional organization under Chapter VIII of the UN Charter for the northern hemisphere from Vancouver to Vladivostock.*

Both this global political change and the institutional adaptation in Europe also have implications for the implementation of German unity.

IMPLEMENTING GERMAN UNITY: THE REQUIREMENTS OF THE 2 + 4 AND THE CFE TREATIES

German unification changed the legal framework and the status of both the forces of NATO allies and of the Soviet forces in Germany, while the 2 + 4 and the CFE Treaties made evident the need for a fundamental reassessment of German defense planning. Moreover, in 1990 and 1991, the bilateral relations between united Germany and the Soviet Union, Poland and Czechoslovakia were adjusted to the new post-cold war environment in a series of bilateral treaties, which created a new political and military context for security policy.

Changes in the Legal Status of Troops of NATO Allies after German Unification

In Art. 7, paragraph 1 of the 2 + 4 Treaty, the four allies terminated "their rights and responsibilities relating to Berlin and Germany as a whole." Paragraph

2 returned to united Germany "full sovereignty over its internal and external affairs." This change in the legal foundations and status of allied forces in Germany resulted in the following agreements and declarations:

On September 25, 1990, the Federal Republic of Germany exchanged verbal notes with Belgium, France, Canada, the Netherlands, the United States of America, and the United Kingdom to extend the agreement among NATO members on the rights of their troops of June 19, 1951 and the additional agreement of August 3, 1959[55] with the restrictions that "Foreign armed forces and nuclear weapons or their carriers will not be stationed in [the former GDR] or deployed there" (Art. 5, paragraphs 2 and 3 of the 2 + 4 Treaty).

In a second verbal note of September 25, 1990, the German Foreign Ministry invited the governments of France, United States, and United Kingdom to keep their troops in Berlin until 1994 under Art. 5, paragraph 2 of the 2 + 4 Treaty.[56]

In a third agreement of September 25, 1990 on the time-limited presence of allied troops in Berlin, the German, French, British, and American governments agreed to adjust the status of allied troops to the legal requirements of Art. 5 and 7 of the 2 + 4 Treaty.[57]

A fourth agreement of September 25, 1990 between the German and allied governments on the Troop Deployment Treaty of October 23, 1954 extends this treaty while granting each party the right of withdrawal within 2 years.[58]

Legal Adjustments in the Status of the Soviet Forces in Germany

On September 24, 1990, a few days before unification, the last GDR Defense Minister Eppelmann and General Lushev, chairman of the Joint Command of the Armed Forces of the Warsaw Treaty Organization, signed a protocol on the withdrawal of the NPA from the WTO.[59] Art. 4 of the 2 + 4 Treaty acknowledges that a united Germany and the Soviet Union will determine both the conditions for the presence of Soviet forces on the territory of the former German Democratic Republic and of Berlin and for their withdrawal to be completed by end of 1994. However, this obligation was linked to the full implementation of the German troop reduction to 370,000.

Both parties negotiated 2 treaties that went into force in March 1991: The agreement on several transitional measures, signed on October 9, 1990 in Bonn,[60] and the treaty on the conditions of the temporary presence and on the modalities of the scheduled withdrawal of the Soviet troops from the territory of the Federal Republic of Germany, signed on October 12, 1990 in Bonn.[61]

The first agreement covers the payments by the German government into a transition fund (1) for the presence of Soviet troops on German soil (3 billion DM and an additional financial credit of 3 billion DM); (2) for the costs of their transportation to the USSR (1 billion DM); (3) for the construction of flats for Soviet officers in the USSR (7.8 billion DM); and (4) for their retraining (200 million DM). The second treaty regulates all the technical issues relating to the continued but temporary presence of Soviet Forces on German soil: their training and scheduled departure, the use of the air space and the bases, police and disciplinary issues, as well as transportation, communication, environmental, health, customs, and judicial concerns. All controversial issues, e.g., the treatment of Soviet deserters or the value of the Soviet-built buildings and of the environmental sanitation costs will be resolved by a joint German-Soviet Commission. On March 4, 1991 both treaties were approved and on April 2, 1991 were ratified by the Supreme Soviet of the USSR and entered into force.

From Opponents to Security Partners: Bilateral Neighborhood Treaties between Germany and the USSR, Poland, Czechoslovakia, and Hungary

In the early 1970s, West German Ostpolitik was based on a network of bilateral treaties with the USSR (August 12, 1970), Poland (December 7, 1970), and Czechoslovakia (December 11, 1974), that eased the way for the Quadripartite Agreement on Berlin (September 3, 1971) and the German-German Basic Treaty (December 21, 1972).[62] The common denominator was an agreement on the territorial status quo and an agreement to disagree on status questions. While West Germany insisted on a peaceful unification, East Germany had demanded the recognition of two Germanys.

With the end of the East-West conflict and the dissolution of the WTO, the political relationship between united Germany and its eastern neighbors is now based on a new network of bilateral treaties. The *Treaty on Good Neighborhood, Partnership and Cooperation* between Germany and the USSR, signed in Bonn on November 9, 1990 by President Gorbachev and Chancellor Kohl,[63] states that both parties will respect the "territorial integrity of all states in Europe in their present borders" (Art. 2): It contains a mutual non-aggression pledge (Art. 3); a commitment to significantly reduced armed forces and armament levels (Art. 4); to gradual development of the CSCE process (Art. 5); for regular consultations at the highest level (between the heads of government, foreign and defense ministers) (Art. 6); and of their bilateral functional cooperation in the economic, industrial, and scientific-technical area (Art. 8–10), on environmental issues (Art. 11), transportation (Art. 12), travel and exchanges (Art. 13–14), in the area of cultural relations (Art. 15–16), on humanitarian (Art. 17–18), and on legal issues (Art. 19) as well as in international organizations (Art. 20).

The *Treaty on the Development of a Comprehensive Cooperation in the Field of the Economy, Science, and Technology* between Germany and the USSR, signed in Bonn on November 9, 1990 by President Gorbachev and Chancellor Kohl,[64] sets a 20-year political framework for the development of comprehensive cooperation in the field of the economy, science, and technology. Both treaties along with the 2 + 4 Treaty were ratified by the Supreme Soviet of the USSR on March 4, 1991 and by the Bundestag in an unanimous vote on April 25, 1990.

Treaties with Poland and Czechoslovakia also have contributed to a new cooperative political context for German security policy in the 1990s. The treaty between the Federal Republic of Germany and the Republic of Poland on their common border of November 14, 1990 defined the external borders of united Germany as "the territory of the Federal Republic, the German Democratic Republic and the whole of Berlin."[65] Germany also signed a second treaty with

Poland on *good neighborhood and amicable cooperation* and several associated agreements on youth exchange, environmental, and regional cooperation on June 17, 1991 in Bonn.[66]

Besides detailed provisions for comprehensive functional cooperation the neighborhood treaty stipulates in the security area: annual consultations among the heads of government as well as the foreign and defense ministers; strict adherence to the goals and principles of the UN Charter; and the Final Act of Helsinki and mutual support for the "buildup of cooperative structures of security for the whole of Europe". Both parties stress their common interest in strengthening stability and enhancing security. They advocate a reduction of armed forces and armaments to the lowest possible level required for defense (but ineffective for attack). They will support multilateral and bilateral extensions of confidence and security building as well as other arms control measures that will enhance trust and contribute to more openness. Whenever one side considers a situation as a threat or a violation of peace both parties will consult closely with the aim of improving the situation. Poland's interest in becoming a full member of the EC is stressed in both the preamble and in Art. 8 where Germany commits itself to support Poland's membership in the EC. Most controversial—primarily within the CDU and CSU factions of parliament—were Articles 20 and 21 that deal with the rights and obligations of the German minority in Poland.

In July 1991, similar treaties have been negotiated between Germany and Czechoslovakia dealing with both the darkest periods of bilateral relations (the Munich Agreement of 1938 and the expulsion of the Germans from Czechoslovakia in 1945) and with the prospects for an intensive functional cooperation in the future.[67] On the same level of the relationship with its immediate eastern neighbors a series of bilateral treaties and agreements were signed with Hungary and Bulgaria.[68] On March 12, 1992, a treaty with Romania was initialed. By March 1992, no similar negotiations had started with Albania.

Impact of the Multi- and Bilateral Treaties for German Defense Planning

In 1988, the last ordinary planning process of the Bundeswehr took place. In spring 1989, in response to the then foreseen manpower shortage[69] and changes in the East-West relationship, Defense Minister Stoltenberg announced a fundamental planning reassessment. In October 1989, the Military Leadership Council (Führungsrat) agreed on a planning directive that was adopted on December 6, 1989 by the Federal cabinet.[70] This plan still assumed a peacetime strength of 470,000 troops by 1995 with 420,000 active soldiers.[71] On July 13, 1990, the draft was reduced from 15 to 12 months, retroactively to October 1, 1989.[72]

After the Berlin Wall had fallen, the cabinet continued to adhere to "Army Structure 2000" (a 12-division force with an enhanced capability for defensive barriers). In spring 1990, Stoltenberg aimed at 400,000 and Foreign Minister Genscher preferred 300,000 soldiers for united Germany while leading spokesmen of the SPD had suggested a size of 250,000 men. In response to the Gorbachev-Kohl agreement of July 17, 1990,[73] on August 31, 1990, Stoltenberg called for a fundamental reassessment of defense policy in a "Basic Guideline for the Planning of the Bundeswehr in united Germany''. Subsequent planning focused on six major aspects:

1. a risk analysis stressing internal instability in the USSR, resource conflicts on the southern flank from Morocco to the Indian Ocean, and the low probability of a major aggression in Europe which ultimately requires a shift to crisis management capabilities to contain crises outside of Central Europe;
2. a transitional force structure until end of 1992 involving the dissolution of the NPA, the destruction of surplus material, and the build-up of a new force structure for former East Germany;
3. personnel planning aiming at a reduction from 521,000 soldiers of both armed forces on October 3, 1990 to 370,000 soldiers by December 31, 1994;
4. the retention of the general draft with a service of 12 months;
5. major hardware reductions per requirements likely to be mandated by CFE I; and
6. probable changes in the planning of NATO allies and potential changes in NATO strategy.

These guidelines required a change in the strategic, doctrinal, and tactical-operative concepts, and a major reorientation, restructuring, and reduction of the Bundeswehr that would lead to base closures and procurement reductions.

On February 4, 1991, Stoltenberg approved the following additional planning elements:

1. reduction and simultaneous differentiation of present and cadred forces;
2. decrease of present ceiling of a mobilized defense manpower from 1,350,000 to 900,000;
3. qualitative upgrade of the reservist components;
4. extension of the Bundeswehr planning to the territory of the new states with minor structural differences;
5. adherence to force integration in NATO including multinational troops;
6. division of labor between NATO and national commanders; and
7. development of both allied and national leadership capabilities.

Longer term planning was based on the assumption of an appropriate German contribution to the security balance in Europe to protect Germany's territorial integrity and to contribute to the protection of NATO's northern and southern flank. On May 17, 1991, Stoltenberg announced the reorganization and basing plan for national command headquarters. On May 24, 1991, he published details of the planned base closures and manpower reductions.[74]

IMPLEMENTING THE 2 + 4 TREATY: MANPOWER REDUCTIONS OF GERMAN FORCES

On October 3, 1990, the united German armed forces counted 525,000 soldiers. In the ten states of Western Germany, the Bundeswehr had already been cut back from 480,000 in early 1989 to 436,000 soldiers and in the five new states the former NPA had shrunk from 170,000 in spring 1989 to 89,000 men. In October

1990, the Army had 302,000 soldiers in the West and 57,300 in the East, the Air Force counted 98,000 men in the West and 22,700 in the East while the Navy had a manpower of 36,200 in the West and 8,700 in the East.[75]

The defense budget outline for 1991 envisaged a reduction of officers and professional soldiers in the West from 89,600 to 78,500; of the short-term soldiers (4 to 15 years) from 145,800 to 115,000; of the volunteers (2 years) from 16,800 to 5,000; and of the draftees from 208,000 to 145,000.[76] By May 1991, the Bundeswehr had dwindled to 462,100 soldiers: 400,000 were stationed in the West, 56,000 in the East, and 6,100 abroad. To implement Art. 3 of the 2 + 4 Treaty, the Bundeswehr's Personnel Structure Model[77] (PSM 370) plans for a peacetime strength of 370,000 by end of 1994. By then, German armed forces will consist of 255,400 Army (69%), 82,400 Air Force (22%), and 32,200 Navy (9%) troops. Beyond 1995, the army will number 260,000, the Air Force 83,800, and the Navy 26,200. PSM 370 plans for 211,000 longer serving and 155,000 draftees serving 12 months of which up to 2,000 will serve 15 or 18 months. Five thousand spaces are available for reservists.[78] (See figure 9.1).

On October 3, 1991, all generals and admirals of the NPA were retired under the unification treaty. Between September 1990 and February 1991, the manpower of the former East German armed forces was reduced from 103,000 by 35,000 to 68,000 soldiers. Of the 32,210 officers of the NPA in September 1990, by February 1991 only 10,500 were still on the rolls, and their numbers will be further reduced to 4,000.[79] As civil servants, the officers in the old Bundeswehr cannot as easily be retired. The manpower build-down in the West will be accomplished by a combination of measures: the early retirement of 6,800 older officers, 48 to 50 years of age,[80] the early retirement of a portion of the soldiers between 1993 and 1997; the voluntary transformation from professional to time limited soldiers between 1992 and 1994; and the voluntary reduction of the service from 1992 to 1994.

The present strength of civilian Bundeswehr employees of 165,000 in the West will shrink by 34,000 to 131,000 jobs by the year 2000. By 1995, 14,000 positions will be cut. In October 1990, the former NPA had 47,000 civilian employees. In Berlin and in the five new states, about 19,500 jobs for civilians will be kept. The total German civilian manpower is scheduled to be reduced from 212,000 in October 1990 by 30% to about 150,500 by the year 2000.

IMPLEMENTING THE CFE TREATY: HARDWARE REDUCTION OF THE BUNDESWEHR

The Bundeswehr acquired 1,300 military sites and 3,300 properties from the former NPA. On July 1, 1991, it still owned 2000 properties of which it plans to retain 700. The Bundeswehr inherited 294,600 tons of munitions, about 11,000 major weapons systems consisting of between 2222 and 2272 tanks, between 5744 and 7831 armored carrier vehicles (ACVs), between 2140 and 2460 artillery tubes, some 400 airplanes and 59 battleships, and more than 1.2 million small arms.[81]

The CFE Treaty requires Germany to withdraw some 11,000 major weapons systems by December 1994 (see Table 9.2). Under present plans the Bundeswehr's structural need for these systems will be below the CFE ceilings. Thus 1930

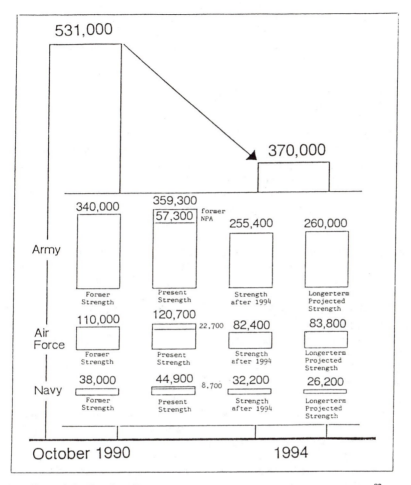

Figure 9.1 The planned manpower reductions of the Bundeswehr 1990–1995[82].

Table 9-2 Arsenal Limitations and Reductions Required by CFE for the Bundeswehr (including Weapons of Former GDR)[83]

	Bundeswehr A	NPA B	Total A + B	Notified[a]	CFE Ceiling	Reduction from A + B	Planned Structural Requirement (% of CFE ceiling)	
Tank	4,799	2,334	7,133	7,000	4,166	2,967 (42%)	3,350	(816) 80.4%
ACVs	3,129	6,469	9,598	8,920	3,466	6,152 (64%)	3,179	(287) 91.7%
Artillery	2,428	2,216	4,644	4,602	2,705	1,939 (42%)	2,077	(628) 76.7%
Helicopter	306	51	357	258	306	51 (14%)	266	(40) 86.9%
Aircraft	656	408	1,064	1,018	900	164 (16%)	416	(484) 46.2%

[a]The notified figure reflects the total for both the Bundeswehr and the NPA that has been submitted in February 1991.

additional major weapons systems will become surplus if the Bundeswehr's planning assumptions of April 1991 are implemented by 1994. The CFE does not cover the destruction of 1.2 million small arms and of 261,000 tons of munitions of the former NPA.[84] Surplus material was shipped to the Gulf coalition.

Revised Force Structure Planning for the Bundeswehr

Defense guidance issued by the defense minister required that the revised force structure must reflect the military tasks, their reconstitutability and the multinational structure, and integration of the forces into NATO. While the basic force structure would remain unchanged, its internal organization and command structure would change. The planned modular structure would contribute to high flexibility. By end of 1994, the manpower of the *Army* in peacetime will be 255,400 (132,025 professionals and 119,375 draftees) and in wartime up to 700,000 soldiers.

The key for the future *Army* structure is the organizational unification of the field and the territorial Army in peacetime. The 26 highlevel army command posts (for three corps, three territorial commands, 12 divisions and eight defense districts), existing in 1991 in the West alone, will be reduced to 13 for united Germany consisting of three combined corps and territorial commands with headquarters in Ulm, Münster, and Potsdam, eight combined division and defense district commands with headquarters in Kiel, Hannover, Düsseldorf, Mainz, Sigmaringen, München, Leipzig and Neubrandenburg, and two division staffs for operative tasks that will be headquartered in Oldenburg and Regensburg. The 48 brigades in the West will be reduced to 28 brigades for united Germany with headquarters in: Boostedt, Wentorf (Schleswig Holstein); Hamburg-Fischbeck; Munster, Oldenburg, Schwanewede, Hildesheim (Lower Saxony); Ahlen, Augustorf (Northrhine-Westfalia); Kassel, Neustadt (Hesse); Saarlouis (Saar); Diez (Rhineland-Palatinate); Calw, Müllheim, Ellwangen (Baden-Württemberg); Veitshöchsheim, Bad Reichenhall, Amberg, Landshut (Bavaria); Erfurt (Thuringia); Frankenberg (Saxonia); Weissenfels (Saxonia-Anhalt); Potsdam (Brandenburg); Stern-Bucholz and Eggesin (Mecklenburg-Vorpomerania). All defense commands at the county level (VKK) will be dissolved. Forty-six defense area commands will have territorial responsibilities.

The new Army will be highly mobile but significantly smaller in size with a broader range of military requirements: (1) an improved technical capability for tactical and operative reconnaissance; (2) a combination of armored troops with air-mobile barriers with a capability for fast concentration; and (3) an enhanced artillery component to improve the capability for widespread barriers. The planning document "Army Structure 5" envisages that seven of the 28 army brigades (three mechanized, two air-mobile, one mountain, one German-French) will be fully active, 19 partly active (18 mechanized and one air-mobile) and two mechanized brigades will be cadred. Thus, the new army will be basically a training army with the capability for appropriate fast mobilization (or reconstitution). With a manpower reduction of 90,000 men, the new structure requires both an increased professional component for the active units and reduced manpower requirements for the partly active and cadred units.[86]

The change in the armed forces between April 1990 and June 1991 was dramatic. In April 28, 1990, the two German defense ministers Stoltenberg and Eppelmann met for the first time. On May 28, 1990, both armed forces initiated an official relationship and on August 20, 1990 a liaison group of the Bundeswehr started to work in Strausberg. On October 3, 1990, Defense Minister Stoltenberg took over the command authority. The former NPA with 800 remaining troop units became the Bundeswehr Command East, commanded by General Jörg Schönbohm with headquarters in Strausberg. Four hundred and fifty of the original 800 troop units were disbanded until July 1, 1991 when the Bundeswehr Command East was dissolved[87] and replaced by the new corps and territorial command in Potsdam, two division and defense area commands VII in Leipzig and VIII in Neubrandenburg, 6 partly active brigades with their headquarters in Potsdam, Hagenow, Eggesin, Erfurt, Weissenfels and Frankenberg that will be assisted by 15 defense area commands.[88] For this territory specific restrictions under Art. 5, paragraph 1 of the 2 + 4 Treaty apply:

> *Until the completion of the withdrawal of the Soviet armed forces from the territory of the present German Democratic Republic and of Berlin . . . only German territorial defense units which are not integrated into the alliance structures to which German armed forces in the rest of German territory are assigned will be stationed in that territory as armed forces of the united Germany. During that period and subject to the provisions of paragraph 2 of this article, armed forces of other states will not be stationed in that territory or carry out any other activity there* (emphasis added).

Allied forces can stay in former West-Berlin until all Soviet forces have left Germany in 1994. However, until then "new categories of weapons will not be introduced there by non-German armed forces" (Art. 5, paragraph 2). After the total withdrawal of all allied troops from Berlin and the five new states.

> *Units of German armed forces assigned to military alliance structures in the same way as those in the rest of German territory may also be stationed in that part of Germany, but without nuclear weapon carriers. . . . Foreign armed forces and nuclear weapons or their carriers will not be stationed in that part of Germany or deployed there. (Art. 5, paragraph 3)*

In an agreed minute it was clarified that any questions with respect to the word *deployed* "will be decided by the Government of the united Germany in a reasonable and responsible way taking into account the security interests of each contracting party as set forth in the preamble."

The restructuring of the German Air Force[89] was initially guided by "Air Force Structure 3" and then "Air Force Structure 4" that aims at a reduction of the fighting aircraft below 500, an enhanced air defense capability, and a reduction of the capabilities for offensive counterair. According to the "Personnel Structure Model 95", manpower will be reduced from 100,000 prior to and 120,700 after unification to 83,800 by end of 1994 (57,775 longer serving and 24,025 draftees and short-term volunteers). Seven command headquarters of the Air Force will be in the West: in Wahn, Kalkar, Münster, Aurich, Karlsruhe, Meßstetten and Birkenfeld, and one in the East in Eggersdorf (Brandenburg).[90] One wing of 24 MIG 29 fighter aircraft will probably be retained and six of the 22 airfields of the NPA are planned for future use.

The structural reorganization of the Navy[91] is based on "Zielstruktur 2005" that aims at a reduction of all boats by half to about 90 units. These cuts will apply especially to those deployed in the Baltic Sea, to its flying components, major cutbacks in the areas of command, support and training. The Navy will maintain its fleet command in Glücksburg and its navy support or logistics command in Wilhelmshaven. The integration of the former NPA navy units will take place in stages: After a survey and evaluation of the exiting hardware under the Bundeswehr Command East, the new Navy structure will be complete by end of 1994. Until then the navy units in the East will be under the navy command in Rostock. After 1994, the navy office will most likely be moved to Rostock. Prior to unification, "Navy Structure 2005" had already envisioned reductions of the Navy from 37,000 men in late 1989 to between 31,000 and 32,000 men. PSM 370 envisages reductions for the Navy down to 32,200 (24,200 career seamen and 7,600 short-term draftees) by 1994. The new German navy will have a fleet command consisting of six commands to be formed from the former staffs of the flotillas and squadrons, three Navy communication districts and 10 ship squadrons. The Navy Logistics Command will rely on three Navy site commands with six harbors, two active and two cadred navy security batallions, and one medical unit. The navy office will be responsible for eight navy schools.

Consequences for Base Planning

The implementation of the new Bundeswehr force structure required a reevaluation of all existing military bases. On May 24, 1991, Defense Minister Stoltenberg presented the base closure plan[92] that was guided by the following goals: The military tasks can be accomplished and the necessary training facilities are available. The new solutions should reflect the fiscal restraints by limiting redeployments to an absolute minimum and the changes should be socially acceptable for the soldiers and the civilian employees. Public acceptance of the Bundeswehr, regional considerations and requirements were also taken into account. Thus, troop units should be redeployed from urban to rural areas to the extent that is militarily justifiable while major command headquarters would remain in the big cities. The old orientation to the former inner-German border in Hesse and Lower Saxonia required major reductions. According to this initial plan, from May 1991 to December 1994, in the West 213 of the 688 military bases will be closed and many others will be drastically reduced. Some 475 military bases will remain in the ten old states and 142 in Berlin and the five new states. After a heated debate and major protests,[93] especially from those communities that were affected by the announced base closures, a revised plan was published in August 1991.[94]

Midterm Defense Planning 1991–1994: Consequences for Procurement and R&D

The percentage of the defense budget of the GNP for West Germany declined steadily since 1982/1983 from 2.78% in 1983 to 2.27% in 1990. The first federal budget for united Germany for fiscal year 1991 projected an increase from 300.1 billion DM in 1990 to 399.7 [411.3][95] billion in 1991 while the defense budget was projected to decline from 54.2 billion in 1990 to 52.6 billion in 1991. The percentage of defense expenditure from the overall federal budget was projected to decline from 17.5% in 1990 to 13.2% [12.8%] in 1991. In NATO criteria, the 1991 defense budget will amount to 68.3 billion DM or 17.1% of the Federal Budget.[96]

On February 20, 1991, the federal cabinet adopted its mid-term budget projection for 1991 to 1994 (see Table 9.3). During the period of the force build-down and force restructuring the defense budget has been projected to decline steadily. While the manpower and the operations and maintenance costs will increase from 66.4% in 1990 to 71.9% in 1991 the procurement and military R&D component is projected to decline from 33.6% in 1990 to 28.1% in 1991. ·

Bundeswehr Planning for Procurement and Military R&D[98]

In the budget request for 1991, the federal expenditure for procurement was projected to decline from 10,902 million DM or 20.1% in 1990 to 9,508 million DM or 17.74% in 1991. The expenditures for military R&D and testing were planned to decline from 3,329 million DM in 1990 or 6.14% to 3,127 million DM or 5.84% in 1991.[99] The most significant defense budget reductions occur in its investive components from 1990 to 1991, i.e., from 19 to 17,3 billion DM. If one adds an inflation rate of 5%, the real reduction is about 15%. In the military R&D budget, real increases could only be observed in the item on the European Fighter Aircraft (EFA) from 560 million DM in 1989, to 700 in 1990 and 800 million DM in 1991.

The three most expensive longer-term R&D projects are the EFA (1984–1999) with projected total costs of 7,050 million DM,[100] the tank defense helicopter PAH-2 (1974–1999) with projected costs of 2,162 million DM and the tank defense missile system PARS LR and PARS MR (1979–1996 or 1998) with projected costs of 1,266 million DM.[101] According to the mid-term financial planning till 1994 additional reductions and cancellations as well as a stretching out over a longer time period will become likely for the defense investment budget.

As a consequence of the 2 + 4 and the CFE treaties, the program and procurement plans of the three services of the Bundeswehr were to be re-assessed in fall of 1991.[102] The changes in the geostrategic context in Central Europe, in NATO's military strategy, doctrine and tactical operative concepts have made many goals and programs obsolete. In April 1991, Defense State Secretary Pfahls offered these four priorities for future armament planning:

improvement of the capabilities for reconnaissance and rapid guidance;

Table 9-3   Mid-term German Budget Planning, 1991–1994 in Current bn DM[97]

	Draft Budget F.Y. 1991	Projected Budgets for F.Y.		
		1992	1993	1994
Federal Budget	399.7	403.0	412.0	421.0
Increase in % to previous year	+5.3%	+0.8%	+2.2%	+2.1%
Defense Budget	52.6	51.1	49.6	48.1
Decrease in % to previous year		−2.9%	−2.9%	−3.9%

improvement of the capabilities for long-range and high-target fire combined with
   the development of intelligent munitions;
a sufficient barrier capability for the Army;
the development of highly efficient mobile weapons systems for all three services
   that permit rapid transportation and force concentration.[103]

Until 1995, major challenges will be the destruction of surplus hardware, the
cutback of defense industrial base both through conversion to civilian production
and manpower layoffs. As 50% of the defense industry is located in the prosperous
southern states of Bavaria and Baden-Württemberg the regional impact will be
minor with the exception to the shipbuilding industry both in the old and in the
new states.[104] The potential for a branching out of the German defense industry to
arms exports is limited for two reasons: the tightened arms exports legislation and
the shrinking global arms export market.[105]

However, the personnel cutback and the announced base closure plan of the
Bundeswehr as well as the withdrawal of 2/3 or 3/4 of the presence of the Western
allies in the ten old states[106] will have a significant regional economic impact,
especially on the rural areas in Rhineland-Palatinate[107] and in Lower-Saxonia.

While the change in the global context, German unification and the strategic
adjustments in NATO have been instrumental for a fundamental change in Bundeswehr manpower, structure, deployment, and procurement planning, the Gulf
War provoked a national political and constitutional debate on the future role of
German forces to repel aggression.

CONSTITUTIONAL CONSTRAINTS FOR GERMAN
FORCES IN INTERNATIONAL CONFLICTS

Prior to and during the Gulf War, Germany was harshly criticized by several
members of the Gulf coalition for not supplying fighting units to the Gulf. Two
factors had an impact on the restrictive official and public German attitude regarding the employment of German troops in conflicts outside of its own or of NATO
territory: (1) Germany's historical legacy in the 20th century; and (2) a multi-party
consensus on a restrictive interpretation of its constitution. This attitude has been
reinforced both in the 2 + 4 Treaty and in the German-Soviet and German-Polish
treaties.

In the first treaty both German governments reaffirmed "their declarations that
only peace will emanate from German soil" and both declared "that the united
Germany will never employ any of its weapons *except in accordance with its
constitution and the Charter of the United Nations*" (emphasis added). In the two
latter treaties, Germany committed itself that its forces should not first be employed in a conflict and only for individual and collective self-defense. Furthermore, its forces should be reduced to a level that is sufficient for defense but not
for offense (Art. 4 of the German-Soviet Treaty of November 9, 1990) that *are
sufficient for defense but incapable of an attack* (Art. 6 of the German-Polish
Treaty of June 17, 1991). These three factors are likely to determine Germany's
attitude with respect to the employment of the Bundeswehr in future conflicts.

The legal foundation for the restrictive interpretation is Art. 87a, paragraph 2
of the German constitution: "With the exception for defense, the armed forces

may only be employed, insofar this Basic Law *explicitly* permits." Whether German forces may be employed

1. as U.N. peacekeeping forces;
2. under U.N. command on the basis of Art. 42 and 43 of the U.N. Charter;
3. as part of military actions outside of the U.N. collective security system but legitimized by the Security Council as in the case of the Gulf War; or
4. in 'out of area' missions in a NATO or a future WEU framework is disputed among German constitutional and international lawyers.[108]

Several decisions of the Federal Security Council were adopted both in the Socialdemocratic-Liberal (Willy Brandt, Helmut Schmidt) and the Conservative-Liberal (Helmut Kohl) coalitions concluding that the Bundeswehr could not be employed for U.N. missions without a change of the constitution that will explicitly permit such an employment. According to this multi-party consensus that existed in Western Germany prior to unification, the Bundeswehr could only be used in the defense of Germany and its NATO allies within NATO territory.[109] Thus both German participation in U.N. missions and in "out of area activities" were not possible for constitutional reasons. Foreign Minister Genscher emphasized this official position in August 1990:

> All federal governments including the present one have held the opinion that the employment of the Bundeswehr outside of NATO territory is not permitted. This reflects the clear wording of our Basic Law. Even those who adhere to a different constitutional interpretation must accept that their opinion is at least doubtful. No government can take the responsibility for such a momentous decision as sending German troops in other regions on a doubtful constitutional basis.
>
> However, through the end of the East-West conflict and German unification the political preconditions have been created that we can participate in future employments based on decisions of the Security Council. Now the constitutional preconditions can be created for such missions.[110]

Since August 1990, Chancellor Kohl has stressed the need for a constitutional clarification that would permit the use of German troops in U.N. missions. In spring 1991, with the exception of the Greens and the PDS, the successor of the Communist Party in the former GDR, all parties in the Bundestag favored a constitutional change. However, they differed on which missions should be explicitly permitted. A conservative MP suggested a general constitutional amendment: "The employment of the Bundeswehr for maintaining world peace and international security in a multilateral framework is permitted.[111]" Such a wide interpretation would allow all U.N., NATO, and possible future WEU and CSCE missions without prior Parliamentary consent.

On May 25, 1991, the Liberals adopted a party resolution that would require a constitutional amendment permitting the Bundeswehr (provided that other EC members join) to participate both in peacekeeping and collective security operations by the Security Council. However, each use would require the support of a Parliamentary majority. On May 31, 1991, the CDU Party Board stressed that as a result of German unification and the acquisition of full sovereignty Germany should fulfill its new global responsibilities through an adequate participation in measures for maintaining and regaining peace in the world.[112]

The SPD was split. While the party leadership (Vogel, Brandt, Bahr) and the foreign policy spokesmen (Gansel and Voigt) supported the first two U.N. missions (peacekeeping operations and enforcement measures under U.N. command), the pacifist wing objected to any constitutional change. On May 31, 1991, after a heated debate, the SPD passed a resolution at its Bremen Party Congress that opposed any extension of the tasks of NATO and the WEU that would permit "out of area" activities and "rapid deployment forces" for this purpose. It also objected to "a German participation in military fighting units commanded or authorized by the U.N." while German participation in peacekeeping operations would be permitted. In each case such an employment would require a majority in the Parliament.[113]

Because each constitutional change requires a two-thirds majority in both the Bundestag and the Bundesrat, no constitutional amendment is possible without the support by the SPD. It is unlikely that the SPD will agree to 'out of area' activities by NATO or to rapid deployment forces for such purposes. However, it is possible that a sufficient number of SPD members in the Bundestag will support a constitutional amendment that would permit not only peacekeeping operations but also enforcement measures under U.N. command or in a future CSCE framework.[114]

In the unification treaty of August 31, 1990, both German governments recommended to the Bundestag to agree within two years to constitutional changes deemed necessary.[115] By summer 1992, these constitutional changes will most likely be passed. The emerging new constitutional consensus on the amendment to Art. 87a, paragraph 2 will have a direct impact on the future global political and military role of a united Germany and on the structure of its armed forces. Given the present political majorities in both houses of Parliament it is unlikely that Bundeswehr units can be employed in rapid deployment forces for 'out of area' operations.[116]

THE RELEVANCE OF NON-OFFENSIVE OR CONFIDENCE-BUILDING DEFENSE CONCEPTS

Since the 1970s, NOD or CBD concepts were developed in Germany and in several other European countries as a reaction to NATO's strategy of Flexible Response and NATO's nuclear first use posture. With the end of the East-West conflict, the disappearance of the Soviet threat, the downgrading of nuclear weapons as "weapons of last resort" in NATO's London declaration of July 6, 1990, the replacement of Flexible Response by a new NATO Strategy in November 1991, and the supersession of the forward defense concept, have specific NOD or CBD concepts and their guiding principles also been overtaken by events? While several tactical operative concepts, such as the official NATO forward defense concept but also Afheldt's techno commando, Löser's area defense, or Hannig's fire barrier model have become irrelevant with German unification and the withdrawal of Soviet troops from Eastern Europe nevertheless the three basic NOD principles: no-target doctrine, inability to attack, and decoupling from the arms race, are even more valid now.

Due to the change in the political context, many proposals of NOD supporters with regard to nuclear weapons have already been realized. INF systems have been destroyed, SNF systems will not be modernized, and all landbased nuclear warfighting systems (both SNF and artillery) will be withdrawn from Europe by the mid-1990s. Nuclear disengagement and a de facto nuclear weapon free zone already exists in Europe after the withdrawal of all Soviet nukes from Germany was completed in 1991.[117] With the withdrawal of Soviet troops and nukes from Hungary and Czechoslovakia, all nuclear targets in these former non-Soviet WTO countries have been taken out from the U.S. nuclear targeting plan (SIOP) in 1991 and the number of targets in the USSR has also been reduced. Whether and which changes were made in Soviet nuclear targeting plans has not been published. Nevertheless, central features of the no target philosophy have already been realized. As suggested by Afheldt in 1976, by C. F. von Weizsäcker, and by this author in the early 1980s, extended nuclear deterrence in Europe will be provided (to the extent that it is still needed) increasingly based on its sea-based component.[118]

The second NOD principle focusing on a military force structure with an inherent inability for attack has been entered at least as a political goal in conventional disarmament talks,[119] into the Joint Declaration of the 22 states of November 19, 1990,[120] into Art. 4 of the German-Soviet Treaty and into Art. 6 of the German-Polish Treaty that suggests a defense "that lacks the capability for attack". In the German force structure planning, the importance of offensive counterair missions was already downgraded. However, so far this second goal did not have any impact on military procurement or research and development projects, e.g., the EFA project that continues irrespective of the global political change. The third NOD principle *decoupling from the arms race* and the criticism of the *overemphasis on balance* considerations in arms control talks[121] has also won increasing public acceptance.

These three NOD principles received some public acclaim in political rhetoric and treaty language, but so far they have hardly affected the weapons modernization process that will determine to a significant respect future military force structures. While procurement projects are being cut the relative importance of R&D projects has increased. Thus, the competition has even more than in the past shifted from quantity to quality.[122] NOD principles and stability considerations have not yet or insufficiently become guiding principles for weapons development (vertical proliferation) and for permitted conventional arms exports (horizontal proliferation). While the specific NOD models designed for the European central front are now dated, NOD concepts have already been discussed for several high conflict areas outside Europe, e.g., between India and Pakistan or for the Middle East.[123]

What role should NOD and CBD concepts and their three basic principles play in the future? The following tasks are worth consideration:

NOD concepts should become a *topic of future CSBM seminars on military doctrine* in the framework of the CPC in Vienna.

For CSCE member states, NOD principles should become the *guiding principles* for (a) the *weapons innovation process,* (b) *force structure planning* and (c) *arms control policy.*

NOD principles should also become the *guidelines for permitted arms exports into crises areas.* Only those weapons systems should be permitted for export that strengthen the defense but that do not foster the capability for offensive operations. Inherently offensive systems like missiles, but also fighter aircraft should become an object of international arms export restraints.[124]

Conetta, Knight, and Unterseher have suggested as part of their proposals for a defensive restructuring in the Middle East a "defensive reorientation of the arms trade" with the goal to extend existing export controls from the three existing control regimes (the London Suppliers' Club for nuclear trade, the Australian Group for biological and chemical trade, and the Missile Technology Control Regime (MTCR) for missiles) to the following offensively oriented conventional weapons systems: heavy and medium battle tanks, heavy and medium infantry fighting vehicles, armored vehicles, attack helicopters, and ground-attack and bomber aircraft with combat radii beyond 800 kilometers. However, those systems that would foster *defensive operations* should remain *uncontrolled:* anti-armor and air-defense weapons, infantry weapons, towed- and self-propelled artillery systems with ranges under 60 kilometers, mines and mine-delivery systems, helicopters for troop transport and mine-delivery and battlefield-interdiction aircraft with radii under 600 kilometers.[125] Negotiated and internationally verifiable limitations on selective export constraints for offensively oriented military weapons would also have an impact on the development and procurement prospects of new offensive weapons systems. If export outlets would disappear, the procurement prices for export-limited items would increase what would again reduce the number of systems produced. As the CSCE countries have supplied more than 80 percent of the arms to developing countries, initiatives for defensively oriented conventional arms export limitations in the CSCE framework are needed. These proposals contradict the lessons that have been drawn from the Gulf War by the defense industry and by MPs that represent hardware interests.[126]

CONCLUSIONS

The change in the East-West context has made old military doctrines and force structures obsolete. While several specific NOD models that offered an alternative to forward defense have become obsolete as well, the basic NOD philosophy and its three major conceptual principles are still valid, not only as guidelines for force structure planning, but increasingly also as guiding principles for controlling both weapons innovation (vertical proliferation) and arms exports (horizontal proliferation).

Since the INF, CFE and START treaties were signed and ratified, economic concerns and often related ethnic conflicts have replaced military hardware issues as priority items on the European policy agenda. A stop to a further economic decline in the new democracies is a precondition to prevent political instability that may well erupt in domestic violence and international conflicts. Thus tremendous resources are needed for rebuilding the collapsing economies.

Given this shift in the political agenda from military concerns to the search for cooperative economic solutions, the major policy center will be the EC in Brussels and increasingly the CSCE both the CPC in Vienna and the Bureau in Prague and less so NATO and the WEU. Both the CSCE and the EC nations will have to develop a new mediating role in containing domestic civil strife as has become obvious during the Yugoslav crisis. The high technology systems employed in the Gulf War will not help in keeping the conflicting parties apart nor will they assist to heal the wounds of ethnic strife. These new conflicts require specific European peacekeeping missions in the CSCE context. In the future, Germany cannot stand aside when peacekeeping missions in a U.N. or a CSCE framework will be necessary. The multinational units currently planned by NATO and discussed within the WEU could partly be tasked with the new common security missions: verification, conversion, peacekeeping, environmental hazards and border crossing catastrophies.[127] However, for these new tasks many weapons systems initiated as follow-on projects during the second Cold War must be reevaluated and canceled in the context of the new NATO doctrine, the emerging new force structures and the evolving new pan-European institutional framework for the solution of a new type of security issues that require cooperation rather than competition.

Due to unification, Germany is experiencing both challenges at once: rebuilding the completely collapsed economic base in the East in the midst of increasing social unrest and winding down the military presence by two thirds within the next forty months. In Europe, the realization of the political visions of Immanuel Kant (1795) of an eternal peace and Dieter Senghaas (1990) of a Europe of democratic states requires both ingenuity and pragmatic problem solutions. If Europe is to avoid the nightmare of the Hobbesian pessimist of moving "back to the future" it must develop new economic, political, cultural and conflict-avoiding and peace-keeping remedies. Structural realism as the analytic tool for security specialists insufficiently addresses the sophisticated social components of national and transnational political processes in Europe and the new cooperative institutional frameworks that have flourished during and partly due to the Cold War: the supranational EC and the intergovernmental CSCE process.

As the "economie dominante"[128], Germany should maintain its low military profile as a country that strictly adheres to its treaty obligations not to develop and acquire ABC weapons. It should employ both its resources and tools to contribute to multinational and cooperative efforts to overcome the economic challenges and instabilities in the new East Central European democracies and to counter many of the economic causes of conflict in the developing countries. In this respect, Germany should participate in self-defense operations with its NATO allies only within NATO's specified territorial boundaries and—whenever requested by the U.N. or the CSCE—both in peacekeeping operations and in enforcement measures under Chapter VII or VIII of the U.N. Charter.

While the politico-military context for European and German security policy has fundamentally changed between 1989 and spring 1992 with the dissolution of the WTO and the dismemberment of the Soviet Union, the remaining security organizations have only slowly adapted to this change. Divergent political interests and assessments have slowed down this adjustment process. While the US appears to interpret any strengthening of the WEU and of the CSCE as a weakening of NATO, and thus of its dominant role in West European security policy, many European states, most particularly France and Germany, have called for more significant institutional adaptations. However, the new challenges, e.g., the civil war in former Yugoslavia and the conflict between Armenia and Azerbeijan over Nagorno-Karabakh, have indicated the political, legal, and operational constraints for existing institutions: NATO, WEU, EC, and CSCE. Europe still lacks a fully operative and capable system of regional collective security as envisaged in Chapter VIII of the UN Charter. In March 1992 at the Helsinki CSCE Review Conference, German Foreign Minister Genscher suggested transforming the CSCE into such a regional system for the northern hemisphere from Vancouver to Vladivostok. Which institutional options for such a new security architecture may gradually be realized till the end of the millenium?

For NATO four options are theoretically foreseeable: a) dissolution, b) maintenance in its present form as a system of collective self-defense, c) transformation into an institution of close transatlantic policy consultation to be used for the solution of economic conflicts between the US and EC, and d) a systemic transformation from an international organization under Article 51 to a security organ of a regional collective security system under Chapter VIII of the UN Charter.

Presently, the first and third alternatives appear unlikely. For Germany's neighbors, Germany's continued NATO membership was a precondition for their consent to unification. In the transition period with its inherent uncertainties until a new stable security architecture has emerged, NATO offers a vital framework for security consultation, cooperation and planning. With the creation of the North Atlantic Cooperation Council, a first step has been made to foster its gradual enlargement. If membership is granted to all CSCE countries, NATO could gradually be converted either into a European-American Treaty Organisation (EATO) or into the security organ of the CSCE under Chapter VIII of the UN Charter. Thus, NATO would change *from an organization of a collective self-defense to an organ of a regional collective security system.*

For the WEU, after the Maastricht summit, three of four possible institutional options have become obsolete: a) dissolution, b) maintenance in its present form as a system of collective self-defense, and c) extension to a pan-European Security Union (ESU). The fourth alternative: the gradual transformation of the WEU from a military alliance under Article 51 into the common security organ of the European Political Union, a federation of independent states with increasingly shared responsibilities, becomes most likely. By 1996, the new institutional setting approved at Maastricht is up for review.

Beyond the initial steps towards an institutionalization of the CSCE process that were approved at meetings in Paris, Berlin, Prague and Helsinki, these proposals may be realized in the 1990s:

> *For each basket of the Helsinki Final Act specific mandates and institutional frameworks should be considered that could lead to the establishment of several pillars of a pan-European process within the CSCE, i.e., for basket 1:*

> *a political pillar (Council) with the Crisis Prevention Center and a possible Arms Control, Disarmament and Verification Agency as implementing organs, and*

> *a military control pillar (European Security Council) with an enlarged NATO as its military planning and implementation agency.*

These two pillars could be the framework for a new European Security Architecture:

> *First, the Conflict Prevention Center should become an early warning system for evolving conflicts for their peaceful settlement, crisis control and conflict termination. (Two specific pan-European institutions should report to the Conflict Prevention Center.*

> *a European Arms Control and Verification Center could be responsible for the cooperative monitoring of the compliance with arms control treaties.*

> *a European Court for the Peaceful Settlement of Disputes among member states.*

Second, a European Security Council *(ESC)—still to be created—would consist of representatives of both the Foreign and Defense Ministries. If an enlarged NATO should become the security institution of the CSCE, this organ could take over the functions of the North Atlantic Council and of the North Atlantic Cooperation Council. To facilitate the decision-making process the ESC could consist of 10–15 of the more than 51 CSCE member states, with 6 permanent members: US, Russia, France, UK, Germany and Italy and 4 or 9 additional states that would be elected for a two year period. However, no member of the ESC should have a veto power. The initiation of peacekeeping operations, for example, could require a majority vote of 50% to 66% and collective security operations a majority vote of 66% to 75%. The following specific institutions could be created to support the ESC in its tasks:*

A Military Council—*with tasks equivalent to those of the Military Staff Committee in Article 47 of the UN Charter—could offer the highest level of consultation and cooperation on the creation of joint military doctrine and on joint peacekeeping operations.*

A European Arms Production and Arms Export Monitoring Center *could be responsible for the monitoring of arms production limitations under a future CFE or CSBM regime and it could function as a European Data Center for all arms exports.*

The institutionalization of the CSCE can hardly succeed if the CSCE Charter remains a legally nonbinding political agreement. A regional collective security system cannot function effectively on the basis of a consensus nor on the veto power of a few members. These changes in the decision-making process are preconditions for a shift from the present collective self-defense to a future regional collective security system.

While systems of collective self-defense are directed *outward* against a common enemy, collective security systems are directed *inward* against a violator in a subregion, a region or on the global level. The past experience both with the League of Nations and during the first 45 years of the United Nations was rather negative. Has this system been too demanding? Was it bound to fail during the prevailing East–West conflict? Was the veto power of its five permanent members the major obstacle in the past?

So far enforcement actions under Chapter VII have not fully been implemented because the institutional requirements, e.g., the Military Staff Committee, are still lacking. Since the end of the East–West conflict, during the second Gulf War, the global collective security system passed a first partial test. The ceasefire and the demilitarization resolutions entered new ground. The UN Special Commission was given a major political task.

On the regional level, few international organizations qualify as regional arrangements under Chapter VIII of the Charter: the OAS, the OAU and the Arab League. Nevertheless, given the implications of the East–West competition on client conflicts, the influence and power for mediation of regional organizations was limited. During the second Gulf War, the Arab League was divided and the Gulf Cooperative Council was helpless to counter the aggression against one of its members.

In Europe, on the subregional level, a spillover from economic cooperation and integration to conflict avoidance could be observed: war as an instrument for conflict resolution has become obsolete among EC members. Thus the enlargement of the EC may also have a positive impact on emerging or subdued conflicts in the new European democracies. The more regional efforts at mediation and conflict resolution succeed, the more the Security Council can focus on major wars that require a broad backing from major weapons suppliers.

To conclude, my preferred conceptual notion is: to strengthen both regional and global efforts for conflict prevention, crisis control and resolution. This requires the gradual development of features of regional collective security systems. However, instead of setting up broad frameworks on paper without a specific institutional backing, a more gradual approach is preferred. In my view the pragmatic *functionalist approach,* implying that *form follows function,* may be more realistic than a *federalist approach,* implying that *functions follow form.*

From a European perspective, NATO as an organization under Article 51 is an institutional remnant of the Cold War era. The CSCE as a legally non-binding political process has gradually developed following the *functionalist path* by creating, first, jointly agreed tasks, and setting up institutions later. As the only organization that comprises NATO and the former WTO countries as well as the CIS it should gradually evolve from a *conference* or *process* to a regional international *organization* that could act under Chapter VIII of the Charter. Thus, NATO should gradually be transformed to the security organ of the CSCE.

There should be a hierarchy of conflict solution efforts: only if the subregional efforts, e.g., the EC or CIS fail, the CSCE should become active, and only if conflicts are beyond the CSCE area or if the CSCE should fail, the Security Council should come in. Thus the problem overload of the Security Council may be reduced. A *functionalist institutional transformation strategy may best contribute to this goal.*

NOTES

*This is a condensed version of two reports that were published as preprints with the title: *The New Europe and Non-Offensive Defense Concepts - Implications for Military Force Planning of United Germany,* AFES-PRESS Report No. 15 (Mosbach: AFES-PRESS, 1991) and *Institutionelle Bausteine einer gesamteuropäischen Sicherheitsarchitektur,* AFES-PRESS Report No. 23 (Mosbach: AFES-PRESS, 1992). This report will be updated with each new reprint. It may be consulted as an update to this chapter. For information contact AFES-PRESS, Alte-Bergsteige 47, D-W-6950 Mosbach, Germany.

1. See my chapter on the developments up to September 1990: "German Unity, Conventional Disarmament, Confidence Building Defense, and a New European Order of Peace and Security", in Hans Günter Brauch and Robert Kennedy eds., *Alternative Conventional Defense Postures in the European Theater, vol. 2:* The Impact of Political Change on Strategy, Technology, and Arms Control (New York: Crane Russak, 1991), pp. 3–44.

2. There is general agreement among observers that an era of world politics has ended. Several analysts in the U.S. reacted in a pessimistic manner, e.g., John J. Mearsheimer, "Back to the Future: Instability in Europe After the Cold War", in *International Security,* vol. 15, no. 1 (Summer 1990), pp. 5–56 (54); Stephan van Evera, "Primed for Peace: After the Cold War", in *International Security,* vol. 15, no. 3 (Winter 1990–91), pp. 7–57(54). Both suggested "the limited and carefully managed proliferation of nuclear weapons in Europe. . . . Ideally [Mearsheimer argued] nuclear weapons would spread to Germany, but no other state." This very policy prescription implies that Germany would have to violate Art. 3, para 1 of the Treaty on the Final Settlement With Respect to Germany (2 + 4 Treaty) in which both German governments "reaffirm their renunciation of the manufacture and possession of and control over nuclear, biological and chemical weapons." These policy proposals indicate a fundamental lack of understanding of German security interests and of the newly emerging post Cold War order in Europe. For a sophisticated theoretical critique of "structural realism", see Ernst-Otto Czempiel, "Gleichgewicht oder Symmetrie?", in Werner Link, Eberhard Schütt Wetschky, Gesine Schwan, eds., *Jahrbuch für Politik (Yearbook of Politics),* vol. 1, no. 1, 1991, pp. 127–150.

3. For a first brief analysis of the international aspects of German unification, see Karl Kaiser: *Deutschlands Vereinigung - Die internationalen Aspekte* (Bergisch Gladbach: Bastei Lübbe, 1991); Elizabeth Pond, *After the Wall - American Policy Toward Germany* (New York: Priority Press, 1990).

4. During the Paris summit, on November 19, the 22 member states of NATO and the WTO

signed the Conventional Forces in Europe (CFE) Treaty and approved a Joint Declaration on CSCE and on November 21, the 34 CSCE member states approved the Vienna Document on Confidence and Security Building Measures and the Charter for a New Europe.

5. "Excerpts From Charter On New Europe Signed In Paris by 34 Leaders," in *International Herald Tribune*, November 22, 1990; "Joint Declaration on CSCE", in: *Survival*, vol. 33, no. 1 (January/February 1991), pp. 79–80.

6. "KSZE-Büro in Polen eröffnet", in *Frankfurter Rundschau*, July 10, 1991.

7. See *Arms Control Reporter*, 1991, Sec. 402. B.280.1; see *Focus on Vienna*, no. 23, May 1991, pp. 6–8.

8. See below on the results of the Berlin CSCE meeting. "Europe Moves on Balkans - New Security Rules to Get First Test in Yugoslav Crisis", in *International Herald Tribune*, June 28, 1991; "Dringlichkeitssitzung in Prag", in *Frankfurter Allgemeine Zeitung*, July 4, 1991; "KSZE-Sitzung über Jugoslawien in Wien - Heftige Attacken Belgrads gegen österreich", in *Neue Zürcher Zeitung*, July 4, 1991; "Die KSZE will Beobachter entsenden - Empfehlung in Prag/Zustimmung Belgrads steht noch aus", in *Frankfurter Allgemeine Zeitung*, July 5, 1991.

9. Jonathan Dean, "Coalitions for Regional Crises", in *The Bulletin of the Atomic Scientists*, vol. 47, no. 5 (June 1991), pp. 33–34.

10. See Brauch, (note 1) pp. 17–18, 52–54 with detailed proposals.

11. "Warsaw Pact Moves to Dissolve Alliance", in *International Herald Tribune*, July 2, 1991.

12. See Hans Günter Brauch, "Nuclear Disarmament Prospects for Europe in the 1990s: Political Change and the Future Role of Nuclear Weapons" in Vilho Harle und Pekka Sivonen (Hrsg.), *Shaping the New Europe* (London: Frances Pinter, 1991).

13. For the details of the negotiations and results, see *Arms Control Reporter*, 1991 and 1992, Sec. 410.

14. *Informationen zur Sicherheitspolitik*, Der Pariser Gipfel, (Bonn: Bundesministerium der Verteidigung, November 1990), p. 6 and 8. For the figures of November 1990, see "Weapons in Europe Before and After the CFE", in *Arms Control Today*, vol. 21, no. 1 (January-February 1991), p. 29. For the revised figures on the reduction liability of February 1991, see "CFE Military Analysis: Revised data summarized", in *ViennaFax*, vol. 2, no. 5 (May 28, 1991). These revised figures have been added in the text.

15. No solution was reached till July 31, 1991. See "Die EWR-Hängepartie", and "Auf den Herbst vertagte EWR-Verhandlungen", in *Neue Zürcher Zeitung* (August 1/2, 1991). On October 21–22, 1991, in separate meetings, the foreign ministers of the EC and EFTA countries approved an agreement for the creation of a common European Economic Space (EES). After objections by the Court of the European Community, the agreement had to be revised during winter 1991/1992. However, the importance of the EES was downgraded after three EFTA members—Austria, Sweden, and Finland—applied for EC membership.

16. "Wirtschaftsgipfel London - Wirtschaftserklärung von London - die Sowjetunion", in *Bulletin*, no. 82 (Bonn: Presse - und Informationsamt der Bundesregierung, July 23, 1991), p. 668; "Gorbatschow überrascht mit dem Antrag auf IWF-Vollmitgliedschaft", in *Frankfurter Allgemeine Zeitung*, July 25, 1991, p. 9.

17. Two treaties between the governments of the Federal Republic of Germany and the German Democratic Republic dealt with the internal aspects of unification: the "Treaty on the Creation of a Currency-, Economic and Social Union of May 18, 1990 and the "Treaty on the Establishment of German Unity- Unification Treaty of August 31, 1990.

18. NATO's London Declaration of July 6, 1990, the continued non-nuclear status of Germany and unilateral drastic troop reductions by united Germany were preconditions for Soviet acceptance of a unified Germany in NATO. See Eduard Schewardnadse, *Die Zukunft gehört der Freiheit* (Reinbek: Rowohlt, 1991), pp. 233–268.

19. "Treaty on the Final Settlement with Respect to Germany (excerpts), 12 September 1990," In *Survival*, vol. 32, no. 6 (November/December 1990), pp. 560–562; see Appendix B in this volume.

20. "Bundeswehr Ost–Der Aufbau der Bundeswehr in den neuen Ländern - Aufgabe, Probleme, Stand, Weiterer Weg", in IAP-Dienst Sicherheitspolitik, Nr. 8-9, May 8, 1991.

21. "USA ziehen mehr Truppen ab - Gesamtstärke in Deutschland wird auf ein Korps reduziert", in *Frankfurter Rundschau*, April 15, 1991. One source points to a future U.S. strength in Germany of some 75.000 soliders, IAP-Dienst, op.cit., p. 12

22. Peter Nonnenmacher, "Großbritannien kündigt Halbierung der Rheinarmee an. London will Streitkräfte insgesamt um ein Viertel reduzieren", in *Frankfurter Rundschau*, June 6, 1990; "Statement

des Oberbefehlshabers der Britischen Rheinarmee, Sir Peter Inge", British Forces in Germany, Public Information- Newsrelease, July 23, 1991.

23. "Frankreich will die Streitkräfte verringen", in *Frankfurter Allgemeine Zeitung*, June 8, 1991, p. 3; "Franzosen bis 1993 abgezogen", in *Frankfurter Rundschau*, July 10, 1991.

24. "Kooperation, Verteidigungsfähigkeit und Dialog sind Elemente der NATO-Politik - Verringerung der Streitkräfte/Sieben Korps in Mitteleuropa", in *Frankfurter Allgemeine Zeitung*, May 31, 1991.

25. Erich Schmidt-Eenboom, "Abzug ausländischer Trupen aus der Bundesrepublik", in *Mediatus*, vol. 10, no. 3-4, 1991, p. 22.

26. Stephen van Evera, "Primed for Peace: Europe After the Cold War", in *International Security*, vol. 15, no. 3 (Winter 1990/91), pp. 7–57.

27. United States Arms Control and Disarmament Agency, *World Military Expenditures and Arms Transfers 1988* (Washington: U.S. Government Printing Office, 1989), p. 22; e.g., Anthony Lewis, "But Look What America was Doing for Saddam," in *International Herald Tribune*, March 16, 1992, p. 6.

28. See the chapters on chemical weapons in the *SIPRI Yearbook World Armament and Disarmament*, 1984-1990. Many references were given in these chapters that were generally ignored by the public.

29. For the abbreviated text of the resolutions see: *Survival*, vol, 32, no. 6 (November/December 1990), pp. 558–559; vol. 33, no. 1 (January/February 1991), p. 78.

30. See: "Growth Trends: U.S. Aerospace Industry", in *Aviation Week and Space Technology*, vol. 134, no. 11 (March 18, 1991), p. 38–39; Clyde H. Farnsworth, "White House Seeks to Revive Credits for Arms Exports", in *New York Times*, March 18, 1991, p. 1; "Bush Proposes Arms Control Initiative for Middle East", in *U.S. Policy Information and Texts*, no. 77. (May 31, 1991), pp. 35–39; "Middle East Arms Control Initiative - Text; White House Fact Sheet", ibid., pp. 41–43.

31. Two reports for the June session of the Assembly of the Western European Union represent the opposite views; e.g., the report by Mr. Martinez (Socialist, Spain) who proposed a conference on peace and security in the Mediterranean region and the Middle East: Assembly of Western European Union, 37th Ord. Sess., first part, *European security and threats outside Europe - the organization of peace and security in the Mediterranean region and the Middle East, Document 1271* (Paris, 13th May 1991) and by Mr. de Hoop Scheffer (Christian Democrat, Netherlands) who suggested new hardware solutions: Assembly of Western European Union, 37th Ord. Sess., first part, *The Gulf crisis - lessons for Western European Union, Document 1268* (Paris, 13th May 1991). Both reports were adopted. *Letter from the Assembly*, no. 8 (Paris, July 1991), pp. 4–7.

32. Alan Riding, "Paris and Bonn Offer EC Security Plan", in *International Herald Tribune*, December 8, 1990; "Deutsch-französische Initiative am Treffen der Außenminister: Vorstoß für eine EG-Sicherheitspolitik", in *Neue Zürcher Zeitung*, February 6, 1991.

33. Jacques Delors, "European integration and security", in *Survival*, vol. 33, No. 2 (March/April 1991), pp. 99–110.

34. Ibid., p. 109. For the Anglo-Italian proposal of October 4, 1991 see: "Italienisch-britische Erklärung zur europäischen Sicherheit und Verteidigung," in: *Britische Dokumentation*, no. D 24/91 (Bonn: British Embassy, October 8, 1991); for the Franco–German initiative of October 14, 1991 see: "Botschaft zur gemeinsamen Außen- und Sicherheitspolitik von Bundeskanzler Helmut Kohl und dem Präsidenten der Französischen Republik, François Mitterrand, an den amtierenden Vorsitzenden des Europäischen Rates und Ministerpräsidenten des Königsreichs der Niederlande, Ruud Lubbers, vom 14. Oktober 1991," in: *Europa-Archiv*, vol. 46, no. 22 (November 25, 1991) pp. D 571–D 574. The conflict was resolved in an appendix to the Maastricht "Treaty on a European Union": "Erklärung zur Westeuropäischen Union," in: *Bulletin*, no. 16 (Bonn: Presse- und Informationsamt der Bundesregierung, 1992), pp. 182–184. For an English summary see: *European union and developments in Central and Eastern Europe. Report by Mr. Goerens for the Political Committee. Document 1293* (Paris: Assembly of the Western European Union, November 27, 1991), pp. 19–22.

34a. The German text of the treaty of Maastricht was published as: "Vertrag über die Europäische Union," in: *Bulletin*, no. 16 (Bonn: Presse- und Informationsamt der Bundesregierung, February 12, 1992), pp. 113–182 (154-156).

35. "NATO Pledges No First Use of Military Force (Text: London Declaration", in *U.S. Policy Information and Texts*, No. 89, July 9, 1990, pp. 15–19.

36. Don Oberhofer, "U.S. Military Strategy Shifts to Large-Scale Mobile Forces", in *International Herald Tribune*, May 20, 1991, p. 1.

37. Joint Chiefs of Staff, *1991 Joint Military Net Assessment* (Washington, D.C.: U.S. Department of Defense, March 1991), pp. 2–5.

38. Erich Hauser, "Beim Thema Friedensdividende graust es den NATO-Militärs", in *Frankfurter Rundschau*, May 23, 1991, p. 8.

39. "NATO Final Communique of May 29", in *U.S. Department of State Dispatch*, vol. 2 no. 23, June 10, 1991.

40. "NATO Meeting 'An Important Milestone' Cheney Says", in: *U.S. Policy Information and Texts*, June 3, 1991, pp. 21–29.

41. Michael Mecham, "NATO's New Strategy Stresses Mobility for 'Crisis' Management", in *Aviation Week & Space Technology*, June 3, 1991, pp. 22–23.

42. "Britische Dominanz bei NATO-Eingreiftruppe - NATO-Streitkräftestruktur mit Fragezeichen, in *Stichworte zur Sicherheitspolitik*, July 1991, pp. 24–25.

43. "NATO will schneller reagieren können - Verteidigungsminister über Eingreiftruppe und multinationale Verbände einig", in *Frankfurter Rundschau*, May 29, 1991; "'Europäische Sicherheitsidentität nur als Pfeiler der NATO' - Verteidigungsminister lehnen Zuordnung der WEU zur EG ab - Integrierte Befehlsstruktur wird erhalten", in *Frankfurter Allgemeine Zeitung*, May 29, 1991; "Dreigliedrige Streitkräftestruktur der Nato - Einigung über die Bildung eines Rapid Reaction Corps", in *Neue Zürcher Zeitung*, May 30, 1991.

44. "NATO Final Communique of May 29", in: *U.S. Department of State Dispatch*, vol. 2, no. 23 (June 10, 1991), pp. 406–408.

45. "NATO, Launching a Command Review, Stresses Urgency", in *International Herald Tribune*, May 30, 1991.

46. "Französische Besänftigungen gegenüber der Nato", in *Neue Zürcher Zeitung*, May 30, 1991.

47. "North Atlantic Council Meeting - Secretary Baker, Communique and Statement", in *U.S. Department of State Dispatch*, vol. 2, no. 24 (June 17, 1991), pp. 427–430; Erich Hauser, "NATO will Partnerschaft mit Osteuropa ohne Sicherheitsgarantie", in *Frankfurter Rundschau*, June 7, 1991; "Die Nato wertet die KSZE auf", in *Frankfurter Allgemeine Zeitung*, June 7, 1991.

48. "Kommunique der Ministertagung des Nordatlantikrats", in *Bulletin*, no. 66 (Bonn, June 11, 1991), pp. 525–529; "Die Nato gesteht Europäern eigene Sicherheitspolitik zu", in *Frankfurter Allgemeine Zeitung*, June 8, 1991; "NATO gibt ihr Feindbild auf. Außenminister beschlossen 'radikalste Strategieänderung'", in *Frankfurter Rundschau*, June 8, 1991.

49. Christoph Bertram, "Nichts vergessen, nichts dazugelernt. Hinter den Zukunftsplanen des westlichen Bündnisses lauert das alte Denken", in *Die Zeit*, June 7, 1991, p. 1; Erich Hauser, "Washingtons Etappensieg", in *Frankfurter Rundschau*, June 3, 1991; "North Atlantic Council Texts, June 7, 1991 - Final Communique", in *U.S. Department of State Dispatch*, vol. 2, no. 24 (June 17, 1991), pp. 428–430.

50. For a detailed analysis of the debate on a European Security architecture till spring 1992 see: Hans Günter Brauch, *Institutionelle Bausteine einer gesamteuropäischen Sicherheitsarchitektur*, AFES—PRESS Report No. 23 (Mosbach: AFES-PRESS, 1992); Hans Günter Brauch, "Elemente einer gesamteuropäischen Sicherheitsarchitektur", in: Michael Kreile (Ed.), *PVS-Sonderheft Europa* (Opladen: Westdeutscher Verlag, 1993).

51. "NATO's New Strategic Concept (Text: Communique)", in: *U.S. Policy Information and Texts*, No. 150 (November 8, 1991), pp. 33–47; "Rome Declaration on Peace and Cooperation (Text: NATO Communique)", in: *U.S. Policy Information and Texts*, No. 151 (November 12, 1991), pp. 19–25; for the German texts see: "NATO-Gipfelkonferenz in Rom", in: *Bulletin*, No. 128 (November 13, 1991), pp. 1033–1048.

52. "Berlin CSCE Council Issues Summary of Conclusions", in: U.S. Policy Information and Texts, No. 87 (June 24, 1991); Marc Fischer, "Moscow Sets Roadblock at Berlin Talks", in *International Herald Tribune*, June 20, 1991; "Das neue Europa auf der Suche nach gemeinsamer Sicherheit", in *Frankfurter Allgemeine Zeitung*, June 19, 1991; Marc Fischer, "Security Talks Settle on Compromise", in *International Herald Tribune*, June 21, 1991; Flora Lewis, "Europe: Collective Security is Taking Shape", in *International Herald Tribune*, June 21, 1991.

52a. For the German text see: "Prager Dokument über die weitere Entwicklung der KSZE-Institutionen und-Strukturen", in: *Bulletin* no. 12 (Bonn: Presse- und Informationsamt der Bundesregierung, February 4, 1992), pp. 83–88; see also: "Letter dated 11 February 1992 from the Permanent Representative of Czechoslovakia to the United Nations addressed to the Secretary-General", UN-GA/47/89 and UN-S/23576 of 12 February 1992.

52b. "Sicherheitsrat verpflichtet sich zur Stärkung der UNO bei der Verhinderung und Lösung von Konflikten", in: *UNO Woche,* vol. 8, no. 6 (February 5, 1992), pp. 2–5.

53. Frederick S. Wyle, "Europhantasien und die Feinabstimmung der europäischen Sicherheit", in *Europa-Archiv,* vol. 46, no. 13, July 10, 1991, pp. 389–394.

54. "Die 'Hexagonale' für eine friedliche Lösung", in *Neue Zürcher Zeitung,* July 30, 1991, p. 2. However, it had no impact on ending the civil war in Yugoslavia.

55. See document 57, in Kaiser, op.cit, pp. 285–287.

56. See document 58, in Kaiser, op.cit., pp. 288–293.

57. See document 59, in Kaiser, op.cit., pp. 293–300.

58. See documents 60 and 61, in Kaiser, op.cit., pp. 300–303.

59. "Protokoll vom 24. September 1990 bei der Herauslösung der Truppen der Nationalen Volksarmee der Deutschen Demokratischen Republik aus den Vereinigten Streitkraften der Teilnehmerstaaten des Warschauer Vertrages", in Karl Kaiser (Ed.), op.cit., pp. 280–282.

60. For the German text, see "Abkommen zwischen der Regierung der Bundesrepublik Deutschland und der Regierung der UdSSR über einige überleitende Maßnahmen, unterzeichnet in Bonn am 9.Oktober 1990", in *Europa-Archiv,* vol. 46, 3/1991 (February 10, 1991), pp. D63–D67; for a shortened version, see document 67, in Kaiser, op.cit., pp. 318–324.

61. For the German text, see "Vertrag zwischen der Regierung der Bundesrepublik Deutschland und der Regierung der UdSSR über die Bedingungen des befristeten Aufenthalts und die Modalitäten des planmäßigen Abzugs der sowjetischen Truppen aus dem Gebiet der Bundesrepublik Deutschland, unterzeichnet in Bonn am 12.Oktober 1990", in *Europa-Archiv,* vol. 46, no. 3, 1990 (February 10, 1990), pp. D67–D85; for a shortened version, see document 68, in Kaiser, op.cit., pp. 325–333.

62. For details see Claus Arndt, *Die Verträge von Moskau und Warschau. Politische, verfassungsrechtliche und völkerrechtliche Aspekte* (Bonn: Neue Gesellschaft, 1982); Arnulf Baring, *Machtwechsel. Die Äa Brandt-Scheel* (Stuttgart: Deutsche Verlagsanstalt, 1982); Peter Bender, *Neue Ostpolitik. Vom Mauerbau bis zum Moskauer Vertrag* (Munich: Deutscher Taschenbuchverlag, 1986); Helga Haftendorn, *Sicherheit und Entspannung. Zur Außenpolitik der Bundesrepublik Deutschland 1955–1982* (Baden-Baden: Nomos, 1983).

63. For the German text, see "Vertrag über gute Nachbarschaft, Partnerschaft und Zusammenarbeit zwischen der Regierung der Bundesrepublik Deutschland und der Regierung der UdSSR, unterzeichnet in Bonn am 9. November 1990", in *Europa-Archiv,* vol. 46, no. 3, 1990 (February 10, 1990), pp. D85–D90; for a shortened version, see document 68, in Kaiser, op.cit., pp. 334–342.

64. For the German text, see *Bulletin,* November 15, 1990, pp. 1382–1387; for a shortened version, see document 72, in Kaiser, op.cit., pp. 346–357.

65. For the German text, see "Vertrag zwischen der Bundesrepublik Deutschland und der Republik Polen über die Bestätigung der zwischen ihnen bestehenden Grenze", in *Bulletin,* November 16, 1990, pp. 1394; see also document 73 in Kaiser, op.cit., pp. 358–359.

66. "Vertrag zwischen der Bundesrepublik Deutschland und der Republik Polen über gute Nachbarschaft und freundschaftliche Zusammenarbeit", in *Bulletin,* no. 68 (Bonn: Presse- und Informationsamt der Bundesregierung, June 18, 1991), pp. 541–547; "Abkommen über das Deutsch-Polnische Jugendwerk", ibid, pp. 547–549; "Vereinbarung über die Bildung eines Deutsch-Polnischen Umweltrats", in ibid., pp. 549–550; "Notenwechsel über die Errichtung der Deutsch-Ponischen Regierungskommission für regionale und grenznahe Zusammenarbeit, in ibid., pp. 550. These treaties have also been published in *Europa-Archiv,* vol. 46, July 10, 1991, pp. D309–D334.

67. "Vertrag zwischen der Bundesrepublik Deutschland und der Tschechischen und Slowakischen Föderativen Republik über gute Nachbarschaft und freundschaftliche Zusammenarbeit", in: *Bulletin,* no. 24 (Bonn: Presse- und Informationsamt der Bundesregierung, March 4, 1992), pp. 233–238.

68. "Vertag zwischen der Bundesrepublik Deutschland und der Republik Ungarn über freundschaftliche Zusammenarbeit und Partnerschaft in Europa", in: *Bulletin,* no. 15 (Bonn: Presse- und Informationsamt der Bundesregierung, February 11, 1992), pp. 105–109; "Vertrag zwischen der Bundesrepublik Deutschland und der Republik Bulgarien über freundschaftliche Zusammenarbeit und Partnerschaft in Europa", in: *Bulletin,* no. 112 (Bonn: Presse- und Informationsamt der Bundesregierung, October 12, 1991), pp. 885–888.

69. See Bernd Grass, "The Personnel Shortage of the Bundeswehr until the Year 2000", in Hans Günter Brauch and Robert Kennedy eds.: *Alternative Conventional Defense Postures in the European Theater. vol. 1.: The Military Balance and Domestic Constraints* (New York: Crane Russak, 1990), pp. 97–112.

70. See the following articles by officers of the Bundeswehr, reflecting the changing planning assumptions: Ulrich Weisser, "Bundeswehr-Planung für die neunziger Jahre", in *Soldat und Technik,*

vol. 33, no. 2 (February 1990), pp. 79–81; Christian Millotat, "Gemeinsame deutsche Streitkräfte. Persönliche Anregungen für einen notwendigen Dialog", in *Soldat und Technik*, vol. 33, no. 6 (June 1990), pp. 410–413; Jürgen Winkelmann, "Die Bundeswehr im vereinten Deutschland", in *Wehrtechnik*, vol. 22, No. 12 (December 1990), pp. 40–43; Wolfgang Schade, "Auftrag deutscher Streitkrafte im Rahmen sich verändernder Sicherheits- und Verteidigungspolitik", in *Wehrtechnik*, vol. 22, No. 12 (December 1990), pp. 54–58; Friedrich Holtzendorff, "Rahmen und Rohentwurf für die kräftige Bundeswehr", in *Europäische Sicherheit/EWK/WWR*, vol. 40, no. 2 (February 1991), pp. 85–87; Harald Wust, "Bundeswehr wohin?", in *Loyal*, no. 4 (April 1991), pp. 4–6; Dirk Sommer, "Neue Aufgaben und neue Lasten für das Heer und die Luftwaffe. Das Konzept der knappen Kräfte", in *Europäische Sicherheit/EWK/WWR*, vol. 40, no. 4 (April 1991), pp. 234–239.

71. Gerhard Stoltenberg, "Die Bundeswehr am Beginn der 90er Jahre - Auftrag und Planung unserer Streitkrafte in einem sich wandelnden Europa", in *Soldat und Technik*, vol. 33, No. 1 (January 1990), p. 10.

72. *Bundeswehr im Wandel (Materialsammlung)* (Bonn: Presse- und Informationsamt der Bundesregierung, Referat Sicherheitspolitik, September 1990), p. 14.

73. See my chapter in volume 2, op. cit. (note 1).

74. Bundesministerium der Verteidigung, *Konzept des Bundesministers der Verteidigung zur Stationierungsplanung der Bundeswehr* (Bonn: Informations- und Pressestab, May 1991).

75. This figure was given by Defense Minister Stoltenberg on November 12, 1990. In a paper of April 1991, the defense department quotes 521,000 and Ulrich Weiser, "Bundeswehrplanung I. Die Weichen sind gestellt. Rahmenbedingungen und Grundentscheidungen zur Bundeswehrgesamtplanung", in *Soldat und Technik*, vol. 34, no. 3/1991 (March 1991), pp. 159–162 (162) gives a number of 531,000 while an information service: IAP-Dienst Sicherheitspolitik, no. 8-9, May 1991, p. 3 counted 588,000 German soldiers in October 1990. In the higher number the time-limited soldiers (4 to 15 years) are included, in the lower number they are excluded.

76. See "Stoltenberg: Sowjetunion verstößt gegen Wiener Abkommen - Militarische Bundeswehreinsätze außerhalb Deutschlands nur durch Freiwillige - Verkleinerung der Armee", in *Frankfurter Allgemeine Zeitung*, February 27, 1991, p. 5; see Burkhardt J. Huck, "Verteidigungsausgaben, Rüstungsplanung und Konversion in der Bundesrepublick Deutschland—Daten und Literaturbericht", *SWP-AP 2700* (Ebenhausen: SWP, May 1991), p. 16.

77. "Bundeswehrplanung: Erklärung von Bundesverteidigungsminister Gerhard Stoltenberg" (Bonn: Presse- und Informationsamt der Bundesregierung, Referat Sicherheitspolitik, November 12, 1990).

78. In late May 1991, the Defense Committee of the Parliament rejected the shift in the relationship in favor of the longer serving officers and the reduced reliance on draftees. "Haushaltsausschuß gegen Stoltenberg", in *Frankfurter Allgemeine Zeitung*, June 1, 1991; "Bundeswehr. Frei zum Abschuß", in *Der Spiegel*, vol. 45, no. 24 (June 10, 1991), pp. 31–32.

79. See IAP-Dienst, no. 8/9, May 1991, op.cit., pp. 4–5.

80. "Verringerung der Bundeswehr strittig", in *Frankfurter Allgemeine Zeitung*, July 21, 1991 "Vorzeitiger Ruhestand für Soldaten - Das Kabinett beschließt Gesetzentwürfe", in *Frankfurter Allgemeine Zeitung*, July 25, 1991, p. 5.

81. Ulrich Weiser, op. cit., pp. 159–162 (162).

82. See Stoltenberg, November 12, 1990, op.cit., p. 4; see also, *IAP-Dienst*, 8-9, May 1991, op.cit., p. 3. On July 1, 1991, Stoltenberg referred to 2,000 properties of which the Bundeswehr plans to retain only 700 at 140 military bases: "Stoltenberg stellt das Bundeswehrkommando Ost außer Dienst", in: *Frankfurter Allgemeine Zeitung*, July 2, 1991.

83. *Informationen zur Sicherheitspolitik*, Der Pariser Gipfel, (Bonn: Bundesministerium der Verteidigung, November 1990), p. 6 and *Arms Control Today*, Vol. 21, No. 1 (January/February 1991), p. 29.

84. See *IAP-Dienst*, No. 8-9, May 1991, op.cit., p. 10–11.

85. See "Konzept des Bundesministers der Verteidigung zur Stationierungsplanung der Bundeswehr", op. cit., pp. 4–6.

86. For the different stages of the planning of the Army, see Henning von Ondarza, "Herausforderung für das Heer. Die Fähigkeit zur Verteidigung in der Ära der Abrüstung", in *Europäische Wehrkunde/WWR*, vol. 39, no. 1 (January 1990), pp. 39–46; Henning von Ondarza, "Heeresplanung 2000. Das Heer hält Kurs", in *Soldat und Technik*, vol. 33, no. 3 (March 1990), pp. 151–156; Henning von Ondarza, "Das Heer in einer Phase des Übergangs. Historische Chancen einer Neugestaltung", in *Europäische Wehrkunde/WWR*, vol. 39, no. 7 (July 1990), pp. 406–411; Henning von Ondarza, "Das Heer auf dem Wege zu seiner fünften Struktur. Parameter der Planung für eine neue Situation", in:

Europäische Sicherheit/EWK/WWR, vol. 40, no. 2 (February 1991), pp. 76–84; Henning von Ondarza, "Bundeswehrplanung II. Das Heer auf dem Weg in das Jahr 2000", in *Soldat und Technik*, vol. 34, no. 4 (April 1991), pp. 230–240; Henning von Ondarza, "Das deutsche Heer auf dem Weg in das Jahr 2000", in *Der Mittler-Brief*, vol. 6, no. 3, 1991, pp. 1–5; Axel Bürgener, "Operationsführung 2000. Gedanken zum künftigen Einsatz des Heeres", in *Soldat und Technik*, vol. 33, no. 4 (April 1990), pp. 231–238; Axel Bürgener, "Strategie im Wandel. Operative Herausforderungen in einer Zeit des Umbruchs für die Streitkräfte", in *Soldat und Technik*, vol. 34, no. 1 (January 1991), pp. 9–12.

87. "NVA-Auflösung abgeschlossen", in *Frankfurter Rundschau*, July 2, 1991; "Stoltenberg stellt das Bundeswehrkommando Ost außer Dienst", in *Frankfurter Allgemeine Zeitung*, July 2, 1991; "Auflösung des Bundeswehrkommandos Ost", in *Neue Zürcher Zeitung*, July 4, 1991; "'Alle bekommen eine faire Chance', *Spiegel*-Interview with General Jörg Schönbohm über Integration der beiden deutschen Armeen", in *Der Spiegel*, vol. 45, no. 27 (July 1, 1991), pp. 78–81.

88. Friedrich Steinseifer, "Streitkräfte im vereinten Deutschland, Integration der NVA", in *Wehrtechnik*, vol. 22, no. 11 (November 1990), pp. 73–78; Friedrich Steinseifer, "Zusammenfügen und verkleinern", in *Truppenpraxis*, no. 1 (January/February 1991), pp. 18–23; Jörg Schönbohm, "Das Bundeswehrkommando Ost - Zentrale Aufgabe - Schaffung einer einzigen Bundeswehr", in: *Wehrtechnik*, vol. 23, no. 5 (May 1991), pp. 4–5; "Bundewehr Ost - Der Aufbau der Bundeswehr in den neuen Ländern", in: *IAP-Dienst Sicherheitspolitik*, no. 8–9, May 8, 1991.

89. For the changes in the planning aims see the following articles by Lt. Gen. Horst Jungkurth, Commander of the German Air Force: "Neue Schwerpunkte für die Planung der Luftwaffe - Luftaufklärung und Luftverteidigung", in *Europäische Wehrkunde/WWR*, vol. 39, no. 5 (May 1990), pp. 280–284; "Die Zukunft der Luftwaffe", in *Wehrtechnik*, vol. 22, no. 7, (July 1990), pp. 18–25; "Luftwaffenplanung im Zeichen epochaler Veränderungen in Europa", in: *Wehrtechnik*, vol. 23, no. 3 (March 1991), pp. 10–14; Hans-Heinz Feldhoff, "Die Herausforderung der militärischen Planung - Vor dem Hintergrund des Wandels in der Sicherheitspolitik", in *Wehrtechnik*, vol. 23, no. 1 (January 1991), pp. 70–73.

90. Karl Feldmeyer, "Ein Meilenstein auf dem schwierigen Weg zur gesamtdeutschen Bundeswehr", in *Frankfurter Allgemeine Zeitung*, July 12, 1991, p. 5.

91. See Otto H. Ciliax, "Planerische Herausforderung der 90er Jahre", in *Marineforum*, vol. 65, no. 1/2 (January and February 1990), pp. 8–11; Völker Hogrebe, "Wiedervereinigung: Folgen für Schiffbau, Schiffahrt und maritime Sicherheitspolitik - Expertengespräch beim Deutschen Marine Institut", in *Wehrtechnik*, vol. 22, no. 11 (November 1990), pp. 66–67; Völker Hogrebe, "Neue Struktur in drei Phasen - Die gesamtdeutsche Bundesmarine", in *Wehrtechnik*, vol. 22, no. 12 (December 1990), p. 75.

92. See: *Konzept des Bundesministers der Verteidigung zur Stationierungsplanung der Bundeswehr*, op.cit., p. 10.

93. "Stoltenberg legt den Stationierungsplan der Bundeswehr vor", in *Frankfurter Allgemeine Zeitung*, May 25, 1991; "Bundeswehr löst 213 Standorte auf", in *Frankfurter Rundschau*, May 25, 1991; "Im Blickpunkt: Truppenverringerung - Niedersachsen aufgeschreckt", in *Frankfurter Rundschau*, May 29, 1991; "Stukturhilfen beim Truppenabzug - Vorschläge der hessischen CDU—Rot-grüne 'Abrüstungskonferenz', in *Frankfurter Allgemeine Zeitung*, June 4, 1991; "Land akzeptiert Bonner Pläne nur zum Teil", in *Rhein-Neckar-Zeitung*, May 25, 1991; Norbert Kostede, "Wenn die Soldaten gehen—Im Süden Niedersachsens wehren sich Kommunen gegen die Schließung der Kasernen", in *Die Zeit*, June 14, 1991, p. 4.

94. "Stationierung der Bundeswehr" in: *Informationen zur Sicherheitspolitik* (Bonn: Federal Ministry of Defense, August 1991).

95. This figure is based on planned increases of the federal budget as of April 1991. Given the economic problems in the five new states, most likely the federal budget will have to be increased above this figure.

96. "Haushalt 1991 des Bundesministers der Verteidigung—Gesetzentwurf der Bundesregierung", (Bonn: Presse- und Informationsamt der Bundesregierung, III B 5, April 1991).

97. "Erläuterungen und Vergleiche zum Regierungsentwurf des Verteidigungshaushalts 1991 (Auszug)", in *Stichworte zur Sicherheitspolitik*, No. 4, April 1991, pp. 26–30.

98. Wolfgang Ruppelt, "Rüstungsplanung in schwieriger Zeit", in *Soldat und Technik*, vol. 33, no. 1 (January 1990), pp. 15–20; Ludwig-Holger Pfahls, "Ende der Ost-West-Konfrontation - Konsequenzen für die Rüstung", in *Soldat und Technik*, vol. 34, no. 4 (April 1991), pp. 227–229.

99. Burkhardt J. Huck, *Verteidigungsausgaben, Rüstungsplanung und Konversion in der Bundesrepublik Deutschland. Daten und Literaturbericht*, SWP - AP 2700 (Ebenhausen: Stiftung Wissenschaft und Politik, May 1991), pp. 10–11.

100. The procurement costs for 200 EFA to be introduced starting in 1997 have been projected at 21 billion DM. However, it is doubtful whether this program will ever be realized. The SPD opposition is opposed and the FDP is extremely skeptical. See Huck, op.cit., pp. 26–29.

101. Huck, op.cit., p. 18.

102. Till March 1992, no final decision had been made. However, in September and in December 1991 a plan for the re-organization of the armament sector was published, see: "Neuorganisation der Territorialen Wehrverwaltung und des Rüstungsbereichs", an: *Informationen zur Sicherheitspolitik* (Bonn: Federal Ministry of Defense, December 1991).

103. Pfahls, op.cit., p. 228.

104. Huck, op.cit., pp. 30–50.

105. Huck, op.cit., pp. 53–57 (with many additional sources); see also Federal Economics Ministry, *Die Reform von Außenwirtschaftsrecht und -kontrolle 1989/1990, BMWi Dokumentation No. 309* (Bonn: BMWi, 1991).

106. See Huck, op.cit., pp. 57–61.

107. See e.g., Marc Weißgerber, *Der Abzug der amerikanischen Truppen aus Rheinland-Pfalz— Probleme einer regionalen Konversion,* AFES-PRESS Report no. 6 (Mosbach: AFES-PRESS, 1991).

108. Dieter Deiseroth, "Was Juristen zu den 'Blauhelmen' sagen - Die Bundeswehr und militärische Einsätze im Rahmen der Vereinten Nationen", in *Frankfurter Rundschau,* June 24, 1991.

109. For a recent response to foreign criticism: Chancellor Helmut Kohl's speech in Washington on May 20, 1990, "Aufgaben deutscher Politik in den neunziger Jahren", in *Bulletin,* Nr.56, May 22, 1991, p. 441–446. For several references to previous restrictive declarations of the federal government on the employment of German troops for U.N. missions, see Deiseroth, op.cit. See e.g., the declaration by the Federal Government of September 17, 1979, in *UN-Document* A/AC.121/30/Add.1.

110. Hans-Dietrich Genscher, as quoted in *Süddeutsche Zeitung,* August 25, 1990.

111. Wolfgang Bötsch, chairman of the CSU members in the Bundestag, in *Bayernkurier,* March 2, 1991, and in *Süddeutsche Zeitung,* March 15, 1991.

112. The quotes are based on a documentation by the Presse- und Informationsamt der Bundesregierung: "Freiheit und Verantwortung gehören zusammen - Materialsammlung zur Diskussion über den Einsatz der Bundeswehr im Rahmen von Systemen kollektiver Sicherheit" (Bonn, June 1991); "Bescheuß des Bundeshauptausschusses der F.D.P.", Hamburg, May 25, 1991, ibid.. p. 19–20; "Beschluß des Bundesvorstandes der CDU", Windhagen, May 31, 1991, ibid., p. 20.

113. "Beschluß zur Außen-, Friedens- und Sicherheitspolitik auf dem SPD Parteitag", Bremen May 31, 1991, in *Documentation,* ibid., p. 20–21; Jürgen Metkemeyer, "SPD befürwortet Blauhelm-Einsätze - Grundgesetz soll geändert werden", in *Frankfurter Rundschau,* June 1, 1991; Dieter Wenz, "Wir sind doch nicht im Besitz einer besonderen Moral - Die Debatte um den Blauhelm-Beschluß", in *Frankfurter Allgemeine Zeitung,* June 1, 1991; Martin Winter, "Koalition beharrt auf Kampfeinsatz der Bundeswehr - Der SPD wegen Blauhelm-Beschlusses Verzicht auf internationale Verantwortung vorgeworfen", in *Frankfurter Rundschau,* June 3, 1991.

114. "Die SPD uneins über Blauhelm-Einsätze", in *Frankfurter Allgemeine Zeitung,* June 12, 1991, p. 5.

115. "Vertrag zwischen der Bundesrepublik Deutschland und der Deutschen Demokratischen Republik über die Herstellung der Einheit Deutschlands - Einigungsvertrag", in *Bulletin* No. 104 (September 6, 1990), pp. 877–1120.

116. In 1990 and 1991, a change in the interpretation of the constitutional provisions could be observed. Members of the German border guard (Bundesgrenzschutz) participated on a voluntary basis in the U.N. observer mission to Namibia. German minesweepers were transferred to the Gulf after the end of the war, Bundeswehr soldiers were sent to Northern Iraq in a humanitarian mission to assist the Kurds, and a German helicopter unit was stationed in Iraq in summer 1991 to transport the U.N. observer team. Obviously German military officials have already planned for contingencies that go beyond the constitutional interpretation that was still valid in July 1991; see "Bundeswehr - Mit Stolz - Die Militärs planen bereits für weltweite Bundeswehreinsätze - ohne politische Vorgaben aus Bonn abzuwarten", in *Der Spiegel,* vol. 45, No. 29 (July 15, 1991), pp. 26–28.

117. "Russian Says Some Nuclear Weapons Are Still in Germany", in *International Herald Tribune,* June 14, 1991; see my proposals in Harle and Sivonen, op.cit., (note 12) pp. 159–202.

118. Horst Afheldt, *Verteidigung und Frieden* (Munich: Hanser, 1976); Carl Friedrich von Weizsäcker, "Zum NATO-Doppelbeschluß. Die neuen Raketen gehörenauf die See", in: *Die Zeit,* no. 22, May 22, 1981; Hans Günter Brauch, "INF and the Current NATO Discussion on Alliance Strategy: A German Perspective", in Hans-Henrik Holm and Nikolaj Petersen eds., The European Missile Crisis: *Nuclear Weapons and Security Policy* (London: Pinter, 1983), pp. 156–202.

119. In the Western position paper to the CFE talks of March 6, 1989, the NATO countries proposed: "In the longer term, and in the light of the implementation of the above measure, we would be willing to contemplate further steps to enhance stability and security in Europe, such as: 1) Further reductions or limitations of conventional armaments and equipment. 2) The restructuring of armed forces to enhance defensive capabilities and further to reduce offensive capabilities. (emphasis added)", in: *Arms Control Reporter,* 407.D.28, 1989.

120. "They undertake to maintain only such *military capabilities* as are necessary to *prevent war and provide for effective defense.* They will bear in mind the *relationship between military capabilities and doctrines* (emphasis added)." For the English text see: *U.S. Policy Information and Texts,* No. 159/ B, November 20, 1990, pp. 17–19.

121. Horst Afheldt, "Conflict of Interest, Nuclear Weapons, and Flexible Response: A Critical German View", in Hans Günter Brauch and Robert Kennedy eds., *Alternative Conventional Defense Postures in the European Theater,* Vol. 2, (New York: Crane Russak, 1992), pp. 111–136. For a theoretical critique of the balance concept in the realist approach see Czempiel, op.cit. (note 2).

122. Hans Günter Brauch, "Compensations for declining defense investment expenditures in the United States: Increasing military R&D and arms exports", in: Hans Günter Brauch, Henny J. van der Graaf, John Grin, Wim A. Smit, eds.: Controlling the Development and Spread of Military Technology—Lessons from the Past and Challenges for the 1990s (Amsterdam: VU University Press, 1992), pp. 17–34.

123. UNIDIR, *Non-Offensive Defense—a Global Perspective: Proceedings of the New York Symposium, 6-8 September 1989* (New York - London: Taylor & Francis, 1990); Carl Conetta, Charles Knight and Lutz Unterseher, "Toward Defensive Restructuring in the Middle East", in *Bulletin of Peace Proposals,* vol. 22, no. 2 (June 1991), pp. 115–134.

124. See the proposals by John Pike and Christopher Bolkom, "Prospects for an international control regime for attack aircraft", in: Hans Günter Brauch, Henny van der Graaf, John Grin and Wim Smit eds., op. cit.

125. Conetta, Knight and Unterseher, op. cit., p. 129.

126. See e.g., John D. Morrocco, "Gulf War Boosts Prospects for High-Technology Weapons", in *Aviation Week & Space Technology,* March 18, 1991, pp. 45–47 and the report by Mr. de Hoop Scheffer to the WEU Assembly (note 31).

127. See my chapter 1 in vol. 2, op. cit., pp. 34–35.

128. Michael Kreile, "Die Bundesrepublik Deutschland—eine 'economie dominante' in Westeuropa", in *Politische Vierteljahresschrift, Suppl. 9* (1978), pp. 236–256.

10

European Security, NATO, and the Future of the New International Cooperative System After the Second Russian Revolution

Robert Kennedy

We are entering an age of epochal international systemic change. The post-World War II bipolar order has ended. The Berlin Wall, symbolic of the division of Europe into two camps, has been razed by a people who refused to remain divided. Subsequently, Germany was reunited. In Eastern Europe, new democratically elected governments have replaced communist-controlled governments subservient to Moscow. The Warsaw Pact has been disbanded. After many years of negotiations, an agreement finally has been reached to reduce substantially the levels of conventional military power on the European continent. Soviet forces already have withdrawn from Hungary and Czechoslovakia and, barring any unforeseen circumstances, also will be gone from Germany and Poland by 1994. It is an understatement to say that the threat of an East-West military confrontation in Europe is greatly diminished.

Perhaps more significantly, the Second Russian Revolution set in motion sweeping changes of historic proportions. The August 1991 coup, orchestrated by Soviet hardliners to remove Union President Mikhail Gorbachev and put an end to reform rooted in greater decentralization and reduced influence of the KGB and the military machine, collapsed within three days. The Russian people, led by Boris Yeltsin, the democratically elected President of the Russian Republic, played a direct and dramatic role in restoring the legitimate government. Moreover, failure of the coup suggested that at nearly all levels of leadership there was a growing recognition that old dogmas had bankrupt the nation economically and politically and that something had to be done. Experiments in political and economic reform had been underway, but there ultimate success now seemed to hinge on a more dramatic systemic change. Seven decades of mismanagement had cost the Communist Party the mantel of leadership. The Communist Party then finally was abandoned by Gorbachev who resigned as its leader and ordered its demise. With the Party's property confiscated, its leadership in retreat, and its institutional association with the military severed, the way was paved for the ultimate demise of the Soviet Union. The end came in December 1991. Mikhail S. Gorbachev resigned as President. The Commonwealth of Independent States (CIS) was formed by eleven of the states of the former Soviet Union and Russia took over the seat held by the U.S.S.R. at the United Nations.

The demise of the Soviet Union and the commitment by Russia and other states of the former Soviet Union to accelerated political and economic reforms offers new opportunities for further accommodation and international cooperation. New relationships between Moscow and the republics are now being drawn. Perhaps most importantly, Cold War confrontation is over. Relationships among the countries of Eastern, Central, and Western Europe are likely to be vastly different than those that have characterized the post-war period.

Change has not been limited to the European system. Advances in transportation and communications and the explosive growth of information technologies have spawned a highly interactive and interdependent world. Water and air pollution, droughts and famine, human rights abuses, and other social and political issues which were formerly unique national concerns become global concerns when aired by the worldwide news media. Economies have become intertwined. Integration into the world economy has become the principal route to rapid economic advancement. Countries that fail to do so risk being marginalized. National boundaries have become permeable. A government can no longer easily shield its citizens from its own political, economic, or social failures by limiting access to knowledge of the successes of others.

Indeed, such changes almost certainly had an impact on "new thinking" in the former Soviet Union and surely contributed to the failure of the coup attempt. Moreover, the emergence of a significant cooperative dimension to Russian foreign policy has presented new opportunities for change in the international community. Radical movements in foreign lands no longer can count on the automatic support of Russia simply by espousing Marxist, anti-American, or anti-West themes. Moreover, the self-admitted failure of the communist system by Soviet leadership and the disdain for communism now shown by people throughout Central and Eastern Europe have undermined Marxism/communism and strengthened democratic movements worldwide.

The combined effects of such changes have dramatically altered the international political landscape. Opportunities abound. The United Nations has been given a new lease on life. Unprecedented cooperation was the hallmark of recent U.N. Security Council efforts to halt and then reverse Iraq's aggression in the Gulf. Regional institutions now also have an opportunity to play expanded roles in fostering international political, economic, and security cooperation. "Zero-sum" game calculations and their military manifestations, characteristic of power politics, are giving way to new modes of thinking. Interstate relations based on mutual benefit may well finally emerge. The operative question today is: Where do we go from here?

THE FUTURE OF EUROPEAN SECURITY

The demise of the Soviet Union, the rise in Central and Eastern Europe of democratic and nationalistic governments no longer subservient to Moscow, the imminent departure of all of the former Soviet Union's military forces from Eastern Europe, and the increased likelihood of further democratization in the CIS raise two major questions concerning Europe's future. What are Europe's future security needs? And what institutions should be relied upon to serve those needs?

The End of History?

Have we reached the end of history in Europe? Will the future simply be that "very sad time" where conflict is replaced by "economic calculations, the endless solving of technical problems, environmental concerns, and the satisfaction of sophisticated consumer demands."[1] Are there any dangers which might threaten the future security of Europe that are worth worrying about?

Even before the demise of the USSR there seemed to be, according to Gary Guertner, a "threat deficit" in Europe.[2] NATO officials had begun to speak of "challenges" rather than threats. With the end of Soviet communism and the likelihood of a full implementation of the Treaty on Conventional Forces in Europe (CFE), few anticipate a renewed Russian threat to the West. This view is further underscored by Russia's tremendous dependence on Western economic aid and largess. Nevertheless, even Boris Yeltsin has warned of the possibility of a reactionary reversal of the current Russian course of political and economic reform and, by implication, accommodation with the West if Russia fails to make significant progress toward reversing its economic decline. Hence, although seldom mentioned publicly, few in Western and Central Europe are prepared to completely dismiss the possibility of future threats to their security emanating from Eastern Europe. Fewer are willing to argue that the nations of Europe need not be concerned about future threats to their security.

Even though the probability of a major war with Russia has greatly diminished, there is little reason to suspect that the century ahead will be any safer than centuries past. Indeed, the Cold War may have had, as one of its primary by-products, the so-called "long peace." Unfortunately the survival of the "long peace" cannot yet be guaranteed, as events in Eastern Europe may now be proving. Stanley Hoffmann, writing before the demise of the Soviet Union, noted that we are entering "a period in which the discrepancy between the formal organization of the world into states and the realities of power, which do not resemble those of any past international system, will create formidable contradictions and difficulties."[3] The Second Russian Revolution and the breakup of the Soviet Union have further altered the realities of power.

Perhaps the greatest danger we now confront is being unable to perceive the dangers that may lie ahead, not just in Eastern Europe but elsewhere in the world. During the Cold War, as Hoffmann has suggested, nothing served to focus the mind more clearly than the threat of a major war in Europe or nuclear war between the superpowers. With the end of the Cold War and the revolutionary events taking place in the CIS, threats have indeed become more diffuse. Nevertheless, the conflictual nature of international politics will remain. The interests of nations will be threatened. Wars will occur. Existing multinational institutions designed to deter aggression, avert conflict, and resolve crises will continue to play an important role in international politics, although they may have to be recrafted to fit contemporary realities. New institutions may be needed. Indeed, one can point to a number of potentially serious future challenges to the security of European states.

Future Dangers

First, there can be little doubt that the nations of the former Soviet Union are entering an era of unprecedented opportunity for democratic change and economic development. Such change, if it comes about, will inevitably lead to a long-term improvement in the political and security climate in Europe. With momentous opportunity comes great risk, uncertainty, and potential instabilities. The path ahead for the Russian people will be a difficult one. The heady days of August and December 1991 have given way to sobering economic realities. The West undoubtedly will increase the level of its economic assistance. But there will be no Marshall Plan success ahead. The Russian economy will not recover easily from nearly 75 years of communism. Russia lacks the infrastructure, human and other, to quickly convert western capital infusions to economic growth. Skilled manpower is in extremely short supply; managerial experience, at every level, in running industries in a market environment is absent. The work ethic has been largely destroyed, as reflected by a saying that had come to characterize the Soviet workplace: "We pretend to work and they pretend to pay us." The transportation system is woefully deficient. Networks for linking suppliers with producers and producers with consumers are virtually non-existent, as are effective means for creating or measuring demand. Frustrations inevitably will grow. Although old reactionary power centers have been greatly weakened, the dynamics of disenchantment will offer new opportunities for those unhappy with the turn of events in 1991. In a system so lacking in democratic experience, the possibility of future coups and renewed confrontation with or disengagement from the West remains. In this regard, one is constantly reminded that Russia remains the largest military power on the continent of Europe. Although its military is in disarray, it remains a strategic nuclear and conventional military power of major proportions.

Perhaps of even greater concern is the possibility of internal conflict within and between the Soviet successor states. The struggle between centripetal and centrifugal forces has not yet been played out. Decentralization has been given a boost by the dissolution of the Soviet Union, but the road ahead remains uncertain and potentially unstable. For example, Belarus, Kazakhstan, and Ukraine all have nuclear weapons. Moreover, the question of whether the Crimea is or is not a part of Ukraine has yet to be resolved.

Second, stability and progress are hardly assured in Central and Eastern Europe. The economic task of rebuilding economies there is enormous. Capital infrastructures, particularly plants and equipments, have suffered enormously after four decades of mismanagement and lack of modernizing investments. Labor, by western standards, is in large measure unskilled and in some cases lacks the work ethic frequently characteristic of western workers. In some cases agriculture is many decades behind Western standards and efficiency. The task of energizing and rejuvenating economies to meet public expectations and demands will place an enormous burden on fledgling democracies of Central Europe as well as on the states of Eastern Europe. There is great potential for political instabilities arising from popular frustrations and disappointments over the pace of progress.

Third, of equal or even greater concern are the forces of fragmentation[4] present in Eastern Europe. Of course, fragmentation and conflict based on nationalism, ethnicism, or religion are not new to Europe. Indeed, such conflicts have been the touchstone of European history. Nor is Western Europe immune from such conflicts, as on-going religious and ethnic difficulties in Ireland, Belgium, and Spain attest. Western Europe states and peoples, however, "are governed by consensus or have well-established political procedures."[5] They also have cooperated freely for over forty years and have seen the benefits of that cooperation. While western

Europeans are not without strong prejudices and national differences, conflicts based on nationalism, ethnicism, and religion within and among Western European states have, in large measure, given way to a significant integration of peoples and nations. Western Europeans also have had time to construct institutions and mechanisms to preserve and advance the cause of integration. For those and other reasons, the degree of pessimism expressed by John Mearsheimer,[6] as regards to Western Europe, is unwarranted.

Eastern Europe is another issue. In eastern Europe, both nationalism and ethnicism were repressed under communist rule. With the demise of the Soviet Union and the end of communist rule in Eastern Europe, old border disputes and revanchist claims are surfacing. Moreover, the intermingling of nationalities within and between states exacerbated by socioeconomic disparities further raises the risk of confrontation within and among the states of Eastern Europe.[7] While pursuing the concept of democracy, Eastern European states lack the democratic experience and popular culture to espouse and nourish concepts of individual guarantees advanced in the Federalist Papers.[8] As a result, minorities in post-Cold War Eastern Europe frequently find themselves economically and politically at the mercy of the majority—a certain prescription for future conflict.[9]

Some analysts have even warned that the very attempt by Eastern European states to establish democracies while administering the shocks necessary to jump-start economies could lead to instability and conflict. British writer Timothy Garton has cautioned that the transition from the moral unity of anti-communist resistance to pluralistic politics is made more difficult by the absence of "many of the elements of civil society" long suppressed under communist regimes. As a result, there is a real danger of authoritarian, antidemocratic regimes taking over.[10]

Finally, there is no shortage of potential scenarios for conflict beyond Europe. Traditional threats based on nationalism, ethnicism, or religious fundamentalism, or based on disputes over resources, or as a result of megalomania, as we have recently witnessed in the Gulf, are likely to abound. One can even foresee potential crises and conflicts emerging in the decades ahead as a result of myriad dilemmas and issues: disparities between the rich nations and the poor, increasing population pressures, disputes over migrations and refugees, disputes over water rights, problems over drug trafficking and control, and conflicts over human rights within states, even over the rights of the majority versus the rights of minorities, to name just a few.

One could argue that many of these non-traditional concerns are potential economic or social problems, rather than military security ones. Perhaps they are. But each harbors the potential for broader regional turmoil with attendant spillover effects which might directly or indirectly threaten the well-being of the Atlantic community. Add to these the potential dangers posed by the increasing availability of advanced conventional munitions and perhaps nuclear weapons and long-range delivery systems and the picture which emerges is not very comforting.

The Tasks Ahead

Unfortunately, it may not be possible for the western democracies to avoid all of these problems simply because none of them, at the present, appears to pose dangers equal to those posed during the Cold War. The question is whether the

Western nations will simply react to events as they take place or play an active role in addressing the potential dangers that lie ahead.

At the laissez faire/retrenchment end of the spectrum, Earl Ravenal offers one potential model for future approaches to security. According to Ravenal, while several types of international systems are possible in the future, "the system that appears to be most probable, in the mid-range of 15–30 years, is what might be called unalignment."[11] Ravenal suggests that such a system would be characterized by a more extensive fragmentation of power and political-military initiative, a variety of power configurations in regions of the world, from hegemony to blocked hegemony and a more even balance of nations, and somewhat wider nuclear proliferation.

In response to such an emerging system Ravenal argues that the United States should design its defense program "to protect the core values of society: the lives and domestic property of citizens, the integrity of national territory, and the autonomy of political processes."[12] The functions of military roles would be restricted to defense of the homeland, including air, land, and sea approaches thereto; deterrence of nuclear, chemical, and biological attacks that might pose direct threats, and deterrence of attacks or pressures against U.S. territory, society, political processes, property, and military forces.[13]

According to Ravenal, such a model would specifically exclude "milieu goals" from the values defense programs would be designed to protect. Presumably, the very adoption of such a model as guide to defense planning, ipso facto, would create the very international system Ravenal forecasts. This system, Ravenal contends, will be "nasty and brutish," but not necessarily short. However, he further notes that on the scale of grand strategy, the problems nations will confront, while vexing and frustrating, will be nuisances when compared with the Cold War period.[14]

The problems with this "head in the sand" approach are many. To mention just a few, it fails to address the impact of the explosive growth of international telecommunications which on a daily basis transform international issues into domestic ones. Furthermore, it ignores the increasingly interactive nature of world politics and the increasing dependence on others for one's security. Nor does it provide an effective hedge against being wrong in our current judgments about the likely future international security environment. While promising, at least in theory, near-term gains in rejuvenating the home front, it sacrifices needed flexibility to deal with unforeseen future challenges to one's security.

In contrast to such a retrenchment approach, a second "active, milieu-oriented" approach to addressing the changes under way in the international system assumes that the international system is foreordained neither by history nor structure.[15] Proponents of such a model concede that it is conceivable, absent the intervention of leadership, that the international system over the next several decades will come to be characterized by what Ravenal calls general "unalignment" and that threats to security may appear more as nuisances than serious security threats. However, proponents also contend that retrenchment is not the ideal approach to preclude minor or nuisance threats from becoming major challenges to international security. Further, they suggest that those who favor retrenchment or renewed isolationism might also be wrong in their estimates of the intensity of the dangers that lie ahead. If so, then "general unalignment" might be among the least satisfactory outcomes for the international system of the future.

Thus, proponents of the "active, milieu-oriented" approach argue that given the opportunities provided by the breakdown of the post-World War bipolar structure, existing frameworks must be revitalized and, as appropriate, new frameworks must be constructed to preserve the peace and enhance future security.

Fortunately, despite the temptation of some Americans to flirt with the concepts of retrenchment, no world leader of consequence—including the American President and his Democratic Party challenger—has adopted such an approach. However, the "milieu-oriented" approach will require leadership, not forecasting, and decisions, not postulation.

SHAPING THE MILIEU OF THE FUTURE

The debate within the western community concerning future security structures has focused on five institutions: the United Nations (U.N.), the Conference on Security and Cooperation in Europe (CSCE), the European Community (EC), the Western European Union (WEU), and NATO.

The United Nations

The successful role played by the U.N. in providing the forum and mechanisms for multilateral action which led to the containment and ultimately the reversal of Iraqi aggression in the Gulf has clearly given new life and meaning to that organization. Some see the U.N. playing an increasingly important role in the security field in the years ahead. They believe new meaning can be given to the U.N. concept of collective security.

There is little doubt that the U.N. has been invigorated by a Security Council not plagued by the East-West conflict. Nevertheless, several factors promise to continue to limit the usefulness of the U.N. in the future. First, the U.N. represents a vast diversity of values and views. The question that remains unanswered is whether harmony during the Gulf crisis was *sui generis* or indicative of a new level of cooperation among the members of the U.N., particularly among the five members of the Security Council. While it is true that a pattern of increased cooperation within the U.N. has emerged since the Iran-Iraq war, in general, the history of the U.N. suggests that achieving sustained agreement in the future on a wide variety of issues likely to affect the security of Western nations will be problematical. Indeed, it is precisely such concerns that encouraged the adoption of Article 51 of the U.N. Charter which permits initiatives under regional security institutions.

Second, the U.N. requires unanimity among all five permanent members of the Security Council, not just a majority consensus. Any permanent member can veto the most insignificant security issue. If those interested in cooperation and closer relations with the West continue to predominate in Russia, then chances are good for stronger cooperation between the West and Russia in the Security Council. However, this will not bridge the gap that frequently exists between the Western members of the Council and China. Moreover, even if Russian hardliners do not return to power, decisive issues may see a rebirth of Russian nationalism and nationalistic interpretations of state interests may undermine future cooperation within the Security Council.

Finally, two of the world's more important powers, Germany and Japan, who by any reasonable standards should sit as permanent members of the Council, have not been accorded that status. In the decades ahead, it would be folly to organize cooperative collective security efforts in an environment where neither Japan nor Germany nor several other major states were full partners to the international decision-making processes.

For the U.N. to play a dynamic role in future international security, its charter would need to be revised. As a minimum, a new means of decision-making within the Security Council which eliminates the power of a single veto must be found. Perhaps as important, the way must be paved for Germany and Japan to sit as permanent members of the Security Council. While a way may be found to solve this latter problem, narrowly conceived state interests will probably block any move to remove or seriously limit the veto power of the permanent members of the Security Council.

The Conference on Security and Cooperation in Europe

Prior to the dissolution of the Soviet Union, Europeans generally agreed that NATO had a continuing role to play in the security of Europe. Today, some Europeans, however, contend that while NATO had played a useful role during the Cold War it is time to move beyond NATO toward a pan-European security structure such as CSCE.

Arguments in favor of an expanded CSCE role usually emphasize several principal factors seen as making CSCE the preferred forum for a future European security system. First, the political situation has changed in Europe. Europe is no longer separated into blocs. The Warsaw Pact is gone. The Council on Mutual Economic Assistance has disbanded. Eastern European states have regained their sovereignty. Germany is reunited. Second, the military situation on the continent has changed. The Soviet Union no longer exists and troops from the former Soviet Union are being withdrawn from Eastern Europe. The negotiations on conventional armed forces in Europe (CFE) have led to a CFE I treaty which will result in a significant reduction of armed forces in Europe. The in-theater military rationale for NATO has ended. Third, CSCE is inclusive. It includes all of the countries of Europe as well as the United States, Canada, and all 15 former republics of the USSR as independent states.[16] Fourth, CSCE reflects the new Europe. It was never organized as a bloc to bloc conference. Therefore, unlike NATO, it does not reflect or attempt to perpetuate the concept of bloc politics characteristic of the Cold War era. CSCE includes NATO countries, the countries of the now defunct Warsaw Pact, as well as the European neutrals. It is a forum of countries from Vancouver to Vladivostok. Fifth, CSCE has been a successful forum during the Cold War period.[17] Finally, Central and Eastern European states and the CIS have expressed strong support for CSCE as an institutional umbrella for a "common European home."[18]

There also have been objections to centralizing CSCE (as the principal bulwark of European security). First, CSCE still lacks the institutional structures which have become the hallmark of NATO. Second, CSCE relies for decision-making on a consensus of 51. When faced with far greater threats to the security of its members NATO, with its years of experience, common values, and well-developed institutional mechanisms to foster cooperation, frequently found it difficult to achieve consensus among its 16 members. Achieving a consensus among 51 nations with values and traditions as disparate as Malta, Albania, Bulgaria, the USSR, France, England and the United States will be far more difficult. Third, if getting NATO's 16 members to agree to address collectively aggression or threats of aggression beyond the immediate European borders of NATO states would be difficult, obtaining the unanimous consent of 51 on such issues will be impossible. Fourth, some argue that emphasis on CSCE will ultimately peripheralize the United States and Canada. As a result, both states already under pressure at home to reduce expenditures, may lose interest and disengage from Europe. This, of course, would not be a desirable situation. Peace and security in the 21st century will require the active, cooperative engagement of the broad community of nations. Europe's future is intimately intertwined with that of the future of the United States and Canada and vice versa. Moreover, Europe's security is intertwined with that of others beyond its borders. By peripheralizing the U.S. and Canada through an emphasis of the CSCE forum, other regions of the world will remain on the margin of European consideration and other countries will be excluded from the security decision-making processes (e.g., Japan, the newly industrialized countries of Asia, China, etc.,) that should be included. Finally, by emphasizing CSCE, many feel that NATO, an institution that on balance has functioned superbly over the last forty-two years, will be undercut.

In recognition of many of the above deficiencies, CSCE members agreed at the Paris summit, November 19–21, 1990, to a series of efforts designed to improve the efficiency and effectiveness of CSCE. In the "Charter for a New Europe" CSCE member states agreed to move forward with a series of measures designed to strengthen CSCE's institutional mechanisms. A Council of Foreign Ministers was created and assigned the role as a central forum for regular political consultation. A Commission of Senior Officials also was created. A permanent CSCE Secretariat was established in Prague. A Conflict Prevention Center (CPC) was established in Vienna. An Office for Free Elections was established in Warsaw.

As of this writing, the Council of Foreign Ministers has met twice–once in June 1991 and again in January 1992. In those meetings the Council, among a variety of initiatives, agreed to increased consultation and cooperation among its members in emergencies and has directed the Commission of Senior Officials to prepare recommendations for the future development of CSCE institutions and structures; set up communications networks among the most important European and trans-Atlantic institutions such as the EC, the ECE (UN Economic Commission for Europe), NATO, and the WEU; and intensify coordination and political consultation among member states.

Furthermore, in response to the Yugoslav crisis, the Crisis Prevention Center met for the first time on July 2, 1991 and the Committee of High Government Officials met in Prague the next day to begin implementing CSCE machinery to help resolve the Yugoslav dispute.[19]

Such efforts undertaken by CSCE members go a long way toward blunting criticism of CSCE's lack of structure and demonstrate CSCE's ability to respond to crises. Indeed, Jonathan Dean contends that the CPC *"could well become the nucleus for a functionally oriented security institution within the CSCE framework that could deal with conflict prevention, crisis management, peaceful settlement of disputes and further conventional disarmament.*[20]

Given CSCE's lack of success so far in dealing with the Yugoslav crisis in Croatia as well as in Bosnia and Herzegovina, the question, however, remains: Can the CSCE make consistent, timely and decisive action and back up those actions with teeth?

European Community

Some see the European Community as the foundation for a new European Security system. Jacques Delors, President of the Commission of European Communities, has noted that the EC has been successful in forging cooperative efforts in the economic arena. In his view, the time has come to move ahead toward broader political cooperation, including security cooperation.[21] Indeed, this view received general endorsement at the December 1990 EC summit in Rome, where member countries were in broad agreement that any future political union would eventually be extended to include security and defense and specific endorsement at the EC summit in Maastricht, the Netherlands, in December 1991. At Maastricht EC member states agreed in the second of three "pillars" of a new European Union that they would "define and implement common foreign and security policies" (CFSP), which would include "the eventual framing of a common defense policy which might lead to a common defense." Furthermore, they agreed to improve cooperation on foreign policy by establishing rules for joint action by EC countries. EC countries specifically marked the areas of arms control, CSCE, nonproliferation, and the "economic aspects of security" to be important areas of initial focus for common policies.

In the lengthy Maastricht agreement EC countries also agreed to develop the WEU as the "defense component of the European Union." However, the Maastricht document also made it clear that further developments in this area must be compatible with the NATO alliance. For the present, foreign and security policies will not be brought under the decision-making apparatus of the EC Commission or the EC Parliament, but rather remain the purview of national governments. Nevertheless, Maastricht represents a giant step in the direction of a harmonization of EC approaches to foreign and security issues.[22]

Stanley Hoffman has argued that the EC may be able to perform two major tasks that "Even the combination of the aging NATO and a strengthened CSCE will not be able to accomplish": to preserve the Western orientation of Germany and to further the integration of Central and Eastern Europe into the rest of Europe.[23]

However, the road ahead toward the development of common foreign and security policies within the EC will be rocky and the task of developing an all-European forum for the discussion of security issues will be of even greater difficulty. As Jenonne Walker and others have noted, devising and implementing joint foreign and security policies will be a lot harder than just agreeing in the abstract to do so.[24] And there is little doubt that this task will grow measurably harder with every expansion of the EC.

In this regard, many members of the EC, while supportive of greater European integration in these fields, disagree over whether the Community should be broadened or deep-end first. For example, Britain and Germany, both for somewhat different reasons, favor a broadening of the EC. Indeed, at the conclusion of the Maastricht meeting British Prime Minister John Major spoke of the need to enlarge the Community to include Eastern European countries and the former EFTA (European Free Trade Association) states and announced that an enlargement of the EC would be something that Britain could carry forward during its presidency in the second half of 1992.[25] Germany, while committed to a deepening of the EC, also would like to keep open the possibility of offering EC membership to Poland, Czechoslovakia, and Hungary.

On the other hand, Belgium and France as well as several other members of the EC believe that a deepening of EC should occur before a significant number of new members is added. In general, they contend that any major expansion of the Community at this time is fraught with a number of social and economic problems. They also see it jeopardizing further political unity. They would prefer that the EC strengthen its institutional relationships before any further expansion takes place. Reflecting this point of view, Belgium's Foreign Minister Mark Eyskens noted:

> *The expansion of the European 12 to new members is desirable but will only be possible if the Community's institutional achievements evolve toward a real political union with a federal character.*[26]

Despite the obvious validity of the arguments of those who favor a deepening of the Community at present, for the EC to function effectively as an *all*-European security structure, it must broaden its membership beyond the current 12. At present not even all of NATO's European members are members of the EC, while one EC member, Ireland, is not a member of NATO. Perhaps more significantly, the EC would have to expand to include Central and Eastern European states as well as Turkey. While some may contend that Turkey need not be included, given the likely development of events in Muslim regions of the former Soviet Union and elsewhere on the periphery of Europe, failure to include Turkey in any *all*-European structure would be a colossal error.

Given the enormous social, economic, and political problems likely to result from such an expansion, a significant and meaningful broadening simply will not happen soon.

Western European Union

Prior to the EC's historic meeting at Maastricht, Willem W. van Eekelen, Secretary General of the WEU, identified a modest role for the organization. He saw three complementary levels around which Europe's security would be organized in the future. First, is the Atlantic level based on NATO. Van Eekelen noted that this is the only organization that binds North America to the defense of Europe. A second level is the pan-European level. This level would be based on CSCE and would bring together all European countries, the U.S., and Canada. Finally, there would be the European level based on the EC and the WEU.[27]

Van Eekelen contended that CSCE would "operate most effectively at the level of 'common principles' and 'prevention.'" However, he did not see the CSCE process providing firm defense guarantees for the whole of Europe. He noted that such guarantees are based on the collective commitments enshrined in the Brussels and Washington treaties which established the WEU and NATO respectively. He further argued that in the future European security architecture, the tasks of defense and deterrence would continue to be shouldered by NATO. Within this context, the European nations of NATO would carry increased responsibilities.[28] It is here that van Eekelen argued that the WEU was increasingly relevant.

The Hague Platform of 1987 made it clear that full European integration presupposes common security and defense. During the 1991 Luxembourg meeting, WEU Ministers agreed that "European political union implies a genuine European security and defense identity and thus greater European responsibility for defense matters." They also contended that the WEU "should be developed in this phase of the European integration process as its defense component."[29]

The EC agreement at Maastricht as well as joint declarations (also made at Maastricht) by the member states of the WEU have set this process in motion. As noted above, for their part, members of the EC agreed to develop the WEU as the defense component of the EC. For its part, the WEU has agreed to:

- build up in stages to be the defense component of the EC;
- synchronize the dates and venues of its meeting and its working methods with those of the EC, as appropriate;
- establish close cooperation between the Council and the General Secretariat of the WEU and the Council of the Union and General Secretariat of the Council of the EC;
- consider harmonizing the sequence and duration of WEU presidencies with those of the EC;
- establish modalities to ensure that the Commission of the EC is regularly informed and consulted on WEU activities; and
- encourage closer cooperation between the Parliamentary Assembly of the WEU and the European Parliament.

The WEU, in parallel with the EC accord at Maastricht, also agreed to be the instrument for a strengthening of the European pillar within NATO, "which will remain *the* essential forum for consultation among its members and the venue for agreement on policies bearing on the security and defense commitments of the Allies under the North Atlantic Treaty." In this regard WEU members affirmed their intention to:

- act in conformity with the positions adopted by NATO;
- intensify coordination among themselves on important Alliance issues with the aim of introducing jointly agreed WEU positions into the process of consultation in the Alliance;
- synchronize the dates and venues of its meetings and its working methods with those of NATO, where necessary; and
- establish close cooperation between the Secretariats-General of the WEU and NATO.

Members of the WEU also have decided to strengthen the WEU's operational role through a variety of means, including:

- the formation of a WEU planning cell;
- closer military cooperation, particularly in the fields of logistics, transportation, training, and strategic surveillance;
- meetings of WEU Chiefs of Defense Staff; and
- the formation of military units answerable to the WEU.

Perhaps more important, in an attempt to overcome one of the principal limitations of the EC as an all-European forum for security and defense issues, the WEU agreed to invite members of the EC that are not WEU members to accede to the WEU or become observers. The WEU also agreed to invite European member states of NATO to become associate members of the WEU "in a way which will give them the possibility to participate fully in the activities of the WEU."[30]

There is, of course, some merit in this: a group of like-minded nations joining together to advance their security interests and in so doing forming the core which will extend to eventually become the security dimension of the EC. The WEU did play a role in orchestrating European participation in both Gulf crises. It also has extended its contacts to Central and Eastern Europe.[31] But it will have a variety of problems to overcome before it can evolve into the European defense pillar within the EC. Just as the EC will have difficulty translating intent to forge common foreign and security policies into practice, the WEU will find it difficult to forge common European defense policies. And this effort will be compounded as membership increases. The unity evident during the Gulf crisis and war may be difficult to duplicate. As a result, it may be no easier to achieve common European defense policies or a strengthening of the European pillar within NATO through the WEU than it might be through the EC or even within NATO itself. In fact, such achievements might be more difficult, depending on the membership composition of the WEU.

Furthermore, as the WEU transforms itself into a more operational organization a host of questions will arise. For example, what will be the tasks of the WEU planning cell? Will it focus its efforts on potential contingencies beyond NATO's traditional concerns, i.e., on so-called out-of-area issues? Or on European contingencies? Or both? If its focus is on European contingencies, will the WEU planning cell duplicate the tasks already undertaken within NATO? If so, why? And perhaps more important, can effective planning be undertaken in the absence of an adequate full range of military assets, including those such as lift and strategic surveillance. Europeans have generally relied heavily, though not entirely, on the U.S. for such capabilities.

Will WEU members be willing to pay for additional military units answerable only to the WEU? This seems unlikely given the changed nature of the security environment and an increased interest in trimming defense budgets. If WEU units are "dual hatted," that is, they are also tasked to respond to NATO commanders, modalities will need to be established in order to decide when it might be preferable for units to train or act under NATO, WEU, or national commands.

Perhaps the most important concern so far expressed has been by those who fear that any attempt to forge common defense policies in a European-only environment will make common decisions more difficult rather than less difficult to achieve within NATO. Thus, rather than enhancing the European pillar of NATO so that the cross-Atlantic bridge of cooperation can be sustained, differences within the Alliance will grow as flexibility is bargained away, particularly in Europe, in attempts to achieve common European positions.

None of these problems is insurmountable, of course. Moreover, van Eekelen contends that the WEU can contribute to a more distinctly European role in a revamped Atlantic Alliance, which "will be of crucial importance for our ability to react adequately to future pan-European and out-of-Europe challenges.[32]

North Atlantic Treaty Organization

Many reasons have already been advanced in discussions (above) for NATO's eminent demise or, at the very least, its supplantation by other inter- and supra-European organizations. Indeed, given the vast changes underway in Europe today, Pierre Harmel rightly has asked the grand question: Does NATO have a future? "Should it continue to exist and for what purposes?"[33] Speaking before the demise of the USSR, Harmel raised the following issues:

> *Faced with the changes in the political regimes of Eastern Europe, the accompanying de-crease in tensions, and now that Germany has been re-united, are we not close to "a peaceful, just and lasting order in Europe, attended by adequate security guarantees?" Was not the meeting of the thirty-five in Paris last November devoted to this order? And have we not consequently achieved the "ultimate goal" described 23 years ago by the report on the future of the Alliance? Hasn't the Alliance now become outmoded and obsolete? Shouldn't we dismantle it in order to re-design new security structures within the framework of the 35?[34]*

Harmel went on to answer these questions by reaffirming his belief in the necessity of the alliance. He suggested that even if Europe is completely at peace by the year 2000, that the countries of Central and Eastern Europe will still have armies. He concluded that there will still be a need to defend the Atlantic area and the freedom of the oceans and the Mediterranean against rising dangers from elsewhere; and that unforeseen adventurism, such as Iraq's, will occur and may deteriorate into global conflicts. According to Harmel such factors will result in great dangers in the Atlantic Ocean and bordering countries.[35]

Certainly NATO has contributed greatly to peace and stability in Europe in the post-war period. Its great strengths lie in its institutions and mechanisms for dis-cussion, consensus, and decision-making which have fostered a truly cooperative political environment: its long experience at dialogue and compromise; its shared values and ideals that transcend national boundaries; its vast experience in military cooperation and joint and combined military operations; and, ultimately, its shared commitment to put community interests above purely national interests. Such strengths have given NATO its durability and flexibility. The question is whether such strengths are relevant to the tasks ahead.

NATO member countries have signaled their belief that they are and have moved to adapt the organization to the changed environment. Indeed, the Alliance has been undergoing a remarkably quick transformation. In July 1990 at the Lon-don meeting of NATO Heads of State and Government, the Alliance was quick to recognize the need to respond constructively to the immense changes then under-way in Central and Eastern Europe. Among a variety of new initiatives, NATO

• proposed a joint declaration with members of the still extant Warsaw Pact ending the adversarial relationship that had existed for well over 40 years;
• invited the Soviet Union and other Warsaw Pact states to establish regular diplomatic liaison with the Alliance;

- signaled its willingness to intensify contacts between military leaders of both Alliances; and,
- informed the USSR that as its troops leave Eastern Europe and the treaty limiting conventional forces in Europe is implemented, Alliance force structures shrink and NATO readiness would be scaled back.

Even before the dissolution of the Soviet Union, NATO Heads of State and Government meeting in Rome in November 1991

- reaffirmed their intention to reduce Alliance nuclear forces by 80%;
- pledged their support for efforts of the Soviet people to transform their society into one based on democracy, human rights, the rule of law, and economic liberty;
- signaled their readiness to assist the Soviet Union along the road to market economic reforms and pledged humanitarian support to help the Soviet people cope with the political and economic crises they are facing;
- agreed on a new strategic concept based on dramatically altered perceptions of risk;
- sketched out a new security architecture in which NATO, CSCE, the European Community, the WEU, and the Council of Europe would complement each other;
- agreed to a further strengthening of the CSCE; and
- affirmed their support for strengthening the European identity in security and defense.

Perhaps even more significantly, a North Atlantic Cooperation Council (NACC) has been established. The NACC now includes the member states of NATO, former non-Soviet members of the Warsaw Pact, and the Soviet successor states. At their first meeting in December 1991 NACC states agreed that the confrontation and division of the past decades has been replaced by a new era of European relations characterized by dialogue, partnership, and cooperation aimed at securing a lasting peace. At a second, extraordinary, meeting held in Brussels in March 1992, NACC states set forth a "Work Plan" designed to intensify consultations between the Central and Eastern European countries and the North Atlantic Council, NATO's various specialized committees, and NATO's Military Committee, as well as to undertake a range of cooperative efforts on political, economic, scientific, social, security, and defense related matters.

If NATO, however, is to deal with the challenges ahead rather than with crises modelled on past political alignments, it will need to undergo further change.

A NEW INTERNATIONAL COOPERATIVE SYSTEM

President Bush has spoken of a new international order. Many have come to use the term. Yet no clear idea of its meaning emerges. Perhaps we are referring to the changes that have taken place as a result of the revolutions in Europe of 1989, 1990, and 1991. Perhaps we are speaking of the new international hierarchy marked by the absence of a second military superpower. If, however, we are referring to the opportunities which are now emerging for the creation of processes which will bring order, dynamic stability, and progress to the international system, then perhaps we would be better served by a different term. "Order" suggests unchanging hierarchy and predictable relationships. Given the broad shift away from totalitarianism and dictatorship and toward democracy, a new hierarchy seems a less stable foundation for future progress than a truly cooperative system. Perhaps we should be seeking a new international cooperative system: a broad partnership of political equals whose relationships are governed by a non-zero-sum calculus and characterized by consensus-building.

If this is the case, then NATO must change to remain relevant. In this regard, I offer some preliminary thoughts. First, the construction of a new international cooperative system cannot be advanced by an alliance which is perceived by some of its members as being dominated by one of them. While, from the U.S. perspective, the problem may be more perception than reality, perceptions have their own reality and therefore must be addressed. NATO must reflect a true partnership among political, if not economic or military, equals.

Second, NATO could benefit from broadening and deepening its institutions at the political level. In the past, the predominant military dimension of the alliance's problems aptly resulted in a progressive expansion of its military instrument. The increasingly political, economic, and social dimensions of the initial phases of the crises we are likely to face in the future demand a broadening and deepening of the political institutions, especially in the field of crisis avoidance, crisis management, and conflict avoidance, containment, limitation, and termination. Such capabilities can complement those developed in CSCE.

Third, while the creation of the NACC as a means of expanding dialogue and cooperation between NATO member states and the states of Central and Eastern Europe has been a successful interim step, the NACC is not likely to be a fully satisfactory solution to the differing security interests of NACC member states. A way will need to be found to more closely integrate into NATO those countries that seek a closer association with the Alliance. Of course, the concern here is as it has been in not offending Russia—in not recreating the "we–they" situation that characterized the cold-war era.

Fourth, since it is conceivable that Western security interests might be threatened by events far from the European heartland, NATO must begin considering what constitutes an appropriate relationship between itself and Japan, China, and other regional powers. Ultimately, NATO may wish to establish at least three levels of association. At the core would be the current 16 members, with rules for expanding membership beyond the current central core. A second "ring" of association might be at the NACC level of regular dialogue and cooperation on specifics associated with a range of political, economic, social, and military issues in one way or another related to European security. An outer, third "ring" of association might be with major regional powers whose cooperation might be necessary if the security interests of NATO member states were threatened by events beyond Europe. Such an association would, as a minimum, involve periodic consultations on problems which, if left untended, might threaten peace. It would most certainly include consultations during crises.

Finally, for NATO to continue to serve the security interests of its members, it must develop a significant capability to deal with out-of-area issues both at the political level and, if need be, with military force. Such a capability is not precluded by the Washington treaty. However, it would require the creation of significant multinational political analysis capability that can develop options and identify acceptable alliance responses to Brussels and national capitals. In short, the alliance will need its own out-of-area expertise for crisis avoidance, crisis management, and conflict management, limitation, and termination.

This hardly suggests that NATO should become the arm of whimsical western intervention around the world. Given the diversity within the alliance and its democratic foundations, this is an unlikely development. However, if history as re-emphasized by Saddam Hussein provides any lessons at all, surely one of them is that conflicts will occur and there will be times when intervention, up to and including the dispatch of military force, will be necessary to secure peace and stability.

CONCLUSIONS

To end where we began, this is not the end of history, rather it is an entirely new era of risks and challenges. Indeed, in Europe in some ways, it is the return of history—a history of national and ethnic conflict in Central and Eastern Europe that had been frozen by 45 years of harsh and sometimes brutal communist regimes. Elsewhere in the world, conflict remains a rather common trait of human existence. Thus, for the foreseeable future there will be a need for institutions and structures to deal with events that threaten the security interests of the members of the "Euro-Atlantic community". Given the complexities of likely future security problems and the limitations of current institutions, it is unlikely that any single institution will suffice.

Given its experience and flexibility, the North Atlantic Alliance will remain a necessary and, with some modifications, effective means of meeting many of the challenges ahead. However, CSCE, EC, the WEU, and indeed the UN can and should play complementary roles in meeting Euro-Atlantic community security needs of the future. Neither Europeans nor North Americans should be forced by ill thought through political bickering, particularly between the United States and France, to have to choose one forum over the others as the sole future security regime. Moreover, rather than arguing over which of the institutions should be the principal organ of Western security, time would be better spent strengthening each of the forums so that they can contribute to a more stable, more secure environment.

NOTES

1. Francis Fukuyama, "The End of History?" *The National Interest* (Summer 1989): 18.

2. Gary Guertner, "NATO Strategy in a New World Order" in Hans Günter Brauch and Robert Kennedy, eds., Alternative Conventional Defense Postures in the European Theater: Volume 2; The Impact of Political Change in Strategy, Technology, and Arms Control (New York: Crane Russak, 1992).

3. Stanley Hoffmann, "A New World and Its Troubles," *Foreign Affairs* 69, no. 4 (Fall 1990): 115–122.

4. For a discussion of the battle between the forces of integration and the forces of fragmentation, see John Lewis Gaddis, "Toward the Post-Cold War World," *Foreign Affairs* 70, no. 2 (Spring 1991): 120–122.

5. Stanley Hoffmann, "The Case for Leadership," *Foreign Policy* 81, (Winter 1990-1991): 27. The problem in Eastern Europe as some see it is that instead of developing into democracies, the regimes in Eastern Europe, for lack of experience and a host of other factors, will evolve into "praetorian states." For a discussion of this concern see Jack Snyder, "Averting Anarchy in the New Europe," *International Security* 14, no. 4 (Spring 1990): 5–41.

6. See John J. Mearsheimer, "Back to the Future: Instability in Europe After the Cold War," *International Security* 15, no. 1 (Summer 1990): 5–56. Also see the responses to Mearsheimer's

contentions by Stanley Hoffmann and Robert O. Keohane and counter response by Mearsheimer in "Correspondence—Back to the Future, Part II: International Relations Theory and Post-Cold War Europe, *International Security* 15, no. 2 (Fall 1990): 191–199.

7. See for example, Daniel N. Nelson, "Europe's Unstable East," *Foreign Policy 822* (Spring 1991): 139–146. Also see Stephen Van Evera, "Primed for Peace in Europe After the Cold War," *International Security* 15, no. 3 (Winter 1990/91): 47–50.

8. See Thomas L. Friedman, "For the Nations of Eastern Europe, the U.S. is More Symbol than Model," *The New York Times* (June 30, 1991): Sec. 4, p. 1.

9. Stephen Larrabee examines ethnic and border conflicts in Yugoslavia, Bulgaria, Romania, Hungary, Greece, and Albania and suggests that political instabilities in Southeast Europe may emerge as the most important threat to European security. F. Stephen Larrabee, "Long Memories and Short Fuses: Change and Instability in the Balkans," *International Security* 15, no. 3 (Winter 1990/91): 58–91. Also see Daniel N. Nelson, *op. cit.*

10. Cited in Stanley Hoffmann, "The Case for Leadership," *op. cit.*: 29.

11. Earl C. Ravenal, "The Case for Adjustment," *Foreign Policy* 81 (Winter 1990-91): 10.

12. *Ibid:* 15.

13. *Ibid:* 15–16.

14. *Ibid:* 14.

15. For a recent critique of structuralism, see Stanley Hoffmann, "The Case for Leadership," *op. cit.*

16. CSCE, originally composed of 35 members, was reduced to 34 with the unification of Germany. Subsequent admissions have raised the total to 51.

17. The formal CSCE process is an outgrowth of agreements reached between Soviet Secretary General Leonid Brezhnev and U.S. President Richard Nixon at the May 1972 Moscow summit meeting. CSCE discussions formally opened in Helsinki on November 22, 1973. The *Final Act* was signed on August 1, 1975. The *Final Act* included agreement in three principal areas, called "baskets." Basket One concerned issues "relating to security in Europe." The second basket addressed cooperation in the fields of economics, science and technology, and environment. The third basket focused on humanitarian issues and cooperation in other fields such as human contacts, information, culture, and education. Final basket contained provisions that called for follow-up conferences. There have been four follow-up meetings (Belgrade, Madrid, Vienna, and Helsinki) and numerous meetings on sub-issues.

18. See for example, Adam Daniel Rotfeld, "The Vienna CSCE Meeting: A Search for a New European Security System," *PISM Occasional Papers No. 11* (Warsaw: Polish Institute of International Affairs, 1989), pp. 9–10. Also see Jiri Dienstbier, "Central Europe's Security," *Foreign Policy* 83 (Summer 1991): 120–121 and Stanley Sloan, *The United States and a New Europe: Strategy for the Future* (Washington, D.C.: Congressional Research Service, May 14, 1990), pp. CRS23–24.

19. For a more detailed discussion of on-going CSCE efforts see Hans Günter Brauch, Chapter 9 of this volume.

20. Jonathan Dean, "Coalition for Regional Crises," *The Bulletin of the Atomic Scientists 7*, no. 5 (June 1991): 33–34.

21. Delors sees the idea of security as "not solely a military one. It involves ideology, values, socioeconomic systems and environment." Jacques Delors, "Europe's Ambitions," *Foreign Policy 80* (Fall 1990): 18.

22. See "Western Europe," *Daily Report*, FBIS-WEU-91-238, Wednesday, December 11, 1991, pp. 4–5. For an excellent discussion on Maastricht and the politics of a European security identity, see Jenome Walker, "Fact and Fiction about the European Security Identity and American Interests." Occasional paper. Washington, D.C.: The Atlantic Interest of the United States, April 1992.

23. Hoffmann, "The Case for Leadership," *op. cit.*: 31–32.

24. Walker, *op. cit.*, p. 8.

25. "Western Europe," *Daily Report*, FBIS, *op cit.*, p. 8.

26. Mark Eyskens, "Europe at the Crossroads," *Le Figaro*, 17 June 1991, p. 2, quoted in Foreign Broadcast Information Service, *Western Europe* (WEU-91-118) June 19, 1991, p. 4.

27. W. van Eekelen, "European Security Developments in the Years Ahead: the Role of the WEU." Address delivered at the AFSOUTH 40th Anniversary conference on "The Alliance and the New European Architecture," June 30, 1991, Naples, Italy. Speaking notes, p. 6.

28. *Ibid*, p. 7.

29. *Ibid*.

30. WEU Related Texts Adopted at EC Summit, Maastricht, December 10, 1991. London: WEU Press and Information Section, undated.

31. Fact finding missions have been conducted by the Secretary Genèral/Presidency of the WEU in Poland, Czechoslovakia, and Hungary and may soon be undertaken to Bulgaria and Romania. The Soviet Union has also expressed an interest in the WEU. See van Eekelen, *op. cit.*, p. 5.

32. *Ibid.*, pp. 7 & 9.

33. P. Harmel, "Remarks," delivered at the AFSOUTH 40th Anniversary conference on "The Alliance and the New European Architecture," June 30, 1991, Naples, Italy, p. 1.

34. *Ibid.*

35. *Ibid.*, p. 3.

Appendix A

Chronology of Political Change in Europe
(January 1991–January 1992)

Hans Günter Brauch and Robert Kennedy

In this chronology of the fundamental political changes in Europe, from January 1991 to January 1992, we have included events relating to the domestic developments in Eastern Europe and on the emerging new democratic governments. We have also incorporated events in East-West diplomacy and in arms control that we consider vital for the emerging new security regime in Europe. Special focus is on the German unification process and on the emerging new political structures of a new order of peace and security with regard to the 35 CSCE member-states. The major events with respect to the Gulf crisis and the second Gulf War have also been included. The first entry refers to where a meeting or event took place. The data have been taken from the chronological sections of the *Europa-Archiv*. The best English source for a chronological account of the CFE and CSBM talks and for the Helsinki process is the *Arms Control Reporter*.

Key to Chronology

A(n)	Albania(n)
ABC	atomic (nuclear), biological, and chemical [warheads/warfare]
Al	Algeria
Amb.	Ambassador
AMF	Allied Military Force [for rapid deployment]
Ar	Armenia
Au	Austria
Az	Azerbaidzhan
B	Bulgaria
Be	Belorussia or White Russia
Bel	Belgium
BC	Baltic Council
BH	Bosnia-Herzegovina
C	Czechoslovakia
Ca	Canada
CC	Central Committee
CE	Council of Europe, Straßbourg (25 members in February 1991)
CFE	Conventional Armed Forces in Europe
CH	Chancellor

Chmn	Chairman
CIS	Commonwealth of Independent States
CM	Council of Ministers of the EC
CoCo	Consultative Committee of Conflict Prevention Center
Com	Commission
CP	Communist Party
CPC	Conflict Prevention Center
Cr	Croatia
CSO	Committee of Senior Officials
CWC	prospective Chemical Weapons Convention
CS	Chief of Staff
CSBM	Confidence and Security Building Measures (talks on)
CSCE	Conference on Security and Cooperation in Europe
CWC	Chemical Weapons Convention
DC	Disarmament Conference in Geneva
Dep	Deputy
DK	Denmark
DM	Denfense Minister/Ministry
DPC	Defense Planning Committee of NATO
E(n)	Estonia(n)
EBRD	European Bank for Reconstruction and Development
EC	European Community
ECC	EC Council
EcM	Economic Minister/Ministry
ECU	European currency unit
Ed	Ireland
EES	European Economic Space [negotiations between EC and EFTA]
EFTA	European Free Trade Association
EM	Environmental Minister/Ministry
EP	European Parliament
EPC	European Political Cooperation
ExCo	Executive Committee
F	France
FeCo	Federal or Federative Council
FI	Finland
FiM	Finance Minister/Ministry
FM	Foreign Minister/Ministry
G	Federal Republic of Germany
G-7	Group of seven leading industrial nations: Canada, France, Germany, Italy, Japan, United Kingdom, United States
G-24	Group of 24 industrial nations
GA	General Assembly of the United Nations
GDR	German Democratic Republic [joined FRG on October 3, 1990]
Ge	Georgia in former USSR
GR	Greece
H	Hungary
HEX	Hexagonale: Group of 6 nations: Italy, Austria, Yugoslavia, Hungary, CSFR, Poland
IGO	International Governmental Organization

IMF	International Monetary Fund
Ka	Kazakhstan
Ky	Kyrgistan
Lic	Liechtenstein
Mac	Macedonia
MBF	Mutual and Balanced Force Reduction Talks
Mol	Moldova
Mon	Montenegro
MP	Member of Parliament
N	Norway
NACC	North Atlantic Cooperation Council
NL	Netherlands
NPT	Nonproliferation treaty
I	Italy
IM	Interior Minister/Ministry
IR	Iraq
Ir	Iran
Is	Israel
Ice	Iceland
J	Japan
K	Kuwait
L	Luxembourg
La(n)	Latvia(n)
Li(n)	Lithuania(n)
NAA	North Atlantic Assembly
NAC	North Atlantic Council
NATO	North Atlantic Treaty Organization
NPG	Nuclear Planning Group
OS	Open Skies negotiations
P	Poland
Parl	Parliament
PB	Politburo
PKK	Communist Party of Kurds in Turkey
PLO	Palestinian Liberation Organization
PM	Prime Minister
Por	Portugal
PR	President
Pres	Presidential
R	Romania
Re(s)	Representative(s)
Rep(s)	Republic (s)
RCC	Revolutionary Command Council
Ru	Russia
S	Spain
SA	Saudi Arabia
SC	Security Council of United Nations
Ser	Serbia
SG	Secretary General
Sl	Slovenia

SLCM	Sea-launched cruise missile
SNF	Shortrange Nuclear Forces
SP	State Presidum in Yugoslavia
START	Strategic Arms Reduction Talks
SuCo	Supreme Council
SuCom	Supreme Command
SuSo	Supreme Soviet
Sw	Sweden
T	Turkey
Ta	Tadzhikistan
Tu	Turkmenistan
Uk	Ukraine
UK	United Kingdom
UN	United Nations
US	United States
USS	Union of Sovereign States, former USSR
USSR	Union of Socialist Soviet Republics, or Soviet Union
Uz	Uzbekistan
V	Vatican
WB	World Bank
WEU	Western European Union
WH	White House [United States]
WTO	Warsaw Treaty Organization, or Warsaw Pact
Y	Yugoslavia
2 + 4	Talks of US, USSR, F, UK, FRG, GDR on German unification.

January 1991

2 IR	S. Hussein meets PLO Chmn Arafat on support for the *intifada* and Gulf crisis.
2 USSR/La	Special units of Soviet IM (Black Berets) occupy the press house in Riga (La).
2 NATO	42 tactical fighers (18 B, 18 G, 6 I) and ground staff as part of AMF will be deployed in Turkey.
3 USSR/Li	Special units of Soviety IM take over the buildings of the Lin CP and its historical institute in Wilna.
3 UK	King Hussein (Jordan) meets with PM Major and FM Hurd to discuss solutions to Gulf crisis.
4-5 COMECON	ExCo agrees on dissolution of COMECON at next Council meeting.
5 US	PR Bush meets UN SG J. Perez de Cuellar on Gulf crisis.
5 P	PM Bielicki presents declaration of government policy; stresses the interest in intensive cooperation with united Germany.
6-7 UK/US	Secretary of State Baker meets with PM Major and FM Hurd and with FMs of S, I, and L, and with NATO SG on Gulf crisis.
7-18 UN	100 nations at partial test ban amendment conference in New York fail to reach a conclusion: US and UK threatened to veto resolution.
8 G/US	Secretary of State Baker meets FM Genscher and CH Kohl to discuss meeting with Iraqi FM Aziz.
8 F/US	Secretary of State Baker meets PR Mitterrand and FM Dumas on Gulf crisis.
8 USSR	V. Landsbergis, Chmn of SuCo of Li, calls on people to protect the SuCo building.
8 US/USSR	WH spokesman Fitzwater protests Soviet violence in Baltic rep.
8-10 IR	Vice PR of RCC, Issat Ibrahim, meets IR PR Rafsanjani on improvement of bilateral relations and on Gulf crisis.
9 US/IR	Secretary of State Baker and FM Aziz negotiate in Geneva on a peaceful settment of Gulf crisis without positive solution. Aziz threatens that if attacked, Iraq would strike against IS.
9 USSR	DM Jasow assures En PM Savisaar no additional paratroopers will be sent to E.
10 USSR	Lin PM Prunskiene resigns, Shimenas is elected as successor. Landsbergis appeals for recognition of Lin independence.
10 Y	PRs of all 6 Y reps hold crisis meeting in Belgrade.
10 F	DM Chevenement appeals to US for acceptance of a Near East peace conference.
10-11 FAL	FM S. A. Ghozali of Al meets FM Dumas on Gulf crisis.
11 USSR	Soviet paratroopers occupy press center and new ministry of national security of Li in Wilna; 13 people are killed and more than 100 wounded: PM Shimenas is replaced by Vagnolius. Three Baltic PRs (Rüütel, Gorbunov, Landsbergis) and PR of

	Russian SuSo Yeltsin protest in joint declaration against use of force.
11 F/UN	UN SG Perez de Cuellar meets PR Mitterand on Gulf crisis prior to his visit to Baghdad.
11 P	Sejm and Senate protest violent repression by Soviet forces in Wilna.
11 US/SA	Secretary of State Baker meets King Fahd after failure of Geneva talks on Gulf war preparations.
11 EC/UN	FMs meet with UN SG Perez de Cuellar on Gulf crisis. EPC declaration on developments in Baltic rep.
12 US	Both houses of Congress authorize PR Bush to start military activities against IR and to liberate K.
12 US	Secretary of State Baker meets PR Assad in Damascus on Gulf crisis.
12-13 UN/IR	UN SG Perez de Cuellar meets FM Aziz and PR Hussein after failure of Geneva talks with Secretary of State Baker on Gulf conflict.
12-13 US/Is	Dep. Secretary of State Eagleburger meets PM Shamir, FM Levy, and DM Arens on Gulf conflict after ultimatum ended.
13 US/T	Secretary of State Baker holds talks on Gulf crisis in Ankara.
13 UK/US	Secretary of State Baker informs PM Major on failure of Geneva talks with Aziz.
13 G/F	FM Genscher and FM Dumas condemn Soviet military activities against democracy and international law in Baltic reps.
14 NATO	NAC adopts declaration condemning developments in Baltic reps.
14 USSR	PR Landsbergis protested to PR Gorbachev against violence of Soviet troops.
14 G	CH Kohl presents a declaration to Parl on Gulf crisis and on Li.
14 F/UN	UN SG Perez de Cuellar informs PR Mitterrand and Chmn of the ECC FM J. Poos (L) on failure of his talks with PR Hussein.
14 F/UK	PR Mitterrand meets PM Major on failure of UN mission and impact on Gulf crisis.
14 Yem/IR	PM Haider A. B. al-Attas of Yemen in peace plan calls for IR troop withdrawal from K.
14 USSR	SuSo elects V. Palov as successor of PM N. Ryshkov.
14 US/J	PR Bush meets FM T. Nakayame (J) on support for Gulf operations.
15 UK/Li	FM A. Saudargas visits Foreign Office to obtain support for Lin independence.
15 IR/T	Iraq closes only frontier crossing point to T.
15 USSR	In Wilna, 10,000 Russians call for intervention of Soviet troops.
15 USSR	SuSo elects A. Bessmertnykh as successor of E. Shevardnadze as FM.
15 UN/SC	Tries to prevent outbreak of military activities in Gulf; F

	presents a six-point plan calling on IR to announce troop withdrawal; plan is opposed by US and UK.
16 F	PM Rocard presents declaration of government policy on Gulf to Parl.
16 C	Parl approves negotiations on immediate dissolution of military structure of WTO, condemns Soviety violence in Li.
16 USSR	PR Gorbachev attacks media and TV reports on events in Li as violations of press law.
16 UN	SG Perez de Cuellar regrets outbreak of Gulf war.
17 IR	Operation Desert Storm begins with allied air attack on Baghdad.
17 EPC	EC FMs support implementation of SC resolution on IR.
17 USSR	PR Gorbachev says Gulf war was a consequence of IR occupation of K.
17 G	CH Kohl, in declaration of government policy on Gulf war to Parl, declares no German soldiers will be involved.
17 NATO	SG Wörner emphasizes NATO will defend T if attacked by IR.
17 WEU	FMs and DMs meet on Gulf war; condemn IR for noncompliance with UN SC resolutions. Coordinate navy activities and logistic support for ground and air forces of WEU member countries involved in war.
17 CSCE	At meeting of high government officials. Soviet re opposes a discussion of developments in Li.
18 T	Parl approves use of bases in Gulf war.
18 IR/Is	IR fires first missiles against Tel Aviv and Haifa.
18 SA	Patriot missile destroys SCUD missile at Dhahran.
18 G	New cabinet of CH Kohl is sworn in, e.g., FM Genscher and DM Stoltenberg.
18 EC	Condemns IR attacks on Is; expresses sympathy for Is and its right to security; hopes that Is will not be drawn into Gulf war.
18-19	US condemns IR missile attacks against Is; will send Patriot to destroy IR missiles.
19 Is	Patriot batteries arrived to protect cities against IR missiles.
20 USSR	Soviet IM units attack Lan IM in Riga; 4 are killed and 10 wounded.
20 F	PR Mitterrand offers full support for allies fighting in the Gulf; stresses IR military industrial complex must be destroyed.
20 UK	FM Hurd explains war aims of Gulf coalition: liberate K. and prevent future aggression by IR.
20 Is/US	Dep Secretary of State Eagleburger stresses US responsibility to protect Is.
20 Y	DMs and IMs of Slovenia and Croatia promise mutual support if attacked by Y. military.
20 USSR	In Moscow, 100,000 demonstrators condemn use of troops in Baltic reps and call for resignation of PR Gorbachev, DM Jasov, and IM Pugo.
21 NATO	NAC meets on developments in Baltic reps.
21 H/P/C	FMs meet in Budapest on developments in Gulf war and in

	Soviet Baltic reps; call for dissolution of the WTO by the end of 1991.
21 C/H	DM L. Dobrovsky and DM L. Für agree on bilateral military contacts and security cooperation for duration of five years.
21 IR/USSR	PR S. Hussein rejects PR Gorbachev's initiative for a cease-fire.
21 G/La	FM Genscher condemns Soviet military violence in Riga.
21-23 UK/La	FM J. Jurkans meets PM Major and FM Hurd on developments in the Baltic reps.
21-25 EP	Supports Gulf alliance and condemns events in Baltic reps.; calls for arms export controls.
22 DC	Spring meeting starts in Geneva.
22 UN	SG sends an urgent appeal to IR to withdraw its troops from K.
22 USSR/La	PM Gorbunov and PR Gorbachev agree on policy of normalization. Gorbachev declares there has been no change in Soviet policy.
23 EC	Chmn of ECC FM Poos (L), comments on Gulf war and Soviet repression in Baltic reps; calls for common European foreign and security policy.
24 F/UK	FM Hurd meets FM Dumas on Gulf war and on postwar regional stability.
24 J	Government announces additional financial support of $9 bn. for multinational forces at the Gulf.
24-25 G/Is	FM Genscher meets PR Herzog, PM Shamir, and FM Levy on aid to Is.
25 T	Government announces Kurdish language may now be used in T.
25 F	PM Rocard and FM Dumas meet FMs of La, J. Jurkans, and Li, A. Saudargas, on independence efforts and Soviet military activities.
26-29 US/USSR	FM Bessmertnykh meets PR Bush and Secretary of State Baker on bilateral relations, military developments in the Baltic reps, on Gulf war; announces postponement of February summit.
29 G	FM Genscher meets with Lan FM J. Jurkans and En FM L. Meri on independence efforts and Soviet military activities.
29 G	Cabinet approves financial contribution of $5.5 billion for first three months of the US Gulf war costs.
29 A/Gr	Gr sends back 5,100 refugees to Albania.
29 US	PR Bush, in his State of the Union speech, emphasizes coalition war aims to force IR withdrawal from K and use opportunity for a new world order.
29 F	DM Chevenement resigns over Gulf war. P. Joxe is sworn in as successor.
29 CE	Parl meeting in Straßbourg will send a delegation to the Baltic reps; calls for a tribunal to prosecute crimes of IR.
29 CSCE	Members criticize USSR because of violent military use in Li and La; USSR is reminded of its obligations under the Paris Charter.

30 IR	PR S Hussein threatens to use missiles with ABC warheads against Is.
30 IR/SA	IR troops take over SA city of Khafji.
30 G	CH Kohl presents government program for next four years.
30 EP	Holds special session on Gulf war and on Baltic reps.
30 G	FM Genscher and FM Hurd meet on developments in Eastern Europe and Gulf War. Genscher offers a financial contribution of DM 800 million and additional equipment for UK Gulf war effort.

February 1991

1 CE/R	Parl Assembly approves special guest status for R, as previously granted to Y and USSR.
1 USSR	FeCo chaired by PR Gorbachev meets; concerned about events in Baltic reps; supports continued dialogue and non-use of force.
1 UK/US	Vice PR Quayle meets PM Major and DM King on Gulf war cooperation.
1 C	FM announces WTO will end its military activity by June 30, 1991.
2 IR/Ir	Dep FM Hammadi meets Ir PR Rafsanjani on Ir mediation efforts in Gulf war and on conditions for a ceasefire.
3 US	Secretary of Defense Cheney accesses USSR of obstructing implementation of CFE Treaty.
3 F/Alg.	FM S.A. Ghozali meets FM Dumas on Gulf war; regrets limited influence of SG of UN in Gulf conflict.
4 ECC	Meets on relationship with USSR and East European countries and financial aspects of Gulf war. FMs Genscher and Dumas table joint proposal for creation of a EC foreign and security policy.
4 EPC	FMs support referenda in Baltic reps; hope for continued dialogue between Reps and Soviet leadership; appeal to the Y government to solve internal problems peacefully; object to dissolution of Y.
4-5 I/P	PR L. Walesa meets with PM Andreotti on develpoments in Baltic and on bilateral and international issues.
6 IR	Breaks diplomatic relations with US, UK, F, I, Egypt and SA.
6 CSBM	Talks are resumed in Vienna.
7 CE/B	CE delegation meets PR Shelev and PM Popov on B application for full CE membership.
7 UK/F	FM Dumas meets FM Hurd on Gulf war and on terrorism.
7 R	FM supports dissolution of military structure of WTO until May 1991.
8 CSCE	Expert meeting on peaceful settlement of conflicts ends in La Valetta with specific proposals for mediation mechanism.
8-10 SA/US	Secretary of Defense Cheney and JCS Powell meet King Fahd, Emir al Sabah and Gen. Schwarzkopf on Gulf war.

9 USSR	In Li 84.5% of 2,654,000 voters take part in referendum; 90.5% support and 6.5% oppose independence.
9 G/C	FM Dienstbier meets FM Genscher on developments in Central and Eastern Europe and on Gulf war.
9-10 SA/UK	FM Hurd meets SA and K officials. K will contribute $1.3 billion to costs of UK war effort.
11 USSR	SuCo with 116 votes and one abstention supports as new name of Li, "Independent Democratic Republic".
11 Ice	Parl approves a resolution in favor of diplomatic recognition of Li.
11 G/UK	PM Major meets CH Kohl on developments in Central and Eastern Europe, of EC and on Gulf war.
11 US/Is	PR Bush meets DM Arens on implications of Gulf war for Is.
11 CFE	CFE IA talks start in Vienna with committee meetings.
11-12 I/G	DM Stoltenberg meets PM Andreotti and DM Rognoni on questions of German security role.
12 US/UK/F	PR Bush meets DM King and DM Joxe on possible extension of Gulf war operations.
12 C/USSR	PR Havel announces that he has word from PR Gorbachev that the military structure of the WTO will be dissolved by April 1, 1991.
12 IR/USSR	PR S. Hussein meets Soviet special envoy J. Primakov on Gulf war.
12 USSR/F	FM Dumas meets PR Gorbachev, PM Pavlov on Gulf war and postwar order in the Middle East.
12 USSR	PR spokesman V. Ignatenko announces that WTO countries will dissolve their military structure by April 1, 1991.
13 G	FM Genscher meets PR Assad of Syria on Gulf war and postwar order.
13-14 G/T	DM Stoltenberg meets PR Özal and PM Akbulut on Gulf war and on German troop deployment in T.
14 UN/SC	Deliberates in closed session on situation in Gulf war.
14 SA/F	PM Rocard and DM Joxe meet King Fahd, Emir of K, and French troops.
14 G	FM Genscher meets King Hussein and FM Masri of Jordan on war and on German aid; disagreement on solution to war.
14 NATO/R	FM Nastase meets with SG Wörner, expresses R's interest in becoming associated with NATO.
14 P	FM Skubiszewski calls for rapid Soviet troop withdrawal; requests a treaty on troop withdrawal and on transit of Soviet units from G.
15 H/C/P	PR Göncz, PR Havel, and PR Walesa discuss cooperation with Western Europe and coordination of efforts of their states for EC membership.
15 IR	RCC announces readiness of IR to accept SC Res. 660, if all foreign troops and supplied weapons would be removed and if Is would give up occupied territories.
15 US	PR Bush rejects IR offer as blunder; appeals to PR Gorbachev to avoid use of force in Baltic reps.

15 G/La	PM Godmanis meets CH Kohl on situation in Baltic reps.
15 F/G	CH Kohl meets PR Mitterrand on Gulf war, development of EC, on Soviet Baltic reps; FMs Genscher and Dumas discuss Gulf war.
16 UN/SC	Meeting on gulf crisis is postponed.
16-17 USSR/EC	Troika (FMs J. Poos (L), G. De Michelis (I), and H. van den Broek (NL)) discuss with Gulf situation PR Gorbachev and FM Bessmertnykh.
16-21 UK/B	PR S. Shelev meets Queen Elizabeth II and PM Major on bilateral relations and developments in Eastern Europe.
17-18 USSR/IR	FM Aziz meets PR Gorbachev and FM Bessmertnykh on Soviet peace plan.
18 NATO/WEU	SG Wörner and SG van Eekelen meet on relationship between EC, WEU, and NATO.
18-20 G	Ir FM Velayati meets PR von Weizsäcker, CH Kohl, and FM Genscher on Gulf war and postwar order.
18-22 EP	Debates results of Troika's visit to Moscow, situation in the Gulf, and postwar order.
19 EPC	Declaration on Gulf war welcomes PR Gorbachev's peace initiative.
19 EPC	Personal res of the FMs consult on political unoin; FM Hurd stresses UK's insistence on independent foreign policy.
19 US	PR Bush rejects PR Gorbachev's Gulf peace plan as insufficient.
19-20 EC/EFTA	Negotiations on creation of a EES; Alps transit for trucks is a major hurdle.
20 A	In Tirana, 100,000 demonstrate against Communist government and topple statue of E. Hoxha.
20 IR	RCC debates Gorbachevs peace initiative; S. Hussein for continued war.
20 CSCE	PR Havel inaugurates new permanent CSCE Secretariat in Prague.
20-21 F	Ir FM Velayati meets PR Mitterrand and FM Dumas on Gulf war, postwar order, and on bilateral issues.
21 CE	Extraordinary ministerial meeting welcomes C as 25th full member; FM Genscher and FM Bessmertnykh meet on bilateral issues and on developments, stability, and security in Europe.
21 CFE	Participants agree to hold no more public meetings.
22 US	PR Bush in ultimatum calls on IR to withdraw from K (until February 23 at noon) to avoid ground war.
22 WEU	Extraordinary meeting of DMs on future role of WEU in European security order; stresses WEU as an integrating component of European integration process, closer cooperation between WEU and NATO is needed.
23 US	PR Bush announces start of ground war for liberation of K.
23-24 UN/SC	Meetings on Gulf crisis end without agreement after ground war.
24 EPC	Declaration on Gulf regrets IR rejection of US ultimatum.

24 A	PR removes PM Carcani; nominates F. Nano as PM and M. Kaplani as FM.
25 WTO	FMs and DMs of WTO states sign agreement in Budapest to dissolve the military structure of WTO by March 31. Political structure will continue to exist until end of 1991.
25 IR	IR troops were ordered to withdraw to line prior to invasion of K.
26 K	US Navy infantry units reach Kuwait City.
26-27 UN/SC	meeting on Gulf war ends without solution.
27 A/USSR	Diplomatic relations are resumed for the first time since 1961.
27 US	PR Bush announces a preliminary ceasefire after the military aims of the Gulf coalition are achieved; liberation of K and defeat of IR.
27 US/UK	Secretary of State Baker meets FM Hurd on developments in Gulf region and on solution of Arab-Israel conflict after war.
28 US/F	PR Bush meets FM Dumas on future peace order in the Gulf.
28 P/C	DM Kolodziejczyk and DM Dubrovsky sign agreement on military cooperation and information exchange.
28 EPC	Declaration on ceasefire in Gulf war brings an end to fighting.
28 EP/NATO/C	FM J. Dienstbier stresses increased importance of NATO after dissolution of WTO; possible risks to former WTO members from developments within USSR. Until a pan-European security system is established, C will enter into bilateral agreements with all neighbors and upgrade relations with NATO.

March 1991

1 USSR	FM Bessmertnykh welcomes liberation of K; stresses need for a regional security system.
1 US/G	FM Genscher meets PR Bush, Secretary of State Baker on elements of a future peace order in Near and Middle East, East-West cooperation, and disarmament.
1-9 A	Refugees try to leave in fishing boats for Italy; harbors are closed.
2 UN/SC	Approves SC Res. 686 on terms of Gulf ceasefire.
3 UN/SC	IR accepts SC Res. 686; trade sanctions against IR continue.
3 USSR	In referendum on independence in E, 82.68% participate and 77.83% vote for independence; in La 87.57% participate and 73.68% favor independence.
3 F	PR Mitterrand TV speech on comprehensive postwar order for Gulf.
3 IR	Ceasefire talks between IR and Gulf coalition forces start in Safwan.
4 USSR	SuSo ratifies 2 + 4 Treaty, treaty on good neighbor policy, partnership, and cooperation, and treaty on German-Soviet economic cooperation. Treaty on Soviet troop withdrawal and on their temporary presence are approved but transferred to Committee for International Affairs.

4 G/P	EM Nowicki meets German EM Töpfer on joint environmental council.
4 EPC	Adopts declaration on referanda in Baltic reps.
4-5 ECC	Agrees on financial aid for Is, Palestinians in occupied territory, relations with T, USSR and Central and East European countries, EES negotiations.
4-5 USSR/UK	PM Major meets PR Gorbachev, PM Pavlov, DM Jasov, and res of Baltic reps on situation in Baltic, Gulf crisis, and Middle Eastern problems.
4-5 UK/Is	FM Levy meets FM Hurd on solution for Arab-Is conflict, regional arms control, negotiations with Palestinians, economic development of region.
5 IR	RCC annuals annexation of K.
5 Y	SP announces efforts to avoid a civil war.
5-6 G/P	PM Bielecki meets CH Kohl on development of actual relations, economic questions, German minority, and Soviet troop withdrawal.
6 US	PR Bush calls on Is and Arab states to compromise, overcome conflict with Palestinians, and create a permanent regional security order.
6 G	Government sends five minesweepers and two support boats to the Gulf.
6 K/UK	PM Major meets with British troops in the Gulf and discusses regional peace prospects.
6-7 SA/UK	PM Major meets King Fahd on Gulf situation after war.
6-7 P/EC	Dep. Chmn of EC Com Andriesen meets PR Walesa and PM Bielecki on planned association with EC.
7 G/T	FM Alptemocin meets FM Genscher on bilateral relations, NATO, European cooperation for creation of a permanent Near East peace order.
7 UK/EC	EC PR J. Delors in speech to IISS addresses fundamental questions of a common EC foreign and security policy; WEU a second NATO pillar.
7 IS/EC	EC Troika (FMs Poos, De Michelis, v. d. Broek) meet PM Shamir, FM Levy on Middle East after Gulf war, peace plan for Near East, and CBMs between Arabs and Israelis.
7 NATO	Permanent council decides to withdraw AMF from Turkey after Gulf war.
7 USSR	SuSo elects 8 members of the new Security Council chaired by PR Gorbachev: G. Janajev (Vice PR of USSR), PM Pavlov, FM Bessmertnykh, IM Pugo, W. Krjutshkov (KGB), DM Jasov, W. Bakatin, and J. Primakov.
8 Y	Parl of Slovenia decides its draftees will serve in territorial defense or police forces of Slovenia instead of Y armed forces.
8-11 SA/US	Secretary of State Baker meets King Fahd on future security order in Gulf region and on efforts for a peace between Is and Arab states.
9-14 Y	Violent clashes in Belgrade between demonstrators and police; opposition leader Draskovic in jail.

9 I	Within a week, more than 20,000 A refugees arrive in I harbors.
9-11 US/F	PM Rocard meets PR Bush on prospects for a permanent Near East peace order.
10 UN/SC	K UN Amb. Abdulhassan requests $100 billion for reparations from IR.
11 G/UK	PM Major meets CH Kohl on end of Gulf war, East-West relations, Eastern Europe, European integration, and bilateral issues.
11 G/F	FM Dumas meets FM Genscher on situation after Gulf war, European unity, and postwar order in Near and Middle East.
11 A/I	Dep PM Martelli meets with PR Alia about development aid. PR Alia and PM Nano assure Martelli there will be no more A refugees.
11 Dk	FM Ellemann-Jensen signs cooperation treaty with En FM L. Meri.
11-12 P/USSR	Dep FM Moissejev meets FM Sklubiszewski and DM Koloziejczyk on Soviet troop withdrawal and on transit of Soviet troops returning from G.
11-12 Is/US	Secretary of State Baker meets PM Shamir and FM Levy on prospects for peace process in Near East, meets Palestinian delegation.
11-13 USSR/T	PR Özal meets Soviet leadership on bilateral relations, economic zone at Black Sea, Gulf conflict, and Near East problems; Özal and Gorbachev sign treaty on friendship, good neighbor policy, and cooperation.
11-15 EP	MPs call for stricter controls of arms exports, destruction of ABC weapons in Near and Middle East, support EES; condemn use of military in Y against demonstrators.
11	Coordinating group of 27 states and three IGOs for financing Gulf war meets in L to upgrade assistance for neighboring states.
13 I/A	FM Kaplani meets FM De Michelis on An refugees.
13-14 C/I	PM Andreotti meets PR Havel and PM Calfa on bilateral and international issues and role of C in Europe.
13-15 G/Is	FM Levy meets PR von Weizsäcker, CH Kohl, FM Genscher on situation in Near East after Gulf war and bilateral issues.
14 F/US	PR Mitterrand meets PR Bush on peace in Gulf region; differences on timing of international peace conference and on Palestinian state.
15 Y	PR Jovic resigns after SP rejects use of armed forces.
15 US/A	FM Kaplani and Under Sec. Seitz resume diplomatic relations.
15 UN/SC	Permanent members consult on ceasefire resolution and on peacekeeping forces.
15 NATO/F	F plans to participate in NATO planning for new strategy.
16 UK/US	PR Bush meets PM Major in Bermudas on conditions for ceasefire with IR; agree on policy of non-intervention in internal affairs of IR.

16 IR	PR S. Hussein admits unrest in the South (Shiites) and North (Kurds).
16 USSR	Secretary of State Baker ends three-day meeting with FM Bessmertnykh and PR Gorbachev on START, CFE, and planned summit.
16 T/US	Secretary of State Baker meets PR Özal on regional security, ABC free zone, Arab-Is conflict and economic cooperation.
16 USSR	FM spokesman supports nuclear-weapon free zone in Middle East; membership of all nations in NPT and in prospective CWC; reduction of troops in, and arms transfers to, the region.
17 USSR	In referendum on a renewed federation of equal and sovereign rep. 76.4% in favor; boycott in Li, La, E, Armenia, Georgia, and Moldavia; SuSo decrees results are binding on whole of USSR.
17 R	PM Roman is elected as new Chmn of Front for National Survival.
17-18 USSR/G	FM Genscher meets PR Gorbachev and FM Bessmertnykh on CFE and illegal transfer of former GDR President Honecker from German prison to USSR.
18 CSCE	CPC is opened in Vienna as agreed in Paris Charter of Nov. 21, 1990.
19 USSR	FM spokesman condemns treaties between Dk and Baltic Reps as breach of international law.
19 G/NL	FM v.d.Broek meets FM Genscher on postwar order in Near and Middle East, future security order in Europe, role of WEU and joint foreign and security policy of EC.
19-22 USSR/UK	FM Hurd meets PR Gorbachev and FM Bessmertnykh on CFE and economic reform in USSR; agree on international conference on Middle East including UN.
19-26 US/P	PR Walesa meets PR Bush on bilateral relations, democratic change in Eastern Europe and security issues; US will cancel 70% of debt amounting to $3 bn.
20 H/P	DM Kolodziejczyk and DM Für sign agreement on military cooperation in weapons production, training of troops and purchase of arms.
20 G/B	FM Walkov meets FM Genscher on economic reform, democratization in B, cooperation with EC and planned membership in CE.
20 EC/C	PR Havel meets J. Delors on special status of C in European integration between association and full membership.
21 NATO/C	PR Havel meets SG Wörner on future Eureopean security order and on security vacuum in Central and Eastern Europe.
21-22 F/G	PR von Weizsäcker meets PR Mitterand, PM Rocard, and FM Dumas on peace settlement in Near East, European integration, and policy toward Eastern Europe.
22 UN/SR	Sanction committee loosens embargo against IR.
22 F/I	PM Andreotti meets PR Mitterrand on European unity, partici-

	pation of East European states, developments in USSR, Y and in Gulf region.
22-23 US/T	PR Bush meets PR Özal on role of T in postwar order in Near East.
22-25 USSR/R	FM Nastase and FM Bessmertnykh initial treaty on friendship and cooperation; Nastase meets leadership in Uk and Mol.
23 F/C	PR Havel meets PR Mitterrand on future European security policy, bilateral relations, political and economic integration of East European states; both support European confederation.
24 US/I	PM Andreotti meets PR Bush on developments in Gulf and postwar order.
25 UN/P	PR Walesa meets SG Perez de Cuellar on cooperation between Western and Eastern Europe.
P 25-26/US/G	Waigel meets PR Bush and FiM Brady on Germany's Gulf war contribution.
26 EC	Informal meeting of FMs in L on future security and defense policy and role of EC in military integration.
26 EPC	Declaration on Y stresses a united Y would have best chances for an integration into new Europe.
28 Y	In Split, PRs of six reps fail in negotiations on future of Y.
29 US/E	PR Rüütel meets PR Bush and Secretary of State Baker on US support for En independence.
31 A	First free Parl election since 1923; CP wins 162, Democratic Party 65, Greek Party 3 of 250 seats; PR Alia loses his seat in Tirana.
31 Y	In gunfire exchange between Serbian and Croatian policemen in Plitvice, 2 are killed and 21 wounded; SP sends army to this region.
31 WTO	Declaration on dissolution of military structure of WTO is published.

April 1991

2 USSR	SuSo ratifies treaties on Soviet troop withdrawal and on temporary presence of Soviet troops.
2-3 CSCE	Parl res from 34 CSCE states agree on creation of a Parl Assembly of CSCE states with 245 members (US and USSR: 17; F, G, I, UK: 13; Ca, S: 10) to adopt resolutions with a majority vote. First meeting in July 1992 in Budapest.
3 G/R	FM Nastase meets FM Genscher on bilateral relations, on situation in Europe, and on CSCE process.
3 NATO/P	PR Walesa meets SG Wörner on elements of a European security system.
3 EPC	Declaration on situation of civilian population in IR; condemns repression of Shiites and Kurds.
3 UN/SC	approves Res. 687 on formal end of the Gulf war with 12 in favor, Cuba opposed, and Yemen and Ecuador abstaining; con-

	ditions foresee a total elimination of IR ABC weapons, reparations for K, and creation of a dimilitarized buffer zone.
3-4 EC/P	PR Walesa meets EC Com PR Delors on closer cooperation with East European states.
4 Y	Meeting of PRs of 6 reps ends without results.
4 USSR/P	PM Bielecki meets PR Gorbachev and PM Pavlov on details of Soviet troop withdrawal.
5 UN/SC	Approves Res. 688 condemning the repression of IR minorities (Kurds and Shiites), with 10 in favor, 3 opposed; Cuba, Yemen, Zimbabwe and China and India abstaining.
5 USSR/R	PR Iliescu and PR Gorbachev sign treaty on cooperation, good neighbor policy and friendship, and an environmental policy agreement.
5 H/Au	FM Mock meets PR Gönz, PM Antall, and FM Jeszenszky on integration of H into European structure, problems of security, and cooperation in Eastern Europe. Antall proposes an East European Union (EEU).
5-6 Y/EC	Troika (FMs Poos, De Michelis, v. d. Broek) in meetings with Y. leadership stresses only a United Y can be integrated into EC.
6 IR/UN	Parl 160 to 31 approves conditions of UN-SC Res. 687.
7-8 T/US	Secretary of State Baker meets PR Özal and PM Akbulut on aid for Kurdish refugees.
8 WEU	FMs discuss Gulf situation and assistance for refugees.
8 EC	Special session of heads of state/government on aid for Middle East. European Council agrees on immediate aid program on DM 300 million.
8 UN/SC	UK, supported by EC, proposes a security zone for Kurds in IR.
8 A	After 2nd ballot for Parl, CP receives 168, Democratic Party 75, Greek Party 5, and veterans 1 seat of 250.
8-10 Is/US	Secretary of State Baker meets PM Shamir, FM Levy on modalities of Near East peace conference; Shamir is opposed to negotiations with Palestinian delegation; Baker meets Palestinians headed by Husseini on peace talks.
9 UN/SC	Approves Res. 689 on sending observer troops (UNIKOM) of 1440 men to be stationed in demilitarized zone between IR and K.
9 P	Soviet troop withdrawal begins. Gen. Dubinin declares that all Soviet nuclear weapons were withdrawn in 1990.
9 USSR	SuSo of Georgia passes a degree on reestablishment of national independence.
9-10 Gr/USSR	FM Bessmertnykh meets PR Karamanlis and PM Mitsotakis on bilateral relations, Cyprus, and developments in Near East after war; FMs initial friendship and cooperation agreement.
9-11 F/P	PR Walesa meets PR Mitterrand, PM Rocard on situation in P, and in bilateral relations; PRs sign a treaty on friendship and solidarity.
10 UN/EC	SG Perez de Cuellar receives PR of EC Com J. Delors and

	Chmn of ECC, FM Poos, on situation after Gulf war and on refugees problem.
11 C/G	FM Genscher meets PR Havel, PM Calfa, and FM Dienstbier on bilateral relations and CSCE process; Genscher and Dienstbier publish Prague theses with basic elements for a new architecture of peace and security in Europe; EC and CE are of major importance for stability in Europe; NATO and WEU will continue to play an important role.
11 Y	PRs of 6 reps agree on separate referenda on future of Y.
11 F	PR Mitterrand notes European security depends on guarantees for minorities.
11 US/UN	SG Perez de Cuellar meets PR Bush on possibility to create a zone of protection for Kurdish refugees in border area.
13 US	PR Bush proposes a "New World Order" based on four principles: 1) peaceful settlement of disputes; 2) solidarity; 3) reduced weapons aresenals; and 4) just treatment of all peoples.
13 USSR	PRs of Baltic reps accept a proposal of Ice for mediation with union leadership.
14 USSR	S. Gamsakhurdia is elected as PR of Georgia by Parl (former SuSo).
15 UK/T	PM Akbulut meets PM Major on zone of protection for Kurdish refugees in Northern IR.
15 ECC	Meets on negotiations on EES, association agreements with P, C, H and on common foreign and defense policy.
15 EBRD	Inaugurated at meeting of heads of states and governments of member states.
15-19 EP	Passes recommendations on control of weapons exports, armaments co-operation of EC.
16 US/R	PM Roman meets Secretary of State Baker on situation and creation of democratic institutions in R, changes in Eastern Europe.
16 US	PR Bush announces creation of zones of protection for Kurds in Northern IR.
16 US/C	FM Dienstbier meets Secretary of State Baker on economic situation in C, European security, and future architecture of Europe.
16 EC	FM Poos submits first draft of a treaty for a political union.
16 EP/UN	SG Perez de Cuellar addresses EP on peace efforts in Gulf, weapons exports, and for cooperation on peace and prosperity.
17 F/USSR	PR Mitterrand receives Russian Parl PR Yeltsin.
17 EC/US	Secretary of State Baker meets EC FMs on peace in Near and Middle East and a Kurdish refugees.
17 G/C	Parl PR A. Dubcek meets CH Kohl on bilateral issues and closer cooperation in Europe.
17-19 F/UN	SG Perez de Cuellar meets PR Mitterand, PM Rocard, and FM Dumas on plan for Kurdish refugees in Northern IR.
17-18 H/B	PR Shelev meets PR Gönzc on bilateral and regional issues in Middle and Eastern Europe.

18-19 R/F	PR Mitterand meets PR Iliescu and PM Roman on bilateral relations and closer cooperation with EC.
18-20 Is/US	Secretary of State Baker meets PM Shamir and FM Levy on details of planned Middle East conference; Baker also meets Palestinian delegation.
19 T/G	FM Genscher meets PR Özal and FM Alptemocin on assistance for Kurdish refugees from IR.
19 G/NATO	SG Wörner meets CH Kohl on European security issues.
22 USSR	PM Pavlov presents the SuSo with anti-crisis plan, approved 323 to 13, with 29 abstentions.
22-26 CE	Meets in Straßbourg on developments in Central and Eastern Europe and integration of these states; PM Mitsotakis (Gr) calls for a conference on security and cooperation in the Mediterranean (CSCM).
23 USSR	PR Gorbachev and PRs of nine union republics, including Yeltsin, sign an appeal to end wildcat strikes.
23-26 UK/P	PR Walesa meets with Queen Elizabeth II. PM Major on bilateral relations, democratization, development in Central and Eastern Europe.
24 F/G	CH Kohl meets PR Mitterand on European unity, peace in Middle East, and Kurdish refugee problems.
24-24 USSR	Meeting of CC of CPSU, PR Gorbachev after attacks from traditionalist wing indicates readiness to resign.
25 USSR	Secretary of State Baker meets FM Bessmertnykh on possibilities to solve the Middle East conflict; both achieve progress on CFE dispute.
25 Y	PR Jovic for an intensified peaceful and democratic dialogue on future of Y.
25 G/USSR	Bundestag approves unanimously treaty of good neighborhood, partnership, and cooperation, and treaty on comprehensive cooperation in the economic, industrial, and scientific fields.
25-26 NATO/C	At invitation of FM Dienstbier and NATO SG Wörner, experts from West, Central, and Eastern Europe discuss on future of European security. PR Havel supports a system of collective agreements to enhance European security.
25-26 Is/US	Secretary of State Baker meets PM Shamir and FM Levy on details of planned Middle East conference.
26 F/H	FM Jeszensky meets FM Dumas on bilateral relations and preparation of a bilateral friendship treaty.
26-27 G/P	FM Skubiszewski meets PR von Weizsäcker, FM Genscher on bilateral friendship treaty.
27 EC	Informal meeting of FMs on situation in Near and Middle East, sending of a police force to Northern IR to protect Kurdish refugees and for creation of a joint weapons export register.
27 C	FM Genscher supports EC membership of C, H, P at founding meeting of the liberal Citizen's Movement.
29 EC/B	PM Popov meets with EC Com members on association with EC.
29-30 EC/USSR	PM Pavlov meets on food aid for Soviet population.

30 UK/G   FM Genscher meets PM Major and FM Hurd on European unity, CSCE process, and on Kurdish refugees.

May 1991

1-2 S/G   Bilateral consultations between CH Kohl and PM Gonzalez on realization of political and economic union in Europe.

3 EPC/Is   Declaration on cooperation with Is criticizes policy in occupied areas; calls for stopping new settlements in occupied areas.

4 A   PR resigns as SG of CP of A.

4 Y   Special meeting of presidium after violence in Brovo Selo (Slovenia) condemns acts of violence and attacks on armed forces.

6-7 USSR/F   PR Mitterand and FM Dumas meet PR Gorbachev on bilateral relations, postwar peace order in Middle East.

6-9 G/H   PR Göncz meets PR von Weizsäcker, CH Kohl on bilateral relations, developments in H, relationship of new democracies to EC; DM Für meets DM Stoltenberg on bilateral military cooperation.

7 US/I   PR Bush meets PR Cossiga and PM Andreotti on European security and developments in Near and Middle East and in Eastern Europe.

7 US   PR Bush meets Lin PR Landsbergis, En PM Savisaar and Lan PM Godmanis on situation in Baltic reps.

7 Y   DM Kadijevic submits an 11-point declaration of armed forces with an ultimatum addressed to presidium to contain violence.

7-8 UK/S   PM Gonzalez meets PM Major on Gibraltar and European issues.

7-8 F/C   FM Dienstbier in meeting with FM Dumas initiates regular political consultations in bilateral, European and other issues, e.g., future European security policy and integration in Europe.

7-9 Y   Presidium agrees on measures to stop tendencies toward civil war; in Crotia police reserves and civilians must be disarmed.

8 EPC/Y   Declaration expresses concern on internal developments in Y.

8 UK/F   PM Rocard meets PM Major on implementation of economic and currency union and preparation of EC summit.

8 G/C   PR Havel meets PR von Weizsäcker on extending bilateral relations.

9 UK/R   FM Nastase meets FM Hurd on assistance, R's relations with USSR.

9 US/UN   SG Perez de Cuellar meets PR Bush on situation of Kurdish refugees in IR and the objection of IR leadership to the deployment of UN police forces in North IR.

9-11 US/G   FM Genscher meets Secretary of State Baker on European security and situation in Middle East; publish joint declaration on future Western security policy with NATO, EC, WEU, CSCE and CE as basic pillars of European stability with NATO re-

	maining the most important forum for policy coordination; support an effective and integrated military structure and further institutionalization of CSCE.
10 UN/G	SG Perez de Cuellar meets FM Genscher on role of UN in catastrophes and on international coordination of assistance programs.
10 Is/USSR	First meeting of a Soviet FM in Is. FM Bessmertnykh and FM Levy discuss improvement of bilateral relations, emigration of Soviety Jews to Is, USSR participation in peace process in Near and Middle East, and situation after Gulf war.
12-13 US/SU	Secretary of State Baker and FM Besmertnykh meet in Cairo on initiation of a peace process in Middle East.
13 US	PR Bush announces a change in U.S. position on CW disarmament.
13 EC/EFTA	Ministerial meeting on EES in Brussels.
13-14 C/Ru	Russian Parl PR Yeltsin meets Havel on economic cooperation and Eureopean integration.
13-17 EP	Discusses a report of the political committee on the establishment of multinational European force for peacekeeping purposes; threatens to stop economic aid to Y if military takes over; condemns Is's policy of settlements in occupied areas.
14-16 Is/US	Secretary of State Baker meets PM Shamir, FM Levy, and DM Arens on Near East conference; meets with Palestinian delegation.
15 F	PM Rocard resigns; Edith Cresson is nominated as successor.
15 Y	Crotian member of presidium S. Mesic is not elected as new PR.
16 USSR/G	EcM Möllemann signs agreement with minister for nuclear energy Konovalov on takeover of Soviet-owned uranium mines in the former GDR.
16 F	PM Cresson presents her cabinet.
16 F/La	Lan PR Gorbunov meets PR Mitterrand on situation in Baltic reps.
16 US/UK	Queen Elizabeth II addresses both houses of Congress with special emphasis on Anglo-American cooperation during Gulf war.
16 DC	US Chief delegate Ledogar introduces PR Bush's CWC proposals, welcomed by USSR chief delegate Bazanov.
16-17 G/F	FM Dumas and FM Genscher hold first joint meeting of Ambs. in Central and Eastern Europe in Weimar on regional political and economic developments, support for reform processes, and "new architecture for Europe".
18 Y	Second attempt to elect S. Mesic as PRSP in Y. fails.
18	FMs of I, Y, Au, H, C [Pentagonale] meet in Bologna on issues of political and economic buildup of former Communist countries and on domestic situation in Y; P participates as an observer.
19 Y	Referendum in sovereignty of Croatia; 84% participated;

	94.3% for sovereignty, 92% oppose membership in a federative Y.
20 US/UK	Secretary of State Baker meets Hurd on developments in Near East and USSR.
20-21 US/G	CH Kohl meets PR Bush and Secretary of State Baker on situation in united Germany, developments in Central and Eastern Europe, Near East, and USSR.
20-21 US/USSR	Soviet CS, Gen. Moissejev meets PR Bush and U.S. military leadership on security policy and disarmament issues.
21 UN	SC decides to establish a fund on consequences of Gulf war into which a part of IR oil export income should be payed.
21-22 F/H	PM Antall meets PR Mitterrand on bilateral relations, H is interested in full EC membership.
21-22 USSR/I	PM Andreotti meets PR Gorbachev, PM Pavlov on bilateral and multilateral economic cooperation and domestic situation in USSR.
22 F/Ar	PR Mitterrand and FM Dumas meet Armenian PR Ter-Petrosjan on situation in USSR and on role of reps.
22-24 EFTA	Liechtenstein becomes seventh member; debate on EES talks with EC.
23 A/CE	CE delegation meets PR Alia, PM Nano, and FM Kaplani on democratization, relationship with CE, and other European institutions.
23 G/NL	FM Genscher and FM v. d. Broek confer on European unity, sign an agreement with PM of North Rhine-Westfalia and Lower Saxony on regional cooperation.
23-24 F/Y	PM Markovic meets PM Cresson on closer cooperation with EC.
24-26 NAA	200 MPs from 16 NATO countries discuss with delegations from B, C, H, P, R and USSR the future of transatlantic relations, new structure of alliances, security and defense after Gulf war, future defense and security identity, cooperation with North America, East European and pan-European security architecture in framework of NATO and CSCE.
25 USSR	Baltic Council meeting in Wilna condemns violent attacks by Soviet forces against border posts.
26 USSR	First direct election of a President in Georgia; with 83.5% voting, S. Gamsakhurdia receives 86.5%.
27 NATO	Eurogroup meeting in Brussels calls on USSR to remove obstacles for ratification of CFE treaty.
27 USSR/G	EcM Mölleman refers with PM Pavlov on prospects of joint economic relations and on participation of German firms in construction of flats for returning families of Soviet officers.
27 F/US	Defense Secretary Cheney meets PR Mitterrand, PM Cresson, and DM Joxe on security political situation after Gulf war and future European security system.
28-29 NATO	Joint meeting of NPG and DPC in Brussels agrees on multinational force structure as an element of future NATO strategy.

28-31 US/USSR	Gorbachev's advisor Primakov meets PR Bush on American financial aid for USSR.
29 US	PR Bush addresses arms limitation in Near East, calls for an end of arms race with ABC weapons and major supplies for constraints in conventional arms transfers.
29 UK/A	A resumes diplomatic relations that were broken off in 1946.
29 USSR	After 46 years, Kaliningrad harbor (Königsberg) is opened to foreign vessels.
29-30 F/G	Bilateral consultations in Lille on situation in Central and Eastern Europe, Near and Middle East, and on European unification; joint appeal to Y. leadership to solve dispute peacfully; support for participation of PR Gorbachev at 6-7 summit in London in July.
30-31 Is/US	Defense Secretary Cheney confers with Is leadership on bilateral military relations; conveys disarmament proposals from PR Bush.

June 1991

1 US/USSR	Secretary of State Baker and FM Bessmertnykh overcome obstacles preventing ratification of CFE; discuss START and peace settlement in Near East.
1 H/A	FM Kapllani meets FM Jeszensky on trade and cultural relations.
2-3 EC	Informal meeting of FMs in Dresden on economic revival of Eastern Europe; preparations of FM conference in Berlin and situation in Y.
2-4 USSR/G	EM Töpfer meets with Soviet leadership on environmental issues at Soviet bases in former GDR. DM Jasov assures Töpfer no Soviet nuclear and chemical weapons are deployed in G.
3 F	PR Mitterrand tables a disarmament plan; supports destruction of all biological and chemical and drastic reduction of nuclear weapons; calls for control of export of missile technology; control of arms exports that violate a regional conventional balance. F will join NPT.
3 A	Government of national concentration is formed, based on CP, and opposition Republican, Agrarian, and Social Democratic parties with Y. Bulfi as PM and M. Kapllani as FM.
3 H/G	FM Genscher meets with PM Antall and FM Jeszensky on EC membership. Genscher proposes a bilateral treaty.
3-6 WEU	Parl Assembly discusses European security identity, role of WEU, and NATO; FM Dumas opposes NATO rapid deployment force.
4 NL/G	FM Genscher meets FM v. d. Broek on joint declaration for Dutch EC presidency and Berlin CSCE meeting; stress importance of European union for integration and European security.
5 N/USSR	PR Gorbachev gives acceptance speech for Nobel Peace Prize

	in Oslo and meets PM Brundtland on bilateral relations, especially on borders in Barent Sea and Kola penninsula.
5 F/Is	FM Levy meets PR Mitterrand on situation in Near East and on participation of EC states in peace process.
5 EC/Is	EC Troika meets in Paris with FM Levy on Near East peace conference.
5 G/F	FM Genscher in consultation with FM Dumas sends letter to PR of EC Com Delor, supporting extended relationship with east European democracies.
5 G/C	FM Genscher meets FM Dienstbier on preparations for CSCE Council of Foreign ministers of Berlin, on bilateral and European issues.
5-7 G/EC	PR of EC Com Delors visits Berlin and five new states; opposes rapid Eastern enlargement of EC; integration of former GDR no model.
6 F/T	PR Özal meets PR Mitterrand on bilateral relations, situation after Gulf war, developments in Eastern Europe, Cyprus, and relations between Gr and T.
6 CFE	Talks on CFE resumed in Vienna; Soviet Amb. Grinewski presents a legally binding declaration on disputed aspects of CFE Treaty.
6 Y	PRs of six reps agree in Sarajevo on continuation of talks.
6 Sw	PR Gorbachev meets PM Carlsson on developments in Baltic reps.
6-7 NATO	NAC meeting in Copenhagen passes declarations on CSCE process and on future roles of NATO.
7 CSCE	Symposium on cultural heritage ends in Krakow with final document.
7-8 Y/USSR	PM Pavlov meets PM Markovic on mutual economic relations.
8 EPC	Declaration on Y.
8 G/UK	FM Genscher meets FM Hurd on CSCE meeting in Berlin and G-7 summit in London; both visit Weimar.
9 UK/G	CH Kohl meets PM Major on EC and G-7 summits and on invitation of PR Gorbachev.
10-14 EP	Passess resolutions on repression in Baltic reps by Soviet leadership.
10 Fi/G	FM Genscher meets PR Koivisto and FM Väyrynen on extension of European integration, defense policy, relations with Baltic reps, and EES talks.
11 UN/SC	Resolves to maintain all sanctions against IR.
11-13 A	Congress of CP, 9 members of PB are expelled. CP is renamed Socialist Party.
12 US/C	DM Dubrovsky meets Defense Secretary Cheney on security in central Europe and future bilateral military cooperation.
12 USSR	First free election of a PR of Russia. Yeltsin obtains 57.3%, Ryshkov 16.85%, and four candidates less than 10%.
12-14 C	Conference on a European confederation cosponsored by PR Havel and Mitterrand meets in Europe.
12-13 T/IR	IR Vice PM Aziz meets with PR Özal, PM Akbulut, and FM

	Alptemocin on bilateral issues, problems of Kurds, reopening of oil pipeline, and U.N. sanctions.
12-13 G/USSR	FM Bessmertnykh meets FM Genscher on bilateral relations, CSCE Berlin conference; Soviet nuclear weapons still in G.
12-14 B	NATO SG Wörner meets PR Shelev, PM Popov, FM Valkov on change in Eastern Europe and European security issues.
13 A/I	FM De Michelis calls upon government to stop flow of refugees; promises food and medical aid of $50 million.
13 P	PM Bielecki meets Lan PM Godmanis on political cooperation; supports participation of La in CSCE.
14 I/A	IM gives orders all boats with refugees have to leave Italian waters.
14 Sw	PM Carlsson announces Sw will apply for EC membership on July 1.
15 A/G	FM Genscher in talks with An leadership; favors membership in CSCE.
16 G/Ca	PM Mulroney meets CH Kohl on developments since unification, and on containment of exports of conventional weapons. Supports stronger cooperation between Europe and North America.
16 G/P	PM Bielecki and CH Kohl meet on bilateral relations and sign treaty on good neighborhood and friendly cooperation.
17 S/H	PM Antall meets PM Gonzalez on bilateral trade relations; calls on West to offer declaration on security for east European states after dissolution of WTO.
17 USSR	PM Pavlov tables SuSo proposal for overcoming economic crisis.
17 T	Pr Özal asks M. Yilmaz to form new government.
17 UN/SC	Approves res. 699 and 700 on IR. IR must pay for destruction of weapons of mass destruction; economic sanctions continue.
17-18 G/US	Secretary of State Baker meets in Berlin with FM Genscher on developments in five new states and economic assistance for USSR.
17-18 EC	Council meets on EES talks.
18-19 EC/EFTA	Ministers meet for EES talks in L.
18-21 US	Russian PR Yeltsin meets PR Bush on future development in USSR.
19-20 CSCE	Meeting of Council in Berlin accepts A as 35th member; approves mechanism for crisis prevention and for peaceful settlement of disputes.
19-20 USSR/EC	PR of Com Delors meets with Soviet leadership on economic cooperation between EC and USSR and on EC economic aid.
20 EC	L presidency tables proposal for treaty on European unity, containing details on future political, and on economic and currency union.
20 G	Parl votes 337 to 320 for Berlin as capital and new government seat.
21 F	PR Mitterrand receives Lin Parl PR Landsbergis on Baltic reps.

21 Y/US	Secretary of State Baker meets separately with PRs of six republics and with PM Markovic and FM Loncar on domestic developments; U.S. will not recognize Slovenia as independent state.
21 A/EC	Diplomatic relations are established.
21-22 F/S	Bilateral consultations on questions of European security and relations with Maghreb countries.
22 A/US	Secretary of State Baker meets PR Alia and PM Bulfi on economic problems and democratization; offers economic aid of $6 million, recommends economic shock therapy.
22 G/USSR	FM Bessmertnykh and FM Genscher hold a joint memorial to observe the 50th anniversary of Germany's attack on USSR. PR Gorbachev and CH Kohl address German and Soviet audiences on TV.
23 G-7	FiMs and heads of currency banks of G-7 meet in London on business cycles and on increase in dollar exchange rate.
23 EC	FMs meet in L on situation in IR and Y; will not recognize a possible unilateral declaration of independence of Slovenia and Croatia.
24 Y	FM of Slovenia regrets EC declaration of Y of June 23.
24 F/UK	PR Mitterrand and PM Major meet in Dunkirk on EC summit.
24 R	Parl condemns annexation of Moldavia in 1946. FM Nastase stressed R has no territorial claims.
24-25 EC	Meeting with EFTA in Salzburg fails on EES over Alps transit dispute.
24-28 I/G	PR von Weizsäcker meets PR Cossiga and PM Andreotti in European unification, support for east European democracies, situation in Y, and on developments for peace in Near East.
25 F/G	CH Kohl and PR Mitterrand discuss EC reform, developments, and cooperation with former USSR.
25 C/USSR	Final protocol on withdrawal of all Soviet troops is signed; mutual financial claims are not yet settled.
25 Y	Croatian Parl approves with large minority decision on sovereignty and independence; Slovenian Parl declares its independence; linkage with Y to be gradually scrapped.
25-27 CE	Parl Assembly meets in Helsinki on European unification and invites PRs of Baltic reps on recent developments; USSR protests against intervention in internal affairs.
26 Y	Federal government rejects declaration of independence of Slovenia and Croatia and orders federal police to take over control of borders on territory of Slovenia; Croita announces violent fighting between Serbs and Croatian police in Glina.
26 US/Y	Secretary of State declares U.S. will not recognize independence of Slovenia and Croatia; continues to support central government in Belgrade.
27 Y	Fighting in Slovenia between Y armed forces and Slovenian territorial defense forces; federal government proposes to stop fighting if Slovenia and Croatia interrupt their independence for three months.

27 USSR	FM declares it will not recognize independence of Slovenia and Croatia; supports continued Y unity.
27 Au	FM Mock called on Y to offer information on military activities, in accordance with the CSCE crisis framework.
27 WEU	Ministerial meeting supports initiation of CSCE mechanism for urgent situations in Y; members stress WEU could function as security component of EC members.
27-29 Au/USSR	PM Pavlov meets PR Waldheim and CH Vranitzky on situation in Y, bilateral issues, European unification, and East-West relations.
28 COMECON	Members meet in Budapest to sign a protocol on its dissolution.
28 Y	EC Troika confers with Y leadership and PRs of Croatia and Slovenia.
28 UN/SC	calls on IR not to obstruct UN experts any longer.
28-29 EC	Summit of European Council focuses on events in Y and Troika's mediation efforts.
30 Y/EC	In presence of Troika, Y presidium meets to elect Mesic as PR; Mesic orders withdrawal of troops from Slovenia and this return to barracks.
30 Au/Y	CH Vranitzky announces forward deployment of 3,000 soldiers to border with Y.

July 1991

1 NL/EC	NL takes over the EC presidency for 6 months.
1 WTO	WTO Political CoCo in Prague approves its dissolution.
1 Y	Y SP calls on Sl to stop encirclement of Y military units. PR of SP Mesic denounces military activities of the federal army; requires measures against Serbian minority in Cr.
1 Y/CSCE	Chmn of CSCE Council FM Genscher meets Y leadership in Belgrade FM Loncar permits visit of EC observers.
1 Y/EC	EC Troika (FMs of L, NL, and Por) receives assurances from the leadership of Sl and Cr to respect the ceasefire.
1 EC/Sw	Sweden applies for EC membership.
1-2 CPC	CoCo of CPC discusses crisis in Y and requests an immediate and comprehensive ceasefire.
1-19 CSCE	Expert meeting on national minorities in Geneva primarily focuses on Y and Baltic reps.
2 EPC	Resolution on Y calls for strict adherence to ceasefire.
2-3 NATO/P	PR Walesa meets SG Wörner on bilateral cooperation.
3 CSCE	CSO meets in framework of its new mechanism for urgent situations; unanimously calls for immediate ceasefire.
3 EC/P	PR Walesa meets PR of EC Com Delors on bilateral relations.
3 US/EC	Secretary of State Baker confers with FM v. d. Broek and Deputy Chmn of the EC Com Andriessen on the crisis in Y.
3 I/NL	PM Lubbers discusses EC attitude on crisis in Y.

3 I/A   PM Bufi talks on An refugees in I and support for An econ-
                 omy.
4 Y/Sl   SP requests Sl to return to situation prior to independence.
4-5 R/NATO   NATO SG Wörner supports democracy and market economy in
                 R.
4-5 USSR/G   CH Kohl and PR Gorbachev discuss Western aid for economic
                 reforms.
5 EPC   FMs sends Troika and monitoring mission to Y; approve im-
                 plementation of CSCE crisis mechanism and weapons embargo
                 against Y.
5 CSCE/CSCO   CSO welcomes EC mission to stabilize ceasefire; offers Y its
                 good offices.
5 EC/Sl   PM Peterle meets with members of EC Com on recognition of
                 Sl.
7-8 Y/EC   At Brioni reps of Sl, Cr, and Ser and EC Troika approve new
                 peace plan. 50 to 60 EC observers will supervise ceasefire in
                 Sl and possibly in Cr.
7-9 USSR/S   PM Gonzalez and PR Gorbachev, PM Pavlov and Ru PR
                 Yelzin meet. Gorbachev and Gonzalez sign bilateral treaty of
                 friendship.
8 Au   CH Vranitzky and FM Mock offer declarations on crisis in Y.
8 CSCE/P   Bureau of Free Elections is established in Warsaw.
8-9 F/UN   Res of five permanent SC members agree on closer coopera-
                 tion on arms exports, especially to Middle East.
9 USSR   PR Gorbachev and res of 10 reps sign program against eco-
                 nomic crisis in USSR.
9 UK   DM King announces major defense cuts and force restruc-
                 turing stressing technological superiority.
10 EC/Y   FMs agree on sending 30-50 civilian and military ceasefire
                 observers; coordinate positions prior to G-7 summit in Lon-
                 don.
10 Ru   Yeltsin is sworn in as first directly elected PR of Ru.
11 G/H   PM Antall meets CH Kohl on economic reforms, situation in
                 Y, and EC membership.
11-14 US/USSR   FM Bessmertnych meets PR Bush and Secretary of State
                 Baker on G-7 summit and on START treaty.
12 B   Parl passes first noncommunist constitution since 1945.
12-13 Y   SP approves peace plan of Brioni and calls on armed groups
                 to hand in their weapons until July 18.
12-13 Por/G   FM Genscher discusses European unification, strengthening
                 of common foreign policy; calls for setting up of European
                 Blue and Green helmets to protect the environment.
14 F/US   PR Bush meets PR Mitterrand on support for USSR, develop-
                 ments in IR, and continuation of UN sanctions.
15 UN   SC discusses secret nuclear installations in IR.
15-17 UK   At London heads of state and governments of G-7 and PR of
                 EC Com and of ECC discuss economic aid to USSR, strength-
                 ening of UN, situation in Central and Eastern Europe, and

	international arms trade. PR Gorbachev participates on July 17.
16 Y	Cr FM Rudolf calls on EC to extend mandate for its observers from Sl to Cr. PM Marcovic states his government has no control over army.
18 F/Y	FM Dumas confers with FM Loncar on situation in Y and on role of F and EC in supporting peace in Y.
18 G/Cr	CH Kohl, FM Genscher confer with Cr PR Tudjman on escalation in Y. Tudjman supports sending peacekeeping forces to Y if federal forces attack Sl and Cr.
18–19 UK/USSR	PR Gorbachev and PM Major meet on economic and trade relations.
18–19 F/R	PR Mitterrand and PM Cresson confer with PM Roman on bilateral economic relations, on situation in R, and on crisis in Y.
18–19 Y	SP decides to withdraw federal army from Sl within 3 months.
18–20 Gr/US	PR Bush calls on both Gr and T to resolve conflict on Cyprus.
20 Sl/Cr/BH	Three PM agree on setting up a joint economic commission.
20–22 T/US	PR Bush and PR Özal agree on new strategic relationship, closer military, political and economic ties, and on 4 party talks (T, Gr, and both groups) on Cyprus.
21–22 Is/US	Secretary of State Baker meets PM Shamir, FM Levy, and DM Arens on creation of a Near East peace conference and then meets with a Palestinian delegation.
22 USSR	PR Gorbachev applies for full membership of USSR in WB and IMF.
22 Y/Cr	Cr PM Tudjman leaves meeting of the Y SP after it rejected immediate withdrawal of federal armed forces from Cr. Tudjman calls on his population to prepare for war.
23 G/F	PR Mitterrand and CH Kohl discuss two EC government conferences on European political and economic and currency union and on Y.
24 F/Au	FM Mock meets FM Dumas on crisis in Y.
24 F/Mac	FM Dumas confers with PR Gligorov on crisis in Y.
25 UN	SC debates sanctions against IR.
25–26 USSR	At plenary meeting of CC of CPSU, SG Gorbachev tables a new draft party program that incorporates domestic and foreign socialist and democratic ideas. It is approved 343–15 as a platform for discussion at next planned party congress.
26 Y/Cr	SP calls for an immediate ceasefire.
30 USSR/US	At a summit in Moscow, several bilateral agreements are signed on technical–economic exchange, mutual assistance in catastrophies, cooperation in medical emergencies, and cooperation against terrorism.
31 USSR/US	PR Bush and PR Gorbachev sign START treaty.
31 Y	At new session of complete SP a new peace plan for Cr is tabled.

29 Au/G	FM Mock meets CH Kohl on crisis in Y and EC membership of Au.
29 Ru/Li	PRs Yeltsin and Landsbergis sign treaty on mutual recognition of sovereignty.
29–30 EPC/Y	FMs discuss with PM Markovic and FM Loncar an extension of the observer missions to 500. A new Troika mission is sent to Y.
30 Y/Cr	PM Tudjman and SP Chmn Mesic leave SP in protest against a massacre by Serbs of Croats.
30 USSR/US	At a summit in Moscow, several bilateral agreements are signed on technical–economic exchange, mutual assistance in catastrophies, cooperation in medical emergencies, and cooperation against terrorism.
31 USSR/US	PR Bush and PR Gorbachev sign START treaty.
31 Y	At new session of complete SP a new peace plan for Cr is tabled.

August 1991

1 B/USSR	Parl repeals 1967 treaty on friendship, cooperation, and mutual assistance with USSR.
1 Cr	PR Tudjman forms a cabinet of national unity and calls on people to be ready for mobilization.
1–2 USSR/Y	PM Markovic and PM Pavlov discuss bilateral relations, situation in Y, and Soviet support for Y unity. ZUSSRPR Gorbachev announces that Ru, Ka, and Uz will sign a new union treaty on August 20.
2–4 Y/EC	Troika (FMs of L, NL, and Por) fails to negotiate a ceasefire in Zagreb and in Belgrade.
4 Y	After ceasefire by SP fighting resumes between Serbs supported by the federal army and the Cr police.
4 Cr	PR Tudjman calls for international peacekeeping force for Cr and a peace conference.
4 T/IR	T army prosecutes PKK rebels in northern IR.
5 Mol/R	PM Roman and PM Muravschi sign a bilateral economic agreement.
5 US	State Department lifts ban on exporting weapons to P, H, and C. PR spokesman says that E, Li, and La were granted most favored nation status.
5 Y/BH	Federal army starts mobilization in BH without government consent.
5I/A	Some 16,000 An refugees arrive by boat in I.
5 EC/NL/Y	EC Troika mission for a new ceasefire failed due to Serbian intransigence.
6 Y	The SP announces new ceasefire.
6 EPC	Failure of EC Troika in Y. FMs call for an active UN and CSCE role. No decision is made on economic sanctions against Ser and on recognition of Sl and Cr.

	CSCE role. No decision is made on economic sanctions against Ser and on recognition of Sl and Cr.
7 WEU	Res of 9 WEU states fail to agree on measures to implement the ceasefire in Y.
8 UN	SC unanimously approves UN membership of North and South Korea.
8 Y/Cr	Cr cabinet rejects the conditions tied to ceasefire.
8–9 CSCE	Crisis committee on Y approves to send monitors, in addition to EC observers, to supervise the ceasefire in Y.
9 I/A	I returns all but 500 Albanian refugees to A.
12 Y	At invitation of Ser PR Milosevic, res of Ser, Montenegro, and of Serbs of BH confer on a new Y.
12 A/I	FM De Michelis offers PR Alia immediate food assistance.
12 Au/Cr	CH Vranitzki meets Cr FM Separovic on international recognition.
14 Ar/Li	PRs Ter-Petrosjan and Landsbergis recognize their sovereignty.
17 I/A	Government returns last 500 An refugees by airplane to A.
17 USSR	Cabinet discusses draft of treaty on new union.
18 USSR/Ge	PM Sigua resigns, FM Choshtarija is ousted by PER Gamsakhurdia.
18 Y	SP once against calls for an immediate ceasefire.
18 USSR	PR Gorbachev is detained after refusing to declare a national emergency and to transfer power to Vice PR Yanayew.
19 USSR	State Committee for the Emergency in the USSR takes over power; prohibits strikes and demonstrations and reintroduces censorship. While USSR cabinet supports the coup, Ru PR Yeltsin denounces members of this committee as traitors and its declarations illegal in Ru.
19 A/I	FM De Michelis discusses with An government In policy of returning refugees and IMs sign agreement on limiting migration.
19 G/US/EPC	CH Kohl, PR Bush, and EPC condemn the coup in USSR.
20 USSR	Ru PR Yeltsin takes over as SuCo of armed forces in Ru; orders all soldiers to remain in their barracks. In a mass demonstration of some 200,000 Yeltsin, Shevardnadze, and Jakovlev condemn the coup.
20 G/Si/Cr	FM Genscher meets with Sl FM Rupel and Cr FM Separovic on Y crisis.
20 EC/USSR	Emergency meeting of FM condemns the coup, calls for return of PR Gorbachev. Economic aid is suspended.
20–21 Y	SP and leaders of six reps agree to end hostilities between Cr and Ser but fighting continues.
21 NATO	FMs in emergency session on coup in USSR initiate CSCE crisis mechanism.
21 USSR	Secretariat of the CC of CPSU calls on Deputy SG Ivaschko to see Gorbachev. At emergency session of SuSo of Ru, PR Yeltsin announces that eight members of state committee were

	caught on their way to the airport. Gorbachev is given back his functions as PR.
22 USSR	PR Gorbachev returns to Moscow. Members of the coup are arrested. IM Pugo commits suicide. Yeltsin bans all CPSU cells in armed forces in the Ru. PR Gorbachev ousts PM Pavlov and PR of SuSo Lukyanov.
22 E/La/Li	Three Baltic states ban CPSU.
22 F/R	PR Mitterrand confers with FM Nastase.
23 USSR	PR Gorbachev confers with PR of nine reps on new union treaty. PR Yeltsin suspends activity of CPSU in Ru.
23 Y/Cr	PR Tudjman calls on Y leadership to end fighting by August 31 an return soldiers to barracks.
24 USSR	PR Gorbachev resigns as SG of CPSU, calls for dissolution of CC, and prohibits all party cells in armed forces, police, and KGB.
24 Ru	PR Yeltsin recognizes the independence of E, La, and Li.
24 Uk	The SuSo announces the sovereignty of the Ukraine provided that it is supported in a referendum by December 1, 1991.
25 Be	SuSo of Bylorussia (Belarus) announces its independence.
26 USSR	Chmn of SuSo of USSR, Lukyanov, resigns. Uk recognizes independence of three Baltic states; Ge recognize E.
26 Ice/FI	FM Hannibalsson confers with FMs of three Baltic states and establishes diplomatic relations. FM Väyrynen follows.
26 P	FM Skubiszewski announces bilateral relations with E, La, and Li.
26 H/Sl	FM Jeszensky and FM Rupel meet on bilateral relations.
27 USSR	DM Shaposhnikov indicated that Soviet forces could be divided among reps but that nuclear forces should be under a central command.
27 EPC	Welcomes independence of E, Li, and La; condemns increasing violence in Cr.
27 Mol	Parl declares its independence; Ge and R recognize Mol.
27 Nor	FMs of Baltic states resume diplomatic relations.
27 Y/Cr	PR Tudjman meets DM Kadijevic. Both agree not to attack first.
27 G/Ser	FM Genscher meets Ser FM Jovanovic on civil war situation.
27–28 EC	FMs meet on situation in the USSR after the coup and on Y crisis.
27–28 G	FMs of E, La, and Li (Meri, Jurkans, and Saudergas) confer with FM Genscher on Baltic reps; establish diplomatic relations.
27–28 Y	SP calls for an end of hostilties and a ceasefire.
27–29 US/UK	PM Major meets PR Bush on developments in and aid for USSR.
28 USSR	PR Gorbachev nominates Amb. Pankin as FM.
28 S	King Carl XVI Gustaf meets with FMs of Baltic states to resume diplomatic relations.
28 F/Cr	PR Mitterrand confers with Cr PR Tudjman on crisis in Y.
29 R/Mol	FM Nastase and FM Tiu open diplomatic relations.

29 USSR	SuSo repeals special powers for PR Gorbachev. He appoints leaders of nine reps and IM Bakatin and Primakov as members of a new security council. SuSo suspends activity of CPSU in USSR. Uk PR Kravchuk and Ru Vice PR Ruzkoy agree to counter uncontrolled disrupture of USSR and call for a new system of collective security. PR Nasarbayev of Ka bans all nuclear tests in Semipalatinsk.
29–30 Li/F	FM Dumas signs a document to resume diplomatic relations.
30 P	PM Bielecki offers resignation to Parl which rejected it.
30 Az/Uz/Ky	SuSo of Az resumes independence of 1918–1920. SuSo of Uz and Ky delcare their independence.
30 Y	Sl, Cr, and federal government of Y support EC peace proposals.
31 Y	Ser accepts proposals for ending hostilities.

September 1991

1 USSR	Special Session of Congress of People's Deputies starts. Ka PR Nasarbayev introduces new draft of union treaty signed by PR Gorbachev and PRs of SuSo of 10 Reps.
1 USSR/UK	PM Major meets Gorbachev and Yeltsin on security of Soviet nuclear arms, economic aid of G-7 for USSR, the Near East, and Y.
1 EFTA	Lie becomes seventh full member of EFTA.
2 USSR	Ru PM Silayev develops concept of a common economic space.
2 USSR/Az	Nagornyi Karabach and Schaumann area declare independence from Az.
2 A/H	FMs Jeszenszky and Bufi confer on crisis in Y.
2 Y/EC	Res of 6 Y reps and EC sign a new ceasefire agreement. All paramilitary forces are to be dissolved and reserve units of Cr national guard must be demobilized. EC ceasefire observers may be active in Sl and Cr.
2 US	PR Bush announces resumption of diplomatic ties to E, La, and Li.
2–5 G/B	PR Shelev confers with PRs V. Weizsäcker and CH Kohl and FM Genscher on reforms in B, bilateral issues, and crises in Y and USSR.
3 UN	E, La, and Li apply for UN membership.
3 USSR/Ru	PR Yeltsin cells for a stop of all nuclear tests.
3 USSR/Mol	Dniester area declares its independence from Mol.
3 NL/P	FM Skubiszewski meets FM v.d. Broek on EC association agreement.
3 Y	Heavy fighting continues in East Cr in Osijek and Okucani.
3 EC/Y	Special session of FMs in The Hague approves a peace conference on Y chaired by FM v.d. Broek and with Lord Carrington as peace mediator.
3–4 CSCE	Crisis committee on Y calls for a weapons embargo to Y.

4 Li/UK	Diplomatic relations were resumed.
4 Li	PR Landsbergis states Li will not joint any Soviet controlled or other alliance. Li aims at a joint defense policy with E and La.
4 CSBM	Negotiations resume in Vienna with focus on events in USSR and Y.
5 CFE	Negotiations resume in Vienna.
5 USSR	Congress of People's Deputies approves establishment of a SuSo with two chambers and other organs, and creation of a common economic space for all ten reps. SuSo is to meet in October to change USSR constitution and to create a USS.
5 F	PM Cresson warns against decline in defense efforts.
5 USSR/Uz	Uz declares its sovereignty with own DM, national guard, currency.
6 USSR	State Council recognizes independence of E, La, and Li. Ge re leave State Council, end all ties to USSR. PR Gamsakhurdia takes over control of IM, FM, DM, Justice Department, and secret police.
6 EC	FMs discuss EC association with P, H, and C; meet FMs of E, La, and Li.
7 R/Mol	PM Roman meets PR Snegur and PM Muravschi on closer cooperation.
7–8 EC/Y	Peace conference in the Hague with members of SP under Chmn v.d. Broek and Carrington is overshadowed by heavy fighting.
8 Az	Elections for PR of Az won by Mutalibov.
8 Mac	Referendum on independence. 95% are in favor.
8 P/Uk	FM Skubiszewski and FM Slenko establish diplomatic relations.
9 OS	Open Sky talks resume in Vienna.
9 USSR/Ta	SuSo of ta supports independence and creation of a sovereign and democratic state.
9 F/G	DM Stoltenberg meets DM Joxe.
9 EFTA	Informal meeting of the FMs in Helsinki on EES and EC membership.
10 USSR/Ge	violence against PR Gamsakhurdia in Tbilisi and in South Ossetia.
10 A/Y	FM protests border incidence with three dead An border guards.
10 La	Parl bans CP and all associated organizations.
10 La/G	FM Genscher meets FM Jurkans on economic aid and EC association.
10 La/US	Secretary of State Baker discusses US assistance and support for a market economy.
10 US/CSCE	At CSCE human rights conference in Moscow E, La, and Li become full CSCE members. Secretary of State Baker confers with PR Gorbachev, FM Pankin, DM Shaposhnikov, General Lobov, and Ru PM Silajevon on foreign policy, defense, arms control, and economic issues.

11 Y	Chmn of SP Mesic orders federal army to return to barracks; accuses army of participating illegally in fighting in Cr.
11 F	PR Mitterrand requests an immediate conference of four nuclear powers in Europe, supports independence of Sl and Cr, proposes a "European confederation", and opposes a rapid EC expansion.
11 F/H	PR Mitterrand and PM Antall sign a bilateral friendship agreement.
11 G/USSR	CH Kohl meets PR Gorbachev's adviser A. Jakovelev.
11 E/G	FM Genscher meets PR Rüütel and FM Meri on economic aid.
11 US/P	PR Bush meets PM Bielecki on Poland; USSR who calls for rapid EC integration and NATO extension to Central and Eastern Europe.
12 Li/G	FM Genscher discusses economic aid and association with EC.
12 Li/US	Secretary of State Baker discusses US assistance and support for market economy.
12 B/R	PM Roman and PM Popow sign a declaration on good neighborhood.
12 Y	DM Kadijevic states that reserves of Cr National Guard must be demobilized first before the army returns to the barracks.
13 USSR/F	DM Joxe and DM Shaposnikov sign agreement on military cooperation.
14 E/US	Secretary of State Baker meets PR Rüütel, PM Savisaar and FM Meri on economic aid.
14 Y/Cr	PR Tudjman claims one-third of Cr is controlled by Serbian fighters. Cr National Guard blocks energy and water supply for federal army.
15 USSR/Ge	PR Gamsakhurdia's majority in Parl calls for withdrawal of Soviet troops from Ge and full UN membership.
16 EC/EFTA	EFTA Chmn PM Aho of Fi meets with EC Com Chmn Delors on EES talks.
16 A/CSCE	A signs Final Act of Helsinki and become full CSCE member.
16 F/S	PM Gonzales meets PR Mitterrand and J. Delors on European unity.
16 UK/Gr	PM Mitsotakis and PM Major support maintaining Y unity.
16 US/G	CH Kohl confers with PR Bush on bilateral issues, situation in Near East, crisis in Y, and developments in USSR.
16–17 USSR	PR Gorbachev chairs state council meetings on food shortage and draft treaty for economic union.
16–17 USSR/US	Secretary of State Baker visits St. Petersburg and Alma-Ata for political talks.
16–18 U/EC	Lord Carrington negotiates a new ceasefire agreement with Ser PR Milosevic, Cr PR Tudjman, and DM Kadijevic.
16–18 C/P	PR Walesa meets PR Havel on EC integration and regional security.
16–19 G/Li	PM Vagnorius meets CH Kohl and FM Genscher on bilateral issues.
17 UN	Seven new members are welcomed: E, La, Li, North, and South Korea, Micronesia, and Marshall Islands; UN member-

	ship increases to 166. The PR of E, La, Li call for withdrawal of Soviet troops.
17 EC/Y	Y Peace conference resumes; forms two tasks forces on constitutional problems and protection of minorities. Sl and Cr withdraw because of permament ceasefire violations.
17 US	PR Bush meets PRs Rüütel, Gorbunov, and Landsbergis on Baltic states, return of frozen currency assets, withdrawal of Soviet troops, and customs benefits.
17 Y/UN	Chmn Mesic calls for emergency session of SC and requests deployment of peacekeeping forces. Serbian members reject request.
17 Y/Cr	Y navy blocks 7 Cr harbors, including Dubrovnik, and attacks a few.
17 B/Mac	PM Klucev meets PR Shelev and PM Popov on Y and bilateral issues.
17–18 Y/BH	Serbs declare several regions in BH as autonomous.
18 NL/UK/Y	PM Major and FM Hurd meet with PM Lubbers and FM v.d. Broek on sending peacekeeping forces to Y.
18 USSR/US	PR Gorbachev nominates Ru PM Silayev as chmn of interrepublican economic committee. US FiM Brady confers with both on Western food and medical aid for USSR.
18–19 G/Mac	PR Gligorov meets FM Genscher on crisis in Y.
18–19 H/Au	CH Vranitzky confers with PM Antall on Y and bilateral economic and trade cooperation.
18–20 G/F	PR Mitterrand meets PR V. Weizsäcker and CH Kohl on EC summit, Y, and aid to USSR. Kohl and Mitterrand support European peace force for Y, possibly in WEU framework.
18–20 R/T	PR Özal and PR Iliescu sign agreement on friendship; confer on bilateral issues, developments in USSR, Y, Middle East, and Cyprus.
19 EPC	FMs hold informal meeting on Y; discuss different options, e.g., emergency session of SC, WEU peacekeeping forces; agree on principles: non-use of force, adherence to existing borders, respect for minorities. WEU will require consent of conflict parties, SC, and CSCE.
19 G/S	PM Gonzalez meets CH Kohl on European unity, Y, aid to USSR, and Near East peace process.
19 Y	PM Markovic requests resignation of DM Kadijevic. Federal army and Cr forces accuse other side of ceasefire violations.
20 UN/SC	Publishes letters from Ca and Au requesting Sc to act on Y.
20 US/B	PR Shelev confers with Vice PR Quayle on situation in B, USSR, and Y.
20 USSR	DM Shaposhnikov states no more CW and nuclear weapons are deployed in former GDR.
20 Y	Chmn of SP Mesic states generals are out of control and are conducting a war against Cr; appeals to soldiers to desert federal army.
20–22 C/T	PR Özal confers with PR Havel on political and economic

	cooperation, situation in Y, USSR, Balkans, and Near/Middle East.
20–23 USSR	Ru PR Yeltsin and Ka PR Nasarbajev mediate in conflict between Ar and Az on Nagorni Karabach; they sign a ceasefire agreement with PR Ter-Petrosjan and PR Mutalibov.
21 USSR	PR Gorbachev appoints interrepublican economic and coordination committee as interim government of USSR.
21 Ar	Referendum on independence: 95.5% participate and 94% in favor.
21 Y/BH	PR Izetbegovic protests troop movements of federal army in BH.
21–22 EC	Informal meeting of FiMs on economic and currency union.
23 Ta	SuSo of Ta ousts PR Aslonov and elects Nabijev as new PR.
23 USSR	PR Gorbachev appoints Shewarnadze, Bakatin (KGB), Popov, Sobchak, and Yakovlev to new political consultative committee.
23–25 Ca/Uk	PR Kravchuk meets PM Mulroney on political, economic relations.
24 Y	Mesics condemns meeting of Serbian members of SP as illegal.
24 H/Mac	PR Gligorov meets PR Gönez and PM Antall on Y and on recognition.
24–25 Gr/B	PM Popov meets PM Mitsotakis on Y, problem of Mac, and bilateral and regional issue.
25 EC/NL	NL table a new draft treaty on political union of EC.
25 UN/SC	Adopts global arms embargo against Y and requests a strict adherence to ceasefire. SC supports peace efforts of EC/CSCE and requests SG to mediate in Y.
25 US/Uk	PR Kravchuk confers with PR Bush on US investment in Uk and withdrawal of nuclear weapons; Uk will become nuclear free state.
25 Ge	After violence PR Gamsakhurdia employees state of emergency.
25 Y	Milosevic, Kadijevic, and Tudjman agree on absolute ceasefire.
25 H/Sl	SR Kucan confers with Hn government on crisis in Y.
25 R	Several thousand mine workers call for resignation of PM Roman. Four people are killed in violent clashes.
25–28 T/Ka	PR Nasarbajev and PR Özal sign a comprehensive cooperation treaty.
26 R	After talk between union leader and PR Iliescu, strike ends; PM Roman resigns.
27 Ca/G/Y	FM Genscher meets PM Mulroney on CSCE and peacekeeping forces.
27 USSR/Ru	Silayev resigns as PM of Russia.
27 EC/Y	Peace conference on Y meets; sets up task force on economic relations between reps.
27 US	PR Bush announces unilateral elimination of all US SNF warheads, removal of SLCM, and cancellation of 24-year-old

	alarm provisions for strategic bombers. Bush calls on USSR to reciprocate these measures. According to DM Cheney, some 1300 warheads for nuclear artillery and 850 for Lance will be destroyed; 500 warheads will be removed from submarine and surface ships.
28 UN/Y	SG de Cuellar meets PR Mesic.
30 WEU	FMs and DMs meet in Brussels on support for EC observers in Y.
30 US/USSR	16th session of talks on space weapons and strategic defense systems resumes in Geneva.

October 1991

1 R	PR Iliescu nominates former FiM Stolojan as PM.
1 EC/EPC	FMs discuss crisis in Y, association of central and east European countries and relations with Baltic states, and negotiations with EFTA on EES.
1 EC	Meeting on political union rejects Dutch treaty proposal.
1 USSR/Au	CH Vranitzky confers with PR Gorbachev on bilateral economic relations and on political situation in Europe.
1 USSR	PR of eight former reps agree to form economic community.
1 Y	SuCo of federal army announces attack of civilian objects in Cr in retaliation for encirclement of barracks, Dubrovnik is target.
1 F/C	PR Havel and FM Dienstbier meet with PR Mitterrand and PM Creason on developments in eastern Europe and USSR and sign a friendship treaty; F supports full integration of C into European institutions.
2–3 F/Sl	PR Kucan meets with PR Mitterrand and DM Dumas on Y and independence of Sl.
2–3 I/Cr	PR Tudjman confers with Italian government on crisis in Y.
2–3 US/G	FM Genscher confers with PR Bush and Secretary of State Baker on disarmament and developments in central and eastern Europe and the USSR. Baker and Genscher propose creation of a NACC for meetings between NATO and former WTO states.
3 Sw	Conservative party leader Bildt is elected as new PM.
3 Y	In absence of PR Mesic and res of Sl and Cr, SP takes over all legislative and executive functions.
3 F/Uk	PR Kravchuk meets with PR Mitterrand and FM Dumas on situation in Uk and recent developments in USSR.
3 UK/EC	PM Major meets J. Delors and PM Lubbers on emergency aid to USSR.
4 EC/Y	Conflict parties agree on new peace treaty and ceasefire requiring disengagement of fighting forces and an end to blocking of barracks of federal army in Cr.
4 UK/I	Publish bilateral initiative on Europe security and defense.
4 CSCE	Final document of Moscow human rights meeting agrees to

	formula: all minus one permitting investigations against a violator.
4 US/H	PM Antall meets PR Bush on closer NATO ties of eastern Europe.
5 USSR	PR Gorbachev announces unilateral disarmament measures: all tactical nuclear weapons delivered by artillery and SNF will be eliminated; all tactical nukes on subarmines and surface ships will be withdrawn; suggest an elimination of these weapons if US reciprocates; stops unilaterally nuclear tests for one year and proposes withdrawal of all airbased tactical nuclear systems.
5 USSR/E	DMShaposhnikov and PM Savisaar agree on Soviet troop withdrawal within a year.
5 Y	PR Mesic calls for a meeting of SP which Serbian members boycott.
5–6 EC	FMs in informal meeting on Y reject Ser occupation of SP; announce economic sanctions violators of agreements of Oct. 4.
5–7 BC	PR of E, La and Li agree on "General security system for Baltic."
6 Y/Ser	Serbian members of SP accept EC guidelines; request parallel mobilization.
6 BH	PR Izegebovic for strict neutrality in war between Ser and Cr.
6 P/C/H	PRs approve close regional cooperation; prefer NATO membership.
7 EC	FiM agree on 2bn DM assistance for USSR.
7 USSR/IMF	PR Gorbachev and IMF sign an agreement on associate membership.
7 Y	Air force attacks PR Tudjman's palace in Zagreb who calls for international military help.
7 B/Gr	PM Mitsotakis and PM Popov sign friendship treaty requiring military cooperation and mutual assistance against an aggressor.
7 G/Gr	FM Separovic meets with CH Kohl and FM Genscher on Y and EC peace conference.
7–11 C/G	PR v. Weizsäcker and PR Havel meet; FMs Genscher and Dienstbier initial treaty on good neighborhood and friendly cooperation.
8 Sl/Cr/G	With end of moratoria agreed with EC, declarations of independence are implemented. Sl PM Kucan and FM Rupel confer with CM Kohl and FM Genscher on Y and on next steps of Sl.
8 T/Gr	PM Mitsotakis meets PM Yilmaz on bilateral issues.
8 UN/Y	SG de Cuellar appoints C. Vance as his special envoy on Y.
9 USSR	USSR enters into diplomatic relations with E and Li.
9 B/G	FM Genscher and FM Walkov sign a friendship treaty requiring close cooperation on the economy, technology, and the environment.

10 CSCE/CSO	Urgent crisis meeting on Y supports goals of EC and discusses setting up a peace force.
10 EPC	Declaration on Middle East peace process calls for active EC role.
10 C/N	PM Brundtland meets PR Havel on security policy issues in Europe.
10 A/F	FM Dumas confers with Pr Alia on crisis in Y.
10 P/Be	PM Kiebitsch and PM Bielecki sign declaration on neighborly relations.
11 EC/Y/NLFM	V.D. Brook confers with PRs of Cr and Ser and with Y DM. Army agrees to withdraw from Cr within a month.
11 P/I	FM De Michelis and FM Skubiszewski sign a treaty on friendship.
11 Uk	SuSo of Uk accepts a concept for national forces with a size of 400,000–420,000 soldiers. Uk aims at a nuclear weapon free status.
12 Ky	In first direct presidential elections, Akayev receives 95%.
12 Y/UN	C. Vance confers with FM Loncar, PM Markovic, and PR Milosevic.
14 EC/Y/UN	At peace conference on Y, Lord Carrington and C. Vance try to arrange a summit of PR of reps with PR of SP.
14 G/F/EC	CH Kohl and PR Mitterrand propose a common European foreign and defense policy and creation of German–French corps; WEU should become defense arm of European Union.
15 USSR	PR Gorbachev meets separately with PR Milosevic and PR Tudjman. At a joint dinner all three agree on new ceasefire.
15 USSR/La	FMs Pankin and Jurkans establish diplomatic relations.
15 Y/BH	60 Serbian members leave Parl in protest. 133 remaining members proclaim BH as a sovereign and democratic state.
15 WB/USSR	Annual conference on WB and IMF in Bangkok focuses on aid to USSR.
16 Ru/Cr	PR Tudjman confers with PR Yeltsin on situation in Y.
16 Ar	In presidential election, Ter-petrossjan receives 80% of votes.
16 F/I	FM De Micheles meets FM Dumas on European summit in Maastricht.
16 R	PM Stolojan presents his cabinet. Nastase remains FM.
16–17 Ka/G	FM Genscher confers with PR Nasarbajev on bilateral relations.
17–18 T/A	PR Alia confers with PR Özal on international issues.
17–18 I/F	PR Mitterrand confers with PM Andreotti on European foreign and security policy and negotiation on economic and currency union.
17–18 NPG	NATO DMs approve a 80% reduction of tactical nuclear weapons but stress substrategic nuclear weapons in Europe should be kept up-to-date.
17–18 SC	Five permanent SC members agree in London on guidelines for arms exports to prevent escalation of international conflicts.
18 Uk/G	FM Genscher confers with PR Kravchuk and FM Slenko on

	economic cooperation. Genscher opens a cultural week in Kiev.
18 USSR	8 of 12 union reps and PR Gorbachev sign treaty on a new economic community. Uk, Az, Mol, and Ce are opposed.
18 Y/Mon	Parl votes for leaving Y. PR Bulatovic supports EC peace plan.
18 EC/Y	Res of all reps and all 8 members of SP participate at EC peace conference. Ser rejects Lord Carrington's prposal for a transformation of Y into a union of sovereign and indepeded states. US and USSR support EC peace efforts.
19 NAA	Annual meeting in Madrid calls for elimination of all land-based SNF in Europe. E, La, and Li become associated members of NAA.
21 Y/Sl	Based on agreement between Sl and federal government on heavy weapons, withdrawal of federal army starts and is completed within a week.
21–22 EC/EFTA	FMs sign the EES agreement.
21–23 Ru/B	PRs Shelev and Yeltsin open diplomatic relations.
21–23 US/C	PR Havel confers with PR Bush and his cabinet on bilateral relations, and situation in Y and USSR. Havel calls for multinational peacekeeping forces to stop fighting.
21–28 USSR	First session of SuSo with res of 7 of 12 reps. Ar and Mol sent observers. Uk and Ge did not come.
22 Y	SP supports DM Kadijevic's request for mobilizing reservists, and boycotts next meeting of EC peace conference.
22 CSCE/CSO	Crisis meeting on Y agrees to send a delegation of Y on adherence to human rights. P proposes setting up a CSCE peace force.
24 Y/BH/Cr	PM Pelivan and Greguric agree on broad economic cooperation.
24 Ru/E	FMs Kosyrev and Meri initiate diplomatic relations.
25 EC/Y	Peace conference continues in absence of Ser res.
25 US/Ky	PR Akayev conveys PR Bush a message from PR Gorbachev on economic and security problems.
25–26 USSR/G	FM Genscher meets PR Gorbachev, FM Pankin, and DM Shaposhnikov on USSR, disarmament agreements, and control of nuclear weapons.
26 USSR/P	Deputy FMs Derjabin and Makarczyk initial an agreement on withdrawal of Soviet forces until the end of 1993.
26 Tu	In referendum 94% of citizens vote for independence.
28 EC	Dutch presidency and presidents of national banks present draft treaty for a currency and economic union.
28 ECP/Y	Declaration notes only Ser opposes EC peace plan. EC opposes creation of a large Serbia. If Ser does not return to negotiations, EC will initiate restrictive measures.
28 US	Vice PR Quayle signs economic agreements with PM of E, La, and Li.
28 USSR	PMs, FiM, and directors of central banks in 12 reps sign an agreement on credits and food supply. Baltic states join as associated members.

28 USSR	Res of 12 union reps sign agreement with deputy FiM of G-7; acknowledge joint and individual responsibility for paying back foreign debt.
28 Ru	PR Yeltsin in opening Ru congress of People's Deputies calls for radical economic reform; takes over tasks of PM and calls for additional powers; prohibits all nuclear tests in Ru for one year. Chasbulatov becomes new Chmn of SuSo.
28 Us/Uk	PRs Karimov and Kravchuk sign a treaty on friendship and economic and environmental cooperation.
29 WEU	In Bonn WEU discusses role in a new European security architecture and French–German initiative.
29 US/USSR	PRs Bush and Gorbachev meet in Madrid on disarmament, Western aid to USSR, and Near East peace negotiations.
30 EC/H	PM Antall confers with Delors on EC association of H, C, P.
30 S	Near East peace conference starts in Madrid in presence of PR Bush, PR Gorbachev, and ECC PR FM v.d. Broek.
30–31 F/USSR	PR Gorbachev confers with PR Mitterrand on peace conference on Near East, mutual relations, and situation in USSR after the coup.
31 G/EC	Delors meets in Potsdam with PMs of five new states on EC aid.

November 1991

1 Ru	SuSo of Ru grants PR Yeltsin (753 to 59) additional powers.
1 USSR	Eight signatories of treaty on an economic community dissolve 80 union ministries until Nov. 15: 36,000 positions are eliminated.
1 Y/EC	SP, representing only Serbs, accepts EC peace plan provided that sections on protection of Serbs in Cr are renegotiated.
1 Sl/I	PR Cossiga meets PR Kucan and PM Peterle.
3–4 T/Az	PM Hassonov confers with PR Ozal and PM Yilmaz.
4 EC	FMs discuss economic sanctions against noncooperating parties in Y. Gr points to negative economic consequences.
4 Uk	SuSo sets up a national guard of 33,000 Uk citizens. Uk DM Martshuk calls for 320,000 UK soldiers; opposes Uk control of nuclear weapons deployed in Ul.
4 F/EP	PR Mitterrand confers with EP PR Baron Crespo on democratization of European institutions and joint foreign and defense policy.
4 Ser/Gr	In meeting with FM Samaras, PR Milosevic opposes ultimatum of EC peace conference.
5 EC/Y	After 12th ceasefire agreement was broken in Y, Lord Carrington asks for postponement. Ser PR Milosevic rejects EC peace plan.
5 USSR/WB	PR Gorbachev and WB director Preston sign agreement for $30 million aid for counseling on economic reform (privatization).

5–6 Y/UN	UN envoy Vance confers with PM Marcovic on peace settlement.
6 USSR	PR Gorbachev appoints Bakatin, Primakov, and Kalinitschenko as heads of three intelligence services replacing KGB.
6 Ru	PR Yetsin takes over control of Ru government and appoints Burbulis as first deputy PM; decrees dissolution of CPSU in Ru.
6 Uk/Mol	Joint treaty for creation of an economic community signed by eight reps on October 18.
6 Uk/Ru	PR Kravchuk and Yeltsin agree on principles of cooperation on economic and trade issues; recognize international agreements (CSCE Final Act) and mutual borders.
6 Y/Cr	PR Tudjman requests US military aid after heavy attacks on Dubrovnik. EC economic sanctions fail to stop aggression.
7 1/Gr	PM Mitsotakis meets FM Andreotti on questions of European security. Gr is interested in becoming a WEU member.
7–8 NATO	Summit in Rome approves new strategy to replace flexible response, Declaration of Rome and declarations on events in USSR and Y.
8 B	Parl elects P. Dimitrov as first noncommunist PM.
8 V/US	Pope John Paul II confers with PR Bush on Near East, USSR, and Y.
8 EPC/Y	FMs decide on economic sanctions against Y.
8–9 EC/US	Support UN register on conventional arms transfers; support peaceful, democratic change in the East based on CSCE principles.
9 Y/Ser	Serbs in SP call on UN SC to send UN forces to Cr.
10 G/UK	PM Major meets CH Kohl on political and currency union prior to Maastricht summit.
10 Cr/EC/UN	FM Separovic calls on UN and EC to stop destruction of Dubrovnik.
11 NATO/P	FM Skubiszewski meets SG Wörner on relationship of P to NATO.
11 T/Az	T recognizes Az diplomatically.
11 I/Y	PR Mesic meets PR Cossiga and PM Andreotti on creating a buffer zone between Cr and Ser; calls for an oil embargo against Ser and federal army.
11 G-24	Meet in Brussels with res of A, E, La, Li, B, R, C, H, and P on economic and political developments in central and eastern Europe. Agree on coordinated economic aid. Aid for Y is stopped.
11–12 C/S	PM Gonzalez meets with PR Havel, PM Calfa, and Parl PR Dubcek on economic cooperation and signs a friendship and cooperation treaty.
11–13 G/USSR	DM Shaposhnikov confers with DM Stoltenberg and CH Kohl on the future structure of Soviet forces and control of nuclear weapons.
12 NATO/E/B	FM Meris and Ganev meets SG Wörner on relationship with NATO.

12 Y/UN	PR Mesic asks SC to send peacekeeping forces to border between Cr and Ser after all peace efforts failed.
12 EPC/Y	Condemns further escalation and attacks on cities in Cr; asks Lord Carrington to evaluate precondition for deployment of international peace forces.
12–13 EC	FMs discuss situation in Y and call for emergency session of SC.
13 Cr/EC	PR Tudjman in talk with Lord Carrington requests international efforts to stop aggression.
13 UN/Y	UN envoy Vance submits his report to SC.
13–14 Y/EC	Lord Carrington states all conflict parties support UN forces.
14 NATO/B	PR Shelev calls for NATO intervention in Y.
14 EC/B	PR Shelev meets EC Com PR Delors on EC association of B.
14 USSR	Seven Republics (Ru, Be, Ka, Ky, Ta, Tu, Az) and PR Gorbachev at State Council meeting agree on a USS, a confederated democratic state with a PR, Parl, common laws, and armed forces.
14 I/Ru	FM Kosyrev discusses bilateral issues with FM De Michelis.
14 US/Ar	PR Ter-Petrossjan meets PR Bush on developments in USSR.
14 G/Y	PR Mesic meets FM Genscher on situation in Y, Cr, and BH. Genscher calls for minority rights and deployment in peace forces in Y.
14 EFTA	Council agrees on economic sanctions against Y.
14–15 G/F	PR Mitterrand, PM Cresson, and 13 cabinet ministers meet their German counterparts on Maastricht summit, crisis in Y, food aid for USSR, and European space cooperation.
15 Ru	PR Yetsin announces liberalization of Ru foreign trade.
17 Y/UN	Vance meets PR Milisevic and PR Tudjman on peacekeeping forces.
17 Ru	PR Yeltsin decrees liberalization of foreign trade.
18 Cr	Vukovar capitulates to federal army.
18 P/Cr	FM Separovic confers with PM Bielecki and FM Skubiszewski on crisis in Y and diplomatic recognition of Cr.
18 Gr/BH	PR Izetbegovic meets PM Mitsotakis on Macedonian question.
18 WEU	FMs meet in Bonn on crisis in Y and European security structure.
18–21 USSR	Res of G-7 confer with PMs of 8 PMs on foreign debt of USSR. G-7 grant a one-year extension for repayment.
19 F/G	FM Genscher meets FM Dumas on Maastricht summit and crisis in Y.
19 USSR	PR Gorbachev reappoints Shevardnadze again as FM.
20 USSR	PR Gorbachev establishes new union command for "Strategic Defense Forces" with authority on ICBM, SLBM, bombers, and nuclear reconnaissance.
20 F/R	PR Iliescu and PR Mitterrand sign a friendship treaty.
20 US/USSR	Government approves financial aid of $1.4 billion for USSR for purchase of wheat, food, and technical assistance.
21 I/Au	CH Vranitzky confers with PR Cossiga. PM Andreotti, and FM De Michelis on crisis in Y and EC membership of Au.

21–23 G/Ru	PR Yetsin meets PR von Weizsäcker, CH Kohl, and FM Genscher on Ru, USSR, and future cooperation.
22 G/BH	PR Izetbegovic meets Ch Kohl and FM Genscher on situation in Y.
22 NATO/Li	Open diplomatic relations.
22 UK/NL	PM Lubbers and FM v.d. Broek confer with PM Major on Maastricht.
23 UN/Y	14th ceasefire agreement negotiated by Vance is signed in Geneva.
23 Uk/IMF	PM Fokin does not oppose repayment of foreign debt.
24 Ta	At presidential election Nabiyev is elected with 56.9% of votes.
25 G/Cr	FM Separovic confers with FM Genscher on mutual relations and increase of humanitarian assistance.
26 US	Senate grants most favored nation status for E, La, and Li.
26 US/Ru	FM Kosyev meets with PR Bush and FM Baker on arms control and US support for reform policy in Ru.
26 USSR	State Council approves draft treaty on USS with joint defense forces and common political and economic space.
26 UN/Y	UN Amb. formally request SC to send peacekeeping forces to Cr.
26 EC/USSR	Signs treaty with USSR onfood aid and credits on 750 mio. ECU.
26 CE/P	P becomes member of CE and signs and European Charter of Human Rights.
27 UN/SC/Y	Calls on Y conflict parties to create preconditions for deployment of UN forces by adhering to ceasefire.
27 G/UK	PM Major meets CH Kohl on preparation for Maastricht summit.
27 I/UK	PM Andreotti and PM Major will recognize Sl and Cr with EC countries.
27–28 R/Gr	PM Mitsotakis and PM Stolojan sign three treaties.
28 G/I	PM Andreotti, FM De Michelis, and five cabinet ministers meet with German counterparts on Maastricht summit and crisis in Y.
28 F/UN	SG de Cuellar meets with PR Mitterrand on peacekeeping forces for Y.
28 EC/R	Credit agreement on 375 million ECU granted by G-24 is signed.
28 EC Com	Publishes critical assessments on drafts for a political and economic and currency union.
29 Y/Gr	PM Mitsotakis meets PR Milosevic; opposes recognition of Sl and Cr.
29 F/G	FM Genscher meets FM Dumas on Maastricht summit, crisis in Y, and recognition of Sl and Cr.
29 USSR	State Bank cannot pay any more for state expenditures in USSR. PR Yeltsin guarantees payment of income of all Union employees, including armed forces.

29 CSCE/CSO   Crisis committee meets in Prague; supports deployment of UN peace fore in Y.

30 H/P/C   Military res of three countries agree on closer cooperation on military, political, and social level.

December 1991

1 HEX   Meeting of FMs in Venic concludes that Y ceased to exist. HEX grants Sl and Cr observer status.

1 Ka   Nasarbayew is elected as PR of Ka by 98.76%.

1 Uk   In referendum on independence and 61.6% for Kravchuk as PR.

1–9 Y/UN   After talks with PR Milosevic, DM Kadijevic, and leadership in Cr, Vance states it is now impossible to send UN peacekeeping forces to Y.

2 UK/F   PR Mitterrand confers with PM Major on Maastricht summit. German–French initiative, and situations in Y and USSR.

2 P/Uk   P government recognizes independence of Uk.

2–3 EC   FMs meet on preparations for Maastricht; exempt four cooperative Y reps from effects of sanctions.

2–3 UK/FI   PMs Aho and Major confer in FI interest in EC membership.

2–5 WEU   Parl Assembly debates European security architecture. FM Dienstbier calls for an extension of European security system to East and full WEU membership of C in 1 or 2 years.

2–6 T/Tu   PR Niyasov meets PR Özal and PM Demirel on bilateral relations.

3 Ru/Uk   Ru PR Yeltsin recognizes independence of Uk.

3 USSR   PR Gorbachev appeals on SuSo to maintain unity of USSR and to sign treaty on USS.

3–4 Ca/H/Uk   Ca and H governments recognize independence of Uk.

3 G/Au   CH Kohl meets FM Mock on Y and on recognition of Sl and Cr.

3 F/Au   CH Vranitzky confers with PR Mitterrand and FM Cresson on Y and Au application of EC membership.

3 F/G   PR Mitterrand and CH Kohl conver on Maastricht summit.

3 G/Sl   PR Kucan meets CH Kohl on international recognition of Sl.

4 Ei/UK   PM Major confers with PM Haughey on Maastricht summit.

4–5 T/B   FM Ganev confers with PR Özal, PM Demirel, and FM Cetin.

4–7 USSR   PMs of 12 union reps meet on economic cooperation and debt repayment and agree on division of foreign debt among states.

5 La/Ru   PR Gorbunov and PM Godmanis meet PR Yeltsin and sign a treaty.

5 La/Li/Uk   Governments of La and Li recognize independence of Uk.

5 B/Uk   Expresso readiness to enter into diplomatic relations.

5 Y/Cr   Parl confirms the resignation of Mesic as PR of Y SP.

5–6 G/Cr   PR Tudjman meets with CH Kohl and FM Genscher on recognition of Cr.

5–9 USSR/H   PM Antall and PR Gorbachev sign a treaty on good neighborhood and cooperation. PM Antall and PR Yeltsin sign bilateral treaty and open diplomatic relations. PM Antall and FM Jeszenszky meet Uk PR Kravchuk, sign a bilateral treaty, and open diplomatic relations.

6 P	J. Olzewski is elected as new PM.
6 Uk	Kratschuk is sworn in as PR. SuSo end union treaty in 1992.
6 F/E/La/Li	PRs Rüütel, Gorbunov, and Landsbergis sign Charter of Paris.
6 US	Announces economic sanctions against Y.
8 R	Referendum hold on new constitution; 67.3 participate; 77.3% are in favor.
8 Cr	Deputy DM Granic announces agreement with Y army on ending blocking of barracks and withdrawal of federal army from Cr.
8 Mol	In presidential election Snegur receives 98.2%.
8 USSR	PR Gorbachev replaces SuCo W. Lobov with V. Samsonov.
8 USSR/CIS	PRs of Be, Uk, and Ru (Shushkewitsh, Kravchuk, and Yeltsin) meet in Minsk on prospects of mutual relations; declare failure of union treaty (USS); establish a "Commonwealth of Independent States" (CIS) open for other states to join.
8 C/Uk	Establish diplomatic relations.
8 EC	Heads of states and governments meet at Maastricht for summit.
9 USSR	PR Gorbachev meets PR Nasurbayev and PR Yeltsin on the Minsk agreement. Kravchuk announces nuclear weapons are under joint control of three PRs of this agreement.
9 Ru/E	PR Rüütel meets PR Yeltsin on bilateral economic relations.
9 UN/GA	Approves an international conventional weapons transfer register.
9 EC/Y	PRs of 6 Y reps meet Lord Carrington who concludes that Y is in dissolution.
9–10 EC	Maastricht summit: heads of states and governments approve political, economic, and currency union; framework for a common foreign and defense policy; majority decisions on selected topics.
10 UN/EC	SG de Cuellar in letter to ECC PR v.d. Broek opposes on early recognition of individual reps in Y.
10 US/USSR	PR Bush signs a law granting USSR most favored nation status.
10–12 Uk/Be/Ru	SuSo of Uk, Be, and Ru ratify the Minsk agreement.
11 Ru	PR Yeltsin stresses SuCo has been retained in the Minsk agreement.
11 Y	FM Loncar formally resigns.
11–12 EFTA	FMs welcome EES treaty with EC.
12 UN/Y	On the basis of Vance's report, SG de Cuellar opposes sending peace forces.
12 US/Gr	PM Mitsotakis meets PR Bush on crisis in Y and Cyprus.
12 Uk	PR Kravchuk takes over command of forces stationed in Uk; Uk recognizes Cr and Sl and enters into diplomatic relations.
12 Ser	Government of PM Zelenovic offers resigniation.

12 Y/CSCE	Delegation investigates situation of human and minority rights.
12–13 NATO	DPC debates new alliance strategy, changes in command structure, results of Maastricht, and control of Soviet nuclear weapons.
12–13 USSR	PRs of five Asian reps meet in Ashkhabad on Minsk agreement; may join the CIS; support central control of nuclear weapons.
13 UN/Gr	PM Mitsotakis meets with SG de Cuellar and Vance on crisis in Y.
13 F/S	PR Mitterrand confers with PM Bildt on interest in WEU membership.
13–14 G/C	FMs Dienstbier and Genscher discuss international issues.
14 EC	EC court challenges the EES treaty with EFTA states.
15–19 US/USSR	Secretary of State Baker meets with PR Yeltsin, PR Gorbachev, DM Shaposhnikov, and PRs Akayev of Ky. Nasarbayev of Ka, Shushkevic of Be, and Kravchuk of Uk.
15 UN/SC/Y	SC decides unanimously to send a small group of UN observers to Y to prepare possible deployment of peacekeeping forces in Y.
16 Ka	SuSo transforms Ka into an independent and democratic state.
16 T	Recognizes all former Soviet reps ad independent states.
16 EC	FMs of P, H, and C sign association agreements with EC as first steps to full EC membership.
16–17 EPC	FMs adopt criteria for recognition of new states in Eastern Europe and in former USSR; respect for UN and CSCE Charter, inviolability of borders, peaceful settlement of conflicts, adherence to disarmament and nonproliferation treaties. EC members will recognize those states that fulfill criteria and ask for recognition by December 23. On January 15, 1992 a joint decision will be made.
16–17 T/Uz	PR Karimov meets PR Özal and PM Demirel on bilateral relations.
16–20 B/T	Chmn of CS of T and B agrees on CSBM and military contacts.
17 Az	PR Mutalibov takes over control of all forces deployed in Az.
17 Ru/Ka/Mol	PR Yeltsin recognizes independence of Ka and Mol.
17 R/Ru/Ka	R recognizes Ru and Ka as independent states.
18 G/H	FM Jeszensky and FM Genscher sign a friendship treaty.
18–19 Y/EC	Lord Carrington holds consultations with governments in Y reps; explains EC decision on recognition of republics; meets with UN observer group.
18–19 Au/B	FM Ganev confers with CH Vranitzky and FM Mock in bilateral issues, crises in Y and USSR, and pan-European process.
19 Ru	PR Yeltsin dissolves FM of USSR and transfer its possessions.
19 Y/Ser	SP rejects EC decision on recognition of individual reps.
19 Ice	FM recognizes Cr and Sl diplomatically.
19 S	Recognizes Ru, Uk, and Be; will recognize Cr and Sl and with EC states.
19 NATO/NAC	Confers on dissolution of USSR, European security, and coop-

	eration issues. Secretary of State Baker reports on his journey to CIS states with nuclear weapons. Uk, Be, and Ka plan to join the NPT as non-nuclear states.
19–20 I/Ru	PR Yeltsin meets PR Cossiga, PM Andreotti, and FM De Michelis on future relations, developments in USSR/CIS, and control of nuclear weapons. I pledges credit for food aid to Ru.
20 NACC	Is inaugurated in Brussels by FMs of NATO, Baltic, and former WTO countries. Informal consultations on recognition of Y reps.
20 Y	PM Markovic resigns. SP opposes recognition of reps.
21 G/Uk	FM Genscher and FM Slenko confer on mutual relations and CIS.
21 USSR/CIS	11 heads of states of former reps: Ar, Az, Ka, Ky, Mol, Ru, Ta, Tu, Uz, Uk, and Be mutually recognize themselves as independent states; dissolve USSR; sign a protocol on CIS membership; agree on joint command on nuclear forces; support Ru taking over USSR seat in UN; establish a council of PRs and heads of states of CIS.
21 EC/US	Biannual meeting in Brussels on GATT and aid for former USSR.
22 Ru/Be/Uk	Decide all nuclear weapons deployed on territory and Be and Uk will be destroyed; tactical nuclear weapons will be taken to central locations for dismemberment by July 1, 1992. Uk and Be join NPT and will submit the START treaty for ratification to their parl.
22 Ge	Violence errupts; opposition requests resignation of PR Gamsakhurdis.
22–26 T/Ky	PR Akayev meets PR Özal and PR Demirel on bilateral relations; signs two treaties on friendship and economic cooperation.
23 Ru/UN	PR Yeltsin informs SG de Cuellar that Ru will take over the seat and functions of USSR in UN.
23 I/Sl	FM De Michelis confers with Sl government on recognition of EC.
23 Sl	Parl approves constitution guaranteeing human and minority rights.
23 EPC	Discusses future status of USSR and its reps; welcome CIS.
25 USSR	PR Gorbachev announces his resignation.
25 US	PR Bush thanks PR Gorbachev for transformation of former USSR.
25 Cr	Cr introduces its own currency.
25 Ca	PM Mulroney recognizes Ru and ten former Soviet reps as independent states and opens diplomatic relations with Ru and Uk.
25 EPC	Declaration recognizes Ru as successor of USSR.
26 USSR	SuSo of reps announce end of USSR.
26 G	Transfers its diplomatic relations with USSR to Ru; recognizes Uk.
26 H/CIS	H recognizes CIS and its members as independent states.

27 C	Recognizes Ru as successor of USSR; Uk and Be are also recognized.
27 F/Uk	F opens diplomatic relations with Uk.
27 CIS	Military leaders of CIS members adopt a common defense policy.
28 Mol/R	PMs Stolojan and Muravshi agree on economic and cultural cooperation.
29 Az	In referendum a large majority vote for independence.
29 Uz	In referendum 95% support independence, Karimov is elected PR by 86%.
30 UN/Y	UN special envoy Vance arrives for his fifth peace mission in Y.
30 CIS	Council of PRs and Council of state governments sign agreement on a joint SuCo on all strategic, military, and border forces, common research, and exploitation of outer space. PR Yeltsin stresses each member may have an independent military policy.
31 EPC/CIS	Recognizes Ar, Az, Be, Ka, Mol, Tu, Uk, and Uz as independent states; indicates readiness to recognize Ta, Ky.

January 1992

1 UN	SG Butros Butros Ghali takes over responsibility.
1 EC	Portugal takes over ECC presidency.
2 Y/BH	Vance persuades Ser and Cr to sign 15th ceasefire as a precondition for sending UN peacekeeping forces.
2 CIS	Members drop price controls.
2–6 Ge	After intense fighting, PR Gamsakhurdia flees and Sigua is Appointed by military council as new PM.
3P/EC/UN	FM Pinheiro confers with Lord Carrington and C. Vance on Y.
3 Ru/US	Open diplomatic relations.
3 Y	Y conference of parties and groups dominated by Serbs in Belgrade.
5 BC	PR of E, La, and Li appeal to CIS to speed up withdrawal of troops.
5–6 G/C	FMs Dienstbier meets Genscher on signing of bilateral treaty.
6 Mac	Changes its constitution to reflect EC conditions for recognition.
7 Y/EC	Y air force attacks EC helicopter and kills five observers.
7–8 EPC/Y/Ge	Expresses concern on attack against EC helicopter; calls for end of fighting in Ge and for national reconciliation.
8 Y	DM Kadijevic is replaced by General Adzic.
8 UN-SC/Y	Condemns attack on EC helicopter; sends 50 officers to Y.
9 BH	Serbs set up autonomous Serbian rep in BH.
9 Y/EC	In meeting with Lord Carrington, PRs of six reps support UN forces to Y and continuation of peace conference.
10 EPC	Special session on Y lifts sanctions against Montenegro.

10 CIS	FMs meet in Moscow on adherence to arms control treaties and division of former Soviet forces.
11 Uk/Ru	Negotiate in Kiev on future control of fleet in Black Sea.
11 Be	SuSo transfers control of forces in Be—except strategic forces—to Be ministerial council.
12 B	Presidential election results: Shelev; 44.8% and W. Wulkanov: 30.1%.
12 Gr/B	FM Ganev disagrees with FM Samaras on recognition of Macedonia.
13 CFE/CSBM	Talks resume in Vienna.
13–14 G/US	DM Cheney meets CH Kohl and FM Genscher on Danger of proliferation of chemical and nuclear weapons of USSR.
14 G/Gr	PM Mitsotakis meets CH Kohl and FM Genscher on peace efforts in Y.
14 G/B	FM Ganev meets FM Genscher on reforms in B and bilateral issues.
14 I/Cr	FMs De Michelis and Separovic agrees on In minority in Cr.
14 Ser/Cr	PM Mitsotakis and PR Milosevic stress continued Y unity.
15 I/Gr	PM Mitsotakis tries to prevent recognition of Mac.
15–17 B/G/I/Ca	Open diplomatic relations with Sl and Cr.
15 G/Ru	FM Kosyrev confers with PR v. Weizsäcker and FM Genscher.
15 F/BH	PR Izetbegovic meets PR Mitterrand on peacekeeping forces for BH.
15 Y/Ec	Government accuses EC of violation of international law by recognizing Sl and Cr.
15 P/Uk	DM Parys and DM Morosow agree on military cooperation.
15–16 G/FI	FM Väyrynen confers with FM Genscher on European integration, CSCE-process, and dissolution of USSR; FI interested in EC membership.
16 Ge	Ousted PR Gamsakhurdia returns; calls for a civil war.
16 Gr/Ser	PR Milosevic meets PM Mitsotakis on mutual friendship.
16 CIS	PRs of 11 CIS states meet in Moscow on military and economic cooperation; sign seven documents.
17 H/Mol	FMs Jeszenszky and Tiu open diplomatic relations.
17 P/F	FM Dumas confers with PR Soares, PM Cavaco Silva, and FM Pinheiro on European integration, CSCE process, and disarmament issues.
18 I/T	FM Cetin confers with PM Andreotti and FM De Michelis on situation in Mediterranean, Near East, and T interest in EC membership.
18 Ka/UK	FM Hurd confers with PR Nasarbayev, Ka will joint NPT.
18 R	Recognizes Sl and Cr as independent states.
19 B	Results of presidential election: Shelev (52.8%), Wulkanov (47.1%).
19 Uk/UK	FM Hurd meets PR Kravshuck and FM Slenko on bilateral relations, developments in CIS; UK offers aid in eliminating nuclear weapons.
19 Be/UK	FM Hurd confers with PR Shushkewitsh and FM Kravtshanka.

10 G/F	FM Dumas meets FM Genscher on CSCE Council meeting in Prague.
20 Be	Recognizes Ky and Ta as sovereign states.
20 Ru/UK	FM Hurd confers with PR Yeltsin and SuCo of CIS forces, Shaposnikov on bilateral relations and controls of nuclear weapons.
20 FI/Ru	PM Aho and Ru Vice PM Burbulis sign trade, border, and political treaty. The 1948 friendship and assistance treaty as invalid.
20–22 Ru/T	FM Cetin confers with FM Kosyrew on bilateral issues.
21 US/EC	FM Baker confers with ECC PR FM Pinheiro on relations between EC/US, crisis in Y, and regional and international issues.
21 Ar/G	Open diplomatic relations.
21 UN/DC	Negotiations on CWC resume in Geneva.
22UK/Li	PM Major states UK will return £ 90, it received in 1941.
22–23 Ru/F	FM Dumas meets PR Yeltsin and SuCo of CIS forces, Shaposhnikov on control of nuclear weapons.
22–23 US	Holds conference on coordiation of assistance to CIS. EC data on aid for CIS: G (57.1%), other EC (18.5%), US (6.5%), and J (3.1%).
23 E	PM Savisaar regions, T. Vähi is elected as new PM.
23 Mac/A	PR Gligorov and FM Bocka discuss situation of An minority in Mac.
23 T/Ser	PR Milosevic meets PR Özal, PM Suleiman on Y and recognition of former reps by T.
23 UN/G	SG Butros Ghali meets FM Genscher on nuclear proliferation issues.
23 UN/Cr/Y	SG Butros Ghali meets separately with Cr PM Greguric and Ser re Jovic on impediments for sending UN peacekeeping forces to Y.
23 UN/SC	Recommends membership for Ka.
23–25 T/Az	PR Mutsalibov and PR Özal sign friendship and cooperation treaty.
24 F/Uk	Open diplomatic relations; FM Dumas meets PR Kravshuck on economic cooperation.
25 F/Ka	Open diplomatic relations.
25 Ka/F	FM Dumas confers with PR Nasarbayev and FM Suleimonov on bilateral relations and transition to a nonnuclear regime in Ka.
25 Mol/R	PR Snegur confers with PR Iliescu on close economic cooperation and creation of bilateral institutions.
25 Au/Uk	Open diplomatic relations.
26–29 Y/UN	Dep SG M. Goulding holds talks with res of Ser, Cr, and federal army on UN peace plan and on peacekeeping forces.
27 Ar/S	Open diplomatic relations.
27 G/Sl	PM Peterle meets CH Kohl, calls for reconstruction aid.
27 B/R	PR Shelev and PR Iliescu sign a friendship treaty and agree to cooperate on economic and environmental issues.

27 B/A	FM Bocka meets PR Shelev, PM Dimitrov and FM Ganev on Y.
27 Ru/Uk	PM Fokin and FM Slenko confer with PR Yeltsin on economic cooperation and on Krim.
27 Ru/Be	Sign agreement on creation of a common economic space.
28 US	PR Bush announces new disarmament measures and cuts in defense spending.
29 Ru	PR Yeltsin responds with new nuclear disarmament proposals aiming at their elimination based on equality.
29 Ru/Por	FM Pinheiro confers with FM Kosyrev on role of Ru in CIS.
29 UN/SC	Recommends membership for Ky, Uz, and Ta.
30 Uk/Ru	PRs Yeltsin and Kravshuck sign declaration on strict control of nuclear weapons and fast implementation of disarmament agreements.
30 F/Be	Open diplomatic relations.
30 I/Uk	Open diplomatic relations. De Michelis talks with Uk leaders.
30–31 I/P	PM Olszewski confers on situation on Eastern Europe and in CIS.
31 Ar/G	Open diplomatic relations.
30–31 CSCE	Council meeting in Prague, accepts 10 new members: Ar, Az, Ka, Ky, Mol, Ta, Tu, Uk, Uz, Be; Ru takes over USSR seat; membership increases to 48; adopts 'Prague Document' on CSCE institutions.
31 UN/SC	First summit meeting of heads of states and governments on regional conflicts, disarmament, and nuclear proliferation. SG is asked to develop proposals for preventive diplomacy and peace creation.

Appendix B

Treaty on the Final Settlement With Respect to Germany

The Federal Republic of Germany, the German Democratic Republic, the French Republic, the Union of Soviet Socialist Republics, the United Kingdom of Great Britain and Northern Ireland, and the United States of America,

Conscious of the fact that their peoples have been living together in peace since 1945;

Mindful of the recent historic changes in Europe which have made it possible to overcome the division of the continent;

Having regard to the rights and responsibilities of the Four Powers relating to Berlin and to Germany as a whole, and the corresponding wartime and postwar agreements and decision of the Four Powers;

Resolved in accordance with their obligations under the Charter of the United Nations to develop friendly relations among nations, based on respect for the principle of equal rights and self-determination of peoples, and to take other appropriate measures to strengthen universal peace;

Recalling the principles of the Final Act of the Conference on Security and Cooperation in Europe, signed in Helsinki;

Recognizing that those principles have laid firm foundations for the establishment of a just and lasting peaceful order in Europe;

Determined to take account of everyone's security interests;

Convinced of the need to finally overcome antagonisms and to develop cooperation in Europe;

Confirming their readiness to reinforce security, in particular by adopting effective arms control, disarmament, and confidence-building measures; their willingness not to regard each other as adversaries but to work for a relationship of trust and cooperation; and accordingly, their readiness to consider positively setting up appropriate institutional arrangements within the framework of the Conference on Security and Cooperation in Europe.

Welcoming the fact that the German people, freely exercising their right of self-determination, have expressed their will to bring about the unity of Germany as a state so that they will be able to serve the peace of the world as an equal and sovereign partner in a united Europe;

Convinced that the unification of Germany as a state with definitive borders is a significant contribution to peace and stability in Europe; Intending to conclude the final settlement with respect to Germany;

Recognizing that thereby, and with the unification of Germany as a democratic and peaceful state, the rights and responsibilities of the Four Powers relating to Berlin and to Germany as a whole lose their function;

Represented by their Ministers for Foreign Affairs who, in accordance with the Ottawa Declaration of 13 February 1990, met in Bonn on 5 May 1990, in Berlin on 22 June 1990, in Paris on 17 July 1990 with the participation of the Minister for Foreign Affairs of the Republic of Poland, and in Moscow on 12 September 1990; Have agreed as follows:

ARTICLE 1

1. The united Germany shall comprise the territory of the Federal Republic of Germany, the Germany Democratic Republic and the whole of Berlin. Its external borders shall be the borders of the Federal Republic of Germany and the German Democratic Republic and shall be definitive from the date on which the present Treaty comes into force. The confirmation of the definitive nature of the borders of the united Germany is an essential element of the peaceful order in Europe.

2. The united Germany and the Republic of Poland shall confirm the existing border between them in a treaty that is binding under international law.

3. The united Germany has no territorial claims whatsoever against other states and shall not assert any in the future.

4. The Governments of the Federal Republic of Germany and the German Democratic Republic shall ensure that the constitution of the united Germany does not contain any provision incompatible with these principles. This applies accordingly to the provisions laid down in the preamble, the second sentence of Article 23, and Article 146 of the Basic Law for the Federal Republic of Germany.

5. The Governments of the French Republic, the Union of Soviet Socialist Republics, and United Kingdom of Great Britain and Northern Ireland and the United States of America take formal note of the corresponding commitments and declarations by the Governments of the Federal Republic of Germany and the German Democratic Republic and declare that their implementation will confirm the definitive nature of the united Germany's borders.

ARTICLE 2

The Governments of the Federal Republic of Germany and the German Democratic Republic reaffirm their declarations that only peace will emanate from German soil. According to the constitution of the united Germany, acts tending to and undertaken with the intent to disturb the peaceful relations between nations, especially to prepare for aggressive war, are unconstitutional and a punishable offence. The Governments of the Federal Republic of Germany and the German Democratic Republic declare that the united Germany will never employ any of its weapons except in accordance with its constitution and the Charter of the United Nations.

ARTICLE 3

1. The Governments of the Federal Republic of Germany and the Germany Democratic Republic reaffirm their renunciation of the manufacture and possession of and control over nuclear, biological and chemical weapons. They declare that the United Germany, too, will abide by these commitments. In particular,

rights and obligations arising from the Treaty on the Non-Proliferation of Nuclear Weapons of 1 July 1986 will continue to apply to the united Germany.

2. The Government of the Federal Republic of Germany, acting in full agreement with the Government of the German Democratic Republic, made the following statement on 30 August 1990 in Vienna at the Negotiations on Conventional Armed Forces in Europe:

"The Government of the Federal Republic of Germany undertakes to reduce the personnel strength of the armed forces of the united Germany to 370,000 (ground, air, and naval forces) within three to four years. This reduction will commence on the entry into force of the first CFE agreement. Within the scope of this overall ceiling no more than 345,000 will belong to the ground and air forces which, pursuant to the agreed mandate, alone are the subject of the Negotiations on Conventional Armed Forces in Europe. The Federal Government regards its commitment to reduce ground and air forces as a significant German contribution to the reduction of conventional armed forces in Europe. It assumes that in follow-on negotiations the other participants in the negotiations, too, will render their contribution to enhancing security and stability in Europe, including measures to limit personnel strengths."

The Government of the German Democratic Republic was expressly associated itself with this statement.

3. The Governments of the French Republic, the Union of Soviet Socialist Republics, the United Kingdom of Great Britain and Northern Ireland and the United States of America take note of these statements by the Governments of the Federal Republic of Germany and the German Democratic Republic.

ARTICLE 4

1. The Governments of the Federal Republic of Germany, the German Democratic Republic and the Union of Soviet Socialist Republics will settle by treaty the conditions for and the duration of the presence of Soviet armed forces on the territory of the present Germany Democratic Republic and of Berlin, as well as the conduct of the withdrawal of these armed forces which will be completed by the end of 1994, in connection with the implementation of the undertaking of the Federal Republic of Germany and the German Democratic Republic referred to in paragraph 2 of Article 3 of the present Treaty.

2. The Governments of the French Republic, the United Kingdom of Great Britain and Northern Ireland and the United States of America take note of this statement.

ARTICLE 5

1. Until the completion of the withdrawal of the Soviet armed forces from the territory of the present German Democratic Republic and of Berlin in accordance with Article 4 of the present Treaty, only German territorial defense units which

are not integrated into the alliance structures to which German armed forces in the rest of German territory are assigned will be stationed in that territory as armed forces of the united Germany. During that period and subject to the provisions of paragraph 2 of this Article, armed forces of other states will not be stationed in that territory or carry out any other military activity there.

2. For the duration of the presence of Soviet armed forces in the territory of the present Germany Democratic Republic and of Berlin, armed forces of the French Republic, the United Kingdom of Great Britain and Northern Ireland and the United States of America will, upon German request, remain stationed in Berlin by agreement to this effect between the Government of the united Germany and the Governments of the states concerned. The number of troops and the amount of equipment of all non-German armed forces stationed in Berlin will not be greater than at the time of signature of the present Treaty. New categories of weapons will not be introduced there by non-German armed forces. The Government of the united Germany will conclude with the Governments of those states which have armed forces stationed in Berlin treaties with conditions which are fair, taking account of the relations existing with the states concerned.

3. Following the completion of the withdrawal of the Soviet armed forces from the territory of the present German Democratic Republic and of Berlin, units of German armed forces assigned to military alliance structures in the same way as those in the rest of German territory may also be stationed in that part of Germany, but without nuclear weapons carriers. This does not apply to conventional weapon systems which may have other capabilities in addition to conventional ones but which in that part of Germany are equipped for a conventional role and designated only for such. Foreign armed forces and nuclear weapons or their carriers will not be stationed in that part of Germany or deployed there.

ARTICLE 6

The right of the united Germany to belong to alliances, with all the rights and responsibilities arising therefrom, shall not be affected by the present Treaty.

ARTICLE 7

1. The French Republic, the Union of Soviet Socialist Republics, the United Kingdom of Great Britain and Northern Ireland and the United States of America hereby terminate their rights and responsibilities relating to Berlin and to Germany as a whole. As a result, the corresponding, related quadripartite agreements, decisions and practices are terminated and all related Four Power institutions are dissolved.

2. The united Germany shall have accordingly full sovereignty over its internal and external affairs.

ARTICLE 8

1. The present Treaty is subject to ratification or acceptance as soon as possible. On the German side it will be ratified by the united Germany. The Treaty will therefore apply to the united Germany.

2. The instruments of ratification or acceptance shall be deposited with the Government of the united Germany. That Government shall inform the Governments of the other Contracting Parties of the deposit in each instrument of ratification or acceptance.

ARTICLE 9

The present Treaty shall enter into force for the united Germany, and the French Republic, the Union of Soviet Socialist Republics, the United Kingdom of Great Britain and Northern Ireland and the United States of America on the date of deposit of the last instrument of ratification or acceptance by these states.

ARTICLE 10

The original of the present Treaty, of which the English, French, German and Russian texts are equally authentic, shall be deposited with the Government of the Federal Republic of Germany, which shall transmit certified true copies to the Governments of the other Contracting Parties.

AGREED MINUTE TO THE TREATY ON THE FINAL SETTLEMENT WITH RESPECT TO GERMANY OF 12 SEPTEMBER 1990

Any questions with respect to the application of the word "deployed" as used in the last sentence of paragraph 3 of Article 5 will be decided by the Government of the united Germany in a reasonable and responsible way taking into account the security interests of each Contracting Party as set forth in the preamble.

IN WITNESS THEREOF, the undersigned plenipotentiaries, duly authorized thereto, have signed this Treaty.

DONE at Moscow this twelfth day of September 1990.

For the Federal Republic of Germany   Hans-Dietrich Genscher

For the German Democratic Republic   Lethar de Maizière

For the French Republic   Roland Dumas

For the Union of Socialist Soviet Republics   Edward Shevardnadze

For the United Kingdom of Great Britain
and Northern Ireland   Douglas Hurd

For the United States of America   James Baker

Appendix C

Treaty Between the Federal Republic of Germany and the Republic of Poland Concerning the Confirmation of the Frontier Existing Between Them

The Federal Republic of Germany and the Republic of Poland,

Anxious to shape their mutual relations in a forward-looking manner in conformity with international law, especially the Charter of the United Nations, and with the Final Act of the Conference on Security and Cooperation in Europe signed at Helsinki, as well as the documents of the follow-up meetings;

Resolved to contribute jointly to the development of a peaceful order in Europe in which frontiers no longer divide, that enables all European nations to live together in mutual trust and engage in comprehensive cooperation for the common benefit, and which ensures lasting peace, freedom and stability;

Deeply convinved that the unification of Germany as a state with definitive frontiers constitutes a significant contribution to a peaceful order in Europe;

Taking account of the Treaty on the Final Settlement with respect to Germany, signed on 12 September 1990;

Recalling that 45 years have elapsed since the end of the Second World War and conscious that the deep suffering caused by the war, especially the loss of their homes suffered by many Germans and Poles through expulsion or forced resettlement, represents a warning and a challenge toward shaping peaceful relations between the two peoples and states,

Desiring, through the development of their relations, to lay firm foundations for living together in friendship and to continue the policy of lasting understanding and reconciliation between Germans and Poles,

Have agreed as follows:

ARTICLE 1

The contracting parties confirm the frontier existing between them, the course of which is specified in the agreement of 6 July 1950 between the German Democratic Republic and the Polish People's Republic concerning the Demarcation of the established and existing German-Polish state frontier, as well as the accords implementing and supplementing the aforementioned agreement (instrument of 27 January 1951, confirming the demarcation of the state frontier between Germany and Poland; Treaty of 22 May 1989 between the German Democratic Republic and the Polish People's Republic on the delimitation of the sea areas in Oder Bay) and in the Treaty of 7 December 1970 between the Federal Republic of Germany and the Polish People's Republic concerning the basis for normalizing mutual relations.

ARTICLE 2

The contracting parties declare that the frontier existing between them shall be inviolable now and in the future and undertake to respect each other's sovereignty and territorial integrity with restriction.

ARTICLE 3

The contracting parties declare that they have no territorial claims whatsoever against each other and that they will not assert such claims in the future.

ARTICLE 4

1. This Treaty is subject to ratification; the instruments of ratification shall be exchanged in Bonn as soon as possible.
2. This Treaty shall enter into force on the date of exchange of the instruments of ratification.

In witness whereof, the representatives of the contracting parties have signed this Treaty and affixed their seals thereto.

Done at Warsaw on 14 November 1990 in duplicate in the German and Polish languages, both texts being equally authentic.

For the   For the
Federal Republic of Germany   Republic of Poland
Hans-Dietrich Genscher   Krzysztof Skubiszewski

Appendix D

Treaty Between the Federal Republic of Germany and the Union of Soviet Socialist Republics on a Good Neighbor Policy, Partnership, and Cooperation

The Federal Republic of Germany and the Union of Soviet Socialist Republics,

Conscious of their responsibility for the preservation of peace in Europe and in the world;

Desiring to set the final seal on the past and, through understanding and reconciliation, render a major contribution towards ending the division of Europe;

Convinced of the need to build a new, united Europe on the basis of common values, and to create a just and lasting peaceful order in Europe, including stable security structures;

Convinced of the great importance of human rights and fundamental freedoms as part of the heritage of the whole of Europe and that respect for them is a major prerequisite for progress in developing that peaceful order;

Reaffirming their commitment to the aims and principles embodied in the United Nations Charter and to the provisions of the Final Act of Helsinki of 1 August 1975, and of subsequent documents adopted by the Conference on security and cooperation in Europe

Resolved to continue the good traditions of their centuries-long history, to make good-neighbor policy, partnership, and cooperation the basis of their relations, and to meet the historic challenges that present themselves on the threshold of the third millennium,

Having regard to the foundations established in recent years through the development of cooperation between the Union of Soviet Socialist Republics and the Federal Republic of Germany as well as the German Democratic Republic.

Moved by the desire to further develop and intensify the fruitful and mutually beneficial cooperation between the two States in all fields and to give their mutual relationship a new quality in the interests of their species and of peace in Europe,

Taking account of the signing of the Treaty of 12 September 1990 on the final settlement with respect to Germany regulating the external aspects of German unity,

Have agreed as follows.

ARTICLE 1

The Federal Republic of Germany and the Union of Soviet Socialist Republics will, in developing their relations, be guided by the following principles:

They will respect each other's sovereign equality, territorial integrity, and political independence;

They will make the dignity and rights of the individual, concern for the survival of mankind, and preservation of the natural environment the focal points of their policy;

They reaffirm the rights of all nations and states to determine their own fate freely and without interference from outside and to proceed with their political, economic, social, and cultural development as they see fit;

They uphold the principle that any war, whether nuclear or conventional, must be effectively prevented and that peace be preserved and developed;

They guarantee the precedence of the universal rules of international law in their domestic and international relations and confirm their resolve to honor their contractual obligations;

They pledge themselves to make use of the creative potential of the individual and modern society with a view toward safeguarding peace and enhancing the prosperity of all nations.

ARTICLE 2

The Federal Republic of Germany and the Union of Soviet Socialist Republics undertake to respect without qualification the territorial integrity of all states in Europe within their present frontiers;

They declare that they have no territorial claims whatsoever against any state and will not raise any in the future;

They regard and will continue to regard as inviolable the frontiers of all states in Europe as they exist on the day of signature of the present Treaty.

ARTICLE 3

The Federal Republic of Germany and the Union of Soviet Socialist Republics reaffirm that they will refrain from any threat or use of force which is directed against the territorial integrity or political independence of the other side or is in any other way incompatible with the aims and principles of the United Nations Charter or with the CSCE Final Act;

They will settle their disputes exclusively by peaceful means and never resort to any of their weapons except for the purpose of individual or collective self-defense. They will never and under no circumstances be the first to employ armed forces against one another or against third states. They call upon all other states to join in this non-aggression commitment;

Should either side become the object of an attack; the other side will not afford any military support or other assistance to the aggressor and will resort to all measures to settle the conflict in conformity with the principles and procedures of the United Nations and other institutions of collective security.

ARTICLE 4

The Federal Republic of Germany and the Union of Soviet Socialist Republics will seek to ensure that armed forces and armaments are substantially reduced by means of binding, effectively verifiable agreements, in order to achieve, in conjunction with unilateral measures, a stable balance at a lower level, especially in Europe, which will suffice for defense but not for attack.

The same applies to the multilateral and bilateral enhancement of confidence-building and stabilizing measures.

ARTICLE 5

Both sides will support to the best of their ability the process of security and cooperation in Europe on the basis of the Final Act of Helsinki adopted on 1 August 1975 and, with the cooperation of all participating states, develop and intensify that cooperation further still, notably by creating permanent institutions and bodies. The aim of these efforts is the consolidation of peace, stability, and security, and the coalescence of Europe to form a single area of law, democracy, and cooperation in the fields of economy, culture, and information.

ARTICLE 6

The Federal Republic of Germany and the Union of Soviet Socialist Republics have agreed to hold regular consultations with a view toward further developing and intensifying their bilateral relations and coordinating their positions on international issues.

Consultations at the highest political level shall be held as necessary but, at all events, at least once a year.

The Foreign Ministers will meet at least twice a year.

The Defense Ministers will meet at regular intervals.

Other ministers will meet as necessary to discuss matters of mutual interest.

The existing mixed commissions will consider ways and means of intensifying their work. New mixed commissions will be appointed as necessary by mutual agreement.

ARTICLE 7

Should a situation arise which in the opinion of either side constitutes a threat to or violation of peace or may lead to dangerous international complications, both sides will immediately make contact with a view toward coordinating their positions and agreeing on measures to improve or resolve the situation.

ARTICLE 8

The Federal Republic of Germany and the Union of Soviet Socialist Republics have agreed to substantially expand and intensify their bilateral cooperation, especially in the economic, industrial, and scientific-technological fields, and in the field of environmental protection, with a view toward developing their mutual relations on a stable and long-term basis and deepening the trust between the two states and peoples. They will to this end conclude a comprehensive agreement on the development of coopeation in the economic, industrial, and scientific technological fields and, where necessary, conclude separate arrangements on specific matters.

Both sides attach great importance to cooperation in the training of specialists and executive personnel from industry for the development of bilateral relations and are prepared to considerably expand and intensify that cooperation.

ARTICLE 9

The Federal Republic of Germany and the Union of Soviet Socialist Republics will further develop and intensify their economic cooperation for their mutual benefit. They will create, as far as their domestic legislation and their obligations under international treaties allow, the most favorable general conditions for entrepreneurial and other economic activity by citizens, enterprises, and governmental, as well as non-governmental, institutions of the other side. This applies in particular to the treatment of capital investment and investors.

Both sides will encourage the initiatives necessary for economic cooperation by those directly concerned, especially with the aim of fully exploiting the possibilities afforded by the existing treaties and programs.

ARTICLE 10

Both sides will, on the basis of the Agreement of 22 July 1986 concerning economic and technological cooperation, further develop exchanges in this field and implement joint projects. They propose to draw on the achievements of modern science and technology for the sake of the people, their health, and their prosperity. They will promote and support parallel initiatives by researchers and research establishments in this sphere.

ARTICLE 11

Convinced that the preservation of the natural sources of life is indispensable for prosperous economic and social development, both sides reaffirm their determination to continue and to intensify their cooperation in the field of environmental protection on the basis of the agreement of 25 October 1988;

They propose to solve major problems of environmental protection together, to study harmful effects on the environment, and to develop measures for their prevention. They will participate in the development of coordinated strategies and concepts for a transborder and environmental policy within the international, and especially the European, framework.

ARTICLE 12

Both sides will seek to extend transport communications (air, rail, sea, inland waterway and road links) between the Federal Republic of Germany and the Union of Soviet Socialist Republics through the use of state-of-the-art technology.

ARTICLE 13

Both sides will strive to simplify to a considerable extent, on the basis of reciprocity, the procedure for the issue of visas to citizens of both countries wishing to travel, primarily for business, economic, and cultural reasons, and for purposes of scientific and technological cooperation.

ARTICLE 14

Both sides support comprehensive contacts among people from both countries and the development of cooperation among parties, trade unions, foundations, schools, universities, sports organizations, churches and social institutions, women's associations, environmental protection, and other social organizations and associations;

Special attention will be given to the deepending of contacts between the parliaments of the two states;

They welcome cooperation based on partnership between municipalities and regions, and between Federal States and Republics of the Union;

An important role falls to the German-Soviet Discussion Forum and cooperation among the media;

Both sides will facilitate the participation of all young people and their organizations in exchanges and other contacts and joint projects.

ARTICLE 15

The Federal Republic of Germany and the Union of Soviet Socialist Republics, conscious of the mutual enrichment of the cultures of their peoples over the centuries and of their unmistakable contribution to Europe's common culture heritage, as well as of the importance of cultural exchange for international understanding, will considerably extend their cultural cooperation;

Both sides will give substances to and fully exploit the agreement on the establishment and work of cultural centres;

Both sides reaffirm their willingness to give all interested persons comprehensive access to the languages and cultures of the other side and will encourage public and private initiatives;

Both sides strongly advocate the creation of broader possibilities for learning the language of the other country in schools, universities, and other educational institutions and will for this purpose assist each other in the training of teachers and make available teaching aids, including the use of television, radio, audiovisual, and computer technology. They will support initiatives for the establishment of bilingual schools;

Soviet citizens of German nationality as well as citizens from the Union of Soviet Socialist Republics who have their permanent abode in the Federal Republic of Germany and wish to preserve their languages, culture or traditions will be enabled to develop their natural, linguistic, and cultural identity. Accordingly, both sides will make possible and facilitate promotional measures for the benefit of such persons or their organizations within the framework of their respective laws.

ARTICLE 16

The Federal Republic of Germany and the Union of Soviet Socialist Republics will advocate the preservation of cultural treasures of each other in their territory;

They agree that lost or unlawfully transferred art treasures which are located in their territory will be returned to their owners or their successors.

ARTICLE 17

Both sides stress the special importance of humanitarian coooperation in their bilateral relations. They will intensify this cooperation with the assistance of the charitable organizations of both sides.

ARTICLE 18

The Government of the Federal Republic of Germany declares that the monuments to Soviet victims of the war and totalitarian rule elected on German soil will be respected and be under the protection of Germany law;

The same applies to Soviet war graves: they will be preserved and tended;

The Government of the Union of Soviet Socialist Republics will guarantee access to the graves of Germans on Soviet territory, their preservation, and upkeep;

The responsible organizations of both sides will intensify their cooperation on these matters.

ARTICLE 19

The Federal Republic of Germany and the Union of Soviet Socialist Republics will intensify their mutual assistance in civil and family matters on the basis of the Hague Convention relating to civil procedure, to which each is signatory. Both sides will further develop their mutual assistance in criminal matters, taking into account their legal systems and proceeding in harmony with international law;

The responsible authorities in the Federal Republic of Germany and the Union of Soviet Socialist Republics will cooperate in combating organized crime, terrorism, drug trafficking, reckless endangerment of civil aviation and maritime shipping, the manufacture or dissemination of counterfeit money, and smuggling, including the illicit transborder movement of works of art. The procedure and conditions for mutual cooperation will be the subject of a separate arrangement.

ARTICLE 20

The two Governments will intensify their cooperation within the scope of international organizations, taking into account their mutual interests and each side's cooperation with other countries. They will assist one another in developing cooperation with international, especially European, organizations and institutions of which either side is a member, should the other side express an interest in such cooperation.

ARTICLE 21

The present Treaty will not affect the rights and obligations arising from existing bilateral and multilateral agreements which the two sides have concluded with other States. The present Treaty is directed against no one; both sides regard their cooperation as an integral part and dynamic element of the further development of the CSCE process.

ARTICLE 22

The present Treaty is subject to ratification; the instruments of ratification will be exchanged as soon as possible in Moscow;

The present Treaty will enter into force on the date of exchange of the instruments of ratification;

The present Treaty will remain in force for twenty years. Thereafter it will be *tacitly* extended for successive periods of five years unless either contracting party denounces the Treaty in writing subject to one year's notice prior to its expiration.

Done at Bonn on 9th November 1990 in duplicate in the German and Russian languages, both texts being equally authentic.

For the
Federal Republic of Germany
Helmut Kohl

For the
Union of Soviet Socialist Republics
Michail Gorbachev

Appendix E

Charter of Paris for a New Europe

CONFERENCE ON SECURITY AND COOPERATION IN EUROPE

Austria, Belgium, Bulgaria, Canada, Cyprus, Czechoslovakia, Denmark, Finland, France, Germany, Greece, the Holy See, Hungary, Iceland, Ireland, Italy, Liechtenstein, Luxembourg, Malta, Monaco, Netherlands, Norway, Poland, Portugal, Romania, San Marino, Soviet Union, Spain, Sweden, Switzerland, Turkey, United Kingdom, United States, Yugoslavia

A NEW ERA OF DEMOCRACY, PEACE AND UNITY

We, the heads of state or government of the states participating in the Conference on Security and Co-operation in Europe, have assembled in Paris at a time of profound change and historic expectations. The era of confrontation and division of Europe has ended. We declare that henceforth our relations will be founded on respect and cooperation.

Europe is liberating itself from the legacy of the past. The courage of men and women, the strength of the will of the peoples and the power of the ideas of the Helsinki Final Act have opened a new era of democracy, peace and unity in Europe.

Ours is a time for fulfilling the hopes and expectations our peoples have cherished for decades; steadfast commitment to democracy based on human rights and fundamental freedoms; prosperity through economic liberty and social justice; and equal security for all our countries.

The Ten Principles of the Final Act will guide us towards this ambitious future, just as they have lighted our way for the past fifteen years towards better relations. Full implementation of all CSCE commitments must form the basis for the initiatives we are now taking to enable our nations to live in accordance with their aspirations.

Human Rights, Democracy, and Rule of Law

We undertake to build, consolidate, and strengthen democracy as the only system of government of our nations. In this endeavor, we will abide by the following:

• Human rights and fundamental freedoms are the birthright of all human beings, are inalienable and are guaranteed by law. Their protection and promotion is the first responsibility of government. Respect for them is an essential safeguard against an over-mighty State. Their observance and full exercise are the foundation of freedom, justice and peace.

Democratic government is based on the will of the people, expressed regularly through free and fair elections. Democracy has as its foundation respect for the human person and the rule of law. Democracy is the best safeguard of freedom of expression, tolerance of all groups of society, and equality of opportunity for each person.

Democracy, with its representative and pluralist character, entails accountability to the electorate, the obligation of public authorities to comply with the law and justice administered impartially. No one will be above the law.

- We affirm without discrimination that every individual has the right to freedom of thought, conscience and religion or belief; freedom of expression; freedom of association and peaceful assembly; and freedom of movement.

- No one will be subject to arbitrary arrest or detention; subject to torture or other cruel, inhuman, or degrading treatment or punishment;

- Everyone also has the right to know and act upon his rights; to participate in free and fair elections; to fair and public trial if charged with an offense; to own property alone or in association and to exercise individual enterprise; and to enjoy his economic, social, and cultural rights.

- We affirm that the ethnic, cultural, linguistic, and religious identity of national minorities will be protected and that persons belonging to national minorities have the right to freely express, preserve, and develop that identity without any discrimination and in full equality before the law.

- We will ensure that everyone will enjoy recourse to effective remedies, national or international, against any violation of his rights.

- Full respect for these precepts is the bedrock on which we will seek to construct the new Europe.

- Our States will co-operate and support each other with the aim of making democratic gains irreversible.

Economic Liberty and Responsibility

Economic liberty, social justice, and environmental responsibility are indispensable for prosperity.

The free will of the individual, exercised in democracy and protected by the rule of law, forms the necessary basis for successful economic and social development. We will promote economic activity which respects and upholds human dignity.

Freedom and political pluralism are necessary elements in our common objective of developing market economies towards sustainable economic growth, prosperity, social justice, expanding employment and efficient use of economic resources. The success of the transition to market economy by countries making efforts to this effect is important and in the interest of us all. It will enable us to share a higher level of prosperity which is our common objective. We will co-operate to this end.

Preservation of the environment is a shared responsibility of all our nations. While supporting national and regional efforts in this field, we must also look to the pressing need for joint action on a wider scale.

Friendly Relations among Participating States

Now that a new era is dawning in Europe, we are determined to expand and strengthen friendly relations and co-operation among the States of Europe, the

United States of America and Canada, and to promote friendship among our peoples.

To uphold and promote democracy, peace and unity in Europe, we solemnly pledge our full commitment to the Ten Principles of the Helsinki Final Act. We affirm the continuing validity of the Ten Principles and our determination to put them into practice. All the Principles apply equally and unreservedly, each of them being interpreted taking into account the others. They form the basis for our relations.

In accordance with our obligations under the Charter of the United Nations and commitments under the Helsinki Final Act, we renew our pledge to refrain from the threat or use of force against the territorial integrity or political independence of any State, or from acting in any other manner inconsistent with the principles or purposes of those documents. We recall that non-compliance with obligations under the Charter of the United Nations constitutes a violation of international law.

We reaffirm our commitment to settle disputes by peaceful means. We decide to develop mechanisms for the prevention and resolution of conflicts among the participating States.

With the ending of the division of Europe, we will strive for a new quality in our security relations while fully respecting each other's freedom of choice in that respect. Security is indivisible and the security of every participating State is inseparably linked to that of all the others. We therefore pledge to co-operate in strengthening confidence and security among us and in promoting arms control and disarmament.

We welcome the Joint Declaration of Twenty-Two States on the improvement of their relations.

Our relations will rest on our common adherence to democratic values and to human rights and fundamental freedoms. We are convinced that in order to strengthen peace and security among our States, the advancement of democracy, and respect for and effective exercise of human rights, are indispensable. We reaffirm the equal rights of peoples and their right to self-determination to conformity with the Charter of the United Nations and with the relevant norms of international law, including those relating to territorial integrity of states.

We are determined to enhance political consultation and to widen co-operation to solve economic, social, environmental, cultural and humanitarian problems. This common resolve and our growing interdependence will help to overcome the mistrust of decades, to increase stability and to build a united Europe.

We want Europe to be a source of peace, open to dialogue and to co-operation with other countries, welcoming exchanges and involved in the search for common responses to the challenges of the future.

Security

Friendly relations among us will benefit from the consolidation of democracy and improved security.

We welcome the signature of the Treaty on Conventional Armed Forces in Europe by twenty-two participating states, which will lead to lower levels of armed forces. We endorse the adoption of a substantial new set of confidence- and security-building measures which will lead to increased transparency and confidence among all participating States. These are important steps towards enhanced stability and security in Europe.

The unprecedented reduction in armed forces resulting from the Treaty on Conventional Armed Forces in Europe, together with new approaches to security and co-operation within the CSCE process, will lead to a new perception of security in Europe and a new dimension in our relations. In this context we fully recognize the freedom of States to choose their own security arrangements.

Unity

Europe whole and free is calling for a new beginning. We invite our peoples to join in this great endeavour.

We note with great satisfaction the Treaty on the Final Settlement with respect to Germany signed in Moscow on 12 September 1990 and sincerely welcome the fact that the German people have united to become one State in accordance with the principles of the Final Act of the Conference on Security and Cooperation in Europe, and in full accord with their neighbors. The establishment of the national unity of Germany is an important contribution to a just and lasting order of peace for a united, democratic Europe aware of its responsibility for stability, peace, and cooperation.

The participation of both North American and European States is a fundamental characteristic of the CSCE; it underlies its past achievements and is essential to the future of the CSCE process. An abiding adherence to shared values and our common heritage are the ties which bind us together. With all the rich diversity of our nations, we are united in our commitment to expand our cooperation in all fields. The challenges confronting us can only be met by common action, cooperation and solidarity.

The CSCE and the World

The destiny of our nations is linked to that of all other nations. We support fully the United Nations and the enhancement of its role in promoting international peace, security and justice. We reaffirm our commitment to the principles and purposes of the United Nations as embodied in the Charter and condemn all violations of these principles. We recognize with satisfaction the growing role of the United Nations in world affairs and its increasing effectiveness, fostered by the improvement in relations among our states.

Aware of the dire needs of a great part of the world, we commit ourselves to solidarity with all other countries. Therefore, we issue a call from Paris today to all the nations of the world. We stand ready to join with any and all states in common efforts to protect and advance the community of fundamental human values.

GUIDELINES FOR THE FUTURE

Proceeding from our firm commitment to the full implementation of all CSCE principles and provisions, we now resolve to give a new impetus to a balanced and comprehensive development of our cooperation in order to address the needs and aspirations of our peoples.

Human Dimension

We declare our respect for human rights and fundamental freedoms to be irrevocable. We will fully implement and build upon the provisions relating to the human dimension of the CSCE.

Proceedings from the Document of the Copenhagen Meeting of the Conference on the Human Dimension, we will cooperate to strengthen democratic institutions and to promote the application of the rule of law. To that end, we decide to convene a seminar of experts in Oslo from 4 to 15 November 1991.

Determined to foster the rich contribution of national minorities to the life of our societies, we undertake further to improve their situation. We reaffirm our deep conviction that friendly relations among our peoples, as well as peace, justice, stability, and democracy, require that the ethnic, cultural, linguistic, and religious identity of national minorities be protected and conditions for the promotion of that identity be created. We declare that questions related to national minorities can only be satisfactorily resolved in a democratic political framework. We further acknowledge that the rights of persons belonging to national minorities must be fully respected as part of universal human rights. Being aware of the urgent need for increased cooperation on, as well as better protection of, national minorities, we decide to convene a meeting of experts on national minorities to be held in Geneva from 1 to 19 July 1991.

We express our determination to combat all forms of racial and ethnic hatred, antisemitism, xenophobia, and discrimination against anyone as well as persecution on religious and ideological grounds.

In accordance with our CSCE commitments, we stress that free movement and contacts among our citizens as well as the free flow of information and ideas are crucial for the maintenance and development of free societies and flourishing cultures. We welcome increased tourism and visits among our countries.

The human dimension mechanism has proved its usefulness, and we are consequently determined to expand it to include new procedures involving, *inter alia,* the services of experts or a roster of eminent persons experienced in human rights issues which could be raised under the mechanism. We shall provide, in the context of the mechanism, for individuals to be involved in the protection of their rights. Therefore, we undertake to develop further our commitments in this respect, in particular at the Moscow Meeting of the Conference on the Human Dimension, without prejudice to obligations under existing international instruments to which our states may be parties.

We recognize the important contribution of the Council of Europe to the promotion of human rights and the principles of democracy and the rule of law as well as to development of cultural cooperation. We welcome moves by several participating States to join the Council of Europe and adhere to its European Convention on Human Rights. We welcome as well as the readiness of the Council of Europe to make its experience available to the CSCE.

Security

The changing political and military environment in Europe opens new possibilities for common efforts in the field of military security. We will build on the important achievements attained in the Treaty on Conventional Armed Forces in

Europe and in the Negotiations on Confidence- and Security-Building Measures. We undertake to continue the CSBM negotiations under the same mandate, and to seek to conclude them no later than the follow-up meeting of the CSCE to be held in Helsinki in 1992. We also welcome the decision of the participating states concerned to continue the CFE negotiation under the same mandate and to seek to conclude it no later than the Helsinki follow-up meeting. Following a period for national preparations, we look forward to a more structured cooperation among all participating states on security matters, and to discussions and consultations among the thirty-four participating states aimed at establishing by 1991, from the conclusion of the Helsinki follow-up meeting, new negotiations on disarmament and confidence and security building open to all participating States.

We call for the earliest possible conclusion of the Convention on an effectively verifiable, global and comprehensive ban on chemical weapons, and we intend to be original signatories to it.

We reaffirm the importance of the open skies initiative and call for the successful conclusion of the negotiations as soon as possible.

Although the threat of conflict in Europe has diminished, other dangers threaten the stability of our societies. We are determined to cooperate in defending democratic institutions against activities which violate the independence, sovereign equality or territorial integrity of the participating States. These include illegal activities involving outside pressure, coercion, and subversion.

We unreservedly condemn as criminal all acts, methods, and practices of terrorism, and express our determination to work for its eradication both bilaterally and through multilateral co-operation. We will also join together in combating illicit trafficking in drugs.

Being aware that an essential complement to the duty of states to refrain from the threat or use of force is the peaceful settlement of disputes, both being essential factors for the maintenance and consolidation of international peace and security, we will not only seek effective ways of preventing, through political means, conflicts which may yet emerge, but also define, in conformity with international law, appropriate mechanisms for the peaceful resolution of any disputes that may arise. Accordingly, we undertake to seek new forms of cooperation in this area, in particular a range of methods for the peaceful settlement of disputes, including mandatory third-party involvement. We stress that full use should be made in this context of the opportunity of the meeting on the Peaceful Settlement of Disputes which will be convened in Valletta in early 1991. The Council of Ministers for Foreign Affairs will take into account the report of the Valletta meeting.

Economic Cooperation

We stress that economic cooperation based on market economy constitutes an essential element of our relations and will be instrumental in the construction of a prosperous and united Europe. Democratic institutions and economic liberty foster economic and social progress, as recognized in the document of the Bonn Conference on Economic Cooperation, the results of which we strongly support.

We underline that cooperation in the economic field, science, and technology is now an important pillar in the CSCE. The participating states should periodically review progresses and give new impulses in these fields.

We are convinced that our overall economic cooperation should be expanded, free enterprise encouraged, and trade increased and diversified, according to GATT rules. We will promote social justice and progress and further the welfare of our peoples. We recognize in this context the importance of effective policies to address the problem of unemployment.

We reaffirm the need to continue to support democratic countries in transition towards the establishment of market economy and the creation of the basis for self-sustaining economic and social growth, as already undertaken by the group of twenty-four countries. We further underline the necessity of their increased integration, involving the acceptance of disciplines as well as benefit, into the international economic and financial system.

We consider that increased emphasis on economic cooperation within the CSCE process should take into account the interests of developing participating states.

We recall the link between respect for and promotion of human rights and fundamental freedoms and scientific progress. Cooperation in the field of science and technology will play an essential role in economic and social development. Therefore, it must evolve towards a greater sharing of appropriate scientific and technological information and knowledge with a view to overcoming the technological gap which exists among the participating states. We further encourage the participating states to work together in order to develop human potential and the spirit of free enterprise.

We are determined to give the necessary impetus to co-operation among our states in the fields of energy, transport and tourism for economic and social development. We welcome, in particular, practical steps to create optimal conditions for the economic and rational development in energy resources, with due regard for environmental considerations.

We recognize the important role of the European Community in the political and economic development of Europe. International economic organizations such as the United Nations Economic Commission for Europe (ECE), the Bretton Woods Institutions, the Organization for Economic Co-operation and Development (OECD), the European Free Trade Association (EFTA) and the International Chamber of Commerce (ICC) also have a significant task in promoting economic cooperation, which will be further enhanced by the establishment of the European Bank for Reconstruction and Development (EBRD). In order to pursue our objectives, we stress the necessity for effective coordination of the activities of these organizations and emphasize the need to find methods for all our states to take part in these activities.

Environment

We recognize the urgent need to tackle the problems of the environment and the importance of individual and co-operative efforts in this area. We pledge to intensify our endeavors to protect and improve our environment in order to restore and maintain a sound ecological balance in air, water, and soil. Therefore, we are determined to make full use of the CSCE as a framework for the formulation of common environmental commitments and objectives, and thus to pursue the work reflected in the report of the Sofia meeting on the protection of the environment.

We emphasize the significant role of a well-informed society in enabling the public and individuals to take initiatives to improve the environment. To this end, we commit ourselves to promoting public awareness and education on the environment as well as the public reporting of the environmental impact of policies, projects, and programs.

We attach priority to the introduction of clean and low-waste technology, being aware of the need to support countries which do not yet have their own means for appropriate measures.

We emphasize that environmental policies should be supported by appropriate legislative measures and administrative structures to ensure their effective implementation.

We stress the need for new measures providing for the systematic evaluation of compliance with the existing commitments and, moreover, for the development of more ambitious commitments with regard to notification and exchange of information about the state of the environment and potential environmental hazards. We also welcome the creation of the European Environment Agency (EEA).

We welcome the operational activities, problem-oriented studies; and policy reviews in various existing international organizations engaged in the protection of the environment, such as the United Nations Environment Programme (UNEP), the United Nations Economic Commission for Europe (ECE), and the Organization for Economic Co-operation and Development (OECD). We emphasize the need for strengthening their cooperation and for their efficient coordination.

Culture

We recognize the essential contribution of our common European culture and our shared values in overcoming the division of the continent. Therefore, we underline our attachment to creative freedom and to the protection and promotion of our cultural and spiritual heritage, in all its richness and diversity.

In view of the recent changes in Europe, we stress the increased importance of the Cracow Symposium and we look forward to its consideration of guidelines for intensified cooperation in the field of culture. We invite the Council of Europe to contribute to this symposium.

In order to promote greater familiarity amongst our peoples, we favor the establishment of cultural centres in cities of other participating States as well as increased cooperation in the audio-visual field and wider exchange in music, theater, literature and the arts.

We resolve to make special efforts in our national policies to promote better understanding, in particular among young people, through cultural exchanges, cooperation in all fields of education and, more specifically, through teaching and training in the languages of other participating states. We intend to consider first results of this action at the Helsinki follow-up meeting in 1992.

Migrant Workers

We recognize that the issues of migrant workers and their families legally residing in host countries have economic, cultural, and social aspects as well as their human dimension. We reaffirm that the protection and promotion of their rights, as well as the implementation of relevant international obligations, is our common concern.

Mediterranean Region

We consider that the fundamental political changes that have occurred in Europe have a positive relevance to the Mediterranean region. Thus, we will continue efforts to strengthen security and cooperation in the Mediterranean as an important factor for stability in Europe. We welcome the report of the Palma de Mallorca meeting on the Mediterranean, the results of which we will support.

We are concerned with the continuing tensions in the region, and renew our determination to intensify efforts towards finding just, viable, and lasting solutions, through peaceful means, to outstanding crucial problems, based on respect for the principles of the Final Act.

We wish to promote favorable conditions for a harmonious development and diversification of relations with the non-participating Mediterranean states. Enhanced cooperation with these states will be pursued with the aim of promoting economic and social development and thereby enhancing stability in the region. To this end, we will strive together with these countries towards a substantial narrowing of the prosperity gap between Europe and its Mediterranean neighbors.

Non-governmental Organizations

We recall the major role that non-governmental organizations, religious, and other groups and individuals have played in the achievement of the objectives of the CSCE and will further facilitate their activities for the implementation of the CSCE commitments by the participating States. These organizations, groups and individuals must be involved in an appropriate way in the activities and new structures of the CSCE in order to fulfill their important tasks.

NEW STRUCTURES AND INSTITUTIONS OF THE CSCE PROCESS

Our common efforts to consolidate respect for human rights, democracy, and the rule of law, to strengthen peace and to promote unity in Europe require a new quality of political dialogue and cooperation and thus development of the structures of the CSCE.

The intensification of our consultations at all levels is of prime importance in shaping our future relations. To this end, we decide on the following:

We, the Heads of State or Government, shall meet next time in Helsinki on the occasion of the CSCE follow-up meeting 1992. Thereafter, we will meet on the occasion of the subsequent follow-up meetings.

Our Ministers for Foreign Affairs will meet, as a council, regularly and at least once a year. These meetings will provide the central forum for political consultations within the CSCE process. The council will consider issues relevant to the Conference on Security and Cooperation in Europe and take appropriate decisions.

The first meeting of the council will take place in Berlin.

A committee of senior officials will prepare the meetings of the council and carry out its decisions. The committee will review current issues and may take appropriate decision, including in the form of recommendations to the council.

Additional meetings of the representative of the participating states may be agreed upon to discuss questions of urgent concern.

The council will examine the development of provisions for convening meetings of the committee of senior officials in emergency situations.

Meetings of our ministers may also be agreed by the participating states.

In order to provide administrative support for these consultations we establish an Office of the Secretariat in Prague.

Follow-up meetings of the participating states will be held, as a rule, every two years to allow the participating states to take stock of developments, review the implementation of their commitments and consider further steps in the CSCE process.

We decide to create a conflict prevention center in Vienna to assist the council in reducing the risk of conflict.

We decide to establish an Office for Free Elections in Warsaw to facilitate contacts and the exchange of information on elections within participating states.

Recognizing the important role parliamentarians can play in the CSCE process, we call for greater parliamentary involvement in the CSCE, in particular through the creation of a CSCE parliamentary assembly, involving members of parliaments from all participating states. To this end, we urge that contacts be pursued at parliamentary level to discuss the field of activities, working methods and rules of procedure of such a CSCE parliamentary structure, drawing on existing experience and work already undertaken in the field.

We ask our Ministers for Foreign Affairs to review this matter on the occasion of their first meeting as a council.

Procedural and organizational modalities relating to certain provisions contained in the Charter of Paris for a New Europe are set out in the supplementary document which is adopted together with the Charter of Paris.

We entrust to the council the further steps which may be required to ensure the implementation of decisions contained in the present document, as well as in the supplementary document, and to consider further efforts for the strengthening of security and cooperation in Europe. The council may adopt any amendment to the supplementary document which it may deem appropriate.

The original of the Charter of Paris for a New Europe, drawn up in English, French, German, Italian, Russian and Spanish, will be transmitted to the government of the French Republic, which will retain it in its archives. Each of the participating states will receive from the Government of the French Republic a true copy of the Charter of Paris.

The text of the Charter of Paris will be published in each participating state, which will disseminate it and make it known as widely as possible.

The Government of the French Republic is requested to transmit to the Secretary General of the United Nations the text of the Charter of Paris for a New Europe which is not eligible for registration under Article 102 of the Charter of the United Nations, with a view to its circulation to all the members of the Organization as an official document of the United Nations.

Done at Paris,
on 21 November 1990,
in the name of

INDEX

About the Editors and Contributors

Editors

Hans Günter Brauch was guest professor of International Relations at the Johann Wolfgang Goethe University in Frankfurt am Main, until March 1991. He was a lecturer at the Institute of Political Science of Heidelberg University. He is chairman of AFES-Press, Peace Research and European Security Studies. Previously he was a fellow of Heidelberg, Stuttgart (FRG), and Harvard and Stanford universities (U.S.). He has taught international relations with an emphasis on international security and arms control matters at Darmstadt, Tübingen, Stuttgart, Heidelberg, and Frankfurt universities. He was a student of political science, modern history, international law, and English language and literature at Heidelberg and London universities and he holds a Ph.D. from Heidelberg University (1976). Dr. Brauch is a member of The International Institute for Strategic Studies, The Pugwash Movement for Science and World Affairs, the International Studies Association, and the International Peace Research Association whose study group on Defense and Disarmament Studies he has been chairing since 1986. He serves on the governing board of the International Security Studies Section of ISA, on the board of editors of the UNESCO Yearbook on Peace and Conflict Studies, and on the board of editorial advisers of the Arms Control Reporter.

Publications: (books only) in English: (ed. with Duncan L. Clark) *Decision-making for Arms Limitation—Assessments and Prospects* (1983); (ed.) *Star Wars and European Defense—Implications for Europe: Perceptions and Assessments* (1987); (with Rip Bulkeley) *The Anti-Ballistic Missile Treaty and World Security* (1988); (ed.) *Military Technology, Armaments Dynamics and Disarmament* (1989); (ed. with Robert Kennedy) *Alternative Conventional Defense Postures in the European Theater, Volume 1: The Military Balance and Domestic Constraints* (1990); *volume 2: Political Change in Europe: Military Strategy and Technology* (1991); *volume 3: Force Posture Alternatives for Europe after the Cold War* (1992), (co-editor with H. J. van der Graaf, John Grin and Wim Smit: *Controlling Military Research & Development and Exports of Dual Use Technologies as a Problem of Disarmament and Arms Control Policy in the 1990s* (1992) (in preparation); in German: *Struktureller Wandel und Rüstungspolitik der USA* (1940–1950) (1977); *Entwicklungen und Ergebnisse der Friedensforschung (1969–1978)* (1979); *Abrüstungsamt oder Ministerium? Ausländische Modelle der Abrüstungsplanung* (1981); *Der Chemische Alptraum oder gibt es einen C-Waffen-Krieg in Europa?* (1982); (co-author with Alfred Schrempf) *Giftgas in der Bundesrepublik* (1982); *Perspektiven einer Europäischen Friedensordnung* (1983); *Die Raketen kommen!* (1983); (ed.) *Kernwaffen und Rüstungskontrolle* (1984); (ed.) *Sicherheitspolitik am Ende?* (1984); *Angriff aus dem All. Der Rüstungswettlauf im Weltraum* (1984);

(co-editor with Rolf-Dieter Müller) *Chemische Kriegführung und chemische Abrüstung* (1985); (ed.) *Vertrauensbildende Maßnahmen und Europäische Abrüstungskonferenz* (1986); (compiler with Rainer Fischbach) *Militärische Nutzung des Weltraums—Eine Bibliographie* (1988).

Robert Kennedy is professor of International Affairs and deputy director of the Center for International Strategy, Technology, and Policy at the Georgia Institute of Technology, Atlanta, Georgia. Previously he served as Civilian Deputy Commandant, NATO Defense College, Rome (1985–1988); Dwight D. Eisenhower Professor of National Security Studies, Department of National Security, U.S. Army War College (1983–1985); Senior Researcher, Strategic Studies Institute, U.S. Army War College (1974–1983); Foreign Affairs Officer, U.S. Arms Control and Disarmament Agency (1974); and as a command pilot on active duty with the U.S. Air Force and later with the reserve forces (1963–1986). Professor Kennedy has also been a Senior Fellow at the Atlantic Council of the United States and Fulbright Scholar in Peru. He holds an M.A. and Ph.D. in political science from Georgetown University and a B.S. from the United States Air Force Academy.

Publications; co-editor with Hans Günter Brauch) *Alternative Conventional Defense Postures in the European Theater, Volume 1* (1990); "The Future of Deterrence in Europe," *Revista Italiana Difesa* (May 1988); "CDI and Realistic Deterrence to the Year 2000 and Beyond," in *The Future of Conventional Defense Improvements in NATO* (1988); (co-editor with Andrew J. Goodpaster and Walter J. Stoessel, Jr.) *U.S. Policy Towards the Soviet Union: A Long Term Western Perspective* (1988); "Nuclear Winter, War Prevention, and the Nuclear Deterrent," in Peter C. Sederberg, *Nuclear Winter, Deterrence and the Prevention of Nuclear War* (1986); and (co-editor with John M. Weinstein) *The Defense of the West: Strategic and European Security Issues Reappraised* (1984). He has also published numerous articles in professional journals and magazines such as the *Marine-Rundschau, Orbis, Air Force Magazine,* and *Parameters.*

Contributors

Horst Afheldt (German) studied physics and law in Strasbourg and Hamburg. He holds a Ph.D. from Göttingen University. From 1970 to 1980 he worked at the Max-Planck Institute on Researching the Living Conditions of the Scientific and Technical World in Starnberg. From 1980 to 1989 he headed the Afheldt Working Group in the Max-Planck Institute of Social Sciences. His writings stimulated research on nonoffensive security structures. He is the author of several books in German and French and of many articles in German and in English.

Steven L. Canby (American), economist and political scientist, is President of C&L Associates, a Washington based research group. Dr. Canby has written extensively in the area of tactics, technology, and manpower, and teaches military history at Georgetown University. Dr. Canby is a graduate of the U.S. Military Academy of West Point and Harvard University.

James M. Garrett (American) is the author of *The Tenuous Balance: Conventional Forces in Central Europe* (Westview, 1989), *Central Europe's Fragile Deterrent Structure* (Harvester-Wheatsheaf, 1990), and several articles on conventional and nuclear weapons as deterrents. He has been a regular U.S. Army officer and a professor of national security policy. He holds a doctorate in international relations and law from Columbia University.

Manfred R. Hamm (German) is an analyst in politco-economic affairs in the Office of the Managing Director of the NEC Germany-GmbH. He was formerly associated with the Stiftung Wissenschaft und Politik in Ebenhausen. Previously he was a senior policy analyst at the Heritage Foundation, and Adjunct Professor in the International Security Studies Program at Georgetown University.

Franz Uhle-Wettler (German), Lieutenant General (retired) served as Commandant of the NATO Defense College in Rome, Italy (1984–1987). Before joining the college, General Uhle-Wettler commanded the 5th Panzer Division (1982–1984). He has also served in the Plans and Policy Division at the Supreme Headquarters Allied Powers Europe (SHAPE) and in similar assignments in the German Ministry of Defense. He has published various books and numerous articles on philosophical, dialectical, and historical materialism, on military history and on a variety of defense issues.

Lutz Unterseher (German) has a Ph.D. in sociology from Frankfurt University. He is a cofounder and the chairman of the Study Group on Alternative Security Policy (SAS), a partner in the consulting firm SALSS. He is an adviser to the German Social Democratic Party on security issues and an editor and author of several books, book chapters, and journal articles in German and English.

John M. Weinstein (American) is Chief of Policy and Programs at the U.S. Nuclear Command and Control System Support Staff in Washington, D.C. He has been involved in most aspects of nuclear weapons policy and planning in prior positions in the nuclear directorates of the Army General Staff, where he served as the army Chief of Staff's SIOP advisor, and in the Office of the Chief of Naval Operations. He also serves periodically in the USSR as an inspector for the On-Site Inspection Agency, monitoring Soviet compliance with the INF Arms Control treaty. Dr. Weinstein is the author of numerous essays in professional journals on U.S. and Soviet military capabilities as well as their nuclear weapons, policies, and plans. He is also co-editor of *The Defense of the West: Strategic and European Security Issues Reappraised.*

Carl Friedrich von Weizsacker (German) was a professor of physics in Strasburg and Göttingen, a professor of philosophy in Hamburg and from 1969–1990 he was the director of the Max-Planck Institute on Researching the Living Conditions of the Scientific and Technical World in Starnberg. He has published numerous books on physics, philosophy, and peace research.

Paul C. Warnke (American) is a partner with the law firm, Clifford and Warnke. He also has served as Director, U.S. Arms Control and Disarmament Agency, March 1977–November 1978 and Assistant Secretary of Defense for International Security Affairs, August 1967–February 1969. He serves on the board of directors/advisory board for a wide variety of organizations and institutions.